T0226186

Lecture Notes in Computer Science   10809

Commenced Publication in 1973
Founding and Former Series Editors:
Gerhard Goos, Juris Hartmanis, and Jan van Leeuwen

Editorial Board

David Hutchison
   Lancaster University, Lancaster, UK
Takeo Kanade
   Carnegie Mellon University, Pittsburgh, PA, USA
Josef Kittler
   University of Surrey, Guildford, UK
Jon M. Kleinberg
   Cornell University, Ithaca, NY, USA
Friedemann Mattern
   ETH Zurich, Zurich, Switzerland
John C. Mitchell
   Stanford University, Stanford, CA, USA
Moni Naor
   Weizmann Institute of Science, Rehovot, Israel
C. Pandu Rangan
   Indian Institute of Technology Madras, Chennai, India
Bernhard Steffen
   TU Dortmund University, Dortmund, Germany
Demetri Terzopoulos
   University of California, Los Angeles, CA, USA
Doug Tygar
   University of California, Berkeley, CA, USA
Gerhard Weikum
   Max Planck Institute for Informatics, Saarbrücken, Germany

More information about this series at http://www.springer.com/series/7409

Jaap Ham · Evangelos Karapanos
Plinio P. Morita · Catherine M. Burns (Eds.)

Persuasive Technology

13th International Conference, PERSUASIVE 2018
Waterloo, ON, Canada, April 18–19, 2018
Proceedings

 Springer

Editors
Jaap Ham (ID)
Eindhoven University of Technology
Eindhoven
The Netherlands

Plinio P. Morita (ID)
University of Waterloo
Waterloo, ON
Canada

Evangelos Karapanos (ID)
Cyprus University of Technology
Limassol
Cyprus

Catherine M. Burns (ID)
University of Waterloo
Waterloo, ON
Canada

ISSN 0302-9743   ISSN 1611-3349   (electronic)
Lecture Notes in Computer Science
ISBN 978-3-319-78977-4   ISBN 978-3-319-78978-1   (eBook)
https://doi.org/10.1007/978-3-319-78978-1

Library of Congress Control Number: 2018937395

LNCS Sublibrary: SL3 – Information Systems and Applications, incl. Internet/Web, and HCI

© Springer International Publishing AG, part of Springer Nature 2018, corrected publication 2018
This work is subject to copyright. All rights are reserved by the Publisher, whether the whole or part of the material is concerned, specifically the rights of translation, reprinting, reuse of illustrations, recitation, broadcasting, reproduction on microfilms or in any other physical way, and transmission or information storage and retrieval, electronic adaptation, computer software, or by similar or dissimilar methodology now known or hereafter developed.
The use of general descriptive names, registered names, trademarks, service marks, etc. in this publication does not imply, even in the absence of a specific statement, that such names are exempt from the relevant protective laws and regulations and therefore free for general use.
The publisher, the authors and the editors are safe to assume that the advice and information in this book are believed to be true and accurate at the date of publication. Neither the publisher nor the authors or the editors give a warranty, express or implied, with respect to the material contained herein or for any errors or omissions that may have been made. The publisher remains neutral with regard to jurisdictional claims in published maps and institutional affiliations.

Printed on acid-free paper

This Springer imprint is published by the registered company Springer International Publishing AG
part of Springer Nature
The registered company address is: Gewerbestrasse 11, 6330 Cham, Switzerland

Preface

In a world in which technology is increasingly present in people's lives, and changing human behavior often is the key to solving many societal and personal problems, studying how technology might be used to influence humans (in their behavior, attitudes, and information processing) is very important. In close multidisciplinary collaboration, researchers study the design, psychology, development, and evaluation of Persuasive Technology, and produce knowledge important for many different application domains (e.g., health care, sustainability, education, or marketing).

PERSUASIVE, the annual international conference on Persuasive Technology is the leading venue for ground-breaking research and novel designs of persuasive technologies. At this annual conference researchers from academia and industry from all over the world discuss the latest persuasive theories, strategies, applications, and artifacts. The conference was organized for the first time in 2006 in Eindhoven (The Netherlands), and then visited Palo Alto (USA), Oulu (Finland), Claremont (USA), Copenhagen (Denmark), Columbus (USA), Linköping (Sweden), Sydney (Australia), Padua (Italy), Chicago (USA), Salzburg (Austria), returning to The Netherlands (Amsterdam) in 2017.

PERSUASIVE 2018 was the 13th edition of the conference, and took place in Waterloo, Canada, in April 2018. The theme of the 2018 edition of the conference "Making a Difference" was both a celebration of what Persuasive Technology has accomplished and a challenge for where Persuasive Technology can make a difference in the future. As a result, Persuasive 2018 invited papers that demonstrate how persuasive technologies can help solve societal issues and ones that explore new frontiers for Persuasive Technology, such as personalized persuasion, new sensor usage, uses of big data, and new ways of creating engagement through gaming or social connection, focussing on a variety of technologies (e.g., Web, wearables, AI, and smart environments). Persuasive 2018 welcomed papers that are grounded in relevant and up-to-date theory, transcending a mere showcasing of applications, and addressing the generalizability of results.

The Doctoral Consortium took place on the 16th of April, where 12 PhD students presented their work to a commitee consisting of Lennart Nacke, Jaap Ham, Harri Oinas-Kukkonen, and Jennifer Boger, chaired by Lisette van Gemert-Pijnen.

On the 17th of April, the conference featured four workshops:

- 6th International Workshop on Behavior Change Support Systems (BCSS 2018): Using Extensive Data in Design and Evaluation of BCSS
- Third International Workshop on Personalizing Persuasive Technologies: A Road Map to the Future
- Persuasive Technology: Making a Difference Together (#MDT2018)
- Uncovering Dark Patterns in Persuasive Technology

On the same day, four tutorials took place:

- Persuasive Systems Design, Evaluation, and Research Through the PSD Model
- Transforming Sociotech Design (TSD)
- Gamification: Tools and Techniques for Persuasive Technology Design
- Combined Toolbox Tutorial

At the two-day main conference (April 18–19) opened by a keynote by Jason Hrera (Head of Product, Behavioral Sciences at Walmart) and closed by a keynote by Julita Vassileva (University of Saskatchewan), the conference showcased 25 oral presentations of accepted papers (short and long) and two poster sessions (pitches and presentations) accommodating 27 scientific posters.

This volume contains the accepted short and long papers presented during the main track of the conference. Of the 59 submitted papers, 25 were accepted, yielding an acceptance rate of 42.4%. Of the submitted papers, 48 were long papers (maximum 12 pages), of which 21 were accepted (i.e., acceptance rate of 43.8%), while of the 11 submitted short papers, four were accepted (i.e., acceptance rate of 36.4%). The 184 authors came from all over the world, and 42 reviewers (all experts in the field of Persuasive Technology) were allowed to indicate their interest for specific (anonymized) papers in a bidding procedure. Selected on the basis of these preferences, and using additional random assignment and excluding conflicts of interest, at least two reviewers evaluated each manuscript. Building on these detailed reviews and numerical rankings, the Program Committee chairs selected the papers to be presented at the conference, and to be published in this volume.

In addition to the papers presented in this volume, the conference also published adjunct proceedings, which include the accepted abstracts of poster submissions, the accepted position papers submitted to the doctoral consortium, as well as contributions about the four workshops and the four tutorials that were accepted for the conference.

This conference was only a success thanks to the great efforts of a large number of people. We would like to thank all authors for submitting their high-quality work, the reviewers for their constructive and extensive feedback, and all scientific and organizational chairs who worked hard to allow this conference to be such an important addition to scientific knowledge and the research and practice community of Persuasive Technology.

April 2018

Jaap Ham
Evangelos Karapanos
Plinio Morita
Catherine Burns

Organization

General Chair

Catherine Burns   University of Waterloo, Canada

Program Chairs

Jaap Ham   Eindhoven University of Technology, The Netherlands
Evangelos Karapanos   Cyprus University of Technology, Cyprus

Organizing Chair

Plinio Morita   University of Waterloo, Canada

Tutorials and Doctoral Consortium Chair

Lisette van   University of Twente, The Netherlands
   Gemert-Pijnen

Workshop Chair

Rita Orji   University of Waterloo, Canada

Social Media Chairs

Agnis Stibe   Paris ESLSCA Business School, France
David Zehao Qin   University of Waterloo, Canada
Dia Rahman   University of Waterloo, Canada

Local Arrangements

Krystina Bednarowski   University of Waterloo, Canada

Steering Committee

Magnus Bang   Linkoping University, Sweden
Shlomo Berkovsky   CSIRO, Australia
Samir Chatterjee   Claremont Graduate University, USA
B J Fogg   Stanford University, USA
Lisette van   University of Twente, The Netherlands
   Gemert-Pijnen
Per Hasle   University of Copenhagen, Denmark

Cees Midden   Eindhoven University of Technology, The Netherlands
Harri Oinas-Kukkonen   University of Oulu, Finland
Manfred Tscheligi   University of Salzburg and AIT, Austria

Program Committee

Raian Ali	Bournemouth University, UK
Nilufar Baghaei	Unitec Institute of Technology, New Zealand
Shlomo Berkovsky	CSIRO, Australia
Samir Chatterjee	Claremont Graduate University, USA
Luca Chittaro	HCI Lab, University of Udine, Italy
Anne-Kathrine Kjær Christensen	Specifii, Denmark
Jacqueline Corbett	Université Laval, Canada
Enny Das	Radboud University, The Netherlands
Janet Davis	Whitman College, USA
Peter De Vries	University of Twente, Netherlands
Alexander Felfernig	Graz University of Technology, Austria
Sandra Burri Gram-Hansen	Aalborg University, Denmark
Ulrike Gretzel	University of Southern California, USA
Stephen Intille	Northeastern University, USA
Anthony Jameson	German Research Center for Artificial Intelligence (DFKI), Germany
Simon Jones	University of Bath, UK
Maurits Kaptein	Tilburg University, The Netherlands
Evangelos Karapanos	Cyprus University of Technology, Cyprus
Pasi Karppinen	University of Oulu, Finland
Saskia Kelders	University of Twente, The Netherlands
Joyca Lacroix	Philips Research, The Netherlands
Sitwat Langrial	Sur University College, Oman
Matthias Laschke	University of Siegen, Germany
Thomas MacTavish	Illinois Institute of Technology, USA
Judith Masthoff	University of Aberdeen, UK
Alexander Meschtscherjakov	University of Salzburg, Austria
Cees Midden	Eindhoven University of Technology, The Netherlands
Alexandra Millonig	AIT Austrian Institute of Technology, Austria
Harri Oinas-Kukkonen	University of Oulu, Finland
Rita Orji	Dalhousie University, Canada
John Rooksby	University of Edinburgh, UK
Peter Ruijten	Eindhoven University of Technology, The Netherlands
Anna Spagnolli	University of Padua, Italy
Agnis Stibe	Paris ESLSCA Business School, France
Piiastiina Tikka	University of Oulu, Finland
Manfred Tscheligi	University of Salzburg and AIT, Austria

Kristian Tørning   Danish School of Media and Journalism, Denmark
Vance Wilson   Worcester Polytechnic Institute, USA
Khin Than Win   University of Wollongong, Australia
Lisette van   University of Twente, The Netherlands
  Gemert-Pijnen

Sponsors

University of Waterloo, Canada
Centre for Bioengineering and Biotechnology
University of Waterloo, Canada

Contents

Personalization and Tailoring

Theoretical Reflections

Thinking About Persuasive Technology from the Strategic Business Perspective: A Call for Research on Cost-Based Competitive Advantage

Xiuyan Shao[(✉)] [iD] and Harri Oinas-Kukkonen

Oulu Advanced Research on Service and Information Systems,
University of Oulu, P.O. Box 3000, 90014 Oulu, Finland
{xiuyan.shao,harri.oinas-kukkonen}@oulu.fi

Abstract. Persuasive system features have been extensively examined, and many of them have been shown to be effective in supporting individuals' achieving their behavioral goals and enhancing system use. Also, companies and organizations have utilized persuasive features in their implementations successfully. However, in order to obtain competitive advantage, organizations need to not only take using persuasive features as differentiation strategy, but also to think about cost of developing persuasive systems. While the research on evaluating persuasive features is important, we argue that previous research has ignored the cost of building persuasive features. As a first step in remedying this gap in research, we present and discuss four research directions for studying cost of developing persuasive systems. This study contributes to persuasive technology field by paving the way for a new research area with highly practical implications.

Keywords: Persuasive technology · Business strategy
Cost-based competitive advantage

1 Introduction

In recent years, technology has been used increasingly to persuade people and motivate them toward various individually and collectively beneficial behaviors in various domains such as healthcare, sustainability, education, and marketing. As a research domain, persuasive technology encompasses disciplines such as social psychology, communication studies, computer science, and information systems [1].

Fogg [2] defines persuasive technology as "interactive computing systems designed to change people's attitudes and behaviors" (p. 1), and Oinas-Kukkonen and Harjumaa [3] define persuasive systems as information systems designed to "reinforce, change or shape attitudes or behaviors or both without using coercion or deception" (p. 486). Using such systems is based on voluntariness [1, 4]; for a system to be effective, it would have to have enough persuasive power.

In an industry context, persuasive technologies play a key role in providing an effective means to employ large scale, personalized interventions [2]. Existing

© Springer International Publishing AG, part of Springer Nature 2018
J. Ham et al. (Eds.): PERSUASIVE 2018, LNCS 10809, pp. 3–15, 2018.
https://doi.org/10.1007/978-3-319-78978-1_1

health-related persuasive technologies in commercial form, such as services, or product-service combinations, make an attempt at influencing people to adopt a healthier lifestyles. The majority of these services use implementations of influence strategies and other theories from motivation and persuasion research to gain compliance and/or change attitudes or behaviors [cf., 1]. Kelders et al. [5] reviewed the literature on web-based health interventions and finds that the differences in technology and interaction predict adherence to a web-based intervention. In their study, increased interaction with a counselor, and more extensive employment of dialogue support significantly predicted better adherence. Likewise, in automotive domain, Wilfinger et al. [6] suggested to widen the scope of automotive persuasive interfaces to persuade drivers to drive safer or in a more sustainable way. Persuasive technology also shows its importance in sales and marketing. Basten et al. [7], through a virtual supermarket simulation, found that triggers co-located with the target product lead to higher sales of that product.

In academic settings, much of the focus in studying persuasive technology has been comparing the effectiveness of technology with and without persuasive function on changing people's behavior. For example, Shamekhi et al. [8] indicated that patients with chronic stress who have medical group visits with a computer-animated conversational agent have more positive stress management behaviors as compared to patients who have usual care (attending regular meetings with their primary care physician). Some of the previous research has focused on explaining a system's success factors. For instance, Karppinen et al. [4] studied user experiences of a web-based health Behavior Change Support Systems (BCSSs) designed as lifestyle intervention targeting obesity, and suggested that self-monitoring, reminders, tunneling, and social support were those system features that especially helped users to achieve their health behavior change goals. Some of the previous studies have focused the usage of individual persuasive features in different application domains. For example, Lehto and Oinas-Kukkonen [9] studied multiple health-related behavior change support systems targeting alcohol misuses and weight loss, and found that reduction and self-monitoring were the most common system features to support accomplishing users' primary task in these domains. Some of the previous studies have addressed the effectiveness of particular persuasive features, and in several cases the results have been promising whereas some of the results have been less clear. For instance, the role of reminders in the context of interventions for weight loss, physical activity, and promoting a healthier lifestyle have been studied. Schneider et al. [10] suggested that email prompts are quite effective in boosting revisits to the program and Fry and Neff [11] reported that together with personal contact with a counselor the periodic reminders increase the effectiveness of the interventions, whereas Griffiths and Christensen [12] reported that while using an information system reduces depressive symptoms weekly reminders makes no difference in its effectiveness.

Previous research on persuasive technology has highlighted the importance of designing persuasion into technologies. However, the selection criterion of particular persuasive features for the systems under development is not limited to their effectiveness on users' behavior change. To obtain competitive business advantage in industry, system development organizations usually have the pressure of developing and implementing the systems within limited time and budget. Industry environment is argued to be important to key constituents involved with information systems and technologies [13]. Industry can influence information technology (IT) artifact, because the design and functionality of most IT applications reflect an industry's core technologies. Besides, market structure influences the features and structure of IT artifacts, for example, when dominant suppliers or customer drive industry standards for electronic data interchange (EDI) and inter-organizational infrastructure. More importantly, system development organizations have to take the industry environment better into consideration to obtain competitive advantage.

In this viewpoint paper, we argue it is time for the field of persuasive technology to more actively think of research from the business strategic perspective. In this paper, we will discuss, under the framework of Persuasive Systems Design (PSD) model [3], how to study the acquisition of competitive advantage by organizations.

2 Conceptual Background: Competitive Advantage

Understanding the sources of sustained competitive advantage has become a major area of study in strategic management. Porter's seminal work does not only address the sources of sustained competitive advantage [14], but also addresses technology, information and competitive advantage in information systems [15]. Porter's generic strategies (see Fig. 1) are the most referred approaches upon the strategies for achieving competitive advantage.

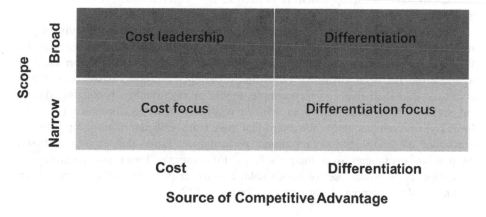

Fig. 1. Porter's generic strategies [16]

According to Porter [14], the key of competitive advantage is the ability to set the position of the business against the competition in the market. Companies achieve competitive advantage either by having the lowest product cost or by having products which differ in ways that are customers value. Porter [16] defined these strategic choices namely as cost leadership strategy and differentiation strategy.

2.1   Cost Leadership

Cost leadership strategy is expressed as cost advantage reflecting selling the goods and services at a lower cost than competitors in terms of design and production [17]. Cost leadership strategy aims to gain competitive advantage by reducing the costs of R&D, service, sales and marketing activities [18]. Companies can get competitive advantage in scale of economics by using effective systems to reduce the cost of human resources and minimizing the costs with cheaper raw material, mass production and distribution [19]. Cost leadership provides competitive advantage in the markets in which the consumers are sensitive to the prices. Firms conducting this strategy aim to reduce all cost in the value chain [20].

2.2   Differentiation

Second generic business strategy is differentiation. In this strategy, an organization aims to be unique in its sector with some characteristics valued by most buyers. It chooses one or more specific characteristics and it positions itself to meet these needs. In the situations where standard goods and services do not meet customer needs, organizations have to find different solutions to their customers' specific needs. This is another way to compete in the market. The basic principle of the differentiation strategy is channeling the customer choices to its goods and services by doing different things from what every rival is doing [21]. Approaches for differentiation can be composed of elements such as brand name, technology, customer services, sales network and other dimensions. The ideal approach is organization's differentiating itself in several dimensions [15].

In this line of research, specific attention has been given to "competitive advantage" from the main elements of which can be labelled as "product-based" and "cost-based". A significant relationship between *product-based advantage* and the performance of organizations has been identified. Firms that experience a product-based competitive advantage over their rivals — for example, higher product quality, packaging, design and style — have been shown to achieve relatively better performance [22, 23]. Similarly, research has further illustrated that there is a significant relationship between *cost-based advantage* and organizational performance. Firms that enjoy cost-based competitive advantages over their rivals — for example, lower manufacturing or production costs, lower cost of goods sold, and lower-price products — have been shown to exhibit comparatively better performance [22, 23].

3   Competitive Advantage in Persuasive Technology Business

To think about persuasive technology from competitive advantage perspective, Fig. 2 summarizes some of the relevant topics. To differentiate, research has already been conducted to evaluate effectiveness of persuasive features, while future research can consider strategically providing persuasive features to customers. To reduce cost of persuasive technology, research can be conducted to investigate cost related with persuasive features, persuasive system development, and strategic cost analysis.

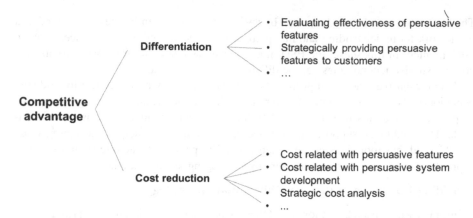

Fig. 2. Competitive advantage in persuasive technology business

Persuasive technology business is still at an immature stage and in many cases a mere provision of persuasive features gives **product-based competitive advantage**. In health BCSSs, mobile applications that incorporate numerous persuasive features that are being used to modify the behavior of users are being developed [24]. These applications are continually improving and are being used more and more by people in their daily lives. Once more evidence becomes available on the costs of producing the product- or service-based advantage, the persuasive technology as a field has reached a much more mature stage. Yet, research into persuasive systems' **cost-based competitive advantage** is still almost non-existent. In this section, we discuss in detail how present persuasive technology research has considered competitive advantage. We first discuss differentiation as the strategy under the framework of PSD model. After that, we suggest how to investigate cost-based competitive advantage in persuasive technology research.

3.1 Differentiation as the Strategy

The differentiation strategy is to create a product or a service, which will differ from the offers by the competitors. In an industry context, designing for persuasion is differentiated from technologies without persuasion or offering a unique persuasive solution. Therefore, this strategy is reflected in persuasive technology research by providing persuasive features and persuasive feature categories that differentiate from competitors.

PSD model. The PSD model [3] is a leading framework in the persuasive systems' field, for designing and evaluating persuasive systems. The PSD model builds on multiple theoretical constructs, such as goal-setting theory [25], the elaboration likelihood model [26], and the theory of reasoned action/planned behavior [27], and it builds upon persuasive technology techniques that Fogg [2], and others define. The PSD model includes a set of seven postulates concerning persuasive systems, and describes 28 potential system features for BCSS, which can be subsumed under the four categories of primary task, dialogue, credibility, and social support features.

The PSD model can be used as a tool by designers and intervention developers and as a framework for understanding and interpreting users' needs and how these needs can be implemented. In this sense, the PSD model serves as a suitable framework to analyze how persuasive technologies can be different from each other.

The persuasive features in primary task support category aim to reflect individuals' behavior goals and track progress toward them. The dialogue support category consists of persuasive features that are related to human-computer interaction and user feedback. The credibility support category includes features that help in designing more credible and thus more persuasive systems. Finally, persuasive techniques in the social support category aim to motivate users by leveraging social influence.

Providing Persuasive Features as Differentiation Strategy

Primary task support. Oduor and Oinas-Kukkonen [28] found that primary task support has the strongest effect on users' continuance intention of using BCSSs among other persuasive feature categories. In health BCSSs, for example, self-monitoring supports a user's primary task and it has been proven to be an effective persuasive feature [4, 12]. It is also the most common persuasive feature implemented in mobile education applications that promote physical activity [24]. In e-commerce, it has been found that primary task support, together with social support, are strong predictors of perceived effectiveness of an e-commerce company like Amazon [30].

Dialogue support. In healthcare, dialogue support features, together with social support features are also frequently implemented. In terms of computer-human dialogue support, applications utilized user data that had been collected to persuade users to engage in their target behavior. A combination of praise, rewards, reminders and suggestion were used to motivate users to achieve their goals [24]. In e-commerce, dialogue support features significantly influence perceived product credibility and perceived review credibility, which both strongly predict system credibility [30].

System credibility support. Twersky and Davis [29] investigated 32 persuasive technology applications, and found that system credibility support features are the most common type of features. In their findings [29], system credibility support features are found mainly in the applications' websites in their use of supporting platforms (such as Twitter or Google Chrome). However, in other industries, like mobile health education [24], credibility support features are the least mentioned. This is confirmed by Adaji and Vassileva [30], which show that in e-commerce perceived system credibility does not influence continuance intention of shoppers in Amazon.

Social support. To explore how social influence design principles affects customer engagement in sharing feedback, Stibe and Oinas-Kukkonen [31] implemented an information system consisting of social influence design principles, and found that social influence could predict even up to 40% of the variance in behavioral intention. For instance, in a persuasive strategy design by Wunsch et al. [32], bikers who received social comparison messages increased their biking compared with control group. They suggested that competition and collective goal elements should be designed to allow social comparison also with familiar besides unknown participants.

Persuasive feature categories are usually implemented dependent on each other to achieve higher effectiveness on persuasion. For example, in health BCSSs primary task support features such as tailoring and monitoring are often present together with dialogue support features such as reminders, rewards and praise [24]. Applications that included self-monitoring features generally included also a feedback mechanism that allowed the users to review their data.

The PSD model suggests that persuasive features have potential to help persuasive technology be effective. Research has already put an effort into investigating how persuasive features make technology more effective in changing people's behavior. To gain some product-based competitive advantage, organizations can simply implement the proven persuasive features into technologies as the first step. Yet, to achieve greater product-based competitive advantage, market analysis of target customer is needed to understand the unique requirements of the group of customers and provide higher quality persuasive technology.

3.2   Cost as the Strategy

To achieve cost-based advantage organizations have to have lower costs than their competitors. Finding the way to lower the cost of production may be the most important question for organizations developing persuasive technology. This urges on estimating the costs of developing persuasive systems and the costs of developing persuasive features into them. But this strategic approach is still quite neglected in persuasive technology research. Here we outline four research directions based on cost-based competitive advantage and PSD model to investigate how to take cost-based competitive advantage into account in persuasive technology research.

Research direction 1: Understanding the cost associated with persuasive technology development. To estimate cost related with persuasive system implementation, software cost estimation models can serve as a foundation. Software cost estimation models attempt to generate an effort estimate, which can be converted into the project duration and cost. Software cost estimation models range from empirical models such as Boehm's COCOMO model [33] to analytical models such as those in Putnam [34], Parr [35], and Cantone et al. [36]. Most software cost models are based on the size measure, such as lines of code (LOC) and function points (FP) within persuasive technology. Software cost estimation models can be applied to understand the cost of developing persuasive features. However, to understand all the relevant costs, it is important to first understand the process of persuasive systems development. Interviews can be done with developers to explore more relevant costs. When conducting interviews, three steps suggested by PSD model for persuasive system development [3] can be used as general framework to design interview questions: (i) analysis of persuasion context and selection of persuasive design principles; (ii) requirement definition for software qualities; (iii) software implementation.

A notable issue related to persuasive technology development is that some persuasive features are considered as popular features [29], and some are usually implemented hand in hand. To evaluate the cost of having multiple persuasive features, simply adding the costs of developing individual persuasive features may not be a correct approach. Cost synergy can be studied in the context of implementing multiple persuasive features from many perspectives. For example, economy of scale explains cost reduction due to the scale of operation [37]. Often there is an optimum design point where costs per additional unit begin to increase. In the context of implementing persuasive features, future research can explore what is the optimum design point for adding more persuasive features. Future studies can also apply other explanations for cost synergy related with persuasive feature implementation.

Research direction 2: Strategic cost analysis for persuasive system development. To stay cost competitive, strategic cost analysis should be considered. Shifts in cost drivers can be identified. Strategic cost drivers include structural cost driver and executional cost driver. Structural cost drivers usually are affected by organizations' external environment, while executional cost drivers are usually affected by the execution of the business activities such as capacity utilization, plant layout, and work-force involvement [38].

To analyze structural cost drivers, it is important to understand customer needs and maintain customer relationship. Customer's Resource Life Cycle [39], for example, can be applied by future research to identify and categorize strategic orientations by focusing on the possible differentiation of organization's product from competitors' products on the basis of customer service. This model considers an organization's relationship with its customers and how this relationship can be changed or enhanced by the strategic application of information system technologies. The four- and thirteen-stage resource life cycles can serve as framework for future case studies.

Interviews conducted in research direction 1 may help understand what are executional cost drivers in the context of persuasive technology development. To manage executional cost drivers, future research may consider factors such as structure and culture of the organization, total quality management, among other issues.

Research direction 3: Empirically validating the price strategy. A third direction of research could adopt a theory-testing research setting and investigate the effectiveness of price strategy. Theories from information systems, marketing, management, and economics can be applied to form a comprehensive analysis framework. The success of price strategy needs to be defined, for instance, based on the goal of persuasive system development. Success elements may include users' actual use of persuasive technology, users' behavioral change, users' satisfaction with the persuasive technology, market share increase. Research in this direction can be quantitative. For instance, a relevant topic concerns about providing different persuasive features and accordingly pricing to different user groups in order to capture a larger portion of the total market surplus. Most persuasive technologies provide the same functions to all customers despite their heterogeneity in willingness to use. While providing persuasive function costs, it is wise to provide a customer the functions that he/she is mostly willing to use. Group pricing (or third-degree price discrimination) refers dividing the market into segments and charges different price to each segment [40], and can be found in many industries today. The travel, hospitality, and entertainment industries commonly offer special corporate or loyalty discount rates; insurance companies use to classify risks and discriminate fees based on the insuree's age, sex, marital status, occupation, etc.

Future research may consider taking experiments in user groups provided with different sets of persuasive features and prices to test their use.

Research direction 4: Theory development. While the third stream of research called for theory testing, we also see that inductive and qualitative approaches are needed. The limitation of the theory-testing setting is that it merely tests if existing theory is supported or not. In contrast, theory development would approach the problem perhaps even from a clean table without any theories in mind by asking persuasive technology development managers report their considerations about competitive advantage. Ideally, a qualitative approach would allow researchers to develop new constructs, concepts, and even theories that explain the persuasive technology design for competitive advantage. Such in-depth interview studies could also reveal a process that covers several rounds of refinement of persuasive technology development. Possible methods for analyzing the interviews includes grounded theory.

It has to be clarified that the new research directions do not refute the importance of previous research on persuasive systems features evaluation. On the contrary, previous research provides fundamental knowledge for new research directions. Although we emphasized that future research on cost-based competitive advantage is needed, we keep it in mind that the flexibility to have "product-based" and "cost-based" strategy may be necessary for persuasive technology business to gain sustainable competitive advantage.

4 Discussion

To gain competitive advantage, a company must either perform these development activities at a lower cost or perform them in a way that leads to differentiation and a premium price [14]. PSD provides a list of persuasive features that offer potential for differentiating persuasive technologies. Numerous studies have investigated effectiveness of these persuasive features on users' behavior change in many application areas. However, so far the research community has paid little attention to the cost of persuasive technology development. The purpose of this viewpoint paper has been to address this oversight and provide research directions for possible future studies. Past research has provided a solid foundation for understanding persuasive features' impact on changing users' behavior, and we now call for new perspectives – especially for analyzing the cost of persuasive features. We argue that to obtain competitive advantage, persuasive technology organizations must not only select from the proven effective persuasive features, but also analyze the cost related with persuasive technology development.

We have framed our arguments through the framework of the PSD model [3], and proposed four research directions for future studies. Although the four proposed research directions have been discussed in isolation, we would suggest that these, and potentially other topics for consideration, might prove fruitful when studied together. For example, research into strategic cost analysis would also appear to link well with the work on understanding costs. As noted, for example, structural cost driver and executional cost driver can be considered in the interviews to understand the cost associated with persuasive technology development. Another area involves consideration of the synergy effect of persuasive features. When multiple persuasive features are implemented, do they lead to more significant impact on users' behavior change, and thus be more cost-efficient? One reasonable explanation can be economies of scale, which are the cost advantage that organizations obtain due to their scale of operation, with cost per unit of output decreasing with increasing scale.

This study offers a valuable contribution to research because previous research on persuasive technology mostly examined the relationship between persuasive features and users' behavior change, leaving external and internal business environment currently absent from the persuasive technology literature. A strategic business perspective is therefore important. Future research should take more industry context into consideration. The proposed research directions will provide implications for practice. Understanding cost of persuasive features offers possibility for development organizations to adjust their system development strategy, and achieve cost efficiency and user satisfaction. This is expected to offer more comprehensive perspective for industry.

5   Conclusion

Persuasive technology literature has put much focus on examining the impacts of persuasive features on users' behavioral change, and this provides significant insights for technology developers. To design a successful persuasive technology, persuasive features can be selected from what's already proved to be effective. To obtain competitive advantage for development organizations, the selection of persuasive features should also consider organizational financial issues and industry environment. We call for research that takes a competitive advantage attitude, especially the cost-based competitive advantage perspective, into persuasive design. As a first step in remedying the gap in our understanding, this study opens up a new research area in persuasive technology field, and our study highlights several directions for future research. First, understanding the cost associated with persuasive technology development. The steps suggested by PSD model can be taken into account when interviewing organizations regarding with the relevant costs. Software cost estimation models can be learnt from. Second, future research could also explore the management of strategic cost. Organization's external environment such as competition shifts should be taken into account. Third, research that empirically validates the price strategy can be done to show if price strategy really matters. Finally, we suggest that future research to develop theory specifically in persuasive technology field related with product-based competitive advantage and cost-based competitive advantage. We believe that the proposed research directions will contribute to the body of knowledge on persuasive technology research.

Acknowledgement. We wish to thank the Finnish Cultural Foundation for supporting this research.

References

1. Oinas-Kukkonen, H.: A foundation for the study of behavior change support systems. Pers. Ubiquit. Comput. **17**(6), 1223–1235 (2013)
2. Fogg, B.J.: Persuasive Technology: Using Computers to Change What We Think and Do. Morgan Kaufmann Publishers Inc., San Francisco (2003)
3. Oinas-Kukkonen, H., Harjumaa, M.: Persuasive systems design: key issues, process model, and system features. Commun. Assoc. Inf. Syst. **24**, 485–500 (2009)
4. Karppinen, P., Oinas-Kukkonen, H., Alahaivala, T., Jokelainen, T., Keranen, A.M., Salonurmi, T., Savolainen, M.: Persuasive user experiences of a health behavior change support system: a 12-month study for prevention of metabolic syndrome. Int. J. Med. Inform. **96**, 51–61 (2016)
5. Kelders, S.M., Kok, R.N., Ossebaard, H.C., Van Gemert-Pijnen, J.E.W.C.: Persuasive system design does matter: a systematic review of adherence to web-based interventions. J. Med. Internet Res. **14**, 17–40 (2012)
6. Wilfinger, D., Gärtner, M., Meschtscherjakov, A., Tscheligi, M.: Persuasion in the Car: probing potentials. In: Spagnolli, A., Chittaro, L., Gamberini, L. (eds.) PERSUASIVE 2014. LNCS, vol. 8462, pp. 273–278. Springer, Cham (2014). https://doi.org/10.1007/978-3-319-07127-5_24
7. Basten, F., Ham, J., Midden, C., Gamberini, L., Spagnolli, A.: Does trigger location matter? The influence of localization and motivation on the persuasiveness of mobile purchase recommendations. In: MacTavish, T., Basapur, S. (eds.) PERSUASIVE 2015. LNCS, vol. 9072, pp. 121–132. Springer, Cham (2015). https://doi.org/10.1007/978-3-319-20306-5_11
8. Shamekhi, A., Bickmore, T., Lestoquoy, A., Gardiner, P.: Augmenting group medical visits with conversational agents for stress management behavior change. In: de Vries, P.W., Oinas-Kukkonen, H., Siemons, L., Beerlage-de Jong, N., van Gemert-Pijnen, L. (eds.) PERSUASIVE 2017. LNCS, vol. 10171, pp. 55–67. Springer, Cham (2017). https://doi.org/10.1007/978-3-319-55134-0_5
9. Lehto, T., Oinas-Kukkonen, H.: Examining the persuasive potential of web-based health behavior change support systems. Trans. Hum.-Comput. Inter. **7**(3), 126–140 (2015)
10. Schneider, F., de Vries, H., Candel, M., van de Kar, A., van Osch, L.: Periodic email prompts to re-use an Internet-delivered computer-tailored lifestyle program: influence of prompt content and timing. J. Med. Internet Res. **15**(1), e23 (2013)
11. Fry, J.P., Neff, R.A.: Periodic prompts and reminders in health promotion and health behavior interventions: a systematic review. J. Med. Internet Res. **11**(2), e16 (2009)
12. Griffiths, K.M., Christensen, H.: Internet based mental health programs: a powerful tool in the rural medical kit. Aust. J. Rural Health **15**(2), 81–87 (2007)
13. Chiasson, M.W., Davidson, E.: Taking industry seriously in information systems research. MIS Q. **29**(4), 591–605 (2005)
14. Porter, M.E.: Competitive Advantage: Creating and Sustaining Superior Performance. The Free Press, New York (1985)
15. Porter, M.E., Millar, V.E.: How information gives you competitive advantage. Harv. Bus. Rev. **63**(4), 149–160 (1985)
16. Porter, M.E.: New global strategies for competitive advantage. Plan. Rev. **18**(3), 4–14 (1990)
17. Wheelen, T.L., Hunger, D.J.: Strategic Management and Business Policy, 8th edn. Prentice Hall, Massachusetts (2002)
18. Rugman, A., Hodgetts, R.: International Business: A Strategic Management Approach, 2nd edn. Prentice Hall, New York (2000)

19. Eraslan, I.H.: The effects of competitive strategies on firm performance: a study in Turkish textile and apparel industry considering the mediating role of value chain activities. Bogazii University Social Sciences Institute, Istanbul (2008)
20. Thompson, A.A., Strickland, A.J.: Strategic Management: Concepts and Cases, 9th edn. Irwin McGraw-Hill, USA (1996)
21. Bal, Y.: The effect of competitive strategies on human resource management practices. Istanbul University Institute of Social Sciences, Istanbul (2011)
22. Gimenez, C., Ventura, A.: Supply chain management as a competitive advantage in the Spanish grocery sector. Published Working Paper. No. 2, 04/2002, Universitat Pompeu Fabra' (UPF), Barcelona, Spain (2002)
23. Morgan, N.A., Kaleka, A., Katsikeas, C.S.: Antecedents of export venture performance: a theoretical model and empirical assessment. J. Mark. **68**, 90–108 (2004)
24. Matthews, J., Win, K.T., Oinas-Kukkonen, H., Freeman, M.: Persuasive technology in mobile applications promoting physical activity: a systematic review. J. Med. Syst. **40**(3), 72 (2016)
25. Locke, E.A., Latham, G.P.: Building a practically useful theory of goal setting and task motivation: a 35-year odyssey. Am. Psychol. **57**(9), 705–717 (2002)
26. Petty, R.E., Cacioppo, J.T.: The elaboration likelihood model of persuasion. Adv. Exp. Soc. Psychol. **19**, 123–205 (1986)
27. Ajzen, I.: The theory of planned behavior. Organ. Behav. Human Decis. Process. **50**(2), 179–211 (1991)
28. Oduor, M., Oinas-Kukkonen, H.: Commitment devices as behavior change support systems: a study of users' perceived competence and continuance intention. In: de Vries, P.W., Oinas-Kukkonen, H., Siemons, L., Beerlage-de Jong, N., van Gemert-Pijnen, L. (eds.) PERSUASIVE 2017. LNCS, vol. 10171, pp. 201–213. Springer, Cham (2017). https://doi.org/10.1007/978-3-319-55134-0_16
29. Twersky, E., Davis, J.: "Don't say that!". In: de Vries, P.W., Oinas-Kukkonen, H., Siemons, L., Beerlage-de Jong, N., van Gemert-Pijnen, L. (eds.) PERSUASIVE 2017. LNCS, vol. 10171, pp. 215–226. Springer, Cham (2017). https://doi.org/10.1007/978-3-319-55134-0_17
30. Adaji, I., Vassileva, J.: Perceived effectiveness, credibility and continuance intention in e-commerce: a study of Amazon. In: de Vries, P.W., Oinas-Kukkonen, H., Siemons, L., Beerlage-de Jong, N., van Gemert-Pijnen, L. (eds.) PERSUASIVE 2017. LNCS, vol. 10171, pp. 293–306. Springer, Cham (2017). https://doi.org/10.1007/978-3-319-55134-0_23
31. Stibe, A., Oinas-Kukkonen, H.: Using social influence for motivating customers to generate and share feedback. In: Spagnolli, A., Chittaro, L., Gamberini, L. (eds.) PERSUASIVE 2014. LNCS, vol. 8462, pp. 224–235. Springer, Cham (2014). https://doi.org/10.1007/978-3-319-07127-5_19
32. Wunsch, M., Stibe, A., Millonig, A., Seer, S., Dai, C., Schechtner, K., Chin, R.C.C.: What makes you bike? Exploring persuasive strategies to encourage low-energy mobility. In: MacTavish, T., Basapur, S. (eds.) PERSUASIVE 2015. LNCS, vol. 9072, pp. 53–64. Springer, Cham (2015). https://doi.org/10.1007/978-3-319-20306-5_5
33. Boehm, B.W.: Software Engineering Economics. Prentice-Hall, Englewood Cliffs (1981)
34. Putnam, L.H.: A general empirical solution to the macro software sizing and estimating problem. IEEE Trans. Softw. Eng. **4**(4), 345–361 (1978)
35. Parr, N.A.: An alternative to the Raleigh curve model for software development effort. IEEE Softw. Eng. (1980)
36. Cantone, G., Cimitile, A., De Carlini, U.: A comparison of models for software cost estimation and management of software projects. Computer Systems: Performance and Simulation. Elisevier Science, Amsterdam (1986)

37. Panzar, J.C., Willig, R.D.: Economies of scale in multi-output production. Q. J. Econ. **91**, 481–493 (1977)
38. Shank, J.K., Govindarajan, V.: Strategic Cost Management. The Free Press, New York (1993)
39. Ives, B., Learmonth, G.P.: The information system as a competitive weapon. Commun. ACM **27**(12), 1193–1201 (1984)
40. Varian, H.R.: Price discrimination and social welfare. Am. Econ. Rev. **75**(4), 870–875 (1985)

What Makes It Persuasive?

Sandra Burri Gram-Hansen(✉), Maja Færge Rabjerg,
and Ea Kirstine Bork Hovedskou

Department of Communication and Psychology,
Aalborg University, Aalborg, Denmark
burri@hum.aau.dk, {mrabje13, ehoved13}@student.aau.dk

Abstract. Based on an analysis of two wearable activity trackers, this papers seeks to contribute to the discussion of characteristics of persuasive design, by arguing that although principles commonly applied in persuasive technologies are present, it may not justify that a technology is defined as persuasive. We refer to the rhetorical concept of peithenanke, in order to explain the subtle nuances of different types of behaviour design, and support previously made arguments that transparency and ethics are fundamental qualities of persuasion, which should not be overlooked neither in theory nor in practice.

Keywords: Persuasion · Persuasive design · Children · Ethics
Peithenanke

1 Introduction

Although persuasion in modern days is most often considered in relation to social psychology, the concept is recognized as being traceable to ancient Greece, the source of not only democracy but also classical rhetoric. Persuasion was central to Aristotle's theory of rhetorical discourse, and the concept remains a dominant tradition in the rhetorical tradition, distinguishing itself from other rhetorical traditions such as politics and marketing [1].

In this paper, we address some of the nuances which constitute subtle yet significant distinctions of persuasion, and discuss these in relation to persuasive technologies. Particular interested is directed towards the persuasive intentions as well as towards the distinction between persuasion and less ethical approaches to influencing the receiver – in classical rhetoric referred to as *peithenanke*. The presented reflections are brought about by a comparative analysis of two wearable activity trackers, from which it was found that often referenced persuasive principles [2, 3] were heavily applied in both systems, but that only one of the trackers might in fact be considered persuasive, when considering the rhetorical nuances of the concept. The persuasive potential of activity trackers is generally acknowledged, however the particular interest of this paper, is the challenges related to devices designed for children – and to discuss whether such devices can in fact be defined as persuasive.

Overall, the goal of this paper is to contribute to the ongoing research and practice in design and evaluation of persuasive technologies, by addressing some of the challenges related to classifying a system as being persuasive. Moreover, we introduce the

© Springer International Publishing AG, part of Springer Nature 2018
J. Ham et al. (Eds.): PERSUASIVE 2018, LNCS 10809, pp. 16–27, 2018.
https://doi.org/10.1007/978-3-319-78978-1_2

rhetorical concept peithenanke, and argue that the rhetorical distinction between pei-thenanke and persuasion may be an important element to consider when evaluating persuasive systems.

2 Family Wearables – A Comparative Analysis of Persuasive Potential

During the past decade, health has been the dominating domain for research and development of persuasive technologies. A review of full papers published in the first decade of Persuasive Technology conferences, indicated that 41 out 133 papers were related to different areas of mental and physical health. Over time, persuasive applications supporting a healthier lifestyle has advanced from simple pedometers and web based diaries for training and diets, to wearable devices and mobile applications which not alone facilitate users in achieving a healthier lifestyle, but also enable them to connect and integrate their activity tracking with additional applications such as calendars, mobile phones and streaming services.

Wearable activity trackers are generally understood as electronic devices which enable the user to monitor physical activity such as walking and running. While early versions of wearable activity trackers mostly targeted ambitious fitness enthusiast aiming to track e.g. their exercise pulse, speed and distance, resent years have shown a developing tendency for activity trackers which target a far wider range of users. With devices, such as Jawbone and Fitbit, wearable activity trackers have become a common household item which furthermore not only provides the user with health-related metrics, but also aim to motivate the user to persuade the user to become even more active. On a more resent scale, wearable activity trackers are now being developed for children, providing them with some of the fundamental features of the adult trackers, but modified in an attempt to meet the practical and motivational requirements of children (e.g. higher durability and use of animations).

In this study, 2 activity trackers (Garmin VivoSmart HR and Garmin Vivofit Jr.) were evaluated and compared in order to identify which persuasive features were incorporated and what parts of the system were seen to have the most significant persuasive impact. The activity trackers are primarily distinguished from each other by the intended users. While the Garmin VivoSmart HR is aimed at adults, the Vivofit Jr is an activity tracker designed for children. Equal for both trackers is that the system consists of the wearable activity tracker (bracelet) and a designated app for mobile devices[1]. Both technologies aim to motivate the user to be more physically active, by tracking activities and providing the user with statistical feedback and motivational triggers. E.g. the Garmin HR will (like many other activity trackers) prompt the user to move regularly, and praise the user when specific goals have been met. The Vivofit Jr. bracelet on the other hand combines activity tracking with assigned chores, and is presented by Garmin as an activity tracker which *"motivates kids with rewards and a mobile adventure trail to unlock"* (Fig. 1).

---

[1] https://buy.garmin.com/da-DK/DK/cIntoSports-c571-p1.html.

Fig. 1. On the left, the Garmin VivoSmart HR, and on the right, Garmin Vivofit Jr

3 Analysing Devices with the PSD Framework

The PSD model [3] was applied as methodological framework for the system evaluation. The evaluation itself was conducted as a group exercise involving both persuasive design experts and information architecture students at Master's levels. Conducting the analysis as a group activity involving different types of expertise, was considered beneficial as the different features of the two systems were more richly discussed. An important element of the PSD model is the encouragement to include an analysis of the intended use and the user context. This was found particularly important to our study as the devices where very similar, and predominantly distinguished by their target users. The evaluation of each system considered the different elements of the PSD framework stringently, and the findings were subsequently compared and discussed. In order to identify where in the system persuasive features are applied, the analysis distinguishes between findings in the mobile app and findings in the wearable activity tracker. To further support the evaluation results, interviews were conducted with 4 adult users and 4 children who were familiar with the two devices. In the following, a very brief overview of the analytical findings is provided. The main goal is to illustrate the extensive commonalities between the two systems, prior to discussing their actual persuasive potential.

3.1 Persuasion Context

Activity trackers are generally applied by user's who wish to increase or monitor their existing level of physical activity. Garmin VivoSmart HR. and similar devices are most often used by adults or young adults who independently make the decision to apply the technology based on an intention to become healthier or increase physical activity. these intentions are seldom shared by children who wear the Garmin Vivofit Jr. For the most part, the decision to provide the child with an activity tracker will be made by an adult, and the intent to increase physical activity is not necessarily shared by the child. Both technologies are meant to be used both day and night, thereby enabling the user to acquire feedback not only about physical activity but also sleep patterns. Whilst the Garmin HR require weekly charging, the Garmin Vivofit Jr requires no charging as the battery will last for approximately 1 year.

An important difference between the two systems, is that whilst they both provide extended feedback through the mobile apps, the Garmin HR app is applied by the user, whilst the Garmin Vivofit Jr app is parentally controlled. Moreover, while the Garmin HR enables the user to integrate content from other health related mobile apps, the Garmin Vivofit Jr is a more closed system. Competition with other users is only possible if the users are connected to the same parental control app (e.g. siblings). Finally, The Garmin Vivofit Jr not only focuses on activity but also on chores, such as doing homework, cleaning room, walking the dog etc. Completed chores can then be rewarded with virtual goal coins.

3.2 Primary Task Support

The primary task support constitutes principles which facilitate the targeted behaviour change. For both technologies, the primary task is identified as supporting the user in increasing physical activity on a daily basis. In our analysis, we focused on identifying which persuasive principles were applied, and in what part of the system (tracker or app) (Tables 1 and 2).

Table 1. Overview of analysis of primary task support principles in Garmin VivoSmart HR

Garmin VivoSmart HR			
Persuasive principle	Example	Tracker	App
Reduction	Complex data is presented in simple visualisations	X	X
Tunnelling	Registration with Facebook, then automatically connected via Bluetooth		X
Tailoring	Activity goals are set individually by the user. User defines what information to be presented in the app and the bracelet	X	X
Personalisation	User name and profile picture + connection to Facebook. Bracelet enables user to receive text messages and email	X	X
Self-monitoring	Steps, stairs, sleep and pulse can be measured. Data is presented for individual days as well as progress over time	X	X
Simulation			
Rehearsal			

As indicated in the tables, the majority of principles categorized as primary task support, was identified in both systems. In most cases the principles were applied in the same manner and with very few adjustments to indicate that one tracker was targeted children. Moreover, it was considered noticeable that while simulation and rehearsal was not identified in the VivoSmart system, all principles within the category was identified in the Vivofit Jr device.

Table 2. Overview of analysis of primary task support principles in Garmin Vivofit Jr

Garmin Vivofit Jr

Persuasive principle	Example	Tracker	App
Reduction	Complex data is presented in simple visualisations	X	X
Tunnelling	Registration requires name and picture, everything is automatic		X
Tailoring	Goal is pre-set for 60 min of daily activity. Chores and rewards are customized in the app	X	X
Personalisation	App has picture of the child, and provides the option to select different colours and customize the app avatar. Name of the user appears on the tracker	X	X
Self-monitoring	Steps and number of coins are visible on the tracker, as well as number of active minutes and completed chores	X	X
Simulation	Coin falls into piggybank	X	
Rehearsal	Same chores are completed every day and activity goal is always 60 min	X	X

3.3 Dialogue Support

The dialogue support constitutes principles which facilitate the communication between the user and the system. Dialogue support particularly aims to maintain user motivation, during the persuasive process (Tables 3 and 4).

Table 3. Overview of analysis of dialogue support principles in Garmin VivoSmart HR

Garmin VivoSmart HR

Persuasive principle	Example	Tracker	App
Praise	Device vibrates when goals are achieved	X	
Rewards			
Reminders	Device reminds user to be active if no activity has been registered for 1 h. User is reminded when the device need to be recharged	X	
Suggestion	Suggestions are provided regarding ways in which the app may be customized		X
Similarity	The design is simple and discrete, thereby being identified as appropriate for everyday use. The app provides an overview of collected data and a neutral presentation of data analysis	X	X
Liking			
Social role	Coach – presentation of data. Assistance in goal setting, motivation and reminders	X	X

Table 4. Overview of analysis of dialogue support principles in Garmin Vivofit Jr

Garmin Vivofit Jr			
Persuasive principle	Example	Tracker	App
Praise	Happy tune when the 60 min are up	X	
Rewards	Coins in piggybank and steps on jungle track	X	X
Reminders			
Suggestion	The app provides suggestions for chores that might be appropriate for the child		X
Similarity	Child friendly avatars and an element of gamification. Piggybank is known by most children, the app has a game like jungle track, and the same ikons are applied throughout the system	X	X
Liking	Happy colours, child friendly ikons. App is highly ikon driven and very simple in its design	X	X
Social role	The appears to take the role of communication facilitator. It eases the dialogue between parents and children, as goals and chores are visualised clearly		X

Dialogue support is identified in both technologies, particularly in terms of praise and rewards. The dialogue support is not limited to verbal feedback, but also physical as the wearable device vibrates when goals are achieved. Reminders are provided through e.g. prompts that the user should move or be active.

While the Garmin HR adopts the social role of a personal trainer, providing feedback on exercise and progress, the Garmin Vivofit Jr is designed in a more game oriented manner, highlighting when the user earns gold coins for completing tasks, and by supplying the user with a game avatar which creates a link to the design of the mobile app. Due to the comprehensive parental control, the Vivofit Jr was identified as a communication facilitator rather than a direct coach or guide for the child.

With regards to the Garmin Vivofit Jr., it was noted that the wearable device itself provides very little feedback for the child. As the mobile application is controlled by the parent, the actual user is provided with very little insight or system transparency. Although the child is provided with information about number of steps completed during a day, the reward is not achieved before the child is provide access to the mobile app, where the steps then enable the child to proceed with a virtual jungle trail. Rewards provided through the wearable device are constituted by virtual coins which the child may earn by completing different chores – chores which have been defined by the parents, and coins which are awarded by the parents rather than the system.

3.4   Credibility Support

Beyond system functionality, credibility is considered a key component in persuasive systems. Harjumaa et al. [4] clarify that credibility may be based on either the manufacturers brand or embedded in the system design. While Garmin is recognized internationally as a highly credible brand in relation to activity trackers, it is by far the only recognized brand. With producers, such as Fitbit, Jawbone and Samsung amongst others also providing users with high quality trackers, the choice of trackers is assumed to very often be based on characteristics such as connecting mobile device (e.g. android vs apple devices, or a wish to connect a Samsung tracker to a Samsung phone for better functionality). Consequently, although acknowledging the brand value in relation to credibility, our analysis has focused more specifically on design based credibility (Tables 5 and 6).

Table 5. Overview of analysis of credibility support principles in Garmin VivoSmart HR

Garmin VivoSmart HR			
Persuasive principle	Example	Tracker	App
Trustworthiness	In general, there is a tendency to trust information from our own phones. The data appears to be detailed and it is possible to test that steps are counted correctly	X	X
Expertise	Garmin is a recognised brand which facilitates the impression of expertise	X	X
Surface credibility	The tracker design appears robust, and professional. The app provides a wide range of information although the visible design is somewhat confusing	X	
Real-world feel			
Authority	Imperative form is applied for messages. Recommendations are very clear. Step goals are not customizable but pre-set based on past days' activity	X	X
Third-party endorsement	Possible to connect to other users through different apps. E.g. Endomondo or Lifesum		X
Verifiability	It is possible to verify if step counting is correct. When connected to other apps, it is possible to verify e.g. distance	X	

Table 6. Overview of analysis of credibility support principles in Garmin Vivofit Jr

Garmin Vivofit Jr			
Persuasive principle	Example	Tracker	App
Trustworthiness	Step count and systematic overview of chores and coins is easily interpreted even by children	X	X
Expertise			
Surface credibility	Tracker is robust and child friendly with no sharp edges. The app is very simple and offers help and guidance	X	X
Real-world feel			
Authority			
Third-party endorsement			
Verifiability			

In the analysis of credibility support, it is particularly noticeable that the majority of principles are identified in the Garmin VivoSmart system. Although recognising that credibility support in general is a significant factor in persuasive system design, it does appear natural that these principles are not heavily applied in a device designed for children, as the intended users are unlikely to weigh them as heavily as adult users.

3.5   Social Support

The final category, social support, is based on Fogg's original principles regarding mobility and connectivity [5]. Fogg argues that networked devices may to facilitate social support, and potentially be more persuasive than technologies that are not connected (Tables 7 and 8).

Table 7. Overview of analysis of social support principles in Garmin VivoSmart HR

Garmin VivoSmart HR			
Persuasive principle	Example	Tracker	App
Social learning			
Social comparison	Compares results to other Garmin users or other trackers through compatible apps		X
Normative influence			
Cooperation			
Social facilitation			
Competition	It is possible to challenge and compete with other users once connected		X
Recognition			

Equal for both devices, social support principles are only scarcely applied. For the VivoSmart HR device, there is an option to share data with others, however the system does not push for the user to do so. We interpret this as a sign of respect that for many users, personal weight and level of activity is a somewhat private topic which the user may comfortably share with the device, but not necessarily with other people. Contrary, for the Vivofit Jr. the little use of social support principles is assumed to be based on a higher focus on security as children may not be fully aware of the consequences of sharing personal information with others. Therefore, sharing is only possible through the mobile app and is as such parentally controlled. Overall, the analysis of the two systems demonstrate an extensive application of persuasive principles, particularly in the categories Primary Task Support and Dialogue Support. Differences are subtle as the principles are often applied in identical manners, it is however noticeable that there is a slight majority of persuasive principles applied in the Vivofit Jr compared to VivoSmart HR.

Table 8. Overview of analysis of social support principles in Garmin Vivofit Jr

Garmin Vivofit Jr

Persuasive principle	Example	Tracker	App
Social learning			
Social comparison	It is possible to compete with other family members on number of steps		X
Normative influence			
Cooperation			
Social facilitation			
Competition	The system provides step challenges and comparison through the app		X
Recognition	The tracker is eye catching and easily recognised by other children in school	X	

4 What Makes It Persuasive?

In spite of the analysis identifying vast commonalities between the two devices, and in spite of persuasive principles being distinctly identified in both activity trackers, the persuasiveness of the Garmin Vivofit Jr. activity tracker was found to be challenged when further considering the intent of applying the device and the transparency of the mobile application. In particular, the parental control of the Garmin Vivofit Jr app imposed challenges, as the majority of persuasive principles were identified in the app, and did as such not necessarily reach the actual user. Moreover, the majority of praise and rewards attained through the activity tracker was related to the chores, rather than to being physically active. Consequently, the potential to motivate children to be more physically active, was found to be surpassed by the more dominating focus on completing chores in order to earn gold coins and eventually receive rewards in real life. The most important challenge however, was found in the overall feedback of the system, which both in relation to chores and in relation to physical activity, primarily focuses on the rewards systems rather than on the targeted behaviour change.

Our reason to contest the persuasiveness of the Vivofit Jr, was further supported by interviews conducted with a group of children and parents who have experience with the device. The group involved 4 children who all used the device, and 2 sets of parents. In all instances, the devices were introduced to the children by parental imitative. In one case, a child had wished for a tracker after being inspired by a sibling who had already been given one. While the parents indicated that the trackers had been given to the children with the intent to motivate more physical activity, the children all stated that their main focus in the system was the rewards in terms of virtual coins in the piggybank. The children showed was very little interest in the jungle track, and neither the children nor the parents had experienced a continuous increase in physical activity amongst the children. On the contrary, one set of parents explained that the activity tracker had made them aware that their children were already extremely active during their school days, and as such it became more acceptable that they felt a need to relax and play with e.g. an IPad once they came home. As such, it appeared that the Vivofit Jr, in spite of a vast use of persuasive principles, had very little persuasive impact in practice, and after a while served more as a parent surveillance tool and a digital resource for rewarding the child when chores had been completed.

Consequently, in spite of the analysis of the Garmin Vivofit Jr. resulting in contradictory results the system is found to not be genuinely persuasive, but rather an example of what is in learning theories referred to as *chocolate covered broccoli* [6]. Rather than have the system motivate and encourage children to be more active, chores and physical activity is made appealing through virtual rewards and animations, comparable to when children are tricked into eating medicine, simply by disguising it in something pleasant such a yoghurt.

In continuation, we refer to distinctions of the concept of persuasion, primarily addressed through classical rhetoric. Rhetoric is understood as the art and science of beautiful communication – in the sense that communication should be not only appealing but also efficient and truthful [7]. In classical rhetoric, persuasion is understood to be an approach to attitude and behaviour change with particularly high ethical standards, as opposed to the concept *peithenanke* which indicates manipulation, or force masked as persuasion [8]. It is important to note however, that in classical rhetoric, truth is considered a far wider concept than for instance logic as the perception of truth is to some extent based on sentiment rather than fact alone [9]. Direct lies are still discarded as untruthful, however classical rhetoric does acknowledge that in some cases, the perception of truthfulness depends on the context and on the rhetorical strategy – a challenge which is well known in e.g. politics, marketing and commercial settings. In contrary, persuasion is argued to distinguish itself through transparency, understood in the sense that the persuadee is fully aware that his or her attitude or behaviour is being changed.

Identifying persuasion as a more ethical approach to behaviour design is by far novel to the persuasive technology community. In a critical review of Fogg's original publication on persuasive technologies [2], Atkinson argues that in order for persuasive technologies to be ethical, some level of transparency is required [10]. Transparency is understood in the sense that users must be aware of the persuasive intent of the technology. Beyond the persuasive conference community, similar arguments have been made by Berdichevsky and Neunschwander (1999), as they stressed that true persuasion does not misinform the user, and that ethical evaluations should include not only the consequences of the persuasive technology but also evaluations of the persuasive intent [11].

To further elaborate on our perception of persuasiveness in comparison to peithenanke, we refer to Spahn's ethical guidelines for persuasive systems:

1. Persuasion should be based on prior (real or counterfactual) consent
2. Ideally the aim of persuasion should be to end the persuasion.
3. Persuasion should grant as much autonomy as possible to the user [12]

In the case of the Vivofit Jr, the problems appear to be multiple. Firstly, the intent of the device is argued to be motivating children to be more physically active, whilst the actual design of the tracking device places a primary focus on the chores and appurtenant rewards, thereby failing to facilitate the primary intention. Secondly, the motivational aspect of the design and the predominant focus on rewards rather than facilitation of knowledge processing regarding progress and health benefits, challenges the persuasiveness as the child is unlikely to identify the intent of the system making it doubtful that the system will result in the child maintaining the intended level of activity and consequently making the persuasive device superfluous [12, 13]. Thirdly, the parental control of the system provides the child with almost no autonomy or ability to consent to the data being collected. While we recognise the safety-concerns leading to this particular element of the design, we find that it gives reason to consider if in fact children can ever be persuadees, before they have the maturity to recognise the implications of the system they are interacting with.

5   Reflections for Future Research

In this paper, we have sought to illustrate that while an analysis of two activity trackers immediately resulted in the impression that they could both be categorized as persuasive systems, the actual persuasiveness is to some extend dependent on the several other factors beyond the distinct system features. To elaborate on the challenges related to identifying a system as being persuasive, we point towards classical rhetoric as well as modern research within the field of persuasion. We find that although some of these thoughts have been presented and discussed previously, they constitute perspective which remains continuously important to revisit, as digital resources become increasingly more pervasive, and as different approaches to behaviour design are constantly emerging. With the dawn of social media, wearable technologies for both adults and children and a constantly increasing use of digital communication platforms in everyday life, we are likely to find that transparency as well as ethics of design and application in general, is challenged. Based on our findings we recommend that future research involves exploring the possibilities and limitations of children as persuadees. The subject has seldom been considered within the persuasive technology community, however with a continuous increase in systems that target a younger audience (e.g. Pokémon Go [14]) we find it to be an important element to consider. In terms of our methodological approach to this research, we found that the PSD model provided a well-structured and systematic framework. However, in our interpretation of the framework, it may be beneficial if the Persuasion Context, is to be considered a reflection benchmark to which all other analytical findings should be related – and potentially a preclusion for further analysis in order to avoid that all interactive systems will potentially be considered persuasive.

References

1. Hogan, M.J.: Persuasion in the rhetorical tradition. In: Dillard, J.P., Shen, L. (eds.) The SAGE Handbook of Persuasion: Developments in Theory and Practice, pp. 2–20. Beverly Hills, SAGE (2013)
2. Fogg, B.: Persuasive Technology, Using Computers to Change What We Think and Do. Morgan Kaufmann Publishers, Burlington (2003)

3. Oinas-Kukkonen, H., Harjumaa, M.: A systematic framework for designing and evaluating persuasive systems. In: Oinas-Kukkonen, H., Hasle, P., Harjumaa, M., Segerståhl, K., Øhrstrøm, P. (eds.) PERSUASIVE 2008. LNCS, vol. 5033, pp. 164–176. Springer, Heidelberg (2008). https://doi.org/10.1007/978-3-540-68504-3_15

4. Harjumaa, M., Segerståhl, K., Oinas-Kukkonen, H.: Understanding persuasive software functionality in practice: a field trial of polar FT60. In: Proceedings of the 4th International Conference on Persuasive Technology. ACM, Claremont, California (2009)

5. Oinas-Kukkonen, H., Harjumaa, M.: Persuasive systems design: key issues, process model, and system features. Commun. Assoc. Inf. Syst. **24**, 28 (2009)

6. Glasemann, M., Kanstrup, A.M., Ryberg, T.: Making chocolate-covered broccoli: designing a mobile learning game about food for young people with diabetes. In: DIS 2010 Proceedings of the 8th ACM Conference on Designing Interactive Systems. ACM, New York (2010)

7. Billig, M.: Arguing and Thinking: A Rhetorical Approach to Social Psychology. Cambridge University Press, Cambridge (1996)

8. Walbank, F.W., et al.: The Cambridge Ancient History, vol. 7. Cambridge University Press, Cambridge (1984)

9. Fafner, J.: Retorikkens Brændpunkt. Rhetorica Scandinavia, vol. 2 (1997)

10. Atkinson, B.M.C.: Captology: a critical review. In: IJsselsteijn, W.A., de Kort, Y.A.W., Midden, C., Eggen, B., van den Hoven, E. (eds.) PERSUASIVE 2006. LNCS, vol. 3962, pp. 171–182. Springer, Heidelberg (2006). https://doi.org/10.1007/11755494_25

11. Berdichevsky, D., Neuenschwander, E.: Towards an ethics of persuasive technology. Commun. ACM **43**, 51–58 (1999)

12. Spahn, A.: And lead us (not) into persuasion...? Persuasive technology and the ethics of Communication. Sci. Eng. Ethics **18**(4), 633–650 (2011)

13. Gram-Hansen, S.B., Ryberg, T.: Acttention – influencing communities of practice with persuasive learning designs. In: MacTavish, T., Basapur, S. (eds.) PERSUASIVE 2015. LNCS, vol. 9072, pp. 184–195. Springer, Cham (2015). https://doi.org/10.1007/978-3-319-20306-5_17

14. Meschtscherjakov, A., Trösterer, S., Lupp, A., Tscheligi, M.: Pokémon WALK: persuasive effects of Pokémon go game-design elements. In: de Vries, P.W., Oinas-Kukkonen, H., Siemons, L., Beerlage-de Jong, N., van Gemert-Pijnen, L. (eds.) PERSUASIVE 2017. LNCS, vol. 10171, pp. 241–252. Springer, Cham (2017). https://doi.org/10.1007/978-3-319-55134-0_19

Sustaining Health Behaviors Through Empowerment: A Deductive Theoretical Model of Behavior Change Based on Information and Communication Technology (ICT)

Ala Alluhaidan[1,2]([envelope]) [iD], Samir Chatterjee[2]([envelope]) [iD], David Drew[2]([envelope]),
and Agnis Stibe[3,4]([envelope]) [iD]

[1] Princess Nourah bint Abdulrahman University, Riyadh 11671, Saudi Arabia
ala.alluhaidan@cgu.edu
[2] Claremont Graduate University, Claremont, CA 91711, USA
profsamirl@gmail.edu,
{ala.alluhaidan,david.drew}@cgu.edu
[3] Paris ESLSCA Business School, 75007 Paris, France
a.stibe@eslsca.fr
[4] MIT Media Lab, Cambridge, MA 02142, USA

Abstract. Theoretical and practical advances have been made within healthcare informatics. Yet, mainstream research has primarily focused on signs and consequences without consideration to causal factors. Likewise, there is an increase demand for better self-management interventions. This demand resulted from the growing elderly populations with chronic conditions that fail to adhere to self-care routine. Still, most of the Healthcare Informatics interventions have achieved short-term success; while the goal is to engage population towards long-term behavior change. This research aims to shed light on the topic of Information and Communication Technology (ICT) empowerment by building and testing a theoretical-model for building intentions to sustain a healthy behavior. With a trial of 174 responses, we found positive results and a promising approach for Empowerment based on this model.

Keywords: Empowerment · Information and Communication Technology (ICT)
Health behavior change · Persuasive wellbeing

1 Introduction

It is not surprising that a chronic disease can tremendously impact life expectancy. Across the world, there is a growing crisis of elderly populations suffering from chronic diseases (such as diabetes, heart failure, etc.); the cost of treating such patients is very high. Additionally, chronic diseases need to be managed and most people fail to adhere to self-management guidelines. In the face of this epidemic, the US healthcare system

The original version of this chapter was revised: The authors corrected Figure 1. The erratum to this chapter is available at https://doi.org/10.1007/978-3-319-78978-1_26

© Springer International Publishing AG, part of Springer Nature 2018
J. Ham et al. (Eds.): PERSUASIVE 2018, LNCS 10809, pp. 28–41, 2018.
https://doi.org/10.1007/978-3-319-78978-1_3

is struggling and trying to find solutions by improving access to timely, quality treatments, at the same time, US healthcare system faces a shortage of clinicians and care-givers [1]:

The global epidemic of chronic disease must, and can, be stopped. This invisible epidemic is an under-appreciated cause of poverty and hinders the economic development of many countries. Chronic disease is responsible for 60% of all deaths worldwide with almost half of chronic disease deaths occurring in people under the age of 70 [1].

Yet, the risk of deteriorating quality of life, readmission to the hospital, or death can be mitigated with proper disease management [2]. There is still a need for a model to detail a technology-enabled empowerment and encourage sustainable behavior change in order to improve self-care management. Home monitoring can transform current practices in chronic disease care to a more proactive approach that empowers patients to take control and improve their health outcomes. This new model in delivering healthcare at home seems convenient because it does not require patients to leave their home and it is more cost effective. While a number of chronic diseases demand daily monitoring, such as Diabetes, Congestive Heart Failure (CHF), Chronic Obstructive Pulmonary Disease (COPD), and Hypertension, research in remote patient monitoring has proven its effectiveness in managing and tracking progress or deterioration [1]. Yet, behavior modification through messages and instructions in the current approaches has only achieved short-term success.

In March 2014, our research team launched MyHeart, a system developed at university lab that has been implemented at Loma Linda hospital to monitor CHF patients' health. An integral part of the system is a smart phone app that displays patient vitals, asks for symptoms, shows motivational messages and reminders, and plots a chart representation of daily vitals and symptoms [3]. Despite MyHeart's effectiveness in tracking patients' health and providing motivational messages, there was an adherence gap for some users of this remote monitoring system. In other words, while some patients adhere to the guidelines, there were many patients that didn't adhere and there is a gap. Based on the feedback from those patients, it was clear that tailored messages could be an effective way of reducing the adherence gap. Thus, we assume empowerment through this approach increases the sustainability of a health behavior.

This has led us to assume we could better empower the patients to remain engaged, build intention to change, and ultimately achieve sustainable positive behavior through this approach. Knowing how to engage and motivate individuals is a complicated process with multiple coinciding elements. Yet, customized messages that matches personal goals can keep an individual active toward his/her plan [4].

Besides the importance of personal goals [3], we also looked at experientially rewarding content and several contextual variables that influence the sustainability of a behavior: social connection, self-efficacy, technology tools, and community support [5, 6]. Then, we built our ICT empowerment model using these latent constructs. This research attempts to find factors that sup-port sustainable health behavior and investigates how empowerment can help people adhere to post-discharge guidelines. Positive behavior change is hard to maintain especially because of factors such as the enjoyment of negative behavior, addiction, or the lack of immediate benefits. About 50% of the population fails to sustain positive behavior changes [7]. Since there is more than one factor that will empower the user to sustain the behavior, these factors may need to match internal feelings and stimulate internal commitment. Additionally, long-term management of chronic conditions is a critical factor in the cost of health-care. In fact, $3 trillion is spent annually in the US for healthcare. Around 30% of this can be avoided with positive health behavior. Moreover, more than $100 billion is spent annually on poor medication adherence, some of which can be corrected [8]. Yet, empowering people to sustain their behavior changes is a complex process. Empow-erment as defined by [9] is the discovery and development of one's inherent capacity to be responsible for one's own life. "Patients are thus empowered when they are in possession of the knowledge, skills, and self- awareness necessary to identify and attain their own goals." [10] Existing research shows that personal goals and customized tailored messages are better perceived by an audience [11]. Hence, we develop a theoretical model for empowerment that provides more insight on how to construct those messages for sustainability.

2 Literature Review

Persuasive design was introduced as one way to encourage adherence and to promote health and health-related behavior [12]. Yet, the concept of persuasive design holds a negative connotation, and therefore, empowerment was introduced to describe the continuous motivation process [13]. Several studies related to empowerment and to the factors related will be described below.

Dempsey and Foreman [14] describe empowerment in clinical literature as a desirable process and outcome of service. Yet, research on empowerment has remained mainly theoretical. In an attempt to operationalize and measure the concept, the Family Empowerment Scale (FES) was developed. This scale defines three constructs: knowledge, behavior, and attitudes on different levels such as family, service systems, and community/politics [15]. Previous research in empowerment was also mainly focused on sharing information and the involvement of parents in decision-making. "This approach refers to empowerment at an individual rather than at an organizational or community level, and will usually include a combination of self-acceptance and self-confidence" [16, 17].

Within healthcare domain, Jerofke's article [18], defines patient empowerment as "(1) helping patients to realize that they can and should participate in their care and treatment planning; (2) providing patients with access to information, support, resources and opportunities to learn and grow; (3) helping to facilitate collaboration with providers, family and friends; and (4) allowing patients autonomy in decision-making" [18]. The article aims to explore the nurses' impact on patient empowerment for a patient who required a self-care management following a surgery. The study used the Patient Perceptions of Patient-Empowering Nurse Behaviors Scale (PPPNBS). The measure of 45 items has seven subscales that cover the following areas: (1) initiation, (2) access to information, (3) access to support, (4) access to resources, (5) access to opportunities to learn and grow, (6) informal power, and (7) formal power" [18]. Jerofke's work [18] focused on nurse-patient relationship and the measurement was conducted after six-weeks on patients who recently underwent a surgical procedure for cancer or cardiac disease.

Within organization domain, Zeglat et al. [19], point to empowerment as "giving employees the possibility of taking necessary actions in modifying the current work processes or employing a new process in order to simplify job-related tasks and decisions." Moreover, the paper defines the psychological/motivational empowerment as "a state of mind in which an employee experiences the feelings of control over how the job can be done, have enough aware to the work tasks that being performed, a great level of responsibility to both personal work outcome and overall organizational advancement, and the perceived justice in the rewards based on individual and collective performance." [19] The study includes within its definition of empowerment: (1) meaning, (2) competence, (3) self-determination, and (4) impact [19]. The experiment is focused on business aspect and encourages implementing better managerial practices such as better job design, the use of up-to date technology, and the revision of job regulations and legislation. This again refers to empowerment as a means of maintaining control over decisions and resources at workspace.

It has been argued that empowerment can hold different meanings and can vary depending on past experiences across time, settings, and population [16, 17, 20]. The definitions of empowerment reveal both diversity and commonality. Still, most definitions focus on matters of gaining power and control over decisions and resources that determines the quality of one's life [21]. In this paper, we look at Empowerment within healthcare, and we define at as having a positive attitude towards life and feeling more capable to achieve positive results. Accordingly, empowerment is looked as a mediating factor for developing intentions to sustain a health behavior. Finding a comprehensive model to evaluate empowerment considering different factors is yet to be found.

2.1 Studies Related to the Concept of Empowerment

An empowerment message, as defined in Chatterjee et al. [13] is a "message sent in good faith and containing no coercion." The goal of empowerment is to direct the receiver without coercing action. Chatterjee et al. [13] suggested that empowerment should be designed after analyzing the momentary experience, which leads to use of a multilevel model and data collection. The study uses a three-layered model that includes: genetics, disease/health state, and social network to evaluate the effectiveness of empowerment technique. These three components are interrelated and essential in designing personalized messages. Persuasiveness is empowering when the message not only matches recipient's long-term goals but also when it is motivating. Messages that make sense and make individuals feel good are believed to be empowering. Chatterjee et al. [13] detail a method of analyzing the outcome using the empowering system that includes constructs of the domain using factor analysis. This research inherits two components from this study - disease/health state and social network in evaluating the empowerment messages, thus factor analysis will be used to validate these domain constructs.

2.2 Experientially Rewarding Content

Messages can create good, happy, and enthusiastic feelings. The experienced feelings resulting from messages or instructions are valuable. "Analyses suggested that whereas experienced outcomes during the learning phase were objectively weighted in children's and adolescents' value estimates, adults biased the weighting of outcomes for the instructed stimulus to be more consistent with the explicit instruction that they had received." [22] This prior research indicates that the feedback is more effective with adults than children and adolescents [22]. Although Author is focused on how individuals would perceive instruction, which is not the primary focus of our research, it points to the importance of feelings embedded in the message and how an individual reacts to the content.

Although empowerment is used widely and referenced with different definitions, concepts, and operations, the hypothesis of employing goal-oriented messages and rewards to empower patients have not been tested. Thus, we hypothesize that goal-oriented messages and experientially rewarding content may enhance self-care management. In the following, we present the literature review of constructs that are strongly related to empowerment.

2.3 Social Connection

In a recent research project at Stanford, Walton [23] identifies that social belonging is an essential factor for human drive or motivation. It mentions the importance of identity belonging (a sense of self and how one gains the feeling of belonging to a family, group, place or community [24] and how social cues such as doing task with others can change behavior [25]. It also points to the lasting effect of interventions with social belonging aspect [23] meaning the higher chance of behavior sustainability with social support. These findings show that it is essential to include social context in the attempt of achieving behavior sustainability.

2.4 Technological Tools

The advantages of technology inventions such as internet, apps, mobile games, and social media include: wide spread reach, low cost, added interactivity, and the ability to quickly provide personalized messages [25]. Technology tools are empowering people with information and knowledge, "Overall, youth perceived computers and the Internet to be empowering tools, and they should be encouraged to use such technology to support them in community initiatives." [9] Digital empowerment is defined as "the ability of an individual to use digital technologies effectively in order to develop life skills and strengthen his or her capacity within the information society" [27]. On the UNICEF website, there is a document indicating the impact of Information and Communication Technology (ICT) on enhancing the cognitive and capacity of individuals' empowerment. The document emphasizes the effectiveness of ICT tools on elevating the society through learning an effective way of performing daily actions such as nutrition tracking and medication consumption [28]. More important, ICT tools can be utilized in supporting individual needs because they are pervasive and easy to customize.

2.5 General Self-efficacy

Another major factor to be considered in an ICT empowerment model, in particular, to perform and maintain a health behavior is self-efficacy, defined as an individual's belief in his or her capacity to execute behaviors [29]. Self-efficacy is an essential factor for feeling empowered and performing and sustaining a behavior. "Perceived self-efficacy has been found to be very important in causing people to form intentions to perform and maintain physical exercise for an extended time." [29] Part of assessing or evaluating self-efficacy is through assessing an individual's confidence and beliefs in their ability to achieve his/her health goals. In this experiment, we chose the self-efficacy measure currently used by the Health Trainer Service. "The Health Trainer Service is designed to train people with the skills they need to set their own health goals and manage and change their behavior." [29] We selected seven items out of the eight questions listed in this measure as they fit the nature of this experiment; specifically, we used the items that address measuring the self-efficacy to achieve a health goal.

2.6 Community Support

"Community empowerment is said to offer the most promising approach for reducing health problems in communities." [30] The need for empowerment approaches in motivating people and especially for patients in their transition to home is notable. "Expansion of empowerment programs in communities is a powerful tool to help improve peoples' health". Health promotions, workshops, drugs prevention programs, and safe community programs are different implementations for community empowerment [30].

The evidence is strong for intervention that is designed to promote individual behavior change, according to the Community Guide [31]. "The recommendation for individually adapted behavior change is based on 18 studies in which the median effect size was a 35% increase in time spent in physical activity and a 64% increase in energy expenditure." [31] These intervention strategies are community-based for increased physical activity, such as the percentage of people starting exercise programs and the frequency of physical activity [31]. Another study states, "participation in school- and community-based sports increases the likelihood that students were active, practitioners should seek to enhance opportunities for participation in and access to these programs in order to increase the level of activity obtained by students" [32]. Therefore, community support is a valuable factor in changing and adopting a behavior.

2.7 Intentions to Sustain a Healthy Behavior

Maintaining a healthy behavior is the optimum goal of any healthcare intervention. The intervention may last a short time period, yet the effect should last longer or for life. In fact, after patients are discharged, self-care management is a main request, especially for the ones with chronic disease. Behavioral intentions, which are indications of how hard people are willing to try to perform a particular behavior, is a key concept in the psychology of behavior change [33]. We refer here to intentions instead of the actual behavior because 19% to 38% of variance in behavior (including health behaviors) can be explained by behavioral intention [34]. In order to build the intention for adherence and instill the behavior in those patients and individuals who seek a better health outcome, many contextual variables such as self-efficacy, social connection, and community support need to be considered. Notably, person-focused behavior change programs proved to be more effective than disease-focused ones [35]. These types of programs appeared to have a lasting effect, because they involve social support, especially from peers, to sustain a behavior. This more focused approach requires customization and more comprehensive intervention considering impactful factors.

3 Objectives and Research Questions

We propose a theoretical model for ICT empowerment to address the adherence gap. We hypothesize that building an intention to sustain a behavior change can be improved with empowerment. The objectives are: To build and evaluate an ICT empowerment theory model using survey that includes the following items:

- A collection of goal oriented messages
- A pool of experientially rewarding types of messages
- Questions about how technology tools, self-efficacy, social connection, and community support can positively increase empowerment feeling which is hypothesized to positively affect the intention to sustain a healthy behavior

The research questions that will guide this research are:

RQ1: How do technology tools, self-efficacy, social connection, and community support positively affect empowerment feeling?
RQ2: Will an empowered individual have a higher probability of forming intention to sustain a behavior?

4 Methodology

This research uses a quantitative survey approach to answer the research questions and build an ICT empowerment theory model. The factors in this model are derived from previous trial results, brainstorming sessions, and a literature review. The theoretical model proposed is demonstrated in Fig. 1.

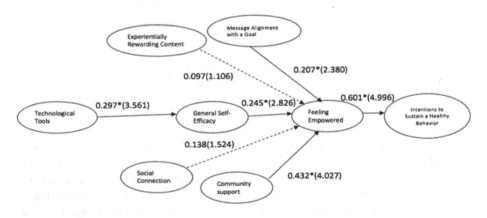

Fig. 1. The proposed theoretical model for ICT empowerment & results

Survey: To answer our research questions, we constructed a survey to measure different constructs and how they contribute to feeling empowered and eventually increase the intention to sustain a healthy behavior.

Prior research has proven that technology tools have an effect on self-efficacy [32, 36] thus, we identify the necessity to include technology tools construct in the ICT empowerment model. Prior research [37] has also proven the strong correlation between social connections and maintaining a behavior; therefore, we include this factor in the model. Community support has also been included in the model for its value in changing a behavior [30]. Lastly, we hypothesize in the model that feeling empowered can positively affects the intention to sustain a health behavior. The survey collects (1) demographic data, (2) current health portfolio, (3) the intervention signified by displaying the different messages, (4) questions on feeling empowered, (5) social connection, (6) general self-efficacy based on the Health Trainer Service Standards, and (7) intention to sustain a health behavior. Because it is hard to identify each individual's goal, we selected one generic commonly identified goal: do physical exercises in a regular manner. The survey was sent via email as an embedded hyperlink to individuals (survey elements are listed in Appendix A).

The survey, which was declared exempt from IRB supervision under the university policy and federal regulations on February 18, 2016, went through internal pilot testing before it was published to public. In two and a half months, we collected 174 completed responses from convenience sample of university students, and the responses were used in SPSS and Amos to perform factor analysis and SEM. The number of responses is sufficient for testing a structural equation model as Boomsma suggests a minimum sample size 100–150 [38, 39].

The result showed that the effects (MA → FE, TT → SE, SE → FE, CS → FE, FE → ISHB) are all significant with $P < 0.05$, SC → FE is abnormal at $P < 0.127$, and experiential rewards (ER) does not have significant effect on empowerment, so we removed this factor. Model fitness indicators are reported below:

The root mean square (RMR) of the model did not show a reasonable fit with the data. However, RMR is a sensitive scale of measurement and it is difficult to establish what a low value is. Thus, this study uses Standardized RMR (SRMR) with recommended values of less than 0.05 signifying a good fit with data. However, this model's SRMR index (0.1257) does not fall within this range. Root mean squared error of approximation (RMSEA) is 0.074, which is below 0.10–the indication of a good fit with the data. X2 and degree of freedom is 1.943, which does not fall within the good index boundary between 2 and 5.

5   Discussion and Conclusion

Empowerment, "respects the right to autonomy, as well as furthering autonomy as ability, it respects the person's dignity, and it reduces inequalities." [40] Therefore, empowerment is preferred for behavior-change interventions [40]. In this study, we present a further step on how to implement such an intervention. Even though we have a small sample size to evaluate the model, we already found interesting results. The significant effects on empowerment from the factors (technology tools, self-efficacy, social connection, and community support) were actually anticipated. Yet, the fact that experiential reward does not have that effect on empowerment was not expected. Since the experiment attempts to define the best way to engage audiences with regard to exercise, the survey was presented as if the messages and rewards were displayed as part of a regular exercise goal. For future trials, we will actually distribute the messages on a smart phone app. Most interventions fail to establish and maintain healthy habits for multiple reasons, such as lacking personalization and motivational perspective. This research brings new light on engaging audiences with meaningful messages and rewarding content and how it can help in forming intention to sustain a behavior. The ICT model proposed here is novel in incorporating personalized goal oriented messages and rewarding content into empowerment. This model also tests the relationship between technology tools, self-efficacy, social connection, community support, feeling empowered, and intention to sustain a healthy behavior in a new way. Ultimately, this model can help in revealing new ways of achieving better health outcomes.

With this research, we expect to contribute to the knowledgebase concerning how to effectively engage target audience using a goal-aligned content towards a better health outcome. Delivering tailored messages towards personal goals on a technology medium has not been established yet by previous research. This novel way of representing motivational content to encourage sustainable health behavior can be utilized to prevent health deterioration and increase the quality of life. This research also points to the importance of considering multiple factors while designing and implementing a changing behavior intervention. Currently, researchers are collecting more data in order to refine the model.

Appendix A: Survey Constructs, Definitions, Elements, Loadings, and Scale

Code	Construct: definition	Items	Loadings	Scale type
MA1	Message alignment with goal: all messages (text) are inline with the subject's goal towards certain behavior (regular exercise)	You should eat five or more servings of fruits and vegetables (combined) daily	.323	Aligned (1 2 3 4 5)
MA2		You should eat foods low in fat	.385	
MA3		Try getting 8 h of sleep a day to keep stress away	.228	
MA4		Drink at least 5 glasses of water a day which reduces the risk for heart attack and stroke by 41% in women and 54% in men	.348	

(*continued*)

(*continued*)

Code	Construct: definition	Items	Loadings	Scale type
ER1	Experientially rewarding: these events, when happened, make the subjects feel good and happy	Spending time with my family gives me motivation to exercise	.487	Important (1 2 3 4 5)
ER2		Getting recognized for my achievements	.869	
ER3		Receiving some award when I achieve my physical exercise goal	.824	
ER4		If you exercise, you will look more attractive	.439	
TT1	Technology tools: we use the term technology in general to refer to smart phones, Internet, computers, televisions, and wearable devices (such as Fitbit)	I am comfortable using technology	.523	Agree (1 2 3 4 5)
TT2		I feel more capable with my smart phone	.580	
TT3		I can accomplish most of my tasks using computers, internet, and technology	.602	
TT4		I often use the internet to look for solutions to problems	.208	
TT5		I feel powerless without technology	.231	
SE1	Self-efficacy: refers to an individual's belief in his or her capacity to execute behaviors	I will be able to achieve most of the goals I set for myself	.354	Agree (1 2 3 4 5)
SE2		When facing difficult tasks, I am certain I will succeed	.445	
SE3		I believe I can succeed at most tasks to which I set my mind	.548	
SE4		I will be able to successfully overcome many challenges	.522	
SE5		I am confident I can manage well many different tasks	.518	
SE6		Compared to other people, I can do most tasks very well	.449	

(*continued*)

(*continued*)

Code	Construct: definition	Items	Loadings	Scale type
SE7		Even when things are tough, I can manage quite well	.414	
SC1	Social connection: the number of family, friends, and social acquaintances that the subject connects to	I have a friend or family member who encourages me to accomplish my goal	.414	Agree (1 2 3 4 5)
SC2		My family members are always there to help and support me	.708	
SC3		In the past month it has been easy to relate to my friends and family	.319	
CS1	Community support: community support implies help from neighborhood, churches, and other social environment	My community helps me to be cheerful	.398	Agree (1 2 3 4 5)
CS2		In my community, I would find a source of satisfaction for myself	.707	
CS3		In my community, I would find someone to listen to me when I feel down	.544	
CS4		In my community, I could find people that would help me feel better	.761	
CS5		In my community, I would relax and easily forget my problems	.337	
CS6		In my community, I take part in activities	.563	
CS7		I respond to calls for support in my community	.467	
FE1	Feeling empowered: having a positive attitude towards life and feeling more capable to achieve positive results	I have a positive attitude towards life	.258	Agree (1 2 3 4 5)
FE2		Having access to information and resources enables me to take properly informed decisions	.344	
FE3		I go out of my way to help others	.238	

(*continued*)

(continued)

Code	Construct: definition	Items	Loadings	Scale type
FE4		I feel the ability to change other's perceptions by democratic means	.437	
FE5		I have a positive self-image and I can overcome stigma	.302	
ISHB1	Intention to sustain a health behavior: forming a plan to maintain the behavior for a long time	I intend to continue to exercise	.279	Agree (1 2 3 4 5)
ISHB2		I intend to eat healthy food from now on	.553	
ISHB3		I intend to keep a work-life balance going forward	.425	
ISHB4		I intend to sleep well and manage my stress from now on	.533	
ISHB5		From now on I will continue to remain healthy	.439	
ISHB6		Technology tools help me better manage my exercise routines	.185	
ISHB7		With or without support, I intend to stay physically fit	.466	

References

1. Gains in managing chronic disease – remote patient monitoring. Telushealth, April 2014. https://www.telushealth.co/item/transforming-healthcare-using-remote-monitoring/. Accessed 17 Jan 2016
2. Center for Disease Control and Prevention: Heart failure fact sheet (2012). http://www.cdc.gov/dhdsp/data_statistics/fact_sheets/fs_heart_failure.htm
3. Alluhaidan, A., Lee, E., Alnosayan, N., Chatterjee, S., Houston-Feenstra, L., Dysinger, W., Kagoda, M.: Designing patient-centered mHealth technology intervention to reduce hospital readmission for heart-failure patients. In: 2015 48th Hawaii International Conference on System Sciences (HICSS), pp. 2886–2895. IEEE (2015). http://ieeexplore.ieee.org/xpls/abs_all.jsp?arnumber=7070164
4. Gómez-Miñambres, J.: Motivation through goal setting. J. Econ. Psychol. 33(6), 1223–1239 (2012)
5. Martire, L.M., Franks, M.M.: The role of social networks in adult health: introduction to the special issue. Health Psychol. 33, 501–504 (2014)

6. Holloway, A., Watson, H.E.: Role of self-efficacy and behaviour change. Int. J. Nurs. Pract. **8**(2), 106–115 (2002)
7. Lofstrom, J.: Chronic disease and social networks. HIMSS.org, 3 December 2012 http:// blog.himss.org/2012/12/06/chronic-disease-and-social-networks/graph-1/. Accessed 25 Nov 2015
8. Patrick, K., Raab, F., Adams, M.A., Dillon, L., Zabinski, M., Rock, C.L., Griswold, W.G., Norman, G.J.: A text message–based intervention for weight loss: randomized controlled trial. J. Med. Internet Res. **11**(1) (2009). http://www.ncbi.nlm.nih.gov/pmc/articles/PMC2729073/
9. Valaitis, R.K.: Computers and the internet: tools for youth empowerment. J. Med. Internet Res. **7**(5), e51 (2005)
10. Wentzer, H.S., Bygholm, A.: Narratives of empowerment and compliance: studies of communi-cation in online patient support groups. Int. J. Med. Inform. **82**(12), e386–e394 (2013)
11. Salovey, P., Rothman, A.J.: Social Psychology of Health: Key Readings. Psychology press, Abingdon (2003)
12. Kelders, S.M., Kok, R.N., Ossebaard, H.C., Van Gemert-Pijnen, J.E.: Persuasive system design does matter: a systematic review of adherence to web-based interventions. J. Med. Internet Res. **14**(6), e152 (2012)
13. Chatterjee, S., Csikszentmihalyi, M., Nakamura, J., Drew, D., Patrick, K.: From persuasion to empowerment: a layered model, metrics and measurement. In: Proceedings of Persuasive 2010, Copenhagen, Denmark, 7–9 June 2010 (2010)
14. Dempsey, I., Foreman, P.: Toward a clarification of empowerment as an outcome of disability service provision. Int. J. Disabil. Dev. Educ. **44**, 287–303 (1997)
15. Koren, P.E., DeChillo, N., Friesen, B.J.: Measuring empowerment in families whose children have emotional disabilities: a brief questionnaire. Rehabil. Psychol. **37**, 305–321 (1992). https://doi.org/10.1037/h0079106
16. Rappaport, J.: Terms of empowerment/exemplars of prevention: toward a theory of community psychology. Am. J. Commun. Psychol. **15**(2), 121–148 (1987). https://doi.org/10.1007/BF00919275
17. Zimmerman, M.A.: Psychological empowerment: issues and illustrations. Am. J. Commun. Psychol. **23**, 581–599 (1995)
18. Jerofke, T.A.: Patient perceptions of patient-empowering nurse behaviors, patient activation, and functional health status after surgery (2013). http://epublications.marquette.edu/dissertations_mu/272/
19. Zeglat, D., Aljaber, M., Alrawabdeh, W.: Understating the impact of employee empowerment on customer-oriented behavior. J. Bus. Stud. Q. **6**(1), 55–67 (2014)
20. Foster-Fishman, P.G., Salem, D.A., Chibnall, S., Legler, R., Yapchai, C.: Empirical support for the critical assumptions of empowerment theory. Am. J. Commun. Psychol. **26**(4), 507–536 (1998). https://doi.org/10.1023/A:1022188805083
21. Oladipo, S.E.: Psychological empowerment and development. Edo J. Couns. **2**(1), 118–126 (2009)
22. Decker, J.H., Lourenco, F.S., Doll, B.B., Hartley, C.A.: Experiential reward learning out-weighs instruction prior to adulthood. Cogn. Affect. Behav. Neurosci. **15**(2), 310–320 (2015)
23. Walton, G.M.: New research on behavior change. Department of Psychology Stanford University (n.d.) http://web.stanford.edu/group/peec/cgi-bin/docs/behavior/workshop/2008/presentations/03-02_New_Research_on_Behavior_Change.pdf. Accessed 14 Dec 2015
24. Introduction to context: identity and belonging. maribsc.vic.edu.au (n.d.). http://www.maribsc.vic.edu.au/sites/default/files/files/Introduction%20to%20Context%20handout.pdf. Accessed 27 Mar 2016

25. Stibe, A.: Towards a framework for socially influencing systems: meta-analysis of four PLS-SEM based studies. In: MacTavish, T., Basapur, S. (eds.) PERSUASIVE 2015. LNCS, vol. 9072, pp. 172–183. Springer, Cham (2015). https://doi.org/10.1007/978-3-319-20306-5_16

26. Franklin, V.L., Greene, A., Waller, A., Greene, S.A., Pagliari, C.: Patients's engagement with "sweet talk": a text messaging support system for young people with diabetes. J. Med. Internet Res. **10**, e20 (2008)

27. Makinen, M.: Digital empowerment as a process for enhancing citizens' participation. E-Learning **3**(3), 381–395 (2006). https://doi.org/10.2304/elea.2006.3.3.381

28. Information and communication technologies. UNESCO. Accessed 15 Dec 2015. http://unesdoc.unesco.org/images/0013/001395/139568eb.pdf

29. Smith, J., Gardner, B., Michie, S.: Self efficacy guidance material for health trainer service. UCL, London (2010). http://healthtrainersengland.com/wp-content/uploads/2014/05/DCRSSelfEfficacyGuidance.pdf

30. Kasmel, A., Andersen, P.T.: Measurement of community empowerment in three community programs in Rapla (Estonia). Int. J. Env. Res. Public Health **8**(3), 799–817 (2011)

31. The CDC guide to strategies to increase physical activity in the community. In: CDC (2011) http://www.cdc.gov/obesity/downloads/PA_2011_WEB.pdf. Accessed 7 May 2016

32. Kurc, A.R., Leatherdale, S.T.: The effect of social support and school-and community-based sports on youth physical activity. Can. J. Public Health/Revue Canadienne de Sante'e Publique, 60–64 (2009)

33. Ajzen, I.: The theory of planned behavior. Organ. Behav. Human Decis. Process. **50**, 179–211 (1991)

34. Behavioral Intention. In: CHIRr (2017). https://chirr.nlm.nih.gov/behavioral-intention.php. Accessed 3 Mar 2017

35. Dixon-Fyle, S., Gandhi, S., Pellathy, T., Spatharou, A.: Changing patient behavior: the next frontier in healthcare value. McKinsey & Company, September 2012. http://healthcare.mckinsey.com/changing-patient-behavior-nextfrontier-healthcare-value. Accessed 8 Nov 2015

36. Shank, D.B., Cotten, S.R.: Does technology empower urban youth? The relationship of technology use to self-efficacy. Comput. Educ. **70**, 184–193 (2014)

37. Cummings, N.G.:. Fostering sustainable behavior through design: a study of the social, psychological, and physical influences of the built environment. University of Massachusetts Amherst (2012). http://scholarworks.umass.edu/theses/885/

38. Boomsma, A.: Robustness of LISREL against small sample sizes in factor analysis models. In: Joreskog, K.G., Wold, H., (eds.) Systems Under Indirection Observation: Causality, Structure, Prediction (Part I), Amsterdam, Netherlands, North Holland, pp. 149–173 (1982)

39. Boomsma, A.: Nonconvergence, improper solutions, and starting values in LISREL maximum likelihood estimation. Psychometrika **50**, 229–242 (1985)

40. Tengland, P.-A.: Behavior change or empowerment: on the ethics of health-promotion strategies. Public Health Ethics **5**(2), 140–153 (2012). https://doi.org/10.1093/phe/phs022

Social Means to Persuasion

Can an Enterprise System Persuade? The Role of Perceived Effectiveness and Social Influence

Jonathan Dabi[1], Isaac Wiafe[2(✉)], Agnis Stibe[3(✉)] [iD],
and Jamal-Deen Abdulai[2(✉)]

[1] Radford University, East-Legon, Ghana
papaakufo@gmail.com
[2] University of Ghana, Accra, Ghana
{iwiafe, jabdulai}@ug.edu.gh
[3] Paris ESLSCA Business School, Paris, France
agnis@transforms.me

Abstract. This study provides an interpretation to empirically explain and predict use continuance intention of students towards an enterprise resource planning (ERP) system. A research model based on the information system continuance, the social identity theory, and the unified theory of acceptance and use of technology was adopted and analyzed using partial least squares structural equation modeling. The analysis uncovered important roles that perceived effectiveness and social influence play in explaining the intention of students to continue using the ERP. Further, the model demonstrated how primary task support contributes to perceived effort, which helps in explaining perceived effectiveness of the system. Computer-human dialogue support significantly contributes to perceived credibility, primary task support and perceived social influence. Social identification of the students significantly predicts perceived social influence. Research related to continuous usage of an ERP system is viable, as it enables designers and developers building more persuasive enterprise and socially influencing systems.

Keywords: Persuasive technology · Enterprise resource planning system
Use continuance · Perceived effectiveness · Social influence

1 Introduction

The design of a hardware and its interface can influence how an individual interacts with it and consequently alter his or her behavior. In addition, persuasive functionalities may also be incorporated into a system's design to change attitude or behavior. Although several studies have been conducted to demonstrate that persuasive technologies are effective in changing human behavior, not much have been done on how an introduction of persuasive features in enterprise systems can promote their use continuance. The acceptance and continuous use of enterprise resource planning (ERP) systems is paramount, as it determines their success or failure.

However, existing theories for measuring acceptance and use continuance of technologies and information systems mostly examine factors that stimulate individuals

© Springer International Publishing AG, part of Springer Nature 2018
J. Ham et al. (Eds.): PERSUASIVE 2018, LNCS 10809, pp. 45–55, 2018.
https://doi.org/10.1007/978-3-319-78978-1_4

to initially adopt them rather than factors that would influence their continuous use [1, 13]. This research therefore seeks to investigate the relationship between persuasive features in an enterprise system and how they impact its use continuance.

2 Background

An ERP system is a software for business management, it include modules for supporting functional areas such as planning, manufacturing, sales, marketing, distribution, financial accounting, human resource management, project management, inventory management, service and maintenance, transportation and electronic business [2]. Many organizations nowadays resort to the implementation of ERP system in order to match up with the competitive environment [21]. The benefit organizations draw from ERP installations may be realized at different levels which include operational, managerial, strategic, infrastructural and organizational [19].

Theories relating to the continuous use of ERP systems include expectation-confirmation theory (ECT) and information system continuance (ISC) model [1]. ECT and ISC were developed for post adaption behaviors. ISC model posits that users' intentions to continue usage of an information system is influenced by three antecedents which are satisfaction, confirmation and perceived usefulness. ISC differs from ECT in several ways including: 1. ISC focuses on post-adoption expectations because users' expectation toward using IS after gaining experience must be different from expectations before usage; 2. post-adoption expectations is represented by perceived usefulness; and 3. perceived performance is not included because it is assumed to be captured in the confirmation construct.

3 Research Model

This study adapted a research model (Fig. 1) that is based on information system continuance, social identity theory, unified theory of acceptance and use of technology, and persuasive technology [14]. According to Robey et al. [3], tried and tested instruments are effective in measurement. The theoretical underpinning for this is that, such instruments enable the researcher to gather enough knowledge and maintain comparability between researches. The scales for measuring the constructs of the research model were also adopted [14]. Questionnaires were designed, and checks indicated that they demonstrated good content validity, i.e. face and expert validity before they were administered. The perceived effort (EFFO) and perceived effectiveness (EFFE) were modified from the unified theory of acceptance and use of technology [26], social identification (SOID) was adopted from the social identity theory, while use continuance intention (CONT) was adopted from expectation-confirmation theory [1].

3.1 Computer-Human Dialogue

Computer-human dialogue support (DIAL) keeps users active and motivated in using an information system [14]. System-to-user prompts, triggers, reminders and positive feedback play an important role in computer-human dialogue support. Information technology artefacts are social actors, according to [16, 18]. Consequently, users envisage their interaction with information technology artefacts to be interpersonal in nature. Furthermore, users tend to see their interaction with information technology artefacts as in social situations [12, 18]. Thus, it is hypothesized that:

H1a: Computer-human dialogue support positively impacts perceived social influence.

Computer-human dialogue support keeps users active and motivate them to perform their primary task. This indicates that computer-human dialogue support encourage students when engaged in activities such as course registration, verification of personal data, checking exam results, etc. Hence, it has a direct link to perceived effectiveness and primary task support. Thus, it is hypothesized that:

H1b: Computer-human dialogue support positively impacts perceived effectiveness.
H1c: Computer-human dialogue support has a positive effect on primary task support.

According to [11], computer-human dialogue support has the potential to influence users' confidence in a system. This means that it will possibly impacts students' confidence in the use of the ERP. Thus, it is hypothesized that:

H1d: Computer-human dialogue support has a positive effect on perceived credibility.

3.2 Primary Task Support

Primary task support (PRIM) is the means given by the system to assist the user to carry out his or her goal [14]. It is related to cognitive fit, task-technology fit, and person-artefact-task [5]. It aids reflection on a user's behavior, personal goal setting, and keeping of track progress towards the goals [15]. It impacts perceived persuasiveness positively [14], whilst perceived persuasiveness and perceived effectiveness are related [19].

This indicates that the ERP provides functionalities for the students to engage in activities such as course registration, checking semester results, uploading and verifying personal data, just to mention a few. Thus, it is hypothesized that:

H2a: Primary task support has a positive effect on perceived effectiveness.

Since primary task support reduces the cognitive burden and disorientation towards the use of the ERP, it is also hypothesized that:

H2b: Primary task support has a positive effect on perceived effort.

3.3 Perceived Credibility

Trust and credibility (CRED) are important and related construct when dealing with the continuous use of an information system. For a system to be credible, it has to build trust in users [4]. The objective of this research does not involve a detailed understanding of trust; therefore, such issues are integrated in perceived credibility. According to Shin [20], perceived trust positively influences user behavior in social commerce environment. This means that the perceived credibility that the Institute's students envisage in the ERP, positively impacts their intention to continuously use the system. Thus, it is hypothesized that:

H3: Perceived credibility has a positive effect on use continuance intention.

3.4   Perceived Effort

In existing technology adoption theories, perceived ease of use, a construct of technology acceptance model [6] and effort expectancy, a construct of unified theory of acceptance and use of technology [27] have proven to be the two basic constructs that explains one's intention to use a system continuously. Perceived effort relates to one of the propositions of expectancy theory of motivation. This implies that, one's effort will result in the realization of desired performance goals, i.e. perceived effectiveness in the case of this research.

It can therefore be concluded that the degree of ease associated with the use of the ERP (perceived effort) motivates the institute's students that the ERP will help them improve their online interactions with the university. Thus, it is hypothesized that:

H4a: Perceived effort has a positive effect on perceived effectiveness.

Effort expectancy positively influences behavioral intention [27]. This logically follows that perceived effort has a direct impact on use continuance intention. Thus, it is hypothesized that:

H4b: Perceived effort has a positive effect on use continuance intention.

3.5   Perceived Social Influence

Most individuals taking part in online social activities are merely readers of discussion forums, searchers of blog posts, or observers of photos or other media [17]. Social influence may be connected with aspects of the social network i.e. groups and families, specific behaviors e.g. emotional or informational support or our perceived availability of support resources [25]. Social influence may also be described as an exchange of resources between two individuals perceived by the provider or the recipient to be intended to enhance the wellbeing of the recipient. It is in the form of encouragement, motivation, information and shared experience [9]. This promotes perceived effectiveness.

Hence, the decision of the institute's students to use the ERP will be influenced by their fellow students and will consequently deepen their desire that the ERP will help improve their online interaction with the university. Thus, it is hypothesized that:

H5a: Perceived social influence has a positive effect on perceived effectiveness.

Social influence is a direct determinant of use intention [27]. Moreover, perceived social influence directly affects use behavior [20]. Thus, it is also hypothesized that:

H5b: Perceived social influence has a positive effect on use continuance intention.

3.6 Social Identification

According to Hogg [10], group cohesion is the sense of members' attraction to the group. It is important to note that group cohesion and social identification are similar constructs. Cohesion strengthens when members in a group perceived that shared goals and objectives can be reached through group action [8]. Group cohesion has a significant effect on task participation and social presence.

This indicates that students' sense of attraction to the use of the ERP is impacted by their colleagues using it. Thus, it is hypothesized that:

H6: Social identification has a positive effect on perceived social influence.

3.7 Perceived Effectiveness

Performance expectancy prognosticates intention to use [27]. The institute's students will continue to use ERP so far as the ERP enables them to perform their online interaction with the university. The construct perceived effectiveness measures students' perceptions regarding whether the ERP is successful in aiding them to register courses, check exam results, verify and upload relevant data. Hence, performance expectancy is equated to perceived effectiveness. It logically follows that, if the students do not perceive the ERP to be effective, they are likely to stop using it. Thus, it is hypothesized that:

H7: Perceived effectiveness has a positive effect on use continuance intention.

4 Methodology

Based on deductive reasoning from earlier research [14], the hypotheses were tested to confirm or refute the proposed relationships. The numerical data collected from participants were used to represent the theoretical constructs and concepts and the interpretation of these values were considered as scientific evidence on use continuance intention on the studied ERP.

The data collection instrument used in this study was questionnaire. Data was collected using an online survey software (google forms). The same tool was used in designing the questionnaire. The questionnaire was administered through email. The process of collection lasted for four weeks. Participation was purely voluntary, and no student was coerced into participating in the research. Undergraduate and graduate students of various faculties were involved. Prior to participation, each student read and completed an informed consent form. Participants were assured of privacy and anonymity. Out of the three hundred (300) questionnaires administered, one hundred and four (104) responses were received and used. The questionnaire consisted of demographic questions and five-point Likert scale items (ranging from strongly agree to strongly disagree).

5 Data Analysis

SmartPLS was used for data analysis, as it contains tools for PLS-SEM that are suitable for predicting outcomes of research models. It employs component-based path modeling, which is robust when it comes to deviation from a multivariate distribution [7].

5.1 Outer Model and Measurement Model

The outer model describes the relationship among the latent variables and their indicators whereas the measurement model is the mathematical equations that express the relationship among the latent variables and their indicators. Table 1 presents the reliability statistical measures for the study.

Table 1. Latent variable coefficients

	Cronbach's alpha	rho_A	Composite reliability	Average variance extracted (AVE)
CONT	0.812	1.086	0.906	0.829
CRED	0.888	0.893	0.922	0.748
DIAL	0.794	0.810	0.865	0.617
EFFE	0.924	0.924	0.952	0.867
EFFO	0.928	0.939	0.949	0.822
PRIM	0.698	0.698	0.833	0.624
SOCS	0.857	0.909	0.913	0.778
SOID	0.785	0.884	0.899	0.817

In Table 2, the calculated value in bold on the diagonal are the square root of AVE for each latent variable. Latent variable CRED has an AVE of 0.748 from Table 1. Hence, its square root is 0.864. This number is larger than the correlation values in the column of CRED i.e. (0.472, 0.702, 0.596, 0.596, 0.417, 0.459) and larger than those in the row of CRED i.e. (−0.396). Similar observation can be inferred from all the other latent variables. This indicates that discriminant validity is well established among the variables.

Table 2. Fornell-Larcker criterion analysis for checking discriminant validity.

	CONT	CRED	DIAL	EFFE	EFFO	PRIM	SOCS	SOID
CONT	**0.910**							
CRED	−0.396	**0.864**						
DIAL	−0.310	0.472	**0.785**					
EFFE	−0.452	0.704	0.566	**0.931**				
EFFO	−0.404	0.596	0.549	0.613	**0.906**			
PRIM	−0.405	0.596	0.579	0.585	0.593	**0.789**		
SOCS	−0.151	0.417	0.594	0.567	0.374	0.457	**0.882**	
SOID	−0.073	0.459	0.566	0.513	0.470	0.450	0.536	**0.903**

5.2   Inner Model and Structural Model

The inner structure describes the relationship among the latent variables that make up the model. The structural model is the mathematical equation that expresses the relationship among latent variables. With the help of bootstrapping procedure, SmartPLS generated a T-Statistics for significance testing of both the inner and outer model. The bootstrapping process resulted in the information provided in Table 3 and Fig. 1.

Table 3. Statistical path coefficients and significance

	Original sample	Sample mean	Standard deviation	T-statistics	P-value
SOID → SOCS	0.294	0.303	0.117	**2.514**	**0.012**
DIAL → EFFE	0.091	0.096	0.114	0.796	0.426
DIAL → CRED	0.472	0.482	0.074	**6.333**	**0.000**
DIAL → SOCS	0.427	0.427	0.103	**4.170**	**0.000**
DIAL → PRIM	0.579	0.585	0.069	**8.415**	**0.000**
PRIM → EFFE	0.198	0.202	0.114	1.746	0.081
PRIM → EFFO	0.593	0.601	0.069	**8.613**	**0.000**
EFFO → EFFE	0.335	0.325	0.124	**2.693**	**0.007**
SOCS → EFFE	0.297	0.300	0.110	**2.696**	**0.007**
CRED → CONT	−0.101	−0.108	0.141	0.715	0.475
SOCS → CONT	0.165	0.178	0.118	1.397	0.163
EFFO → CONT	−0.184	−0.185	0.120	1.539	0.124
EFFE → CONT	−0.362	−0.364	0.147	**2.467**	**0.014**

The values in the 'T-Statistics' column determines if the path coefficient of the inner model is significant or not. Using a two-tailed t-test with a significance level of 5%, the path coefficient will be significant if the 'T-Statistics' is larger than 1.96 (marked as bold in Table 3). Two different values are indicated on each arrow line in Fig. 1. The upper ones represent structural path significant strength among the constructs or latent variables in the model (T-statistics). The higher values represent more significance and vice versa. The values in the variables represent the coefficient of determination, R^2. These values explain the percentage of variance. The lower ones represent inner model path coefficient size. Standardized path coefficients value lower than 0.1 indicates that path is statistically not significant. Based on the results of the PLS-SEM analysis (Fig. 1), the following conclusions were drawn on use continuance intention of the ERP that was studied. The coefficient of determination, R^2, for continuance intention is 0.253 (see Fig. 1). This indicates that the exogenous or independent variables, i.e. CRED, EFFO, SOCS and EFFE moderately explain 25.3% of the variance in CONT (continuance intention). An endogenous variable is the same as dependent variable. SOCS, DIAL, PRIM and EFFO together explain 54.1% of the variance of EFFE, (i.e. Perceived Effectiveness). DIAL and SOID together explain 41.2% of the variance of SOCS (i.e. Perceived Social Influence). DIAL alone explains 33.5% of the variance of PRIM (i.e. Primary Task Support). Whilst DIAL explains 22.2% of the variance of CRED (i.e. Perceived Credibility). Primary Task Support (PRIM) accounts for 35.1% of the variance of Perceived Effort (EFFO).

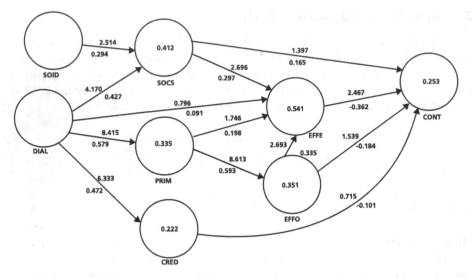

Fig. 1. The research model with the results of the PLS-SEM analysis

The inner model suggests that perceived social influence (SOCS) has the strongest impact on continuance intention with a value of 0.165. On the other hand, perceived effectiveness, perceived effort and perceived credibility have no significant impact on continuance intention because they are negative values i.e. −0.362, −0.184 and −0.101 respectively. The relationship between perceived social influence and continuance intention is statistically significant. However, the one between perceived effectiveness and continuance intention, perceived effort and continuance intention, perceived credibility and continuance intention are all statistically not significant. This is because their standardized path coefficients are lower than 0.1. Perceived social influence is moderately strong predictor of continuance intention, but perceived effectiveness, perceived effort and perceived credibility do not predict continuance intention directly.

6 Discussion

In this study, a research model proposed [14] was adopted to explain and predict use continuance intention of an ERP. The outcomes of the analysis confirmed most of the hypotheses. All the constructs of the research model have a significant impact. With human-computer dialogue support, the system must provide relevant, motivating feedback to the students via words, images, sounds and other forms of media. Its role in the adopted model is significant in that, it affects perceived social influence. Perceived social influence strongly influences use continuance. Through social identification, students easily relate to the experiences of their colleagues on the ERP platform. It is evident in the structural model that social identification influence use continuance indirectly through other constructs.

A strong positive connection from social identification on perceived social influence was confirmed. This agrees with the idea that information technology artefacts can be designed to perform as social actors [22]. Tuunanen et al. [24] found that students rarely use any information system in isolation but would like to connect with others. Computer-human dialogue support plays a key role when it comes to students' intention towards the ERP. Students need to be prompted, suggested to and reminded of necessary tasks that they need to perform. Looking at the results carefully, social identification and computer-human dialogue support explains considerably 41.2% of the variance of perceived social influence. Perceived credibility involves how trustworthy, reliably, believable and credible the ERP should be. As seen in the model, (Fig. 1) perceived credibility has significant relationship to continuance intention. However, computer-human dialogue accounts for 22.2% of the variance of perceived credibility.

This study contributes to the research of continuous use of ERP systems, which can be promoted by incorporating suitable sets of persuasive mechanisms into it design. Perceived social influence was found to be the stronger construct that impacts use continuance. This is indicative of the fact that persuasive features promote use continuance intention, as it has similarly been confirmed in other recent research work related to behavioral intentions [10, 14, 20] and user engagement [23].

To further gain insights into the underlying persuasive mechanisms, multi group analysis was performed on the demographic data available. Gender, age range and level of study were the focus, which helped to uncover several interesting observations. For the male participants, perceived effort had a strong impact on use continuance. For the female participants, perceived social influence strongly impacts use continuance. Whereas for participants under age of 26, perceived social influence strongly impacted use continuance. Amongst graduate students, perceived effort strongly impacted use continuance, while within undergraduate students, perceived social influence was the main contributor for use continuance.

7 Conclusions

After the empirically examination of users' continuance intention towards a selected ERP system, it has been established that the introduction of persuasive features into enterprise systems can promote use continuous. As such, ERPs must be designed to possess features that engage and retain students in order to take full advantage of its use. Persuasive features are keys factors that motivate student continuance use of such systems. User resistant to use in the post implementation process has been identified as one of the root causes of ERP implementation failure. For the ERP to continue to serve its purpose, users must be motivated by embedded persuasive mechanism.

Although this study has provided empirical evidence that supports the fact that the introduction of persuasive features into enterprise systems can help promote continuous use, there is the need for further studies to be conducted to ascertain whether this notion may hold for other systems. This is because mostly ERPs are used in business and industries where the users (employees) often do not have the choice to avoid using it. However, within the academic industry, students are a special type of customers who also ends up being products of the same institution. Hence the type of psychological contract that exist between the students and their institution may differ from the one between a typical employer and employee. It is therefore recommended that future research should focus on non-academic industry to verify whether the findings of this study holds among all industries.

References

1. Bhattacherjee, A.: Understanding information systems continuance: an expectation-confirmation model. MIS Q. **25**, 351 (2001). https://doi.org/10.2307/3250921
2. Botta-Genoulaz, V., Millet, P.A.: An investigation into the use of ERP systems in the service sector. Int. J. Prod. Econ. **99**, 202–221 (2006). https://doi.org/10.1016/J.IJPE.2004.12.015
3. Robey, D., Ross, J.W., Boudreau, M.C.: Learning to implement enterprise systems: an exploratory study of the dialectics of change. J. Manag. Inf. Syst. **19**, 17–46 (2002)
4. Everard, A., Galletta, D.F.: How presentation flaws affect perceived site quality, trust, and intention to purchase from an online store. J. Manag. Inf. Syst. **22**, 55–95 (2005)
5. Finneran, C.M., Zhang, P.: A person–artefact–task (PAT) model of flow antecedents in computer-mediated environments. Int. J. Hum. Comput. Stud. **59**, 475–496 (2003). https://doi.org/10.1016/S1071-5819(03)00112-5
6. Davis, F.D.: Perceived usefulness, perceived ease of use, and user acceptance of information technology. MIS Q. **13**, 319–340 (1989)
7. Gefen, D., Rigdon, E.E., Straub, D.: Editor's comments: an update and extension to SEM guidelines for administrative and social science research. MIS Q. **35**, 3–14 (2011)
8. Hsu, C.-L., Lu, H.-P.: Consumer behavior in online game communities: a motivational factor perspective. Comput. Hum. Behav. **23**, 1642–1659 (2007). https://doi.org/10.1016/j.chb.2005.09.001
9. Hwang, K.O., Ottenbacher, A.J., Green, A.P., Cannon-Diehl, M.R., Richardson, O., Bernstam, E.V., Thomas, E.J.: Social support in an Internet weight loss community. Int. J. Med. Inform. **79**, 5–13 (2010). https://doi.org/10.1016/J.IJMEDINF.2009.10.003
10. Jin, X.-L., Lee, M.K.O.: Cheung, C.M.K: Predicting continuance in online communities: model development and empirical test. Behav. Inf. Technol. **29**, 383–394 (2010)
11. Kahn, B.E., Isen, A.M.: The influence of positive affect on variety seeking among safe, enjoyable products. J. Consum. Res. **20**, 257–270 (1993)
12. Kang, Y.S., Hong, S., Lee, H.: Exploring continued online service usage behavior: the roles of self-image congruity and regret. Comput. Hum. Behav. **25**, 111–122 (2009). https://doi.org/10.1016/J.CHB.2008.07.009
13. Karahanna, E., Straub, D.W., Chervany, N.L.: Information technology adoption across time: a cross-sectional comparison of pre-adoption and post-adoption beliefs. MIS Q. **23**, 183 (1999). https://doi.org/10.2307/249751
14. Tuomas, L., Oinas-Kukkonen, H.: Explaining and predicting perceived effectiveness and use continuance intention of a behaviour change support system for weight loss. Behav. Inf. Technol. **34**, 176–189 (2015)
15. Locke, E.A., Latham, G.P.: Building a practically useful theory of goal setting and task motivation: a 35-year odyssey. Am. Psychol. **57**, 705–717 (2002). https://doi.org/10.1037//0003-066x.57.9.705
16. Nass, C., Moon, Y.: Machines and mindlessness: social responses to computers. J. Soc. Issues **56**, 81–103 (2000)

17. Preece, J., Shneiderman, B.: The reader-to-leader framework: motivating technology-mediated social participation. AIS Trans. Hum.-Comput. Interact. THCI **1**, 13–32 (2009)
18. Al-Natour, S., Benbasat, I.: The adoption and use of IT artifacts: a new interaction-centric model for the study of user artifact relationships. J. Assoc. Inf. Syst. **10**, 661–685 (2009)
19. Shang, S., Seddon, P.B.: A comprehensive framework for classifying the benefits of ERP systems. In: Association for Information Systems AIS Electronic Library (AISeL), vol. 1, pp. 1–11 (2000)
20. Shin, D.-H.: User experience in social commerce: in friends we trust. Behav. Inf. Technol. **32**, 52–67 (2013). https://doi.org/10.1080/0144929X.2012.692167
21. Spathis, C., Constantinides, S.: The usefulness of ERP systems for effective management. Ind. Manag. Data Syst. **103**, 677–685 (2003). https://doi.org/10.1108/02635570310506098
22. Stibe, A.: Towards a framework for socially influencing systems: meta-analysis of four PLS-SEM based studies. In: MacTavish, T., Basapur, S. (eds.) PERSUASIVE 2015. LNCS, vol. 9072, pp. 172–183. Springer, Cham (2015). https://doi.org/10.1007/978-3-319-20306-5_16
23. Stibe, A., Larson, K.: Persuasive cities for sustainable wellbeing: quantified communities. In: Younas, M., Awan, I., Kryvinska, N., Strauss, C., Thanh, D. (eds.) MobiWIS 2016. LNCS, vol. 9847, pp. 271–282. Springer, Cham (2016). https://doi.org/10.1007/978-3-319-44215-0_22
24. Tuunanen, T., Myers, M.D., Harold, C., Cassab, H.: A conceptual framework for consumer information systems development. Pacific Asia J. Assoc. Inf. Syst. **2**, 47–66 (2010)
25. Uchino, B.N.: Social support and health: a review of physiological processes potentially underlying links to disease outcomes. J. Behav. Med. **29**, 377–386 (2006). https://doi.org/10.1007/s10865-006-9056-5
26. Venkatesh, V., Thong, J.Y.L., Xu, X.: Consumer acceptance and use of information technology: extending the unified theory of acceptance and use of technology. MIS Q. **36**, 157–178 (2012)
27. Venkatesh, V., Morris, M.G., Davis, G.B., Davis, F.D.: User acceptance of information technology: toward a unified view. MIS Q. **27**, 425–478 (2003)

Is It My Looks? Or Something I Said? The Impact of Explanations, Embodiment, and Expectations on Trust and Performance in Human-Robot Teams

Ning Wang[1(✉)], David V. Pynadath[1], Ericka Rovira[2], Michael J. Barnes[3], and Susan G. Hill[3]

[1] Institute for Creative Technologies, University of Southern California, Los Angeles, USA
nwang@ict.usc.edu
[2] U.S. Military Academy, West Point, USA
[3] U.S. Army Research Laboratory, Hillandale, USA

Abstract. Trust is critical to the success of human-robot interaction. Research has shown that people will more accurately trust a robot if they have an accurate understanding of its decision-making process. The Partially Observable Markov Decision Process (POMDP) is one such decision-making process, but its quantitative reasoning is typically opaque to people. This lack of transparency is exacerbated when a robot can learn, making its decision making better, but also less predictable. Recent research has shown promise in calibrating human-robot trust by automatically generating explanations of POMDP-based decisions. In this work, we explore factors that can potentially interact with such explanations in influencing human decision-making in human-robot teams. We focus on explanations with quantitative expressions of uncertainty and experiment with common design factors of a robot: its embodiment and its communication strategy in case of an error. Results help us identify valuable properties and dynamics of the human-robot trust relationship.

1 Introduction

Trust is critical to the success of human-robot interaction (HRI) [1]. To maximize the performance of human-robot teams, people should trust their robot teammates to perform a given task when robots are more suited than humans for the task. If the robots are less suited, then people should perform the task themselves. Failure to do so results in *disuse* of robots in the former case and *misuse* in the latter [2]. Real-world case studies and laboratory experiments show that failures of both types are common [3].

Research has shown that people will more accurately trust an autonomous system if they have a more accurate understanding of its decision-making process [4]. The Partially Observable Markov Decision Process (POMDP) is one such

© Springer International Publishing AG, part of Springer Nature 2018
J. Ham et al. (Eds.): PERSUASIVE 2018, LNCS 10809, pp. 56–69, 2018.
https://doi.org/10.1007/978-3-319-78978-1_5

decision-making process, providing optimized decision making that is commonly used by robots, agents, and other autonomous systems [5]. Unfortunately, the quantitative nature of POMDP algorithms and their results makes them hard for people to understand. Furthermore, while a robot could learn to improve its POMDP model, such changes in its decision-making only exacerbate the lack of transparency. Fortunately, recent research has shown promise in calibrating human-agent trust by automatically generating explanations of POMDP-based decisions [6].

In this work, we seek a deeper understanding of the factors leading to the effectiveness (or lack thereof) of such automatically generated explanations. We specifically focus on explanations that provide quantitative information on uncertainty and two factors related to common robot design decisions: its embodiment and its communication strategy in case of errors. We seek to understand how a robot's coping strategies after making an error may interact with its transparency communications in calibrating a human teammate's trust in it. We implement a specific trust-repair strategy inspired by prior work in organizational trust: an acknowledgement of a mistake, paired with a promise to improve [7]. We thus can study differences in the effect of such an error acknowledgment and promise to learn when preceded by different types of explanations of the robot's decision-making.

In addition, people have been observed to react differently to robot teammates based on their appearance [8]. There are clear behavioral differences for many people when interacting with more human- or animal-like robots, in contrast to their interactions with more "mechanical" robots. In fact, trust in human-animal interaction shares some characteristics with trust in human-robot interaction, in that both seek to augment human skills and abilities in order to better accomplish a particular task [9]. It has been suggested that human-animal interactions may represent a suitable metaphor for human-robot interactions (for review, see [10]). Of course, the roles that each entity fills depend on its capabilities, skills, and affordances [11,12]. Thus we consider how the robot's embodiment will affect the interpretation and effectiveness of its explanations. In particular, we draw inspiration from studies showing that dog-like robots are treated differently from those with a more traditionally robotic appearance [11,12]. We can therefore quantify the potentially different effects of POMDP-based explanations when coming from robots with different embodiments.

To quantify the impact of these variables, we expand our measures to consider self-reported trust as well as behavioral measures of human decision-making, such as compliance with the robot's recommendations, correct decisions by the human teammate, and correct diagnosis of the robot's failures by the human teammate. By looking at where these behavioral measures deviate from self-reported measures, we can better drill down into the mental states of the human teammates, into the antecedents of trust.

2 Related Work

Existing studies have shown that a human's ability to understand its agent teammate has a clear impact on trust [4]. Hand-crafted explanations have shown to contribute to that understanding in a way that provides transparency and improves trust [13]. Automated, domain-independent methods for generating explanations have a long history within the context of rule- and logic-based systems, like expert systems [14]. There has been more recent work on generating explanations based on Markov Decision Problems (MDPs) [15]. Our previous work automatically generated explanations from Partially Observable MDPs [6], which provide a more realistic model for HRI domains, due to the inherent uncertainty in the robots' operating environment. The existing evidence is encouraging as to the potential success of applying a general-purpose explanation on top of an agent's decision-making process.

To identify the most effective content for such AI-based explanations, we look to studies that measure the impact of various forms of explanation on people's perceptions of risks and uncertainties when making decisions. A survey of these studies indicates that "people prefer numerical information for its accuracy but use a verbal statement to express a probability to others." [16]. On the other hand, one of the studies in the survey contrasted a numeric representation of uncertainty with more anecdotal evidence and found that the numeric information carried less weight when both types were present [17]. A study of risk communication in medical trade-off decisions showed that people performed better when receiving numeric expressions of uncertainty in percentage (67%) rather than frequency (2 out of 3) form [18]. In translating our robot's POMDP-based reasoning into a human-understandable format, our explanation algorithms use natural-language templates inspired by these various findings in the literature.

Previous studies of automatically generated explanations in HRI used a fixed robot, with a traditionally mechanical appearance. However, people react differently to robot teammates based on their appearance. Prior studies have shown that some people show a marked preference for more mechanical-looking robots, while others are more comfortable interacting with humanoid robots [8]. Such observations have prompted other technological attempts to emulate the physical, behavioral, and cognitive aspects of biological entities within robots. Studies have found that humans tend to describe their relationships with robotic animals as similar to those with biological animals [11,12]. These studies found that people will often attribute some (but not all) dog-like qualities to robots who look like dogs. In fact, in many domains, human-animal trust can be viewed as a better model for HRI than human-human trust [10].

Given the uncertain nature of the robot's decisions, they will inevitably turn out to be wrong from time to time. Reinforcement learning has enabled many robots to improve from their mistakes (e.g., [19,20]). While such learning is likely to complicate the robot's effort to reason transparently with human teammates, it does provide an opportunity to repair trust that has been damaged by robot errors. Our investigation into the interaction between explanations and trust repair is inspired by work on the latter within organizations [7,21]. Prior research has found that timely trust-repair actions are critical to effectively maintaining trust within HRI [22].

In this paper, we discuss the impact of a robot's embodiment, its explanation, and its promise to learn from mistakes on trust and team performance.

Based on results from previous studies of robot explanations and trust [23], we hypothesize that:

H1: Compared to a robot who offers no explanations of its decisions, a robot who offers explanations can help its teammate better calibrate trust and produce better team performance.

Additionally, we hypothesize that a robot that looks like an animal, such as a dog, will help human teammates establish a trust relationship with it similar to the one they would have with a real dog. We therefore hypothesize that:

H2: A robot's embodiment will impact trust in the robot and team performance. Specifically, a robot whose appearance shares that of an animal will foster a stronger trust relationship than one with a more mechanical appearance.

Finally, a robot can acknowledge its mistakes and promise to learn from them, so as to indicate that it is aware of its limitations and knows how to improve. Such indications can potentially improve its teammate's trust in its ability. We hypothesize that:

H3: A robot that acknowledges each mistake it makes and promises to learn from them will improve its trust relationship with its human teammates.

3   HRI Testbed

We evaluate our hypotheses in the context of an online HRI testbed [24]. For the current study, we used the testbed to implement a scenario in which a human teammate works with a different robot across eight reconnaissance missions (Fig. 1). Each mission requires the human teammate to search 15 buildings in a different town. The virtual robot serves as a scout, scans the buildings for potential danger, and relays its findings. The robot has an NBC (nuclear, biological, and chemical) weapon sensor, a camera that can detect armed gunmen, and a microphone that can identify suspicious conversations.

The human must choose between entering a building with or without protective gear. If there is danger in the building, the human will be injured if not wearing the protective gear, and the team will incur a 3-min time penalty. However, it takes time to put on and take off protective gear (20 s each). The human teammate must enter all 15 buildings within 10 min; otherwise, the mission is a failure. So the human is incentivized to consider the robot's findings before deciding how to enter the building.

We model this task as a POMDP, which is a tuple, $\langle S, A, P, \Omega, O, R \rangle$ [5]. The state, S, consists of objective facts about the world, such as the presence of dangerous chemicals in the buildings. The robot's available actions, A, correspond to the possible decisions it can make. Upon arrival at a new building, the robot makes a decision as to whether to declare it safe or unsafe for its human teammate. We model the dynamics of the world using a transition probability function, P, that captures the uncertain effects of the robot's actions. A recommendation that a building is safe (unsafe) has a high (low) probability of decreasing the teammate's health if there is, in fact, danger present.

The robot has only indirect information about the true state of the world, through a subset of possible observations, Ω, that are probabilistically dependent (through the observation function, O) on the true values of the corresponding state features. For example, if dangerous chemicals are present at its current location, then the robot's chemical sensor will detect them with a high probability. There is also a lower, but nonzero, probability that the sensor will not detect them.

The robot's reward, R, is highest when all buildings have been explored by the human teammate. This reward component incentivizes the robot to pursue the overall mission objective. There is also a positive reward associated with the human teammate's health. This reward component punishes the robot if it fails to warn its teammate of dangerous buildings. Finally, there is a negative reward that increases with the time cost of the current state. This motivates the robot to complete the mission quickly.

An agent can generate behavior based on its POMDP model by determining the optimal action based on its current beliefs, b, about the state of the world [5]. In particular, our robot will consider declaring a building dangerous or safe by combining its beliefs about the likelihood of possible threats in the building with each possible declaration to compute the likelihood of the outcome (i.e., impact on teammate's health and time needed to search the building). It will finally combine these outcome likelihoods with its reward function and choose the option that has the highest reward.

While the scenario is military reconnaissance, it is simple enough that it does not require prior experience to complete the mission in the study, e.g., the task does not need knowledge of procedures for searching buildings. The participant needs to decide only whether to trust the robot's findings (safe/dangerous) and press a button to enter/exit the room. In the current study, we fixed the observations the robot receives to be accurate 80% of the time. As a result, the robot makes incorrect assessment of the danger level for 3 out of 15 buildings in each town. Research on automation reliability on trust and human-automation team has indicated that a reliability of 80% [25] or above 70% [26] to be a suitable setting for similar studies.

Fig. 1. Human robot interaction simulation testbed with HTML front-end.

4   Evaluation

The domain of the testbed scenario is relevant to the military, so we recruited 61 participants from a higher-education military school in the United States. Participants were awarded extra course credit for their participation.

Design: We varied the robot's embodiment (robot vs. robot dog), explanation (no explanation vs. confidence explanation) and acknowledgement to learn from mistakes (no acknowledgement vs. acknowledgement). The aforementioned testbed was used in the study. Because individual differences often impact trust in automation [27], a $2 \times 2 \times 2$ within-subject design is used in the study. Each participant completed 8 missions. In each mission, a different variation of the robot worked with the participant. A total of 8 variations of robot were used (hence 8 missions). While the task and environment of mission 1 through 8 were fixed, the order of the robot variations was counter-balanced. At the beginning of each mission, participants were told that they were working with a new robot for the first time (e.g., not the same robot from previous missions).

Embodiment: Two robot embodiments were used in the study, illustrated in Fig. 2. One robot was designed to look like a dog, with ears, nose, and highlighted eyes, suggesting possibly embedded sound, NBC, and vision sensors. The second robot was designed to have the appearance of a typical robot-looking robot on wheels.

Explanation: Existing algorithms explain an agent's decision-making by exposing different components of its POMDP model [6]. In this study, the explanation variable has two levels: no explanation and a confidence-level explanation. At both levels, the robot informs its teammate of its decision (e.g., "I have finished surveying the doctor's office. I think the place is safe."). Under the confidence-level explanations, the robot augments this decision with additional information that should help its teammate better understand its ability (e.g., decision-making), one of the key dimensions of trust [28]. The confidence-level explanations augment the decision message with additional information about the robot's uncertainty in its decision. One example of a confidence-level explanation would be:

Fig. 2. The two embodiment of the robots used in the study: a robot (left) and a robot dog (right).

"I have finished surveying the Cafe. I think the place is dangerous. I am 78% confident about this assessment." Because the robot's one faulty sensor will lead to occasionally conflicting observations, it will on those occasions have lower confidence in its erroneous decisions.

Acknowledgment: The acknowledgement variable has two levels: no acknowledgement and an acknowledgement that a mistake has been made along with a promise to learn from the mistake. This acknowledgement is given every time the robot makes an assessment that turned out to be incorrect. The team searches 15 buildings during each reconnaissance mission. In each mission, the robot makes an incorrect assessment of three buildings. An example of the robot's acknowledgement is "It seems that my assessment of the informant's house was incorrect. I will update my algorithms when we return to base after the mission".

Procedure: Participants first read an information sheet and filled out the online background survey. Next, participants worked with a simulated robot on 8 reconnaissance missions. In each mission, a variation of the simulated robot (with a different combination of embodiment, explanation, and acknowledgment to learn from its mistakes) was presented. The order in which the robots were presented was counter-balanced across participants. After each mission, participants filled out an online post-mission survey. The study was designed to be completed in 2 sessions, 120 min total.

Measure: The Background Survey included measures of demographic information, education, video game experience, military background, predisposition to trust [29], propensity to trust [30], complacency potential [31], negative attitude towards robots [32], and the uncertainty response scale [33]. Because the impact of individual differences on trust is not the focus of this paper, such analyses and results are not included.

In the Post-Mission Survey, we designed items to measure participants' understanding of the robot's decision-making process. We modified items on interpersonal trust to measure trust in the robot's ability, benevolence, and integrity [28]. We also included the NASA Cognitive Load Index [34], Situation Awareness Rating Scale [35], and trust in oneself and teammate [31]. We have also collected interaction logs from the testbed.

The dependent measures discussed in this paper are listed below. Trust can be measured via both self-report [28] and behavioral indicators, such as compliance. Both of these measures used in the study are discussed below. Because transparency is hypothesized as the "mediating" factor between explanations and trust, we also included transparency as one of the outcome measures. The investigation is carried out in the domain of a human-robot team, because the goal of designing explanations to improve transparency and trust relationship is to improve team performance. Thus, we include two team-performance measures as outcome measures, shown below.

Trust: Trust in the robot's ability, benevolence, and integrity was measured by modifying an existing scale [36]. Each factor of trust was calculated by averaging corresponding Post-Mission Survey items collected after each of the 3 missions.

The explanations compared in this paper are designed to influence perceptions of the *ability* factor of trust, and do not explicitly target *benevolence* and *integrity*. So we focus on only the *ability* component of trust in this paper. The value ranges from 1 to 7.

Transparency: This is measured using items (along a 1–7 Likert scale) on the understanding of the robot's decision-making process, designed by the researchers. A sample item from this measure is "I understand the robot's decision-making process".

Transparency Test Score: We designed a question to assess participant's understanding of the robot's decision-making process. The question asks the participants to name the components of the robot that need repair. The components include the NBC sensors, audio and video processing units, etc. For the current study, only the audio/video processing units are faulty. Participants receive either 0 or 1 on this test.

Compliance: This is calculated by dividing the number of participant decisions that matched the robot's recommendation by the total number of participant decisions in the interaction logs collected in each mission (15). The value ranges from 0 to 100%.

Correct Decisions: This measure is calculated by dividing the number of correct decisions (e.g., ending in safety) by the total number of participant decisions in the interaction logs collected in each mission (15). The value ranges from 0 to 100%.

5   Results

Data from 61 participants are included in the analysis (14 women, 39 men, $M_{age} = 19.2$ years, age range: 18–23 years). 2 participants answered that they had worked with an automated squad member (such as a robot) before. 3 participants had reconnaissance or search and rescue training, and 1 was actively involved in such missions.

We conducted a General Linear Model analysis with Repeated Measures and Bonferroni corrections, using explanation, embodiment, and promise to improve as within-subject factors, and trust, transparency, compliance, and correct decisions as dependent variables. Results show that explanation had a significant impact on trust ($F(1, 60) = 118.68$, $p < .0001$), transparency ($F(1, 60) = 33.82$, $p < .0001$), transparency test score ($F(1, 60) = 11.72$, $p = .001$), compliance ($F(1, 60) = 66.31$, $p < .0001$), and correct decisions made ($F(1, 60) = 83.90$, $p < .0001$). As shown in Table 1, participants reported a higher level of trust in the robot's ability when it offered explanations on its decisions. Participants also reported that they felt that they understood the robot's decision-making process better when the robot offered explanations. Additionally, when the robot offered explanations, the human teammate made better decisions, as reflected in the percentage of correct decisions. The explanation also helped the human teammate calibrate when they should trust robot, as indicated by the combination of compliance rate and percentage of correct decisions. For each mission, 80% of the robot's decisions are correct (12 out of 15). We can see from Table 1 that when the robot offered no explanations, the participants over-trusted the robot (89.3%), resulting in poor decisions (69%). In contrast, when the robot offered explanations, the compliance rate (78.9%) is much closer to the robot's correctness rate (80%). On the other hand, when the robot offered no explanations, participants scored higher on the transparency test score, compared to when explanations were offered.

Table 1. The effect of explanation on trust, transparency, compliance, and correctness.

	No explanation	Confidence explanation
Transparency	2.75 (out of 7)	3.65 (out of 7)
Transparency test score	.414 (out of 1)	.275 (out of 1)
Trust	2.99 (out of 7)	5.07 (out of 7)
Compliance	89.3%	78.9%
Correct decisions	69%	85.1%

The main effect of the promise to learn from mistakes was not statistically significant for any of the dependent variables. The robot's embodiment had a marginally significant effect on trust ($F(1, 60) = 3.64$, $p = .061$) and no significant main effect on the rest of the dependent variables. With a dog-like embodiment, participants reported a lower level of trust, compared to that reported for the machine-like robot embodiment ($M_{dog} = 3.96$, $M_{robot} = 4.10$).

There was a marginally significant interaction between the robot's promise to improve and its explanations on trust ($F(1, 60) = 3.85$, $p = .054$). As shown in Table 2, when the robot offered explanations, additional acknowledgment of error and promise to learn from it did not make much difference in the self-reported trust in the robot. However, when the robot did *not* offer explanations, acknowledging that an error was made and promising to improve did lead to higher self-reported trust by the participants.

Table 2. Interaction between the robot's explanations and acknowledgment on participants' trust.

	No explanation	Confidence explanation
No ACK.	2.86 (out of 7)	5.09 (out of 7)
With ACK.	3.13 (out of 7)	5.05 (out of 7)

The analysis of the main effect of embodiment shows that there was a marginally significant impact of the robot's embodiment on trust, as we originally hypothesized. The rationale of the hypothesis is that participants will carry their trust relationship with the real animal over to the animal-like robot. Such carry-over may last only a short period of time after the initial interaction, as over time, it will be overcome by the actual behavior of the robot. We plotted the self-reported trust over the course of 8 missions between interactions of robots with different embodiments. As Fig. 3 shows, this hypothesized decaying effect is indeed the case. Initially (i.e., during the first mission), the trust level differed significantly between the two robot embodiments. An ANOVA with explanation, embodiment, and acknowledgement as fix factors and self-reported trust right after the first mission as the dependent variable shows a significant main effect of the robot's embodiment ($M_{dog} = 3.58$, $M_{robot} = 4.39$, $F(1, 60) = 6.48$, $p = .014$) and the explanation offered ($M_{none} = 2.91$, $M_{confidence} = 5.00$, $F(1, 60) = 47.47$, $p < .001$). However, over time (in fact, starting from the second mission), the impact of the robot's embodiment is overtaken by the robot's behavior. And the difference in the level of trust in the robot is dominated by the difference in the robot's behavior, in this case, mainly the explanations offered by the robot (Fig. 3). The aforementioned ANOVA tests on self-reported trust after subsequent missions indicated only a significant main effect of the robot's explanations. Additionally, we did not observe a significant impact of embodiment on the other dependent variables during the first mission or over the course of 8 missions.

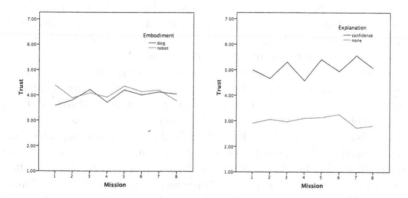

Fig. 3. Left: self-reported trust in the robot between two different robot embodiments. Right: self-reported trust in the robot between a robot offering confidence-level vs. no explanation.

6 Discussion

It is intriguing that explanation had a significant effect on transparency and self-reported trust. The explanation offered by the robot indicates only its confidence in its own assessment, not any information about what the assessment was based on or how the assessment was made. However, participants still reported that they felt that they understood the robot's decision-making process better when such an explanation was offered. Furthermore, such explanations do not indicate which component of the robot is faulty. This is reflected in the generally low scores on the transparency tests ($M = .344$). It may be somewhat surprising that when the robot offered explanations, participants actually scored lower on the transparency test. Perhaps, during these times, participants relied on the robot's explanation to guide their decisions, without thinking about where its recommendation came from. When the robot offered no explanations, the participants had to rely on experience with the robot to make future decisions, and, in the process, tried to figure out what was wrong with the robot. Additionally, by offering explanations of its decisions, the robot helped its teammate calibrate a proper compliance rate (e.g., when and when not to follow its recommendations), resulting in better decision-making by the human teammate. Finally, without receiving explanations from the robot, the participants overused the robot, i.e., they followed the robot's recommendations even when the robot was wrong. Such participants also reported a lower level of trust in the robot, most likely due to the fact that over-relying on the robot during the mission resulted in poor decision-making.

Embodiment had an only marginally significant impact on self-reported trust. In particular, participants reported a lower level of trust in a robot with a dog-like appearance, compared to a robot with a machine-like appearance. This difference in trust levels did not translate to a difference in perceived transparency, compliance, or percentage of correct decisions. The direction in which the self-reported trust differed is contrary to our hypothesis. We hypothesized that one would trust a robot that looks like a dog more because of the existing trust relationship between humans and their best friend. The fact that participants trusted a machine-like robot more indicates that trust in the robot's ability could be context- and task-dependent. A machine-like robot may give the initial impression of a technological advantage offered by more sophisticated sensing equipment, which would be relevant to the reconnaissance task, compared to a dog-like robot. However, the effect of embodiment on self-reported trust is most pronounced at the beginning of the interaction. After interacting with the robot in the first mission, the robot's embodiment made no significant difference in the teammate's trust. The robot's behavior, particularly the explanations, which are highly relevant to the teammate's decision-making and team performance, became the deciding factor on transparency, trust, compliance, and teammate's decision-making for the following missions. This is congruent with the notion that trust is built based on past experience and first impressions based on appearance may not last.

Acknowledging a mistake and promising to learn from it had no significant effect on any of the dependent measures in the study. This is contrary to our hypothesis. Perhaps this is due to the fact that the participants interacted with each robot in only one mission. While the robot promised to update its decision-making algorithms to reflect the experience during the mission, the participants never got to witness any change after that mission. Making such acknowledgment had a significant interaction effect with the robot's explanations on self-reported trust. Particularly, when no explanations were offered, making such acknowledgment and promise can help restore some trust and perhaps instill some hope in the robot. However, when the robot offered explanations with its recommendations, such acknowledgement and promise did not make any significant impact. Perhaps the explanations alone were enough to steer the trust relationship.

We experimented with a robot that acknowledged its errors and promised to learn from them after the mission. However, it did not change its behavior within the mission, possibly accounting for the lack of any significant effect of such an acknowledgment/promise. Our robot's POMDP model can support such a dynamic behavior with some straightforward modification. In the next iteration of this study, we will expand the robot's POMDP model to include an explicit representation of the possibility of a sensor failure. The standard POMDP belief-update algorithms could then allow this robot to decrease its confidence in its vision system after each false negative it receives [5]. In general, we can allow our robot to perform model-based *reinforcement learning* to update any aspect of its POMDP model [37]. Introducing the ability for the robot to change its decision-making model will no doubt raise new challenges for maintaining transparency and trust for human teammates.

Acknowledgment. This project is funded by the U.S. Army Research Laboratory. Statements and opinions expressed do not necessarily reflect the position or the policy of the United States Government, and no official endorsement should be inferred.

References

1. Lewis, M., Sycara, K., Walker, P.: The role of trust in human-robot interaction. In: Abbass, H.A., Scholz, J., Reid, D.J. (eds.) Foundations of Trusted Autonomy. SSDC, vol. 117, pp. 135–159. Springer, Cham (2018). https://doi.org/10.1007/978-3-319-64816-3_8
2. Parasuraman, R., Riley, V.: Humans and automation: use, misuse, disuse, abuse. Hum. Factors **39**(2), 230–253 (1997)
3. Lee, J.D., See, K.A.: Trust in automation: designing for appropriate reliance. Hum. Factors **46**(1), 50–80 (2004)
4. Lee, J., Moray, N.: Trust, control strategies and allocation of function in human-machine systems. Ergonomics **35**(10), 1243–1270 (1992)
5. Kaelbling, L.P., Littman, M.L., Cassandra, A.R.: Planning and acting in partially observable stochastic domains. Artif. Intell. **101**(1), 99–134 (1998)
6. Wang, N., Pynadath, D.V., Hill, S.G.: The impact of POMDP-generated explanations on trust and performance in human-robot teams. In: International Conference on Autonomous Agents and Multiagent Systems (2016)
7. Schweitzer, M.E., Hershey, J.C., Bradlow, E.T.: Promises and lies: restoring violated trust. Organ. Behav. Hum. Decis. Process. **101**(1), 1–19 (2006)
8. Walters, M.L., Koay, K.L., Syrdal, D.S., Dautenhahn, K., Boekhorst, R.T.: Preferences and perceptions of robot appearance and embodiment in human-robot interaction trials. In: AISB Symposium on New Frontiers in Human-Robot Interaction Convention, pp. 136–143 (2009)

9. Bruemmer, D.J., Marble, J.L., Dudenhoeffer, D.D.: Mutual initiative in human-machine teams. In: IEEE Conference on Human Factors and Power Plants, pp. 7-22–7-30. IEEE (2002)
10. Billings, D.R., Schaefer, K.E., Chen, J.Y., Kocsis, V., Barrera, M., Cook, J., Ferrer, M., Hancock, P.A.: Human-animal trust as an analog for human-robot trust: a review of current evidence. Technical Report ARL-TR-5949, Army Research Laboratory (2012)
11. Kerepesi, A., Kubinyi, E., Jonsson, G., Magnusson, M., Miklosi, A.: Behavioural comparison of human-animal (dog) and human-robot (AIBO) interactions. Behav. Process. **73**(1), 92–99 (2006)
12. Melson, G.F., Kahn, P.H., Beck, A., Friedman, B., Roberts, T., Garrett, E., Gill, B.T.: Children's behavior toward and understanding of robotic and living dogs. J. Appl. Dev. Psychol. **30**(2), 92–102 (2009)
13. Dzindolet, M.T., Peterson, S.A., Pomranky, R.A., Pierce, L.G., Beck, H.P.: The role of trust in automation reliance. Int. J. Hum.-Comput. Stud. **58**(6), 697–718 (2003)
14. Swartout, W.R., Moore, J.D.: Explanation in second generation expert systems. In: David, J.M., Krivine, J.P., Simmons, R. (eds.) Second Generation Expert Systems, pp. 543–585. Springer, Heidelberg (1993). https://doi.org/10.1007/978-3-642-77927-5_24
15. Elizalde, F., Sucar, L.E., Luque, M., Diez, J., Reyes, A.: Policy explanation in factored Markov decision processes. In: European Workshop on Probabilistic Graphical Models, pp. 97–104 (2008)
16. Visschers, V.H.M., Meertens, R.M., Passchier, W.W.F., De Vries, N.N.K.: Probability information in risk communication: a review of the research literature. Risk Anal. **29**(2), 267–287 (2009)
17. Hendrickx, L., Vlek, C., Oppewal, H.: Relative importance of scenario information and frequency information in the judgment of risk. Acta Psychol. **72**(1), 41–63 (1989)
18. Waters, E.A., Weinstein, N.D., Colditz, G.A., Emmons, K.: Formats for improving risk communication in medical tradeoff decisions. J. Health Commun. **11**(2), 167–182 (2006)
19. Matarić, M.J.: Reinforcement learning in the multi-robot domain. Auton. Robots **4**(1), 73–83 (1997)
20. Smart, W.D., Kaelbling, L.P.: Effective reinforcement learning for mobile robots. In: IEEE International Conference on Robotics and Automation, vol. 4, pp. 3404–3410. IEEE (2002)
21. Lewicki, R.J.: Trust, trust development, and trust repair. In: Deutsch, M., Coleman, P.T., Marcus, E.C. (eds.) The Handbook of Conflict Resolution: Theory and Practice, pp. 92–119. Wiley Publishing (2006)
22. Robinette, P., Howard, A.M., Wagner, A.R.: Timing is key for robot trust repair. Social Robotics. LNCS (LNAI), vol. 9388, pp. 574–583. Springer, Cham (2015). https://doi.org/10.1007/978-3-319-25554-5_57
23. Wang, N., Pynadath, D.V., Hill, S.G.: Trust calibration within a human-robot team: comparing automatically generated explanations. In: The Eleventh ACM/IEEE International Conference on Human Robot Interaction, Piscataway, NJ, USA, pp. 109–116. IEEE Press (2016)
24. Wang, N., Pynadath, D.V., Hill, S.G.: Building trust in a human-robot team. In: Interservice/Industry Training, Simulation and Education Conference (2015)

25. Rovira, E., Cross, A., Leitch, E., Bonaceto, C.: Displaying contextual information reduces the costs of imperfect decision automation in rapid retasking of ISR assets. Hum. Factors **56**(6), 1036–1049 (2014)
26. Wickens, C.D., Dixon, S.R.: The benefits of imperfect diagnostic automation: a synthesis of the literature. Theor. Issues Ergon. Sci. **8**(3), 201–212 (2007)
27. Pop, V.L., Shrewsbury, A., Durso, F.T.: Individual differences in the calibration of trust in automation. Hum. Factors **57**(4), 545–556 (2015)
28. Mayer, R.C., Davis, J.H., Schoorman, F.D.: An integrative model of organizational trust. Acad. Manag. Rev. **20**(3), 709–734 (1995)
29. McKnight, D.H., Choudhury, V., Kacmar, C.: Developing and validating trust measures for e-commerce: an integrative typology. Inf. Syst. Res. **13**(3), 334–359 (2002)
30. McShane, S.L.: Propensity to trust scale (2014)
31. Ross, J.M.: Moderators of Trust and Reliance Across Multiple Decision AIDS. ProQuest, Ann Arbor (2008)
32. Syrdal, D.S., Dautenhahn, K., Koay, K.L., Walters, M.L.: The negative attitudes towards robots scale and reactions to robot behaviour in a live human-robot interaction study. In: Adaptive and Emergent Behaviour and Complex Systems (2009)
33. Greco, V., Roger, D.: Coping with uncertainty: the construction and validation of a new measure. Pers. Individ. Differ. **31**(4), 519–534 (2001)
34. Hart, S.G., Staveland, L.E.: Development of NASA-TLX (task load index): results of empirical and theoretical research. Adv. Psychol. **52**, 139–183 (1988)
35. Taylor, R.M.: Situational awareness rating technique (SART): the development of a tool for aircrew systems design. In: Situational Awareness in Aerospace Operations (1990)
36. Mayer, R.C., Davis, J.H.: The effect of the performance appraisal system on trust for management: a field quasi-experiment. J. Appl. Psychol. **84**(1), 123 (1999)
37. Kaelbling, L.P., Littman, M.L., Moore, A.W.: Reinforcement learning: a survey. J. Artif. Intell. Res. **4**, 237–285 (1996)

Building Online Platforms for Peer Support Groups as a Persuasive Behavior Change Technique

Amen Alrobai, Huseyin Dogan(✉), Keith Phalp, and Raian Ali

Bournemouth University, Poole, UK
{aalrobai, hdogan, kphalp, rali}@bournemouth.ac.uk

Abstract. Online peer group approach is inherently a persuasive technique as it is centered on peer pressure and surveillance. They are persuasive social networks equipped with tools and facilities that enable behaviour change. This paper presents the case for domain-specific persuasive social networks and provides insights on problematic and addictive behaviour change. A 4-month study was conducted in an addiction rehab centre in the UK, followed by 2-month study in an online peer group system. The study adopted qualitative methods to understand the broad parameters of peer groups including the sessions' environment, norms, interaction styles occurring between groups' members and how such interactions are governed. The qualitative techniques used were (1) observations, (2) form and document analysis, and (3) semi-structured interviews. The findings concern governing such groups in addition to the roles to be enabled and tasks to be performed. The Honeycomb framework was revisited to comment on its building blocks with the purpose of highlighting points to consider when building domain-specific social networks for such domain, i.e. online peer groups to combat addictive behaviour.

Keywords: Online peer groups · Behaviour change · Addictive behaviour

1 Introduction

Online peer groups exhibit their own characteristics which necessitate revisiting their design principles in comparison to general purpose social networks. Social surveillance differs from traditional surveillance in terms of the power, hierarchy, and reciprocity [1]. Traditional surveillance involves, for example, corporations monitoring populations for the purposes of law enforcement, while social surveillance is the process of monitoring activities for the purpose of influencing individuals' behaviours, i.e. persuasion through "overt" observation [2] and it is usually done by peers not only authorities. Online social surveillance utilises digital traces left by users to investigate behaviours and activities, also known as "dataveillance" [3]. The tools that social software offers, e.g. sharing and commenting, are the functional utilities that facilitate online social surveillance. Yet, they still lack theory-based solutions and best practices on how to employ such utilities. The high volume, speed, traceability and process-ability are all new features which necessitate a revision of the known principles and models for traditional social surveillance.

© Springer International Publishing AG, part of Springer Nature 2018
J. Ham et al. (Eds.): PERSUASIVE 2018, LNCS 10809, pp. 70–83, 2018.
https://doi.org/10.1007/978-3-319-78978-1_6

The Honeycomb framework [4] proposed to understand social media platforms from a functional perspective. Previous work on social informatics reviewed and suggested adding extra blocks, e.g. social objects [5] and collaboration, to help designers shifting from Social Computing to Socially Aware Computing [6]. Socially aware systems are supposed to be socially responsible, universal and entirely satisfying users requirements [7]. Social interactions are driven by or revolve around a shared "object(s)", e.g. topic, idea, event or public figure [6]. Social objects help to maintain the focus of a social interaction [5]. This aligns with the use of social networks for domain-specific purposes such as persuasive online peer groups where the group is driven by a specific goal and centred on main issue. However, despite this recognition, there is still lack of enough practice and engineering principles on how to develop such platforms to boost positive behaviour and prevent side-effects [8].

This paper presents the results of a 4-month study that was conducted in an addiction rehab centre in the UK. An observational study was performed followed by practitioner interviews. This study was complemented by 2-months study on an online system for peer support group. The findings focus on group governance, roles to be enabled and tasks to be performed. The Honeycomb framework [4] was revisited to comment on its building blocks with the purpose of highlighting points to consider when building domain-specific social networks for such domain, i.e. online peer groups to combat addictive behaviour.

1.1 Addictive Behaviour Change

Behavioural change theories are mainly used to bridge the gap between attitudes and behaviours. These theories aim at reducing discrepancies between these two conceptual constructs such as, for example, the gap between the intention to change a behaviour and the act of actually doing so [9]. This is achieved by encouraging individuals to create a plan to achieve the targeted behaviour. These theories include (1) Theory of Planned Behaviour which emphasises the role of the intention to predict actions [10], (2) Social Cognitive Theory which also relates to the theory of planned behaviour but places a greater emphasis on the self-efficacy [11], (3) Control Theory which requires goal(s) as a reference value to assess the current rate of the behaviour [12], (4) Transtheoretical Model which suggests that an individual can be mapped to one of the five milestones: pre-contemplation, contemplation, preparation, action, and maintenance [13], (5) Goal Setting Theory which suggests that goals setting can positively impact the performance [14], and (6) Health Belief Model which requires feeling vulnerable to a health threat, in order to perform protective measures [15].

Online peer groups are a type of social software that utilises certain mechanisms, such as social pressure through surveillance [2], to change negative behaviours or to reinforce positive ones [8, 16]. Online interactions differ from face-to-face (AKA FTF) setting as they are performed in a less restrictive environment leading to more self-discloser [17]. Traditional online peer groups are used as forums to host treatment practice, such as counselling, which could be helpful for providing care and assisting positive behaviour in remote settings. Despite the new facilities online peer groups can provide, e.g. real-time and intelligent interventions enhanced by gamified and persuasive experience, designing them as typical social networks could lead to adverse side-effects [18]. This includes the spread of negative emotions, misleading peer comparisons, and spreading and justifying negative behaviours.

2 Methodology

The performed studies adopted qualitative methods to understand peer groups including the session environment, interaction styles occurring between groups' members and how those interactions are governed. The first study was on FTF peer groups for treating substance and behavioural addiction, followed by an interview with an addiction counsellor. This study was complemented by a document analysis method mainly for the forms and diaries used in the daily practice. These three methods were applied in iterative style, i.e. after each observation session and its analysis, an interview was conducted. A referral to the documents and diaries used by the practitioners was also used when needed, before or after the observation sessions and the interviews to support the preparation and the analysis, respectively. The second study concerned the analysis of online peer groups designed for treating problematic gambling to compare the practices in both the physical space and the cyberspace.

The data collected were textually analysed using qualitative content analysis technique, i.e. the priori coding technique. The contextual dimension, which focuses on the *"structural descriptions to various properties of the social, political or cultural context"* [19], was also considered in the analysis. Analysing the data textually and contextually is also known as discourse analysis [19]. The goal was to understand the main processes and activities of online peer groups as an approach to overcome addictive behaviours and the motivation of each process and what considerations to be taken into account.

More information about the research settings and full analysis of the data collected can be found in [20].

2.1 First Study: Traditional Rehab Centre

A 4-months observational study at an addiction treatment centre was performed to better understand the different stages of treatment. In the rehab centre, therapeutic sessions had a minimum of 7 participants and a maximum of 15, mixed genders, aged between 19 and 56 years old. Some of the clients were experiencing parallel addiction, such as problem gambling and alcohol abuse. Participants in the peer groups were selected so that different levels of addiction are included in the same group, i.e. some were at the prescribed medical detoxification stage arranged with the GP to treat withdrawal symptoms, while others were in the advanced stage of the treatment. The stages of treatment, e.g. Transition, Stabilisation were based on the model proposed in [21, 22]. All group therapy sessions were facilitated by a qualified therapist, with over 13 years of experience in this field. The therapist's role is to listen and when appropriate confront clients on the issues and problems they raise, in a process known as reflective listening. The observation study included 14 sessions for two groups, where each session lasted for an average of two hours.

The treatment of the first group was based on Marlatt and Gordon's model [23] for relapse prevention. The model explains the relapse process, which can occur as a result of the immediate determinants (e.g. high-risk situations and outcome expectancies) and covert antecedents (e.g. stress and urges). The treatment of the second group, the therapist utilised The GORSKI-CENAPS Clinical Model [24], particularly the Relapse Prevention Therapy (RPT) [25]. The observation study results were refined based on the interviews with the rehab centre specialists. The aim was to articulate common practices, especially focusing on the group activities, communications, and individuals' attitudes of clients. A set of documents were also analysed as a complementary approach for a holistic view. These documents comprise the initial warning signs list, warning sings analysis, and warning sign management and planning.

2.2   Second Study: Online Peer Groups

Another observational study was performed on an online peer group facilitated by an expert therapist to deal with problematic gambling behaviour. The aim of this study was to explore the practices in handling addiction in the online space. Gambling addiction is a behavioural addiction as well which part of the generic theme of digital addiction. Rather than the group evolvement over time, this study was focused on the general practices and communication styles and facilities, both those done by the therapist and those which can be facilitated through the online platform. The study was conducted over the period of two-months to enable capturing practices. The study was conducted in an online forum for a gambling addiction treatment charity that provides emotional support and practical advice on gambling to people affected by problem gambling throughout the world. The therapy provides text-based live support forum and consultations in addition to the wide verity of online support groups. These support groups run at various times of the day and facilitated by trained members of the therapy. The users participate online, and their identity is kept anonymous. The study followed non-participant observation to avoid any potential effect on the users' interactions and to avoid disrupting group work.

3   Results

This analysis concerned the various design aspects of peer support groups as a persuasive social network to change addictive behaviours. For this paper, we will present part of the findings focusing on: *tasks, roles, interaction styles, group evolution and stages* and *governance*.

3.1   Frist Study Results – Traditional Peer Groups

Group Development and Interaction
Tuckman's model [26] of group development was the approach adopted in the rehab centre. Accordingly, and to help new clients reaching performing stage in a shorter period, they were introduced to the groups already at that stage. While this strategy

seems to require a high level of moderation, it helps to maintain established norms where new clients can start "performing" after a couple of days.

Interactions that indicate any form social hierarchy were deliberately avoided, i.e. status and power, within the group peers. The social hierarchy may emerge when a group includes new and senior peers. Senior peers refer to those who spent a longer period in the group. The social hierarchy may, also, naturally emerge from interactions such as in the case of peers with dominant character. Such social properties should not provide peers with any privileged position or extra influence. Indeed, senior peers are expected to hold more responsibility as they are considered role models. For example, as the counsellor commented: "*sleeping during the session* [for a senior member] *will not be tolerated like someone who just started the treatment*". Also, commented that "*they* [those who have been in treatment for six to eight weeks] *would be more challenged compared to someone who is just coming to the door*".

Figure 1 provides an overall picture of group therapy in terms of the group development and the change in the interaction scope over time. Our model highlights four main stages of the rehabilitation path: (1) The pre-contemplation stage: users are in the active addiction with the lack of perceived need or intention to change, (2) Stabilisation stage: users are supported to "*regaining the biopsychosocial balance required to maintain abstinence*" [21, 22], and obtaining healthy coping skills to manage thoughts and feelings, (3) Active rehab: users are supported to understand and recognised addiction symptoms, promote and build a balanced lifestyle, learning management strategies and how to create a plan and maintain it, and (4) Aftercare: users are provided with additional support to build self-esteem and stay motivated while facing real life challenges. It involves follow-up meetings to prevent relapse.

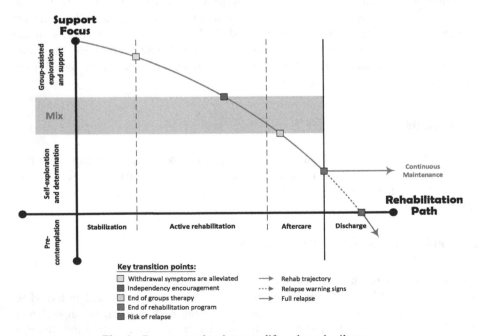

Fig. 1. Peer group development lifecycle and milestones

During this lifecycle, users pass four transition points as shown in Fig. 1. Also, the focus of the treatment changes as users proceed through these points. Clients remain engaged in group facilitated activities once they join the group and continue till the aftercare stage by taking a couple of follow-up group sessions. However, users' participation in group work is expected to decrease over time. So, they can focus on the self as they proceed to the discharge stage. In the active rehab stage, after passing more than half of the treatment programme, the journey enters the mixed phase. In this phase, users are actively engaged in group work and are also offered opportunities to do a variety of self-care and self-assessment tasks which increases over time.

Figure 1 is meant to provide designers of online peer group platforms with a high-level guide to how the system should operate and what features and functionalities need to consider for different stages. For example, general purpose social networks, Facebook, for example, are designed to encourage an increased participation and networking activities while online peer groups as a domain-specific social network shall be designed to deliberately reduce social activities over time and to start encouraging more self-focused activities.

Tasks Considerations

Three dimensions characterize the tasks performed by clients in the rehab centre. The first concerns the immediate motivators of the assigned task or activity, e.g. ice breaking, hope installation, and norms maintenance. The second concerns the interaction style or mode of delivery that is also should be planned to mediate planned purposes, e.g. discussion, confrontation, competition, and collaboration. The third concerns the functional activities that support achieving the planned purpose(s), i.e. the method of delivery, e.g. problem solving, diaries, and groups versus individuals' competition.

Over the period of the observation study, it was also observed that starting the sessions with *check-in* activity is a good practice where each client is given a chance to mainly describe their current emotional state. The reason is *"to ensure that clients focus on where they currently are and what they intend to do* [when addressing negative emotions]". Clients shall be aware that *"addiction, in a way, is running out from painful emotions"*. By performing this activity, clients are taught to recognise their actual emotional state and given a chance to voice it. Throughout the observation study, addicts seemed, normally, willing to talk about what makes them happy but hide and avoid talking about their negative emotions, e.g. sadness, shyness, being upset and worried because there seem to be difficulties in expressing that fully. Being able to express that is a way of coping. As such, regular practising of this simple activity will address this side of addicts' ability. While some purposes are decided based on the group or individual needs, some tasks such as "check-in" are compulsory.

The peer groups in the rehab centre were based on the mainstream 12 steps programme of Alcoholic Anonymous (AA) and the group's interactions revolved around those 12 principles. A special focus in the observation study concerned step 4 of the Gorski's model [25] which was applied to the group at the rehab centre. In this step, clients are required to write a list of their personal warning signs that could lead to a relapse. This can be mapped to the step 12 of the AA which reads: "Continue to take personal inventory and when we were wrong promptly admitted it". Both the 12th step programme of the AA and step 4 of Gorski's model are mainly focussed on relapse prevention. In the rehab centre, the last 30 days of the treatment were focused on step 4 of Gorski's mode. After that, clients are gradually moved to the aftercare treatment by attending additional sessions in the aftercare groups. The clients of these groups were fairly known to each other and shared membership in similar groups in the past which was an important aspect to maintain group cohesion in the aftercare sessions.

Steps 11th and 12th of the AA are focused on spiritual practices that can be performed outside the rehab centre. What is mentioned above suggests the need to consider the steps from 1 to 10 when designing the tasks of peer groups activities as well as paying attention to the sequential order of these steps. This will ensure a logical evolution of group envelopment. For example, asking clients in the early stages of the treatment to write personal inventory would not yield any improvement as clients are still in their biased perception. Another example concerns the step 1 of the Alcoholic Anonymous which read: "we admitted we were powerless over alcohol - that our lives had become unmanageable". Each client performs this step individually with the counsellor through writing examples of bad personal behaviours. This was one of the crucial preconditions to be admitted into the treatment programme. This suggests that the 12th steps of the AA are stage-based with admittance and help-seeking being a key requirement. Online peer group design should support a managed dialogue and evolve its allowed set of interactions as time passes and as progress is made.

Roles considerations
There are different types of roles that can exist within small groups for behavioural change. Bates [27] defined the term *role* as a part of social status within a social structure. A social structure consists of distinguished behavioural expectations, i.e. norms. Here, the researcher refers to the roles that define the self [28] and are associated with a set of expectations, such as acted roles, e.g. group 'facilitator'. However, Callero [28] pointed out some roles are not formal and hard to be fully defined with regard to expectations only, such as the roles that can evoke complex feelings and can be unconsciously played. Some roles are subject to behaviour impulses and arise during the interaction, such as most of the roles addicts may play, e.g. 'relapsed'.

Hare [29] proposed a set of guidelines to classify roles within small groups. These guidelines suggest that roles should be either "functional", "communication-based", "emotional" or "dramaturgical". For the case of online peer groups, these categories for changing addictive behaviours, e.g. introducing gatekeeper and facilitator as functional roles. Furthermore, this paper introduces *stage-related roles* as a new family of roles related to the stages of treatment, e.g. senior and relapsed. This list of roles, which were derived from our study shall guide in the design of online peer groups. Table 1 summarizes the list of roles in their four categories.

Table 1. Social roles classified into four classes.

Functional Roles: they refer to roles involving status, control and access to recourses. Each member in the group can play one role only, except the role *"peer"* who can be temporally assigned as a *"leader"*

Gatekeeper	A person who has the authority and control over particular resources
Facilitator	An assigned person who is expected to lead, guide and provide knowledge
Co-facilitator	An assigned person who is expected to help and support the facilitator
Peer	A person who shares similar behavioural issues and experience
Observer	A person who is permitted to join temporarily for observational learning
Leader	A temporary role played by all senior clients

Stage-Related Roles: they refer to roles associated with stage of treatment. Each member in the group can play one role only, except the role "new peer" who can also be "in-Detox" as well

Recovered	A peer who can be described as recovered based on the current behaviours
Senior	A peer who has spent longer time in the treatment and adopted healthy behaviours
New peer	A peer who is new to the group
in-Detox	A peer who is in the process of medical remodelling (i.e. removal of toxic substances)
Relapsed	A peer who experienced very recent relapse episode

Communication Roles: they refer to the roles related to interaction. Peers play multiple roles at once

Role model	A peer who is expected to be an example to be imitated and inspire others
Isolates	A peer who refuses/has not developed the ability to interact with others
Sociable	A peer who is willing to talk, engage and collaborate with others
Complying	A peer who adheres to rules and norms to achieve personal goals rather than to recover
Scapegoat	A peer who is deliberately excluded on the group basis
Rejected	A peer who is deliberately excluded on the individual basis
Withdrawing	A peer who tends to withdraw from activities or participate passively
Competing	A peer who tends to compete in different tasks for the sake of having power
Disrupting	A peer who disrupts group natural development
Dominant	A peer who attains high degree of influence in a group and wants to heave the control
Denying	A peer who is in extreme conscious denial to avoid consequences

Emotional Roles: they refer to roles representing emotional themes. Peer can play multiple roles at once

Attention seeker	A peer who wants to be the centre of attention in the group
Avoidant	A peer who has a false feeling of inadequacy and uses avoidance to cope
Victim	A peer who believes that he is always treated unfairly or taken advantage of
Crisis	A peer who is always expressing negative thoughts
Follower	A peer who admires a particular person or believes in system of ideas
Fixer	A peer who prevents other peers from expressing their emotions, e.g. "do not worry!"
Helper	A peer who supports other peers and encourage a positive behaviour

3.2   Second Study Results – Online Peer Groups

The second study revealed two additional facets, which will require both management and design consideration when facilitating peer support groups by online platforms.

Online Support
Online media can provide more access to help by reducing time, costs, and personal barriers, such as reluctance to seek help, stigmatisation and confidentiality concerns. Unlike the FTF peer groups, online groups are more agile and open where users are free to join as much as they like without progressive protocol that controls the process. This has its benefits and limitations. Examples of different aspects of help provided include emotional support and practical tips, and understating causes and consequences of the behaviour with the aid of qualified counsellor. Overall, the current online support is typically more concerned with *informing* users and helping them to decide goals and provide an environment for social enforcement. The support in its current status and with the lack of dedicated platforms would mainly work for post-residential support and outreach for clients. In our observed system, users were only able to use the system to interact with each other during the pre-arranged meetings.

Online support groups are typically not intended to substitute intensive psychological treatment; but more as complementary by helping users who are less motivated to start the therapy, and perhaps need support. It could be also helpful for after-care treatment to avoid relapse. The pillars of the online support within the observed platform can be outlined as being not judgemental, less confronting, comforting, practical information, requires the help-seeking attitude and focused on awareness building.

Interaction Environment
Similar to most available online health forums, the interface of the online peer group observed was relatively simple. They offer the main interface that shows actual live conversations and recommendations. They also offer a limited amount of pictorial representation of facial expressions. The interfaces are designed in a way that avoids providing users with immersive experience. The interface facilitates finding out who is online during the group meeting as well as who moderates the session. The group's interactions are typically facilitated using synchronous text-based communication. These systems are mainly designed as a group chatting service.

Similar to the traditional rehab centre, users are not allowed to create their own chat rooms, and no private communication features shall be offered. This is to avoid promoting bad behaviour and distraction. For example, the following features were not offered: *poking, who is viewing my profile* and *private chatting* including the so-called *whispering* feature which enables a user to communicate to another user without a publicly visible dialogue. The platform observed was designed to discourage in-person communication, and all interactions were mediated using the online system. In online peer groups, there seem to be communication norms followed. For example, the use of capital letter which were perceived as shouting and aggressive behaviour. While this depends on the context, it can create misunderstanding. These cyber norms seem important to ensure friendly environment but can be easily missed. Other types of communications include *actions* by adding words between brackets or stars, e.g. *thumbs up*. However, users were reminded that this is a support service rather than a medium for social networking. Hence, these must be used in moderation.

4 Designing Online Peer Groups as a Social Software

4.1 Online Peer Groups as a Social Software

In the light of the results obtained from the conducted observational studies and the findings from [8, 18], this research concluded eight essential building blocks for such platforms: conversation, sharing, reputation, identity, presence, collaboration, awareness and assessment. The first five blocks exist in the original honeycomb framework, while (collaboration, assessment and awareness) are the added ones. The blocks (groups and relationships) were excluded. Let's start discussing these exclusions first.

In online peer groups, the *group* block is an integral basic attribute, i.e. part and parcel of this social context. As such, the analyses of the persuasive mechanisms should always consider group dynamics and social psychology influences as a central perspective in these systems. Providing this type of users with the means to form communities can be very risky to the individuals and to the group performance.

Typically, forming *relationships* between users during intensive rehab treatment is discouraged, unless it is defined and moderated by therapists. Personal relationships could lead to deep intimacy, which may create a risky situation in the recovery process. The literature of computer-mediated communication already points out that visual anonymity and self-disclosure are likely reciprocated and could lead to high level of intimacy [30]. Combining that with the opportunities the system may provide to form a one-to-one relationship in online space can be very negative. In more liberal governance styles of peer groups [8], relationships might be allowed with precautionary measures, such as implementing auditing features to emphasise the element of authoritative surveillance.

According to the honeycomb framework, voting features such as "like", "re-tweet" and "share" aggregate counts to reflect the *reputation* of social entities. This is the implicit representation of the honeycomb framework blocks. Users are provided with "Flagging" tools to report offensive and harming digital materials. This is a kind of governance mechanism to support social responsibility in dealing with the massive collections of user-generated content. "Flagging" in this sense is not a technical feature only, but a socio-technical mechanism that enables users to express their concerns. Individuals values, social norms and community guidelines play a role in setting standards to assess content and actions according to these bodies of moral values [31].

In peer groups, assigning users to different groups is based on assessment procedures. This entails commencing with user assessment through personal interviewing for severe cases or screening questions for moderate ones. Then, assessment of the suitability for a particular user to a specific group. As such, this paper argues the need for introducing the *assessment* block to the framework.

Users in such systems are expected to collaborate with each other to progress in the treatment. In peer groups, collaboration is a critical element to help boosting group performance [6]. *Sharing*, which is another standalone block, can be seen as a functional trait within the collaboration block in online peer groups. Unlike groups in open forums, the avoidance of sharing, e.g. self-disclosing, is seen as a form of resistance.

The *identity* block as Kietzmann et al. [4] explains revolves around self-disclosure. However, in peer groups, this block should be less emphasised over time as a member approaches the aftercare stage and then to be completely removed, i.e. the member profile, after their discharge. In the case of relapsing after the discharge, a new identity would need to be created, since the relapsing is a process that could start with negative behaviours and then moving to many critical warning signs before a full relapse.

Peers' accomplishment, goals and the overall treatment progress would have a direct influence on the *self-awareness*. This can lead to greater adherence to the treatment goals and correlate to functional features of the online platform. Other features can support *social awareness*, e.g. a system showing accomplishments of others based on their competence in certain tasks that may create an opportunity for collaboration.

The social *presence* which can include encouraging self-disclosure and communication are important aspects of the peer group environments. "*Personal isolation is a strong aspect of addiction*" as a therapist highlighted in the treatment centre. These indicate the importance of considering the *conversation* block on the online platform.

4.2   Online Peer Groups as a Tunnelling-Based Persuasive Technique

Tunnelling is a persuasive technique that aims at "*using computing technology to guide users through a process or experience provides opportunities to persuade along the way*" [2]. Some characteristics of the persuasive techniques include: (1) Applying high

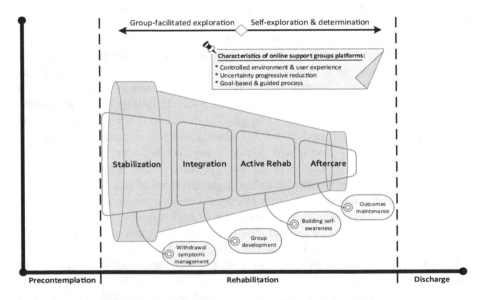

Fig. 2. Online peer groups as a tunnelling-based technology

control over the interaction environment where the persuasion expected to occur, (2) Reducing the level of uncertainties along the way of the tunnel, (3) Controlling and guiding the user experience through staged-based processes, and (4) People voluntarily enter the tunnel, i.e. people in online peer groups are characterised as help-seekers [2]. In the peer groups, people give up "*a certain level of self-determination*", exposed to a predetermined experience that increases the opportunities for persuasion. Tunnelling can be useful persuasion strategy.

Figure 2 proposes a reference model for how online peer groups should look like when viewing it through the lenses of tunnelling persuasive technology. The online peer group platforms can guide users through the various steps to analyse their behaviour, set up goals, and decide the plans to achieve these goals. It could also guide users through a series of questions designed to identify problematic triggers, personal traits and habits and make tailored suggestions to improve them.

5   Conclusion

Social software systems are expected to provide interactive tools to build and maintain social connections and facilitate mass interactions and collaboration among individuals. The results suggest that the design constructs of social software are not sufficient enough to influence behaviours for users who want to achieve specific goals and make positive change. Using such systems to mediate behavioural change may lead to negative concrescences as they were not built for this purpose. This paper calls for an exploration into the theoretical aspects of social software design to enable building systems that mediate persuasive messages to the targeted audience. This paper highlights the lack of frameworks for designing social software for specific purposes.

Acknowledgment. This work was partly sponsored by the EROGamb project, funded jointly by GambleAware and Bournemouth University. We also thank StreetScene Addiction Recovery and the Gambling Therapy for their support.

References

1. Marwick, A.E.: The public domain: social surveillance in everyday life. Surveill. Soc. **9**, 378–393 (2012)
2. Fogg, B.J.: Persuasive Technology: Using Computers to Change What We Think and Do (Interactive Technologies) (2002)
3. Leth Jespersen, J., Albrechtslund, A., Øhrstrøm, P., Hasle, P., Albretsen, J.: Surveillance, persuasion, and panopticon. In: de Kort, Y., IJsselsteijn, W., Midden, C., Eggen, B., Fogg, B.J. (eds.) PERSUASIVE 2007. LNCS, vol. 4744, pp. 109–120. Springer, Heidelberg (2007). https://doi.org/10.1007/978-3-540-77006-0_15
4. Kietzmann, J.H., Hermkens, K., McCarthy, I.P., Silvestre, B.S.: Social media? Get serious! Understanding the functional building blocks of social media. Bus. Horiz. **54**, 241–251 (2011)
5. Cetina, K.K.: Sociality with objects: social relations in postsocial knowledge societies. Theory Cult. Soc. **14**, 1–30 (1997)

6. Pereira, R., Baranauskas, M.: Social software building blocks: revisiting the honeycomb framework. In: 2010 International Conference on Information Society (i-Society). IEEE (2010)
7. Baranauskas, M.: Socially aware computing. Presented at the Proceedings of VI International Conference on Engineering and Computer Education (2009)
8. Alrobai, A., McAlaney, J., Phalp, K., Ali, R.: Online peer groups as a persuasive tool to combat digital addiction. In: Meschtscherjakov, A., De Ruyter, B., Fuchsberger, V., Murer, M., Tscheligi, M. (eds.) PERSUASIVE 2016. LNCS, vol. 9638, pp. 288–300. Springer, Cham (2016). https://doi.org/10.1007/978-3-319-31510-2_25
9. Webb, T.L., Sniehotta, F.F., Michie, S.: Using theories of behaviour change to inform interventions for addictive behaviours. Addiction **105**, 1879–1892 (2010)
10. Ajzen, I.: The theory of planned behavior. Organ. Behav. Hum. Decis. Process. **50**, 179–211 (1991)
11. Bandura, A.: Social Foundation of Thought and Action: A Social-Cognitive View. Prentice-Hall, Englewood Cliffs (1986)
12. Carver, C.S., Scheier, M.F.: Control theory: a useful conceptual framework for personality–social, clinical, and health psychology. Psychol. Bull. **92**, 111–135 (1982)
13. Prochaska, J.O.: Transtheoretical model of behavior change. In: Gellman, M.D., Turner, J.R. (eds.) Encyclopedia of Behavioral Medicine, pp. 1997–2000. Springer, New York, New York, NY (2013). https://doi.org/10.1007/978-1-4419-1005-9_70
14. Strecher, V.J., Seijts, G.H., Kok, G.J., Latham, G.P., Glasgow, R., DeVellis, B., Meertens, R.M., Bulger, D.W.: Goal setting as a strategy for health behavior change. Health Educ. Behav. **22**, 190–200 (1995)
15. Janz, N.K., Becker, M.H.: The health belief model: a decade later. Health Educ. Q. **11**, 1–47 (1984)
16. Davidson, L., Chinman, M., Kloos, B., Weingarten, R., Stayner, D., Tebes, J.K.: Peer support among individuals with severe mental illness: a review of the evidence. Clin. Psychol. Sci. Pract. **6**, 165–187 (2006)
17. Al-Deen, H., Hendricks, J.A.: Social Media: Usage and Impact (2011)
18. Alrobai, A., McAlaney, J., Phalp, K., Ali, R.: Exploring the risk factors of interactive e-health interventions for digital addiction. Int. J. Sociotechnol. Knowl. Dev. **8**, 1–15 (2016)
19. Lupton, D.: Discourse analysis: a new methodology for understanding the ideologies of health and illness. Aust. J. Public Health **16**, 145–150 (1992)
20. Alrobai, A.: Engineering Social Networking to Combat Digital Addiction: The Case of Online Peer Groups (2018)
21. Gorski, T.: Passages Through Recovery. Hazelden Publishing, Center City (2009)
22. Gorski, T.: Recovery From Addiction: Gorski's Operational Definition. https://terrygorski.com/2013/10/15/recovery-from-addiction-gorskis-operational-definition/
23. Marlatt, G.A., Gordon, J.R.: Determinants of relapse: implications for the maintenance of behavior change (1978)
24. Gorski, T.: The GORSKI-CENAPS Clinical Model. http://www.tgorski.com/clin_mod/clin_mod.htm
25. Gorski, T.T.: Relapse prevention planning: a new recovery tool. In: Alcohol Health and Research World-National Institute on Alcohol Abuse and Alcoholism (1986)
26. Tuckman, B.W., Jensen, M.A.C.: Stages of small-group development revisited. Group Organ. Manag. **2**, 419–427 (1977)
27. Bates, F.L.: Position, role, and status: a reformulation of concepts. Soc. Forces **34**, 313–321 (1956)
28. Callero, P.L.: From role-playing to role-using: understanding role as resource. Soc. Psychol. Q. **57**, 228–243 (1994)

29. Hare, A.P.: Types of roles in small groups: a bit of history and a current perspective. Small Group Res. **25**, 433–448 (1994)
30. Joinson, A.N.: Self-disclosure in computer-mediated communication: the role of self-awareness and visual anonymity. Eur. J. Soc. Psychol. **31**, 177–192 (2001)
31. Crawford, K., Gillespie, T.: What is a flag for? Social media reporting tools and the vocabulary of complaint. New Media Soc. **18**, 410–428 (2016)

Nudging and Just-In-Time-Interventions

A Decision-Making Perspective on Coaching Behavior Change: A Field Experiment on Promoting Exercise at Work

Chao Zhang[✉], Armand P. Starczewski, Daniël Lakens,
and Wijnand A. IJsselsteijn

Eindhoven University of Technology, 5612 AZ Eindhoven, The Netherlands
c.zhang.5@tue.nl

Abstract. We discuss a decision-making perspective on coaching behavior change and report a field experiment following the perspective in which we promoted physical exercises at work using an e-coaching app. More specifically, we investigated what are the important attributes that influence the attractiveness of exercise options, and whether showing an extreme option would nudge users to do more exercises (a.k.a. compromise effect). Seventy participants were coached by the app *BeActive!* for 10 days to consider taking breaks at work twice a day to do simple exercises. Through choice modeling, it was found that people cared more about whether the exercise options would reduce their productivity at work and whether doing the exercises were socially embarrassing, than the health benefits of the exercise options. The results did not reveal the compromise effect, but rather an effect in the opposite direction, supporting an alternative model that people make decisions hierarchically. Potentials and challenges of taking the decision-making perspective in behavior change research are discussed based on what we learned from the experiment.

Keywords: Choice architecture · Compromise effect · Physical activity
E-coaching · Option generation

1 Introduction

Healthy lifestyle is highly promoted in today's society and is also well-accepted by individual members in our society. Yet, in terms of realization, many people do not live up to the standard of a healthy lifestyle. For example, according to World Health Organization, 23% of adults and 81% of school-going adolescents are not physically active enough [1]. To explain the puzzling gap between what people want and what they actually do, traditional theories of behavior change mostly focus on the desired behavior per se. In Fogg's behavior model [2], for example, exercise behavior is jointly determined by motivation towards exercise, ability to exercise, and triggers of exercise behavior. However, taking a different perspective, it is important to realize that desirable healthy behaviors are not in a vacuum, but always complete with other behaviors. In other words, people almost always make decisions in daily life with the presence of competing behavioral options that satisfy different personal goals. For example, when you consider taking a break for a walk on a normal working day, you

© Springer International Publishing AG, part of Springer Nature 2018
J. Ham et al. (Eds.): PERSUASIVE 2018, LNCS 10809, pp. 87–98, 2018.
https://doi.org/10.1007/978-3-319-78978-1_7

are choosing between two options – taking a walk or continuing working. Sometimes, even when taking a walk is both attractive and actionable, the option of continuing working on your tasks may still be preferred, if being productive at work is a more important goal to you. Following this reasoning, we consider decision-making as a natural but overlooked perspective in the domain of persuasive technology and behavior change research. In this paper, we report a field experiment of promoting exercise at work, with the goal to validate a choice modeling paradigm in daily environments. More specifically, we use the choice modeling method to determine attractive coaching options and to test a subtle form of persuasion by manipulating choice architecture.

1.1 E-Coaching and Option Generation

E-coaching systems in the health domain can be defined as a type of persuasive technology that aims at promoting sustainable positive behavior change [3], rather than achieving single-time persuasion success (e.g., purchasing of a product on an e-commerce website). From a decision-making perspective, Kamphorst and Kalis have conceptualized e-coaching systems as technologies that interfere with users' natural processes of *option generation* [4]. In natural daily environments, before any decisions can be made, behavioral options have to be generated from a person's long-term memory. In the health domain, option generation is often the bottleneck of behavior change, because a person may simply not be aware of potential healthy behavioral options in contexts where default behaviors are in dominance. For example, in an afternoon on a working day, keep working may be a very strong default, and you may never consider to take breaks to exercise. In this case, e-coaching systems are good at disrupting the default behavior and to generate relevant behavioral options for users to consider.

However, when the suggested options are considered, they still need to compete with default options generated by the users themselves before they can achieve positive effects. Thus, for system designers, it is important to ensure that the recommended options are sensible and would be valued by the users. In a framework proposed by Kamphorst and Kalis [4], the best options are those that are unknown to the users, but would be endorsed by the users when they are known. For example, a user may have never considered to take a walk after lunch in the past (high novelty), but a suggestion of doing so can be found to be attractive (high endorsement). Although this principle is appealing, in practice, determining what options would be liked by a given user is not easy. In this paper, we will explore what factors determine the attractiveness of options in the context of promoting exercise at work.

1.2 The Case of Promoting Exercise at Work

We chose to study the case of promoting exercise at work based on both practical and theoretical considerations. From an application perspective, taking breaks at work and doing moderate exercise, such as walking and climbing stairs, are beneficial and relevant for everyone who sits most of the day to work or study. As doing at least 30-min moderate physical exercise is widely recommended for long-term health benefits [5], taking 2–3 active breaks per working day would fulfill this requirement. Moreover, taking active breaks may also offer immediate benefits, such as releasing body tensions caused by long period of sitting and refreshing one's mind for more productive work after the breaks. A final practical advantage is that exercise behavior at work can be repeated frequently, such as once or twice a day. Thus, it enables us to quickly collect enough ecologically valid data to evaluate theories and applications.

From a theoretical perspective, exercise at work is a relatively simple case where we can try out the approach of conceptualizing behavior change and its coaching as a decision-making problem. In the terminology of decision-making, people make choices from a set of options by evaluating a set of attributes that are relevant to their personal goals [6]. Thus, it is easier to apply the decision-making perspective if options and attributes for a given behavior can be clearly defined. In our case, the decisions can be described as choosing between the option of continuing working (non-exercise option) and one or more exercise options. For attributes, the case is a bit more complex than the typical cases in decision-making research, such as choosing between two cameras. In the latter case, because options are homogeneous (all cameras), concrete attributes can be easily defined, such as image quality and price. In our case, the non-exercise option creates heterogeneity because it is a very different behavior from other exercise behaviors. Thus, when the non-exercise option is considered, people may focus on more abstract attributes that are defined as attainments of personal goals, such as being productive at work and being physically active. In contrast, when two or more exercise options are compared, concrete attributes are likely to be considered, such as time cost and required skills. We include both abstract and concrete attributes in the experiment.

When options and attributes are defined, according to a class of utility-based models [6], a person would combine individual attributes to evaluate the total utilities of all options, and to choose the option with the highest utility. In calculating total utilities, some attributes may be considered to be more important than others, and the weights given to different attributes may also differ greatly between people. In applied research, it is very useful to enumerate all relevant attributes and to determine their weights in decisions. Instead of directly asking users what attributes are important, the decision-making perspective allows one to derive decision weights more objectively by modeling actual choices with measured attributes [7]. The methodology is similar to conjoint analysis frequently used in marketing research [8], but attributes in our case are self-reported rather than manipulated.

1.3   Choice Architecture and Compromise Effect

By modeling exercise behavior at work as a decision-making process and its e-coaching as interventions on option generation, a new persuasive technique becomes possible through the manipulation of choice architecture. In decision-making research, choice architecture refers to the structure of choice-sets and the way that are presented to the decision-makers [9]. It is now well-established that people's decisions do not always comply with classical utility theories, but can be influenced through the manipulations of what constitutes the option-attribute matrices in choice-sets [10]. In other words, a person's preference towards a certain option can be affected by the simultaneous presence of other options, often known as context effects [10]. We will focus on one famous context effect called *compromise effect* in this paper. Compromise effect describes what happens when a new choice option is included in a choice-set, which makes one of the two original options appear to be a compromise [11]. As an example, one can consider the case of choosing a camera, assuming only two attributes are relevant to consumers, price and image quality. In making a purchase decision, there is often a trade-off between price and image quality, when one camera (A) is cheap ($400) but mediocre (8 megapixels) and another one (B) is excellent (20 megapixels) but expansive ($900). When a third extremely high-quality and expansive camera (C; 30 megapixels and $2000) is added to the choice-set, compromise effect emerges as people start to prefer the "compromise" option (B) more, so that the choice share of B relative to A would increase. As a quite robust effect in marketing research [11, 12], adding an extreme option can be used as a technique to promote the sales of mid-range products. Theoretical explanations have also been proposed to explain compromise effect, including the theory of reason-based decision [12] and a dynamic computational model called Associative Accumulation Model [10].

It is yet unknown whether compromise effect would hold for the case of exercise decisions at work, and especially when choice data are collected in the field rather than in the lab. For example, if walking 30 min is provided as an option, would people find the option of walking 10 min to become more attractive? The answer to this question may be less straightforward when compared with the case of choosing cameras. Again, because of the inclusion of the option to continue working, two different models of how users would make decisions can be proposed. The first model assumes that people decide among three options (two exercise and one non-exercise) simultaneously, focusing mainly on the two high-level attributes concerning goal attainment (*direct model*). The direct model would predict the emergence of compromise effect. However, the second model would posit that people make decisions hierarchically by first choosing between an exercise category and a non-exercise category based on the high-level attributes, and when the exercise category is preferred a further choice is made between the two exercise options by evaluating some concrete attributes (*hierarchical model*). Given the hierarchical model, compromise effect becomes irrelevant as only two choice categories are compared first. Rather, as would be predicted by nested logit models in econometrics [7], the presence of a second exercise option (e.g., 30-min walk) would substitute more choices to the other exercise option (e.g., 10-min walk), which is nested in the same exercise category, than to the non-exercise option. Thus, testing compromise effect in our case provides a way to evaluate the truthlikeness of two competing decision models. Practically, if the effect can be reproduced, it can be applied to e-coaching systems as a subtle way of persuasion.

1.4   The Current Study

In the study, we use the choice modeling method to determine the relative importance of different attributes in people's exercise decisions at work, and to test whether compromise effect holds for such decisions. Although similar works have been done extensively in other domains (e.g., consumer choices) where the decision-making perspective is dominating, the research questions are novel to the health domain, especially in the context of e-coaching. It is also valuable to know whether the methodology as well as the compromise effect can be applied in field studies where people make decisions in natural environments, rather than in artificial choice experiments in the lab. We answer the two research questions in a field experiment where we use a simple mobile e-coaching system to promote exercise behavior at work.

2 Method

2.1 Participant and Study Design

Seventy-two participants were recruited to join a two-week intervention program with a goal of becoming more active at work[1]. There were 50 males and 21 females, with age ranged from 18 to 32 years old (*Mean* = 23.88, *SD* = 2.50). All the participants were students, except for two. Participants met the recruitment criteria that they spent most of their weekdays sitting to work or study and were motivated to be more active. The sample size was planned based on a power analysis using a simulation approach. Basically, we used the Associative Accumulation Model [10] to simulate how hypothetical participants would make decisions in the same situations as defined by the experiment design, and the hypothetical participants' perceptions of attributes of the behavioral options were bootstrapped based on data from a pilot study (to be discussed in some details later). Assuming that each participant makes 20 decisions, to produce a significant compromise effect at alpha level of 0.05 required 70 participants to achieve 80% power and 90 participants to achieve 90% power. As this was an exploratory study, we aimed for 80% power.

The 72 participants were randomly assigned to either a two-option condition or a three-option condition. In the two-option condition, the participants were present with a no-exercise option (continuing working) and one exercise option with moderate intensity (e.g., walking for 10 min). In the three-option condition, a third exercise option with relatively extreme intensity (e.g., 30-min walking) was added to the former two options. The order of the options were randomized. All participants were prompted by an e-coaching app 2 times a day to make decisions for 10 working days.

2.2 The E-Coaching System and Exercise Options

A simple mobile e-coaching app called *BeActive!* was developed specifically for this study. The mobile app was a Cordova app based on the Experience Sampler framework [13] and was compatible with both Android and iOS phones. The main function of the app was simply to prompt users with exercise decisions at the scheduled time and to provide exercise options (see Fig. 1). Because we focused on compromise effect, more advanced features of the system such as feedback and educational messages were not used.

In order to select appropriate exercise options to be used in the app, a pilot study was performed to explore possible options in an attribute space with the two high-level attributes (being active and being productive). From an online survey of

---

[1] All materials of the study are open at Open Science Framework: https://osf.io/aybuw/, including pilot and main experiment data, scripts of power analysis and modeling, and a pre-registration.

55 participants, results indicated that people could indeed evaluate exercise options on the two high-level attributes and it was possible to create three-option choice-set with compromise configuration by manipulating the intensity of exercises. The final exercise options used in the studies were from 4 types of exercise with two variants in terms of intensity: *walking* (10 min or 30 min), *climbing stairs to another floor and back* (2 times or 6 times), *squats* (10 times or 30 times), and *jumping jack* (10 times or 30 times). In the three-option condition, the two exercise options in a choice-set were always from the same exercise type. The relatively unfamiliar ones, squats and jumping jacks were explained visually to the participants during the set-up of the app (see Fig. 1).

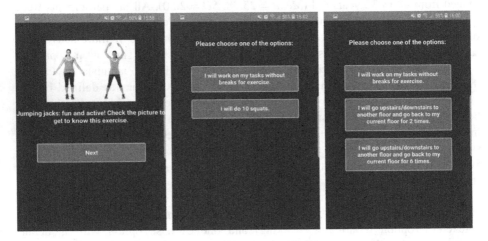

Fig. 1. Screenshots: instruction (left), two-option choice (middle), three-option choice (right)

2.3   Measurements

When participants were prompted to make exercise decisions, their choices were recorded by the app as they clicked on one of the option buttons on the screen. If they choose (one of) the exercise options, they were asked to report whether they indeed did the exercises or not within two hours of the initial notifications. Although a limitation was that it the actual exercise behaviors were not possible to access objectively, self-indicated choice data as used often in decision-making experiments were nonetheless informative, and even if potential self-presentation bias was inevitable the examination of compromise effect and attribute importance were not affected.

Participants were also asked to rate all the exercise options (including the non-exercise option) on two abstract attributes – their affordance to the goal of being physically active and the goal of being productive at work, as well as on a set of more concrete attributes. According to the results of the pilot study, the two least important concrete attributes - *physical effort* and *skill required*, were excluded in the main study. *Immediate benefit* was also excluded as it was relatively unimportant and correlated highly with *long-term health benefit*. The final set of concrete attributes used in the main study were *time cost*, *enjoyment*, *social embarrassment*, and *long-term health benefit*. For each options used, these attributes were rated on 10-point scales (1-not at all, 10-very much).

2.4   Procedure

Participants were invited to the lab in groups of 1–4 where they were introduced to the study procedure and were asked to install the mobile app *BeActive!*. The field study formally started on the next day and lasted for two weeks. On the 10 working days, participants received 2 prompts per day, one at 10 a.m. and one at 2 p.m., to make decisions regarding whether to take breaks for exercises or not. At the end of the study, they completed an online questionnaire about attributes of the suggested exercise options (including the non-exercise option). They received 10 euros for their participation.

2.5   Data Analysis

We started our analyses by simply describing and plotting data in terms of response rate, exercise frequency over the days, and popularities of different exercise options, in order to gain a general understanding about the effectiveness of the e-coaching app. Next, to answer the two main research questions, we built mixed-effect logit models [7], in which actual choice (choosing the moderate exercise option or the non-exercise option) was the outcome variable, while attribute perceptions and experimental condition were the predictors. The regression coefficient obtained for each attribute would indicate the decision weight given to the attribute and the direction of its effect. In addition, compromise effect was tested by examining the coefficient of condition as a predictor in the model. Since compromise sets could be defined by either using the objective exercise intensity (e.g., 10 versus 30 min), or by the subjective perceptions of attributes, similar models were built for the whole dataset and also for the subset where compromise sets were justified by participants' perceptions. All analyses were done in R version 3.3.3, and using the package *mlogit*, version 0.2–4.

3   Results

3.1   Descriptive Results

Participants responded to 65.3% of all the prompts sent from the app, resulting in 941 valid observations of choices. Among the choices made, 71.9% of the time, participants chose one of the exercise options over the option of continuing working. When all prompts were considered, participants were successfully persuaded by the app to take physically-active breaks about half of the time (47.7%). Over the two weeks, response rate gradually decreased, but when participants did respond to the prompts, decisions to do exercise or not remained stable, while exercising in the morning was slightly preferred over exercising in the afternoon ($B = 0.33$, $p = .03$; see Fig. 2). Among all the exercise options, moderate options were clearly more favorable than the more extreme ones (see Fig. 2). Walking was the most popular exercise category, followed by climbing stairs, jumping jack, and squat.

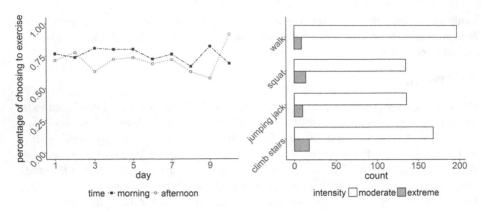

Fig. 2. Descriptive results: temporal trend of exercise choice (left); popularity of options (right)

3.2 Modeling Decisions and Testing Compromise Effect

Table 1 presents the choice modeling results for the full dataset (left) and for the 251 observations when the choice-sets were perceived by participants as compromise sets, based on the attributes of being active and being productive (right). In general, participants chose to do exercises more often than choosing to continue working, as indicated by the significant negative intercept ($B = -1.33$, $p < .001$; $B = -1.18$, $p < .05$), and this effect of favoring exercise options differed significantly among participants, as indicated by the significant random effect of intercept ($B = 1.02$, $p < .001$; $B = 0.56$, $p < .05$). With both methods, results revealed robust influences of the attributes of being productive and social embarrassment on actual choices. When an option tended to satisfy the goal of being productive, participants were more likely to choose the option ($B = 0.17$, $p < .001$; $B = 0.28$, $p < .001$). Moreover, when the execution of an option is socially embarrassing (e.g., doing jumping jack in front of an office-mate), participants were less likely to choose that option ($B = -0.09$, $p < .001$; $B = -0.10$, $p < .05$). When the full dataset was analyzed, long-term health benefit of options also had a small positive effect on actual choice ($B = 0.10$, $p < .05$), but the effect was not found for the subset. When the subset was analyzed, a considerable positive effect of the attribute of being active emerged. When an option better satisfied participants' goals of being physically active, they chose the option more often ($B = 0.24$, $p < .01$).

More critically, when the influences of all attributes were controlled, a significant positive coefficient for experiment condition (with the two-option condition as the reference level) would support the presence of a compromise effect. However, this was not the case using both approaches. When the full dataset was analyzed, there was a significant effect of condition in the opposite direction to the compromise effect ($B = 0.54$, $p < .01$) – when a third extreme exercise option was added to a choice-set, the choice-share of the moderate exercise option, relative to the non-exercise option, decreased slightly (from 74.3% to 68.0%). In other words, it seemed that the inclusion of the extreme exercise options competed more with the moderate exercise options rather than with the non-exercise option, thus taking more share from the former than the later. This pattern would be predicted by the hierarchical model of decision in which participants first decided on whether to exercise or not, and then chose which exercise option to execute. When the perceived compromise subset was analyzed, experiment condition had no effect on the relative share of moderate exercise options, supporting neither the compromise effect nor the prediction from the hierarchical model.

Table 1. Results of choice modeling

	Full dataset	Compromise subset
	Coefficient (SE)	Coefficient (SE)
Fixed-effect		
Intercept (non-exercise)	−1.33 (0.21)***	−1.18 (0.56)*
Being active	0.05 (0.13)	0.24 (0.08)**
Being productive	0.17 (0.03)***	0.28 (0.08)***
Time cost	−0.03 (0.04)	−0.06 (0.11)
Long-term health benefit	0.10 (0.05)*	−0.02 (0.10)
Enjoyment	−0.03 (0.03)	−0.04 (0.06)
Social embarrassment	−0.09 (0.03)***	−0.10 (0.05)*
Condition	0.54 (0.18)**	0.06 (0.39)
Random-effect		
Intercept (non-exercise)	1.02 (0.14)***	0.56 (0.27)*
McFadden R^2	0.094	0.079

Note: significance level (two-tail) is coded as *.05, **.01, ***.001.

4 Discussion

In a field experiment where we persuaded participants to do exercises at work using an e-coaching system, we investigated what influenced option attractiveness and whether compromise effect could be replicated and utilized in the context of promoting physical activity. By modeling choice with a mixed-effect logit model, we found that two attributes - being productive and social embarrassment, were most important for participants' decisions. Compromise effect was not replicated in the experiment, but rather the results supported a hierarchical decision process in the current context.

4.1 Implications for Designing Attractive Exercise Options

In designing effective persuasive technology or e-coaching systems, it is crucial to understand what makes attractive choice options for specific behavior and context [4]. In this study, we provide an example of determining option attractiveness through choice modeling. Our results suggest that when people are considering whether to accept the advice of taking active breaks at work from an e-coaching system, they care mostly about whether the action would cost their productivity at their main tasks (e.g., doing assignments) and whether the action is socially embarrassing. Health-related attributes, such as being active and long-term health benefit, seem to have much smaller influences on decisions. Time cost and hedonic aspects of the exercise options, according to our model, are not considered in actual decisions. When designing exercise options, designers can use our results to evaluate the potential attractiveness of new options. This can be done by calibrating new options on the two most important attributes (being productive and social embarrassment), and for example, asking people to judge their attribute scores and comparing the scores with the known options (e.g., 10-mins' walk scored 6.9 on being productive and 3.5 on social embarrassment). More generally, the results indicate that at least in the case of exercising at work, rather than trying to persuade people about the health benefits of taking active breaks, it is more important to trigger some actions at the time when exercising would not hinder their productivity [14], and when the actions are not considered socially awkward. For example, although jumping jack is a fun and easy-to-do exercise, an e-coaching app should recommend it only when it can detect that a user is alone in the office.

It is important to note that the estimated importance of attributes based on the models differed a lot from the self-reported importance of attributes. Although being productive and social embarrassment were rightly judged as highly important, and enjoyment was rightly judged as less important by participants, the rated high importance of health benefit and time cost did not match the results obtained from the model. Thus, we consider the choice modeling method as an alternative and perhaps superior to self-report method since it is based on actual choice and is not contaminated by social desirability. Although choice modeling method has been used extensively in lab experiments in marketing research [8], we might be the first to modeling attribute importance using real choice data in people's daily environments, and in the context of promoting health.

4.2   Implications for Decision-Making Process and Persuasive Techniques

We designed the study with the hope that compromise effect as often found in decision-making research can be replicated in the current context and can be used as a persuasive technique to promote more active lifestyle. If adding one extreme option can nudge people to perceive the moderate exercise option to be more attractive for the sake of balancing conflicting goals (being active and productive at the same time), it would be useful to implement it in the design of e-coaching systems. However, we were aware of the difference between our case and the classical case of compromise effect – the non-exercise option is of a different category than the exercise options, and that people may make decision in a hierarchical fashion. Although compromise effect is not replicated, our result is informative in a way that it helps to shed light on the cognitive mechanism underlying decision processes when people are faced with one or more options from e-coaching systems. Compared with our even prior beliefs about the two possible mechanisms – a direct model versus a hierarchical model, the latter should be considered to have a much higher truthlikeness after obtaining the data. Our result is consistent with a fundamental property of the nested logit model in econometrics that choice options nested in the same category compete more with each other than with options from a different category [7] (e.g., bus competes more with metro than car). It is interesting to note that the opposite effect was not found when only analyzing the compromise subset. The null effect might be simply due to the much smaller sample size for the subset, but it might indicate that both hierarchical decision process and compromise effect played a role to offset each other when choice-sets were actually perceived to be compromise sets.

4.3   Reflections on the Decision-Making Perspective

Connecting the domain of behavior change and persuasive technology with decision-making is a natural and potential rewarding journey, but not without challenges. Besides the contribution of revealing context-specific attribute importance, we are able to validate a decision-making paradigm to study behavior change and e-coaching in the field. It is an important first step as it is a non-trivial task to transform a paradigm from exclusive lab experiments where options, attributes, and contexts can all be controlled by researchers, to messy and unpredictable daily contexts. Although compromise effect was not reproduced, we have demonstrated that quality data can be collected using the paradigm, which can be used to explore other persuasion techniques by manipulating choice architecture [9].

Throughout this project, one central challenge is that unlike the domains where attributes of options can be objectively defined, in the health domain most attributes are only meaningful as subjective perceptions. This challenge raises a difficult question of how to truly create choice-sets that are supposed to produce compromise effect or other context effects. In the domain of consumer behavior, this can be easily done by manipulating, for example, the prices and image qualities of three cameras. In our case, the same three options may appear as a compromise set to some people, but not to others. It was why we used two data analysis strategies to test compromise effect, and yet it is hard to know which strategy was better. Until future research can provide definite answer to this issue, it is better to analyzing data in both ways whenever possible. A related challenge is that when studying health-related behaviors in real-life environments, such as in a field experiment, attributes of options as perceived can change greatly across contexts. In this study, for example, the attribute of being productive was judged by participants only once for each exercise option, but the real value of the attribute could fluctuate depending on what type of tasks a participant was doing at hand. Indeed, although we found some of the attributes had significant influences on decisions, the effects were small and based on the McFadden R^2, much of the total variance in choices was not explained. This does not have to mean that there are other important attributes that we omitted, but rather than the values of these attributes may change greatly from one context to another. Thus, for e-coaching systems to be truly effective, the capacity of knowing user context and context-specific attribute values is important and warrants more research [14, 15].

4.4   Conclusion

From a decision-making perspective, a pivotal task of lifestyle e-coaching is to alter people's choices between default unhealthy behavioral options and healthy options. In a field experiment to promote physical exercise at work, we have provided practical insights into the design of attractive options, and tested a theory-driven persuasive technique - compromise effect, for the first time in the field. We hope our work will stimulate more research in the direction to apply theories and methodologies from decision-making research to the field of behavior change and e-coaching.

References

1. World Health Organization: 10 facts on physical activity, pp. 99–110 (2016)
2. Fogg, B.J.: A behavior model for persuasive design. In: Proceedings of the 4th International Conference on Persuasive Technology. ACM, Claremont (2009)
3. IJsselsteijn, W., de Kort, Y., Midden, C., Eggen, B., van den Hoven, E.: Persuasive technology for human well-being: setting the scene. In: IJsselsteijn, W.A., de Kort, Y.A.W., Midden, C., Eggen, B., van den Hoven, E. (eds.) PERSUASIVE 2006. LNCS, vol. 3962, pp. 1–5. Springer, Heidelberg (2006). https://doi.org/10.1007/11755494_1
4. Kamphorst, B., Kalis, A.: Why option generation matters for the design of autonomous e-coaching systems. AI & Soc. 30(1), 77–88 (2015)
5. Clinkenbeard, D., Clinkenbeard, J., Faddoul, G., Kang, H., Mayes, S., Toygar, A., Chatterjee, S.: What's your 2%? A pilot study for encouraging physical activity using persuasive video and social media. In: Spagnolli, A., Chittaro, L., Gamberini, L. (eds.) PERSUASIVE 2014. LNCS, vol. 8462, pp. 43–55. Springer, Cham (2014). https://doi.org/10.1007/978-3-319-07127-5_5
6. Oppenheimer, D.M., Kelso, E.: Information processing as a paradigm for decision making. Annu. Rev. Psychol. 66, 277–294 (2015)
7. Train, K.E.: Discrete Choice Methods with Simulation. Cambridge University Press, Cambridge (2009)
8. Green, P.E., Srinivasan, V.: Conjoint analysis in marketing: new developments with implications for research and practice. J. Mark. 54, 3–19 (1990)
9. Johnson, E.J., Shu, S.B., Dellaert, B.G., Fox, C., Goldstein, D.G., Wansink, B.: Beyond nudges: tools of a choice architecture. Mark. Lett. 23(2), 487–504 (2012)
10. Bhatia, S.: Associations and the accumulation of preference. Psychol. Rev. 120(3), 522 (2013)
11. Simonson, I.: Choice based on reasons: the case of attraction and compromise effects. J. Consum. Res. 16(2), 158–174 (1989)
12. Shafir, E., Simonson, I., Tversky, A.: Reason-based choice. Cognition 49(1), 11–36 (1993)
13. Thai, S., Page-Gould, E.: ExperienceSampler: an open-source scaffold for building smartphone apps for experience sampling. Psychol. Methods (2017). Advanced online publication
14. Ham, J., van Schendel, J., Koldijk, S., Demerouti, E.: Finding Kairos: the influence of context-based timing on compliance with well-being triggers. In: Gamberini, L., Spagnolli, A., Jacucci, G., Blankertz, B., Freeman, J. (eds.) Symbiotic 2016. LNCS, vol. 9961, pp. 89–101. Springer, Cham (2017). https://doi.org/10.1007/978-3-319-57753-1_8
15. Intille, S.S.: Ubiquitous computing technology for just-in-time motivation of behavior change. Medinfo 107, 1434–1437 (2004)

Towards Finding Windows of Opportunity for Ubiquitous Healthy Eating Interventions

Nađa Terzimehić[✉], Christina Schneegass, and Heinrich Hussmann

Media Informatics Group, LMU Munich, Munich, Germany
{nadja.terzimehic,christina.schneegass,hussmann}@ifi.lmu.de

Abstract. Persuasion towards healthier eating decisions is a challenging field of research, depending on various internal and external factors. Recent advances in sensor-enriched mobile devices and wearables enable persuasive techniques to predict and influence people's food decisions. One such technique, just-in-time adaptive interventions (JITAIs), provide users with personalized and situation-related content and thus, exploit windows of high user receptiveness for persuasion. This work's aim is to shed light on context characteristics of such windows by analyzing 469 meal decisions as well as relating in-depth interviews on eating behaviour. We derive and describe four interesting windows in which JITAI's could be effective: (1) Lack of Alternatives, (2) Unawareness of Alternatives, (3) Evening Cravings, and (4) Social Pressure. On the basis of these situations, we postulate recommendations for timing and content of JITAIs for healthy eating. We plan to use the findings to implement and evaluate ubiquitous nutrition-supportive interventions in the future.

Keywords: Persuasive technologies · Just-in-time interventions
Context · mHealth · User-centered design

1 Introduction

Inadequate diets can increase the risks for diseases such as diabetes, some forms of cancer, and cardiovascular problems [11]. By using computationally powerful smartphones, an increasing number of smaller sensors, affordable consumer health wearables, and machine learning algorithms, advances in proactive persuasive systems in the area of nutrition become possible. In particular, such systems could go beyond recording and evaluating past nutritional behavior [3,6], and offer on-spot and in-time support towards healthier eating, that is, even before a food choice has been made. The premise is that such, technology-supported, Just-In-Time Adaptive Interventions (JITAIs) could proactively offer highly effective support in windows of high user receptiveness [19]. Within persuasive technology, such windows are known as *kairos* - "the brief, decisive moment which marks a turning-point in the life of human beings" [13]. Hence, in the food choice process,

© Springer International Publishing AG, part of Springer Nature 2018
J. Ham et al. (Eds.): PERSUASIVE 2018, LNCS 10809, pp. 99–112, 2018.
https://doi.org/10.1007/978-3-319-78978-1_8

the long term vision is that JITAIs could automatically sense user's internal and surrounding factors affecting their food choice and deduce opportune moments, *kairos*, to offer the most effective decision support.

Nutritional science already offers insights into the factors underlying (deliberate) food choices and their interplay [20]. Still, there is a surprising lack of *empirical evidence* regarding the presence of patterns in everyday food-choice situations, and how these patterns affect the healthiness of the food. For example, at what time or place do people eat? To what extent does this routine enable a healthy nutritional behavior? How do people react to other people cooking them meals they do not like? We could assume that all about-to-eat moments are *kairos*, but what about that birthday cake? If we had this knowledge, we would be able to inform JITAI designers regarding people's *kairos* for food choices. Hence, we offer insights to the answers of following questions:

1. Where and when in the real world are the windows of opportunity for a ubiquitous healthy eating intervention to intervene - and where and when not?
2. How do these windows of opportunity differ regarding their social, spatial, temporal, and environmental context?

To answer these questions, this work contributes the results of an exploratory study evaluating every meal of 14 participants over an 8-day period. We (1) collected 469 food choice moments regarding the participant's environmental and individual context, and (2) had participants reflect in-depth on the reasons and appropriateness of food choices. By using a contextual inquiry data analysis approach, we observe four distinct opportunity windows for healthier food choices and discuss the fit of various JITAI methods.

2   Background and Related Work

Fogg already highlighted the importance of identifying the right time for suggestions in persuasive technologies to increase the probability that a user performs a suggested action [8]. Intervening at the right moment is especially important in mobile persuasion due to the ubiquity and availability of mobile devices.

A persuasive strategy often used for persuading into healthy nutrition is self-monitoring of food intake [12]. Current apps such as FitBit[1] or MyFitnessPal[2] rely on this strategy as well. As such, the opportune moment is assumed to be *after* the user had a meal. Hence, the system targets behaviour change *passively* in a long term perspective by reviewing previous behaviour. However, once the food is served, more than 9 out of 10 people will eat the whole content of the plate [22]. In a recent survey [16], users expressed the desire for nutritional interventions to take place *before* a meal has been taken. Moreover, a previous

---

[1] https://www.fitbit.com/de/app.
[2] https://www.myfitnesspal.com/.

study on *kairos* for smoking interventions has shown the opportune moment to be way before 'bad' behavior occurs [17].

Besides timing, JITAIs also focus on various other internal and external contextual factors, likewise activity level, sleep, heart rate, location, routines etc. As result, JITAIs are to be triggered in moments of user's high receptiveness and intervention's high effectiveness [19]. As recent studies demonstrated, both external [10] and internal [6] contextual information is an important identifier of opportune moments to maximize persuasive technologies' effectiveness. For example, when triggered in an appropriate location, persuasive technologies are more successful [2]. Yet, the context of people's meals and influencing factors on food choice are so multifaceted [20], that they change between and within individuals, with different weekdays, seasons, and events. Thus exists a lack of knowledge on individual differences regarding receptiveness and reactions on eating interventions, which makes it difficult to determine *kairos*.

We intend to contribute to closing this gap by exploring *kairos* for eating interventions in *breadth*. We differentiate from previous work by taking one step back and scanning people's eating routine to identify a gallery of potential *kairos* moments, rather than examining or predicting solely one use case. Moreover, we discuss how the deduced *kairos* differentiate regarding contextual attributes. Finally, we explore the fit of various intervention manners for the found *kairos*. With the data provided in this paper, we aim to support persuasive designers in finding the appropriate time and manner for persuasive technology to provide decision support for every day meal choices.

3   Methodology

3.1   Procedure

The study consisted of two main parts, a self-reporting field study and a post-study interview in order to reflect on the food choices made within the period of the field study. General demographics data was collected throughout a short questionnaire. Participants were rewarded with either a 15€Amazon voucher or student participation points.

Food Monitoring. To simplify the meal reporting process, we implemented a smartphone application (iOS & Android) similar to [7]. The participant could, by using the app, (1) take a new photo or upload an existing meal photo from the gallery; (2) supplement the photo with contextual information evolving the food choice and finally (3) send the photo along with the information about the context via email to the study designers. The collected contextual data is depicted in Table 1. To sufficiently cover all nuances of moods, we followed a classification of secondary emotions by [18], who divided these among the coordinate axes of intense-mild/pleasant-unpleasant and chose some of all quarters. All input fields were optional, but we encouraged participants to provide data as thoroughly as possible. Participants who had troubles with installing or using the app were given the option to send the meal pictures along the context data via WhatsApp messages. Three participants used this option.

Table 1. Overview of the collected contextual variables in the smartphone food journal app

Contextual variable	Examples of value
Description	Open text-field
Sort of meal	Breakfast, lunch, dinner, snack
Occasion	Regular meal, family dinner, business meeting etc.
Location	Home, work, restaurant etc.
Number of people present	0, 1–3, 4–6, 7+
Social surroundings	None, partner, friends etc.
Activity during meal	None, watching TV, phone-call etc.
Level of hunger	5-point likert scale
Mood before eating	Angry, sad, bored, tired, happy etc.
Additional information	Open text-field

Post-study Interview. Once the 8-day reporting period was over, we invited the participants to a post-study interview. Initially, we asked the participants about themselves, including questions about the lifestyle change they were going through. We then invited participants to pick up to five pictures of meals they perceive as healthy and up to five pictures of meals they perceive as unhealthy. We stressed several times during the interview that the food choices will not be judged but rather be explored with particular interest on their surrounding context. Following, we encouraged the participants to explain more profoundly the reasoning on why they chose these particular food pictures, going one by one in chronological order. We asked participants whether they would, in retrospect, change something about their choice. Finally, we asked if they could imagine a technology intervention that could have nudged the participant towards a healthier meal, i.e., to encourage a continuance towards making healthy decisions.

3.2 Participants

The study was conducted in Germany. We recruited students or young professional that were undergoing major lifestyle change(s) within the previous year, such as start of studies, new employment, or major exams. As research shows, such transition is a groundbreaking period for young adults, as they start facing the process of making own food choices [1]. As major lifestyle alterations are connected to changes in routine behavior, they likely provide influence on long-lasting behavior changes [15], hopefully in a positive way. Out of sixteen recruited participants, fourteen have sent at least one food picture (four male). We therefore consider only the remaining fourteen as our study participants. The age of participants ranged from 18–32 years, with a mean of 25.7 years (SD = 3.75). Eight participants were exclusively students. Recruiting was accomplished via university mailing lists and a university Facebook group which also includes alumni. To record people's natural eating behaviour, we excluded those who must follow a strict diet for both medical and well-being reasons (i.e. diabetes, heart diseases etc). However, participants with steady nutritional habits or preferences were allowed to participate (i.e. vegetarians, vegans, intolerances etc.).

3.3 Data Analysis

We collected all sent meal pictures and according data into one data source. In order to find recurring patterns within the conducted qualitative interviews, we followed the contextual inquiry method [4]. Each examiner first listened to the recorded interview in order to record key statements. For each food choice labeled by the participant as a healthy or a unhealthy meal (that is, up to ten meals), the examiner wrote down the statements participants have made concerning one of the following topics: (1) the reason(s) why that food choice was made, (2) the reason(s) participants would, or would not, in retrospection, change the chosen food choice, (3) the time ahead of which the food decision was made, and (4) the hypothetical, technological, intervention methods that could have convinced the participant to choose a healthier food choice instead of the selected unhealthy decision, that is, to continue making healthy decisions in similar situations. Each statement covering one single information was written on one sticky-note. The sticky-notes for healthy and unhealthy food choices were differently coloured in order to easily differentiate them in an affinity diagram, as in Fig. 1.

To assure a high consensus in the interpretations of both examiners, statements from two of the fourteen interviews were transcribed by both examiners. The interrater-reliability is calculated based on the following metric proposed by [5], since their experimental setup was similar to our approach:

$$coding\ agreements \div (coding\ agreements + coding\ disagreements)$$

According to this metric, we achieved a mean reliability of 88% (91,24% + 86,37%) for both interviews. In most cases where the two examiners did not agree, the doubt was whether to count a statement as containing one or two key pieces of information. Although the reliability is not perfect, we concluded that no data would be lost in the process in case only one examiner evaluated the qualitative interviews.

4 Results and Discussion

During the one week study we collected 469 food snaps from the fourteen participants. On average, users sent 33.5 snaps in total $(SD = 10.2)$ or 4.2 per day. This correlates nicely with the common perception of three main meals and one or two snacks per day. Since all participants assured that they took a photo of every meal they consumed, we assume the list of meals to be complete.

Fig. 1. The resulting affinity diagram of JITAI support methods

4.1 Tendencies for Healthy Eating Decisions

Within our data, tendencies can be seen towards factors and situations fostering healthy eating decisions. These include (1) the level of hunger right before consuming a meal, (2) the occasion for the eating event, and (3) the reason(s) for eating the particular food.

(1) Level of Hunger
For each meal, the participants were asked about their hunger level ranging from "not hungry at all" to "very hungry" on a 5-point Likert scale. The distribution, as displayed in Table 2, shows that the meals marked as healthy were much less likely to be consumed when (rather) not hungry in comparison to unhealthy meals. Without physiological hunger, the reason for eating lies in other factors, as for example social pressure or cravings.

Table 2. Level of hunger before a meal categorized by healthy, unhealthy, and all food choices.

Hunger	Healthy	Unhealthy	All
Not hungry at all	0	**3**	39
Rather not hungry	3	**10**	46
Neutral	20	23	134
Hungry	**28**	18	192
Very hungry	8	8	42

(2) Occasion of Meal
Within the food monitoring application, the participants had to characterize the occasion of the logged meal as either one or more of the following: (1) regular meal, (2) business meal, (3) meal with family/friends, (4) date, (5) ravenous appetite (craving), or (6) other. As the distribution of occasions displays in Table 3, participants more likely had a healthy meal if it was regularly scheduled,

i.e. for breakfast, lunch or dinner. Surprisingly, the number of unhealthy meals resulting from cravings seems oddly low, as one expects unhealthy meals to happen because of a ravenous appetite rather than regular meals. The follow-up interviews revealed, that the actual occasion of the meals was often indeed the need for a regular meal, but the choice of food was the result of a craving. For example, P3 was hungry and had a schnitzel for lunch. So he marked the schnitzel as a regular meal, although he chose the schnitzel out of a craving.

Table 3. Occasion of a meal categorized by healthy, unhealthy, and all food choices.

Occasion	Healthy	Unhealthy	All
Regular meal	**52**	30	237
Ravenous appetite (craving)	7	4	47
Meal with family/friends	3	**14**	61

(3) Reasons for Healthy Meals
Eight of the thirteen participants (P1, P2, P3, P7, P11, P12, P13 and P15) stated eating healthy because of **preparation** in advance (in 15 situations). The situations ranged from lunch, dinners and snacks, and were consumed at home, at work, or on a trip, at various times with various people. All but one were regular meals and 7 out of 15 meals happened when the participants were (very) hungry.

Another similar reason to choose a meal is because it was in stock at home. Therefore, all but one of the twelve healthy meals classified as **in stock** were also consumed at home. In eight cases the participants were relaxed, eating either alone, with a partner, or family. All but two meals were regular lunch or dinner (one breakfast & one snack).

Three participants (P2, P8, P13) stated **exercise** as the reason for their food choices. For example, P8 stated she adapts her breakfast in terms of fats and proteins on the days she exercises, preferring almond and banana milk. In opposite to P8, P3 stated to have routinized his breakfast, eating cereals with cream cheese, eggs, water, and coffee every day. Moreover, P4 and P6 classified their breakfast as **routine** meals at home or at work, all of them being very hungry at the time of the meal.

4.2   Tendencies for Unhealthy Eating Decisions

Contrary to the factors fostering healthy eating decisions, the following circumstances can contribute to an unhealthy eating decision.

(1) Meal of the day
When looking at the distribution of the meal categories (breakfast, lunch, dinner, snack), the "snack"-category covers interesting remarks. Only six snacks were

marked as a healthy food choice, opposed to 22 unhealthy ones. In ten of 22 unhealthy snacks, the consumption followed a desire for that particular food. From those ten, only two were no sugar cravings. Seven out of ten eating events occurred after 5 pm. In 19 snack cases, participants' hunger level was neutral or lower. Seven snacks were connected to a feeling of fatigue/sleepiness, three during late afternoons and the others in the evening.

(2) Reasons for unhealthy meals
Participants stated various explanations regarding reasons for their unhealthy food choices. One food choice could have been justified with more than one reason.

We called one heavily advertised reason **appetite & desire**, stated by eleven participants (P1, P2, P3, P4, P5, P6, P8, P9, P11, P12, P13, P15). In total, nineteen unhealthy food choices were the result of a craving. The food consumed ranged from chocolate, to pizza, cake, burger, gummibears or schnitzel. This aligns well with the nutritional body of research stating that the energy density of foods craved was more than twice as high as food consumed as regular meal [9]. In ten out of these 19 cases, the meals were classified as snacks and in eleven cases the level of hunger was described as "neutral". The situations in which these cravings occurred were very diverse regarding location, occasion, number of people present etc. In six meals, participants stated that the food happened to be there and available (at home). Time-wise, seven out of these nineteen meals based on desire happened before 5 pm, two before 1 pm.

Another reason for unhealthy food choices stated frequently (twelve times) by the participants was **social pressure**. In these situations the participants were accompanied by at least one and max three other people which were either partner, friend(s), or family members. Additionally, social pressure includes cases in which food was cooked for the participant and they felt uncomfortable to reject the food (three occurrences). Similar to the meals chosen by desire, only two of these meals were consumed before 3 pm. In eight cases the participants consumed the meal at home and in all but three situations they experienced only positive emotions like happiness and relaxation. Likewise, participants engaged in unhealthy meals out of time-saving/practical-to-prepare food motives. Six out of eight times, participants were alone, evenly during lunch and dinner.

We find worth mentioning that five unhealthy occurrences were consequences of a **shortage of healthy alternatives** in the participant's immediate surrounding. All of these occurred while the participant was away from home. Two incidents happened as result of hunger prevention, that is, participants claimed that they were not hungry at that point in time but assumed hunger in a moment when no food would be available. Other reasons were less popular, for example, P5 and P13 stated she likes trying new food out of **curiosity**. If the food is something they are interested in and want to try, it does not matter if it is healthy or unhealthy. P1 and P8 named **boredom** as a reason to eat chocolate while watching TV.

4.3   Food Choice Timing

We classified the answers to the question: "How long in advance have you decided to eat that particular food?", into three time categories, according to the time distance between the food decision and the actual eating event. Food decisions made less than 30 min before were categorized as spontaneous. Additional categories included decisions made within the same day of the eating event, that is, one or more days ahead respectively.

Unsurprisingly, the further ahead the meals were planned, the higher was the fraction of healthy food decisions within a certain time category, as shown in Fig. 2. This makes us discuss the timing of a JITAI for healthy food choices. One could assume that the just-in-time in JITAI denotes the time shortly before the eating event. However, if a JITAI could make the user rethink and plan his meals ahead, we could expect an increase of healthier food choices. This way, JITAIs time frame should ideally shift to the earliest moment possible, for example, support the participant already while grocery shopping or even grocery planning.

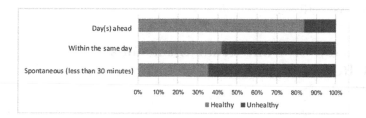

Fig. 2. Food choice decision timing relative to the actual eating event

4.4   Alteration of Food Choice

As expected, participants were happy with their healthy choices in 80% and would not change anything about them. A distribution of all participants' statements on whether they would alter their food choice is displayed in Fig. 3. Within the remaining 20% of healthy choices, participants would have changed the meal because they mostly did not like the taste (4 instances) or because the food amount was insufficient (3 instances). Three healthy meals were labelled as "maybe" to be changed. Participants either perceived the amount of food as too much, or either the meal as unnecessary or the amount of healthy components as insufficient.

Within unhealthy meals, participants claimed that in 31 out of 62 unhealthy labeled food choices, they would not opt for any meal alteration. The reasons for these claims include self-made, conscious decisions to indulge in unhealthy meals, routine, lack of time, and social pressure. In four cases participants hesitated to modify the unhealthy food choice. Two stated further explanation: (1) if more information at that particular moment was available, the participant would not

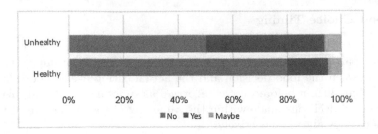

Fig. 3. Participants' statements on whether they would change their food choices in retrospect.

have taken the food whereas the other person stated that (2) the amount could have been reduced. On the other hand, participants expressed the desire to alter something in 27 food choices. In seven cases, the meal was marked as unnecessary. Four meals should have been substituted with a healthier alternative. A caloric reduction was mentioned three times. The remaining three modifications included an increase of healthier foods in the meal, better planning, and more information respectively.

5   Summary of Contextual Situations and Recommendations for Intervention Methods

In each following subsection, we discuss a *kairos* that emerged as a JITAI's window of opportunity from our observation. We back these up with anecdotal evidence from the interviews (quotes are translated to English when necessary) and examine the fit of intervention methods suggested from the participants.

Kairos 1: Lack of (Practical) Alternatives in Immediate Surroundings.
According to comments of participants, unhealthy food decisions were likely to occur in situations without healthy alternatives in their immediate surroundings. For example, P1 named at least two situations where she was home eating chocolate and gummibears after 8 pm because *"[They were] just there"*. P12 recalled a frozen pizza consumption at 10:26 pm: *"[The pizza] was just there for such cases [of late dinner] and it is easily prepared in no time"*. P15 recalls a Sunday afternoon on which he was really hungry and decided to eat a big Subway sandwich as "the next best thing", since the usual bakery where he could have gotten a bun and salad was closed.

All three participants proposed a planning tool as their favoured JITAI method. If the tool could automatically detect events ahead, by for example syncing with the participant's calendar, it could propose healthier evening snacks (in case of P1's situation), more diverse food (P12) or just prompt the user that no shops will be working on certain days (P15). It is to be noted, that in Munich most grocery shops close after 8 pm Mon-Sat and Sunday all day. When planned right, eight out of thirteen participants stated eating healthy because of preparation in advance (15 situations). Unsurprisingly, the further ahead the meals were planned, the higher was the fraction of healthy food decisions (>80% vs. 35% healthy meals when planned day(s) ahead vs. less than 30 min). This data backs up the participants desire for a planning ahead tool.

Kairos 2: Unawareness of Alternatives in Immediate Surroundings. Although our participants preferred eating at home (almost 60% of all reported eating events had home as location), sometimes they had meals at other locations. Five unhealthy food choice occurrences were consequences of a shortage of healthy alternatives when our participants were away from home. More precisely, participants P2, P11, P13 and P15 all stated having an unhealthy meal in eating situations around unknown locations. For example, P13 implied: *"It was already after 8 pm, [shops were closed] and I just looked around the main train station where I could get something to eat [...] and I decided to take a noodle box which was relatively cheap and easily accessible."*

All participants wished for a JITAI that displays eating opportunities around the unknown location beforehand. P2 could have benefited from more information the day before, as he wanted to be more prepared when deciding where to eat with colleagues. P11 would prefer an intervention right before making a decision on where to eat: *"I" was in a [pizza] restaurant ... in itself I do not like to go to the pizzeria but I did not have so much choice around [that area].* For P13, it is important that the suggestions accustom her taste preferences and include places all along her way to home from work.

Kairos 3: Spontaneous Cravings as Snack in the Evenings. Cravings were a reason perceived as responsible for nineteen unhealthy food choices. Even though participants were not hungry, they still snacked, majorly in the evenings (12 were after 5 pm). For example, P8 stated for a snack at 7 pm that she *"was bored and then the cookie came to my mind and it did not go away [from my mind] anymore."* P15 similarly recounted a situation when he came home around 6 pm and had his *"most unnecessary meal of the whole week, because I knew I was meeting friends for dinner in less than 3 hours [...], a frozen pizza".* P15 added that the meal was not based on a desire for pizza, but rather a craving for food in general.

Eleven participants claimed they would have changed something about an unhealthy food choice rooted in cravings. Participants articulated hunger re-examination as a desirable intervention method. P4, P8, P11 and P15, all desired a system that could detect a craving and pop a question whether that food really is necessary at that moment. P11 was more extreme, describing a system that would lock her 'stack' of unhealthy food and make it inaccessible. P3, P5, P11 and P13 proposed an intervention with the aim of calorie reduction, that is, a food saturation predictor. However, in 7 out of 19 unhealthy food choices, participants would not have changed anything. As P2 stated: *"A pizza [or something" similar] from time to time is not wrong"* and P1 and P13 complemented an unhealthy meal as reward for good behavior. An ideal JITAI would, therefore, be able to detect the craving as well as its ineffectiveness and therefore, decide not to intervene.

Kairos 4: Social Pressure in Various Situations. Social pressure has been recognized twelve times as a stimulus towards unhealthy food choices. For example, in the three cases other people have cooked for our participants, participants were mostly not willing to pursue anything out of social stigma or time saving reasons. Both P11 and P4 assumed a JITAI to be of no help in such situation. On the other hand, P8 and P15 observed that they tend to eat more when in company. Therefore, a proper JITAI could provoke self-control measures by evoking personal goals or, more drastically, predict food saturation. It could state when the participant had enough for the aim of food intake reduction. Yet participants are sometimes also fine with consuming more food in company (P5).

Sometimes, food is a reason for gathering of friends and family. P8 considered a JITAI, that suggests healthier alternatives to coffee and sweets when meeting friends and family, as probably useful. However, she emphasized the importance of a *"decent alternative for coffee and cake, and not exactly an apple."* Finally, even though she was aware the coffee and cake she had were unhealthy, she would not have altered anything in her choice. In eight out of twelve cases, our participants experienced only positive emotions like happiness and relaxation. JITAI designers therefore have to carefully design the JITAI in order to not harm such positive emotions and strengthen negative ones.

6   Limitations

Although self-report is a common approach for gathering information on eating behaviour, self-reported data can be (1) inaccurate, (2) influenced by recall bias [14] or (3) influenced by social desirability [21]. We did however stress the importance of a complete dataset as well as our position as neutral and not-judgmental observers. We also asked the participants for their honesty in regards to the correct and complete data we received from them. In addition, participants were asked in the interviews to choose each five rather healthy and unhealthy meals. We therefore cannot assure if these meals were actually healthy, but we did not want to put unnecessary "judgmental" pressure.

Moreover, confusion may have appeared with the participants regarding the terminology of the questions, leading to confusion especially when deciding the meal category and occasion as outlined in 4.2 (1). In many cases, meals had both purposes, namely, to (1) reduce hunger as a regular meal does and (2) fulfill a craving.

To conclude the limitations, we observe that our results may not generalize due to the rather homogeneous study sample and 8-day study duration. Still, we are confident that our exploration gives directions for future work on proactive persuasive technologies.

7   Conclusions and Future Work

We performed an exploratory approach towards finding windows of opportunity for proactive persuasive technologies, that is, JITAIs encouraging healthy eating behaviors. Within a collection of 469 food choice moments from 14 participants and in-depth reflections on the participants' reasons and appropriateness of food choices, we examined the broadness of real-life eating events and their contextual fit for healthy eating JITAIs. As result, we deduced four windows of opportunity (i.e. *kairos*), with potentially high JITAI effectiveness. We discussed how these windows distinguish themselves within their timely, spatial and social characteristics. Furthermore, we collected and mapped a space of intervention techniques to the observed opportunity windows. For future work, we suggest to include additional context factors we discovered during the study such as the emotional value of food (e.g., the cookie for children linked to childhood memories [P5]) and the strength of a craving (e.g., would a person walk all the way to the next store just to get chocolate?). In addition, further differentiation between appetizer, regular meal, and dessert might be helpful. All factors could be good indicators for people's willingness to withhold or indulge their cravings. An additional point for future work would be to investigate how *kairos* differs regarding people's short-term (eg. emotions) and long-term (eg. character, social background) personal characteristics.

In general, we find that in particular designers of persuasive technologies can benefit from the observed information. Within our research, we plan to use the findings to implement and evaluate ubiquitous nutrition-supportive interventions using current mobile and sensor technology. We hope to evaluate the JITAIs' success within changing nutritional behavior across a diverse population in the future.

References

1. Baker, S.: College cuisine makes mother cringe. Am. Demogr. **13**, 10–11 (1991)
2. Basten, F., Ham, J., Midden, C., Gamberini, L., Spagnolli, A.: Does trigger location matter? The influence of localization and motivation on the persuasiveness of mobile purchase recommendations. In: MacTavish, T., Basapur, S. (eds.) PERSUASIVE 2015. LNCS, vol. 9072, pp. 121–132. Springer, Cham (2015). https://doi.org/10.1007/978-3-319-20306-5_11
3. Bentley, F., Tollmar, K., Stephenson, P., Levy, L., Jones, B., Robertson, S., Price, E., Catrambone, R., Wilson, J.: Health mashups: presenting statistical patterns between wellbeing data and context in natural language to promote behavior change. TOCHI **20**(5), 30 (2013)
4. Beyer, H., Holtzblatt, K.: Contextual Design: Defining Customer-Centered Systems. Morgan Kaufmann Publishers Inc., San Francisco (1997)
5. Campbell, J.L., Quincy, C., Osserman, J., Pedersen, O.K.: Coding in-depth semistructured interviews: problems of unitization and intercoder reliability and agreement. Sociol. Methods Res. **42**(3), 294–320 (2013)
6. Carroll, E.A., Czerwinski, M., Roseway, A., Kapoor, A., Johns, P., Rowan, K., Schraefel, M.: Food and mood: just-in-time support for emotional eating. In: Proceedings of the ACII 2013, pp. 252–257. IEEE (2013)

7. Cordeiro, F., Bales, E., Cherry, E., Fogarty, J.: Rethinking the mobile food journal: exploring opportunities for lightweight photo-based capture. In: Proceedings of the CHI 2015. ACM (2015)

8. Fogg, B.J.: Persuasive Technology: Using Computers to Change what We Think and Do. Interactive Technologies. Morgan Kaufmann Publishers (2003). ISBN: 9781558606432, ICCN: 2002110617. https://books.google.de/books?id=9nZHbxULMwgC

9. Gilhooly, C., Das, S., Golden, J., McCrory, M., Dallal, G., Saltzman, E., Kramer, F., Roberts, S.: Food cravings and energy regulation: the characteristics of craved foods and their relationship with eating behaviors and weight change during 6 months of dietary energy restriction. Int. J. Obes. **31**(12), 1849–1858 (2007)

10. Ham, J., van Schendel, J., Koldijk, S., Demerouti, E.: Finding kairos: the influence of context-based timing on compliance with well-being triggers. In: Gamberini, L., Spagnolli, A., Jacucci, G., Blankertz, B., Freeman, J. (eds.) Symbiotic 2016. LNCS, vol. 9961, pp. 89–101. Springer, Cham (2017). https://doi.org/10.1007/978-3-319-57753-1_8

11. World Cancer Research Fund International: The link between food, nutrition, diet and non-communicable diseases (2014). www.wcrf.org/sites/default/files/PPA_NCD_Alliance_Nutrition.pdf

12. Lehto, T., Oinas-Kukkonen, H.: Persuasive features in six weight loss websites: a qualitative evaluation. In: Ploug, T., Hasle, P., Oinas-Kukkonen, H. (eds.) PERSUASIVE 2010. LNCS, vol. 6137, pp. 162–173. Springer, Heidelberg (2010). https://doi.org/10.1007/978-3-642-13226-1_17

13. Panofsky, E.: Studies in Iconology, vol. 198. Harper & Row, New York (1962)

14. Paulhus, D.L., Vazire, S.: The self-report method. Handb. Res. Methods Pers. Psychol. **1**, 224–239 (2007)

15. Prochaska, J.O.: Transtheoretical model of behavior change. In: Gellman, M.D., Turner, J.R. (eds.) Encyclopedia of Behavioral Medicine, pp. 1997–2000. Springer, New York (2013). https://doi.org/10.1007/978-1-4419-1005-9_70

16. Rahman, T., Czerwinski, M., Gilad-Bachrach, R., Johns, P.: Predicting about-to-eat moments for just-in-time eating intervention. In: Proceedings of the Digital Health 2016, pp. 141–150. ACM (2016)

17. Räisänen, T., Oinas-Kukkonen, H., Pahnila, S.: Finding kairos in quitting smoking: smokers' perceptions of warning pictures. In: Oinas-Kukkonen, H., Hasle, P., Harjumaa, M., Segerståhl, K., Øhrstrøm, P. (eds.) PERSUASIVE 2008. LNCS, vol. 5033, pp. 254–257. Springer, Heidelberg (2008). https://doi.org/10.1007/978-3-540-68504-3_25

18. Russell, J.A.: A circumplex model of affect. J. Pers. Soc. Psychol. **39**(6), 1161–1178 (1980)

19. Spruijt-Metz, D., Wen, C.K., O'Reilly, G., Li, M., Lee, S., Emken, B., Mitra, U., Annavaram, M., Ragusa, G., Narayanan, S.: Innovations in the use of interactive technology to support weight management. Curr. Obes. Rep. **4**(4), 510–519 (2015)

20. Stroebele, N., De Castro, J.M.: Effect of ambience on food intake and food choice. Nutrition **20**(9), 821–838 (2004)

21. Tourangeau, R., Yan, T.: Sensitive questions in surveys. Psychol. Bull. **133**(5), 859 (2007)

22. Wansink, B., Johnson, K.A.: The clean plate club: about 92% of self-served food is eaten. Int. J. Obes. **39**(2), 371–374 (2015)

Influencing Participant Behavior Through a Notification-Based Recommendation System

Venkata Reddy[1], Brian Bushree[2], Marcus Chong[2], Matthew Law[3],
Mayank Thirani[2], Mark Yan[2], Sami Rollins[2(✉)], Nilanjan Banerjee[1],
and Alark Joshi[2]

[1] University of Maryland, 1000 Hilltop Cir, Baltimore, MD, USA
[2] University of San Francisco, 2130 Fulton Street, San Francisco, CA, USA
srollins@cs.usfca.edu
[3] Cornell University, Ithaca, NY, USA

Abstract. Behavioral recommendations for achieving energy savings in the home are extremely common, however how to effectively influence users to adopt such recommendations is not well understood. In this work, we present the results of a feasibility study, conducted over a 4-week period, that deployed a phone-based recommendation system designed to encourage participants to follow the popular utility-company recommendation: *Consider dimmer switches to adjust the light to the lowest level necessary for an activity*. We found that the system did influence participants to follow the recommendation and some even realized that they preferred dimmer lighting, suggesting that recommendation systems can serve to demonstrate to participants that they can maintain comfort even with lower energy consumption levels.

1 Introduction

Recommendation-based approaches for influencing user behavior toward energy savings are common, however most are either manual—relying on the user to apply a static recommendation—or automatic—for example, the Nest thermostat. Manual solutions may inconvenience the user, while automated systems often cause frustration. In this work, we report results of a feasibility study of a hybrid, in-situ recommendation system to provide cues to help participants follow a popular utility company recommendation - *Consider dimmer switches to adjust the light to the lowest level necessary for an activity*. Our system measures the brightness of a light bulb and uses a heuristic to determine whether the bulb is brighter than necessary. If so, a recommendation to dim the bulb will be delivered via a phone notification. Our study was conducted over a four-week period during which we collected data on the light bulb usage and, after which, we conducted in-person interviews with the participants from our study.

Our results show that our recommendations *did* influence participant behavior and increased their awareness towards the use of a smart home automation systems. Additionally, we show that participant-in-the-loop systems can

© Springer International Publishing AG, part of Springer Nature 2018
J. Ham et al. (Eds.): PERSUASIVE 2018, LNCS 10809, pp. 113–119, 2018.
https://doi.org/10.1007/978-3-319-78978-1_9

avoid frustrations caused by automated smart home and energy saving systems. Finally, we demonstrate that the content of the recommendations and their frequency of delivery are two key attributes that must be properly designed for a recommendation system to be useful in the context of home energy management systems.

2   Related Work

Our paper builds on previous work on home energy systems. Several papers study which recommendation attributes are effective for long term adoption. For instance, Abrahamse et al. [1] study several types of interventions: goal-setting, information tailoring, modeling, and feedback. Allcott [2] study personalized recommendations based on historical usage patterns and demographics. Castelli et al. [3] prototype a context-based recommendation system on a smartphone, and Costa and Kahn [4] and Gonzales et al. [5] discuss the effectiveness of nudging and social cognition and persuasion in increasing the effectiveness of recommendation systems. Most of the research in this field is based on mock prototypes and does not involve any real end-to-end system deployment and evaluation.

A group of previous work focuses on designing automatic energy management systems. The approach taken is to model energy consumption behavior using machine learning techniques and predict future energy usage [6,7]. Based on our results, we find that such automatic systems can frustrate the participants and, while human-in-the-loop system are more cumbersome to use, they are more effective in changing energy use behavior.

3   Study Setup

Our goal in this work is to explore whether a lighting recommendation-based system is a plausible approach for influencing energy decisions. We focus on one appliance—a dimmable light bulb—and our findings focus on the benefits and limitations of this type of system. Our goal is *not to quantify energy savings*, but to better understand whether this type of system can influence behavior.

Our system measures the brightness of a dimmable light bulb and calculates an ideal level based on the time of day and local weather—other contextual cues like activity performed by the user are not considered in this study. The system then sends a phone notification recommending that the participant reduce the brightness of the bulb. As shown in Fig. 1, the system uses the Philips Hue infrastructure to measure and control a light bulb, which interfaces with a Node.js API through a Java client running on a Raspberry Pi 3. For the purposes of our study, the system records the brightness level of the bulb every 30 s, which allows us to determine whether the participant accepted or overrode any given recommendation.

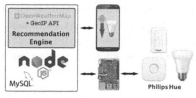

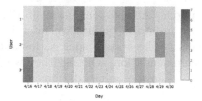

(a) Client side System   (b) Brightness Override Frequency

Fig. 1. (a) The client-side system consists of a Raspberry Pi 3 interfaced with a Philips Hue light bulb via a wireless Hue bridge. (b) This heat map represents the brightness override frequency for 'automatic' participants in Phase 1. Each row represents one participant and the intensity of the color for a segment the number of times the participant overrode the system on that day. (Color figure online)

Study Design: We performed a small-scale deployment over four weeks with eight participants (three females) who received a Philips Hue bulb, a physical dimmer switch, a Raspberry Pi and, if necessary, an Android phone. To study interactions between recommendations and automation through our system we designed the following four treatments: (1) **Manual** - no recommendations are communicated to the participant. Participant uses a physical dimmer switch to manually adjust the brightness of the bulb. (2) **Automatic** - recommended light levels are sent directly to the participant's lighting system, which *automatically* adjusts the brightness of the bulb. Participants may override the setting using the physical dimmer switch. (3) **Recommendation+Manual** - recommendations are sent to the participant's phone. To apply a recommendation, the participant must manually adjust the light using the physical dimmer switch. (4) **Recommendation+Automatic** - recommendations are sent to the participant's phone, and s/he may use the phone to accept the recommendation. If accepted, the system will automatically adjust the brightness of the bulb to the recommended level.

The study was organized into two-treatment within-participant tracks (automatic and manual), each of which introduced recommendations in the *second* phase. Thus, one group successively underwent treatments (1) and (3) mentioned above, and the other (2) and (4), as described below.

Phase 1: In the *manual* group, five participants were given the equipment and encouraged for the first phase to use the physical dimmer switch to adjust the brightness of the lamp to a comfortable level. No further instructions or recommendations were provided. The remaining three participants (in the *automatic* group) were informed that their lamp would automatically adjust to the recommended level, which they could override at any time.

Phase 2: In this phase, participants installed either the *manual* (Treatment 3) or *automatic* (Treatment 4) version of the recommendation application on the phone. At the conclusion of Phase 2, each participant participated in a 15-min in-person qualitative interview during which we collected feedback on aspects of the system such as instances when they followed or did not follow a recommendation, whether they would continue to use such as system, and if they had any recommendations for us.

4   Findings

Insight 1: Recommendations may influence participant behavior either directly or indirectly by increasing their contextual awareness.

We observed changes in participant behavior due to the introduction of recommendations in **both** manual and automatic groups, however we observed a fair amount of variance. Table 1 displays the mean light bulb brightness level (from 0 to 255) for each participant during Phase 1 (no phone recommendations) and Phase 2 (recommendations). We exclude readings below light level 10 as one participant appeared to have turned her light to the lowest brightness setting rather than completely off in Phase 1. We observed that over 78% of the dim events occurred within 20 min of a notification, implying a probable causation between the participants dimming the bulb and receiving a notification.

Table 1. Mean bulb brightness and number of participant dim events during Phase 1 and Phase 2 of the study. **Dim Events** are when a participant adjusted their light by following a recommendation or manual. Participant #7 encountered technical difficulties and was unable to complete Phase 2.

Group	ID	P1 mean level	P2 mean level	P1 dim events	P2 dim events
Automatic	1	156	216	n/a	3
	2	183	198	n/a	2
	3	194	199	n/a	8
Manual	4	157	96	4	2
	5	254	254	0	0
	6	252	234	0	2
	7	210	n/a	4	n/a
	8	198	184	7	11

The observed changes in light levels suggest that recommendations could affect participant behavior in ways that could either reduce *or increase* energy usage. In the manual group, participants almost uniformly exhibited a *reduced mean light level* in Phase 2. In the automatic group, surprisingly, we observe an increase in mean light level for all three participants. This is particularly interesting, considering participants had the choice to override automatic light levels at any time. Nonetheless, frequent participant overrides (Fig. 1(b)) hint at the possible influence of an over-aggressive dimming algorithm, with at least one participant expressing gratitude for the control afforded by the recommendations. It is worth noting that, even with the increase, light levels were still below the maximum (255) for all three participants in Phase 2 (when they received recommendations). Overall, these two seemingly discordant trends could suggest that recommendations offer participants opportunities to discover ways to reduce consumption, while giving them the freedom to adapt consumption more closely to their needs than an automatic system.

In the post-study interviews, two participants cited the potential of the system to provide contextually meaningful nudges. One participant remarked, *"The chiming sound of the recommendation otherwise was useful because it reminded me that oh maybe I don't need it to be this bright."* Another participant observed that, when he changes context, i.e. finishes studying and begins relaxing, the brightness of the bulb may not be on his mind but when he receives the notification it reminds him *"...I don't need that much light at that time"*.

Three of the eight participants reported preferring dimmer lights as a result of their experience in the study, suggesting that timely recommendations can serve to demonstrate possibilities for lower consumption without discomfort. One participant observed, *"After using this device I prefer using a dimmer switch so I can set it to a [...] low setting, especially at night."*. Another participant noted, *"I kinda got used to it, and once your eyes adjust to it, it really doesn't make too much of a difference."*. Despite the possibility of some initial discomfort, this participant continued, *"I wish that I had dimmers on more of my lights, just because when you are aware of the fact [...] a little less power getting consumed and if I could do this with all of my lights I definitely would."*.

Insight 2: Participant-in-the-loop systems can help to avoid participant frustration caused by automatic solutions, but must be carefully designed to avoid inefficiencies.

Our follow up interviews confirmed that two of three automatic participants did prefer the automatic system, however one participant's comments suggested that the automatic system may not be widely accepted. He expressed frustration with the automated system, noting it was not *"what [he] wanted"* and further explained, *"I think I liked phone recommendation more 'cause [...] I have access to say yes or no."* Automatic participants' override behavior (Fig. 1(b)) supports this observation. Even though one participant reported infrequently overriding our settings, there were several overrides most days for all three participants. This raises the concern of long-term frustration with the system.

Though a participant-in-the-loop system may overcome many of the challenges of an automated system, care must be taken that it does not enable self-defeating usage decisions. In our study, most reported behavioral changes were positive, however some participants reported behavioral changes that could increase energy usage. One participant noted, *"I probably had the light on more or later in the night"* due to the ability to choose a lower setting when he didn't want full brightness. Without a baseline for typical usage, it is difficult to quantify if this participant's overall consumption dropped or increased as a result, but it is reasonable to imagine how increased usage could offset brightness reductions.

Insight 3: The recommendation content, frequency and delivery mechanism are critical system design components.
The content of the recommendation itself is critical for behavioral change. One participant reported that our simple notification—We recommend you dim your light— *"...didn't really motivate me to want to override my choice."* and another stated, *"I want to know more information, like how much I need to dim the light."* Another participant reported feelings of guilt when he chose not to follow the recommendations noting that he was, *"nervous when the notification came... It made me feel bad."* These observations point to the need to provide motivation, such as potential savings in terms of energy or cost, as well as the potential for using positive reinforcement rather than negative reinforcement to suggest behavioral change.

The frequency and timing of notifications should be carefully tuned to avoid participant frustration. Participants complained that recommendations were made too frequently (every 30 min) or too quickly after the light was switched on. One participant requested a "busy mode" to pause recommendations for a longer period of time. Several participants also commented on the fact that a recommendation would happen immediately after the light was switched on. One participant even began to distrust the system due to the immediate notifications, declaring that *"...I don't know whether that is, that is more smarter decision or it just popped out no matter, every time you just open the light."* There is a tradeoff between frequent notifications that may frustrate the participant, and infrequent notifications that may miss opportunities to save energy.

A feature-rich phone application is a good choice for delivering recommendations, however variance in participant preferences suggests the need for a customizable delivery mechanism. Five of eight participants responded positively to a question asking them whether phone-based notifications were their preferred option. One participant would have preferred to view and interact with his data on the phone app, while others wanted to have more control of the light from the app. The majority of the six participants that were loaned Android phones asserted that they would have preferred to use their personal phone. Participants had other suggestions for recommendation delivery such as an ambient sound, fixed device near the light, and an Xbox. Overall, the diversity of desires articulated by participants in response to our system point to the need to provide multiple options for participants and allow personalization based on preference.

5   Conclusions

In this paper, we present the results of a deployment of an energy-based recommendation system and its feasibility for changing energy usage behavior. We show that human-in-the-loop energy saving systems can influence human behavior. However, it is important to design feature rich recommendations and carefully control the frequency of generating these recommendations. Future directions for this work include studying how personal characteristics, for example vision, affect how the system is used; how the system would influence behavior over time; and the effect the system has on energy use.

References

1. Abrahamse, W., Steg, L., Vlek, C., Rothengatter, T.: A review of intervention studies aimed at household energy conservation. J. Environ. Psychol. **25**(3), 273–291 (2005)
2. Allcott, H.: Social norms and energy conservation. J. Public Econ. **95**(9), 1082–1095 (2011)
3. Castelli, N., Stevens, G., Jakobi, T., Schönau, N.: Switch off the light in the living room, please!-Making eco-feedback meaningful through room context information. In: EnviroInfo, pp. 589–596 (2014)
4. Costa, D.L., Kahn, M.E.: Energy conservation "nudges" and environmentalist ideology: evidence from a randomized residential electricity field experiment. J. Eur. Econ. Assoc. **11**(3), 680–702 (2013)
5. Gonzales, M.H., Aronson, E., Costanzo, M.A.: Using social cognition and persuasion to promote energy conservation: a quasi-experiment. J. Appl. Soc. Psychol. **18**(12), 1049–1066 (1988)
6. Ozturk, Y., Senthilkumar, D., Kumar, S., Lee, G.: An intelligent home energy management system to improve demand response. IEEE Trans. Smart Grid **4**(2), 694–701 (2013)
7. Choi, J., Shin, D., Shin, D.: Research and implementation of the context-aware middleware for controlling home appliances. IEEE Trans. Consum. Electron. **51**(1), 301–306 (2005)

Using Visual Cues to Leverage the Use of Speech Input in the Vehicle

Florian Roider[1,2]([⊠]), Sonja Rümelin[1], and Tom Gross[2]

[1] BMW Group Research, New Technologies, Innovations, Munich, Germany
`florian.roider@bmw.de`
[2] Human-Computer Interaction Group, University of Bamberg, Bamberg, Germany

Abstract. Touch and speech input often exist side-by-side in multi-modal systems. Speech input has a number of advantages over touch, which are especially relevant in safety critical environments such as driving. However, information on large screens tempts drivers to use touch input for interaction. They lack an effective trigger, which reminds them that speech input might be the better choice. This work investigates the efficacy of visual cues to leverage the use of speech input while driving. We conducted a driving simulator experiment with 45 participants that examined the influence of visual cues, task type, driving scenario, and audio signals on the driver's choice of modality, glance behavior and subjective ratings. The results indicate that visual cues can effectively promote speech input, without increasing visual distraction, or restricting the driver's freedom to choose. We propose that our results can be applied to other applications such as smartphones or smart home applications.

Keywords: Visual cues · Prompts · Speech input · Triggers
Persuasive

1 Introduction

Touch input has become the state of the art input modality for interaction with many devices over the last decade. More recently, speech input is about to emerge as a full-fledged alternative to touch input, supported by the success of voice based systems such as Amazon Alexa, Apple's Siri or the Google assistant. Besides mobile devices or smart home applications, touch and speech have evolved as the dominating input modalities in the automotive domain. The latest models of many manufacturers integrate large touch based screens and intelligent speech based systems, but there is no or only little interplay between both modalities at the moment. Touch is usually the primary input mode, while speech input is mostly a less used alternative path for specific use cases that work independently of the touch interaction.

© Springer International Publishing AG, part of Springer Nature 2018
J. Ham et al. (Eds.): PERSUASIVE 2018, LNCS 10809, pp. 120–131, 2018.
https://doi.org/10.1007/978-3-319-78978-1_10

There is a number of advantages of speech compared to touch input that support the driver's safety. Speech input reduces visual distraction, it allows drivers to keep both hands on the steering wheel, and it offers a fast and convenient way to achieve many tasks in the vehicle, especially those that require the driver to enter text in any forms (e.g. when giving destinations, searching for contacts, or composing text messages). However, for some tasks, especially those that require the user to express spatial information, touch input is suited much better [14]. Furthermore, it has been shown that speech input is not free of distraction either and that situational influences can impair the suitability of speech input [10, 12]. Finally, speech input still faces some technical challenges such as understanding heavy dialect or recognition in noisy conditions.

In order to cope with such problems it makes sense to integrate both input modalities in the car. The challenge is to find a seamless and efficient interplay between alternative input modalities, so that users can actually benefit from the many possibilities they have. The "user should be made aware of alternative interaction options without being overloaded by instructions that distract from the task" [9]. In this work, we address the question if visual cues provide an effective, but unobtrusive way to leverage speech input while driving.

2   Related Work

Fogg describes the likelihood of influencing peoples' behavior as product of three factors [4]. Besides sufficient motivation and the ability to perform a target behavior, effective triggers are necessary. There are three types of triggers: *sparks* motivate behavior, *facilitators* make behavior easier, and *signals* simply remind people to perform a behavior [4]. In the case of speech input while driving, reduced distraction and increased safety provide a strong motivation. Furthermore, we assume that people have the ability and know-how to use speech input. In this case, visual cues are signals that just remind people to use speech input now. But they can also serve as facilitators, that make the target behavior easier to do. By displaying possible voice commands they help reducing the effort for formulating words ourselves, reduce the thinking effort and thus increases the likeliness that speech input is used.

2.1   Effects of the Prompt Modality

Why do people rather interact via touch instead of speaking to current cars in regard of these benefits? A psychological explanation is the cognitive mapping of visual stimuli to manual responses [13, 14]. Large touch-sensitive screens in current vehicles provide visual stimuli that provoke direct touch input. The other way around, auditory stimuli are most compatibly mapped to speech responses [13, 14]. Accordingly, one way to remind users to use speech input is to prompt them with auditory cues, such as spoken prompts or earcons. Yet, visual cues have some major advantages over spoken or auditory cues: Visual cues are faster.

Users can benefit from preattentive processes that support rapid pattern recognition and thereby absorb information at one glance [8]. Furthermore, auditory prompts are short term and sequential by nature and thus make heavy demands on human working memory [1]. Visual cues, in contrast, do not have this temporal relation and can be displayed permanently. At the same time, they are less disruptive than acoustic prompts. Playing a sound or spoken prompt whenever the user should use speech interaction can be very annoying. Parush compared spoken and visual prompts for speech dialog interaction in multitasking situations such as driving [8]. They found that speech interaction with spoken prompts took longer than with visual prompts, whereas the driving performance was better with spoken prompts. Their study also showed that the difficulty of the tracking task affected these results. They conclude that multitask situations must not always have spoken prompts. Especially novice users can profit from visual cues for speech interaction [15]. In multimodal systems, this allows to display the names of possible selections to suggest or explicitly indicate what users can say.

2.2 Implicit vs. Explicit Prompts

Explicit prompts stand in contrast to implicit prompts that help to direct user input in a more reserved way. Yankelovich proposes that those are not two distinct categories but spoken prompts rather fall along a continuum from implicit to explicit [15]. The most explicit form of prompts are directive prompts. They tell user the exact words they should say. Descriptive icons such as microphones or speech bubbles are one potential way to notify users to begin speaking [9]. Kamm concludes that directive prompts can facilitate the "ease of use" of voice interfaces [6].

Explicitly telling people what to do can potentially result in the exact opposite behavior. Prompts that are perceived as restricting to ones's freedom (to choose the input modality) can arouse reactance [3]. Reactance is an unpleasant motivational arousal that serves as a motivator to restore ones freedom e.g. by not following what the system suggests [11]. The extent to which a message is perceived as threatening to one's freedom finally influences peoples' behavior to follow or not follow the advice of the message [11].

2.3 Summary

Although research has shown that speech interaction leads to a safer and more efficient interaction, there are many situations where drivers do not decide to use their voice intuitively. We assume that this could be changed by providing a suitable trigger. Visual cues have some advantages over auditory cues that make them a promising means for triggering speech input. They can range from implicit hints to very explicit directive prompts. The latter ones are potentially more effective, yet they might draw too much of the driver's attention, or arouse reactance so that user will eventually not follow the system's advice.

3   Method

We conducted a user experiment that investigated the efficacy of visual cues to leverage speech input while driving. In order to address this research question in a differentiated way, we propose five hypotheses:

H1: Visual cues increase the amount of speech interactions.
H2: Explicit visual cues result in higher speech rates than implicit ones.
H3: Additional audio signals result in higher speech rates than only visual cues.
H4: Explicit visual cues cause higher visual distraction than implicit ones.
H5: Explicit visual cues induce a higher threat to freedom than implicit cues.

3.1   Participants

45 participants, 17 females and 28 males, with a mean age of 30.2 years ranging between 21 and 58 years took part in the study. All of them were either native German speakers or had excellent knowledge of the German language and none of the participants had motor impairments of the upper limbs, which would have shifted their decisions towards either touch or speech input. Participants' self-reported data showed about the same openness to touch and speech input with a slight advantage for touch. Tendencies to use rather speech or touch input while driving was balanced over all participants.

3.2   Experimental Design

The experiment used a within-subject design. Each participant completed 64 tasks that were displayed on a secondary display while they were driving. For every task, participants had to decide whether to use speech or touch input. Tasks varied in presence and explicitness of visual cues (none, implicit cues, explicit cues, implicit and explicit cues). In order to create a greater generalizability of our results, we additionally included two task types (selection, text input) and two driving scenarios (easy, difficult) and varied the presence of an additional audio signal (none, audio). Each specific configuration occurred twice to each participant. All tasks were counterbalanced in order to prevent ordering effects.

In both driving scenarios, participants followed a leading vehicle on a highway with three lanes and slight curves. In the easy scenario, the leading vehicle moved with 100 km/h, it stayed on the rightmost lane and did not overtake. There was only few traffic. In the difficult scenario, there was more traffic. The leading vehicle moved at 130 km/h and it used all three lanes to overtake slower cars. The audio signal was the standard earcon of a current BMW 7 series for pressing the push-to-talk button on the steering wheel. Task types and visual cues will be explained in detail in the following sections.

3.3   Experimental Tasks

We used two task types in our experiment. The *selection task* is well suited to be solved with touch input, while the *text input task* is better solved using speech. By including these very different task types we aim to achieve a better generalizability of our results for a broader range of tasks. The speech recognizer was active as soon as a task appeared.

(a) Selection task   (b) Text input task

Fig. 1. The selection task displayed three big elements that displayed gas stations (example in the figure) or restaurants. The text input task displayed an input field and a virtual keyboard to search a destination city (example in the figure) or a contact name. (Color figure online)

The goal of the *selection task* is to make a selection out of three elements. It is illustrated in Fig. 1a. The task displayed either three gas stations or three restaurants. Participants were instructed, which elements to select for the gas stations ("Total") and the restaurants ("Seehaus"). Selections were made by saying the name of the instructed element or by touching the according tile whenever this screen would appear.

In the *text input task*, participants had to enter a short text in form of a contact name or a destination. It is illustrated in Fig. 1b. They were instructed to enter "Lisa" for contacts and "Jena" for the destination by either saying the requested entry or by typing it on the keyboard. Both instructed texts have four letters. We assume that current intelligent text input systems propose a small selection of possible words about three letters. They only require the user to tap a forth time to select out the correct proposition.

3.4   Visual Cues

In a preceding brainstorming session, we identified interface elements in touch based systems that users associate with the use of speech input. Identified elements were split in two groups: implicit cues and explicit cues.

Implicit cues are more subtle adaptations that refer to speech input without explicitly telling the user what to do. In the experiment, three types of adaptions were made when implicit cues were used. First, the highlighting of touch elements such as buttons was reduced. Touchable areas are often highlighted in brighter

Fig. 2. Both tasks with increasing levels of visual cues. From left to right: implicit, explicit, implicit and explicit. (Color figure online)

colors, which creates a visual stimulus that makes users more likely to touch them. Second, more emphasis was put in visible text on the screen by highlighting possible commands with quotation marks, making it easier for users to remember potential commands. Third, text was rephrased to be rather conversational and therefore promote a spoken answer. For example, instead of "Search city" the text input task displayed "Which city?".

Explicit cues, in contrast, are more noticeable and directly prompt the user to use speech input. Again, there were three adaptations made in conditions with explicit cues. First, a notification banner was displayed on the top of the screen to catch users' attention. Second, on the banner, there was a microphone symbol orange color. Third, there was a short text displayed, that prompted users to name the desired selection or text.

Figure 2 displays the application of implicit and explicit cues on the two experimental tasks. The most left picture illustrates the task with implicit cues (Imp). The next one shows the explicit cues (Exp). Finally, the most right picture integrates both, implicit and explicit cues (ImpExp). Together with the basic version of each task (see Fig. 1), both rows illustrate four rising levels within the continuum from implicit (left) to explicit adaptions (right).

3.5 Apparatus

The experiment was conducted in a static high-fidelity driving simulator illustrated in Fig. 3. The driving scene was projected on a 180° canvas in front of the vehicle mock-up. There were two displays in the cockpit: the instrument cluster displayed a speedometer and rounds per minute, the central information display in the dashboard showed the experimental tasks. The latter was a 10.1 inch *Faytech capacitive touch display*[1] with a resolution of 1280 × 800 pixels. The experimental tasks were integrated in a special application implemented in *Unity3D*. Speech recognition was achieved using the built-in speech

---

[1] https://www.faytech.com/de/katalog/product/101-capacitive-touch-monitor-ft10wtmbcap/.

engine in *Unity3D* which uses the Windows speech recognition engine in combination with a *Rode SmartLav+*[2] clip on microphone. The users' glance behavior was recorded with *Dikablis Essential*[3] eye tracking glasses in combination with infrared markers.

Fig. 3. The cockpit in the experimental setup. The experimental tasks were displayed on the central display and participants decided whether to use touch or speech for interaction. Glance behavior was recorded using a head-mounted eye tracker.

3.6   Procedure

Participants completed a short form covering demographic data before they were introduced to the experimental tasks. They were shown all tasks (selection-gas stations, selection-restaurant, text-contacts, text-destination) in the basic version, without any visual cues and without an audio signal (as illustrated in Fig. 1). They were instructed to memorize the correct selection for each of the four tasks. Participants were *not* told that there will be additional visual cues, but the examiner emphasized that participants *always* have the choice to use either touch or speech input. Tasks appeared automatically on the central display after a random wait time between 10 and 15 s. This varying wait time avoided that participants got used to a certain rhythm, and ensured that there was sufficient time between tasks, so that each task was handled independent of the previous one. As soon as the task was displayed participants looked at the screen to identify the task, decided whether to use touch or speech, and made their input. Tasks disappeared after the selection or text input was completed and participants turned back to driving until the next task appeared. After all

---

[2] http://de.rode.com/microphones/smartlav.
[3] http://www.ergoneers.com/eye-tracking.

tasks had been completed, participants were shown all possible combinations of task type, visual cue and audio signal on a laptop display without driving. This way they could concentrate on the illustration of tasks. For each specific illustration, they rated the suitability of touch and speech input, as well as the threat to freedom. The order in which tasks appeared was counterbalanced.

3.7   Data

There was a total number of 2880 choices (45 participants*4 visual cues*2 scenarios*2 task types*2 audio signals*2 choices per configuration) and 90 choices for one specific configuration. The Eye Tracking system recorded the total glance time per task, which is the average duration that a participant looked on the display while a task was active. Finally, there were participants' self-reported assessments about the perceived threat to freedom that is caused by a specific illustration of a task. They are based on the ratings of four items, each on a 5-point Likert scale from -2 (strongly disagree) to 2 (strongly agree) [3].

4   Results

4.1   Choice of Input Modality

The choice of input modality was encoded in a binary variable ($0 =$ touch input, $1 =$ speech input). Figure 4 illustrates the percentage of speech inputs depending on the visual cue, the driving scenario, the task, and on the occurrence of an audio signal. The percentage of speech input grew with increasing level of the visual cues. The maximum increase was 16% for the selection task and 15% for the text task. This effect can be observed for both task types and both driving scenarios. The results of a Friedman test show that the visual cues had a significant influence on the choice of input modality ($\chi^2 = 13,904, p = .003, r = 2.07$). Additional Wilcoxon signed-rank tests were used to compare implicit cues to those conditions with explicit cues. They show that only explicit cues ($Mdn = 0.69$) did not result in significantly higher percentage of speech input than implicit cues ($Mdn = 0.56$). Instead, implicit and explicit cues ($Mdn = 0.69$) led to a significant rise of the speech rates compared to implicit cues ($Z = -2.48, p = .013, r = 0.37$). The level of significance was corrected according to Bonferroni.

Additionally, a logistic regression was performed to analyze the influence of all factors on the participants' modality choice. The results show that both the logistic regression model $\chi^2(4) = 350.00, p < .001$, as well as the individual coefficients (except the audio signal) were statistically significant. The model correctly classified 66.8% of the cases. Increasing the explicitness of visual cues by one level rises the relative probability to choose speech input by 17.4%. In the difficult driving scenario the relative probability to choose speech is 54.2% higher than in the easy one. Finally, the task-type had the greatest impact. Choosing speech for text input was 290.0% more likely than for the selection task. R^2 (Nagelwerke R square) is 0.155, which indicates a strong effect [2].

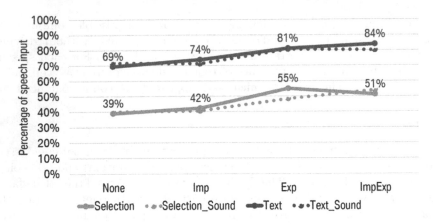

Fig. 4. The percentage of speech input depending on the visual cues, the task-type and the audio signal (dotted line).

In line with these findings, a Wilcoxon signed-rank test between conditions with acoustic signal ($Mdn = 0.59$) and without acoustic signal ($Mdn = 0.56$) showed no significant differences ($Z = -0.87, ns.$).

We can summarize that the task type was the most decisive coefficient, followed by the driving scenario. Visual cues play a smaller, yet decisive role in influencing the participants' decision. Moreover, the model shows that the probability to choose speech input rises with the level of visual cues. The additional audio signal did not influence the participants' decisions.

4.2 Glance Duration on the Display

The average glance duration in both driving scenarios was between 0.83 and 0.89 s for the selection task and between 1.41 and 1.83 s for the text entry task. Figure 5 illustrates the total glance times for both tasks individually. We observe a light tendency that glance times decrease with increasing level of visual for the text input task, while the selection task remains constant. Glance data was not normally distributed. Results of a Friedman test showed that the average glance duration on the display was not significantly affected by the visual cues ($\chi^2 = 2.32, ns.$). Wilcoxon tests confirmed that the total glance duration without visual cues did not significantly differ between implicit cues ($Mdn = 1.03$) compared to Explicit cues ($Mdn = 1.13$) or implicit and explicit cues ($Mdn = 0.99$). The duration that participants looked on the display did not depend on the type or presence of visual cues.

4.3 Perceived Threat to Freedom

The perceived threat to freedom was measured with the mentioned four questions. Ratings were very diverse because some participants did not feel any

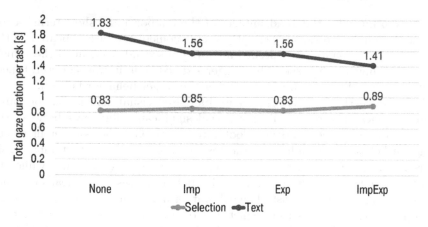

Fig. 5. Total glance time (TGT) on the display while a task was active. Visual cues did not significantly affect TGT.

restriction, while others reported that they felt like being influenced or urged to behave in certain way. The data was not normally distributed. A Friedman test indicted that the average ratings were not significantly affected by the visual cues ($\chi^2 = 5.49, ns.$). Accordingly, results of Wilcoxon tests showed that explicit cues ($Mdn = 0.00$) or implicit and explicit cues ($Mdn = 0.19$) were not associated with a higher threat to freedom compared to implicit cues ($Mdn = 0.00$).

5 Discussion

The first hypothesis H1 proposes that visual cues increase the amount of speech input used. Our results show that the user's choice of input modality was mainly determined by the task type and the driving scenario. Still, the visual cues had a significant influence, which can be classified as a strong effect based on the estimated effect size of the Friedman test [2]. Furthermore, the results of the logistic regression model and Fig. 4 indicate that implicit cues can already increase speech usage and we can accept H1.

H2 claimed that explicit cues would be more effective to promote speech input than implicit ones. The logistic regression model supports this thesis, but additional pairwise comparisons showed that the increase of speech rates for explicit cues compared to implicit cues was not significant. Based on these findings we do not accept H2. However, *extending* implicit cues by explicit ones (ImpExp) led to a significant increase of speech interaction. This suggests that the effects of implicit and explicit cues complement one another. The combination of both led to overall highest speech input rates.

H3 proposed that additional audio signals increase the amount of speech input used. However, the results show that they did not have a statistically significant influence on the participants' decisions. This was surprising, given the fact that speech input is mostly prompted using audio signals. At the same time, it is in line with the disadvantages of the temporal and short term nature of audio [1]. The audio signals were played the moment the task appeared on the screen, but participants often needed a couple of seconds to control the vehicle before attending to the task. The trigger existed, but it was not well-timed, which is one possible reason why achieving the target behavior fails [5].

H4 proposed that explicit cues cause increased visual distraction compared to implicit ones. The results did not reveal significant differences between the four levels of visual cues. A deeper look into glance data shows different trends for glance behavior depending on the task in Fig. 5. For the text input task, the usage of speech input rises with increasing level of visual cues while the average glance times for both, speech and touch decreases. This means that not the actual glance times per task changed, but rather the amount of (less visually distracting) speech inputs rose, which led to an overall decrease of the total glance time. The fact that this affects only the text input task shows that glance times for touch and speech input for the selection task were similar, since the higher percentage of speech selections did not reduce the overall glance duration. In summary, explicit cues did not result in longer or more glances on the display, but they reduced the overall visual distraction by increasing the amount of speech usage. For these reasons, we do not accept H4.

H5 assumed that explicit visual cues induce a higher threat to freedom than implicit ones, which increases the likeliness to show reactance and that participants will not follow the systems' advice. The average ratings from participants' self-assessed threat to freedom did not differ significantly between conditions. This indicates that the design of our visual cues did not have a big influence on the perceived freedom to choose themselves. A limiting factor might be that participants were explicitly told that they can always decide freely. Moreover, previous work in this field notes under-reporting as potential problem for participants' self-reported data. This might also contribute the missing variance in this case [7]. Therefore, we do not accept H5.

6 Conclusion

In this experiment, we explored the influence of visual cues on the users' choice whether to use speech or touch input. Our results show that visual cues can significantly contribute to leverage speech input while driving. This effect can be observed across different task types and different driving scenarios. At the same time, visual cues did not cause increased visual distraction. In contrast, there is a tendency that the overall glance time away from the street can be reduced for text input tasks by using explicit visual cues. We conclude that visual cues are an effective means to influence the user's choice of input modality and thereby to support users by emphasizing suited input modalities. The system can guide users in an unobtrusive way so that they can benefit from the whole range of input modalities, without concerning themselves with the decision. Our study showed that visual cues increased the amount of speech input used, decreased visual distraction on the road, and thereby contributed to the driver's safety.

While this experiment was conducted in the automotive domain, our results can be applied in other domains that offer speech along with other input modalities such as smartphones or smart home devices. This experiment served as a first try to test the potential of simple graphical adaptions. Future experiments should explore the full potential of visual cues, to see if incorporating animations or context sensitivity can further increase their persuasive influence.

References

1. Bradford, J.H., James, H.: The human factors of speech-based interfaces. ACM SIGCHI Bull. **27**(2), 61–67 (1995)
2. Cohen, J.: A power primer. Psychol. Bull. **112**(1), 155–159 (1992)
3. Dillard, J.P., Shen, L.: On the nature of reactance and its role in persuasive health communication. Commun. Monogr. **72**(2), 144–168 (2005)
4. Fogg, B.J.: A behavior model for persuasive design. In: Proceedings of the 4th International Conference on Persuasive Technology, p. 1. ACM Press, New York (2009)
5. Fogg, B.J.: Creating persuasive technologies: an eight-step design process. In: Proceedings of the 4th International Conference on Persuasive Technology, vol. 91, pp. 1–6 (2009)
6. Kamm, C.: User interfaces for voice applications. Proc. Nat. Acad. Sci. **92**(22), 10031–10037 (1995)
7. Miranda, B., Jere, C., Alharbi, O., Lakshmi, S., Khouja, Y., Chatterjee, S.: Examining the efficacy of a persuasive technology package in reducing texting and driving behavior. In: Berkovsky, S., Freyne, J. (eds.) PERSUASIVE 2013. LNCS, vol. 7822, pp. 137–148. Springer, Heidelberg (2013). https://doi.org/10.1007/978-3-642-37157-8_17
8. Parush, A.: Speech-based interaction in multitask conditions: impact of prompt modality. Hum. Factors **47**(3), 591–597 (2005)
9. Reeves, L.M., Martin, J.-C., McTear, M., Raman, T.V., Stanney, K.M., Su, H., Wang, Q.Y., Lai, J., Larson, J.A., Oviatt, S., Balaji, T.S., Buisine, S., Collings, P., Cohen, P., Kraal, B.: Guidelines for multimodal user interface design. Commun. .ACM **47**(1), 57–59 (2004)
10. Roider, F., Rümelin, S., Pfleging, B., Gross, T.: The effects of situational demands on gaze, speech and gesture input in the vehicle. In: Proceedings of the 9th International Conference on Automotive User Interfaces and Interactive Vehicular Applications, pp. 94–102. ACM Press, New York (2017)
11. Steindl, C., Jonas, E., Sittenthaler, S., Traut-Mattausch, E., Greenberg, J.: Understanding psychological reactance: new developments and findings. J. Psychol. **223**(4), 205–214 (2015)
12. Strayer, D.L., Drews, F.A., Crouch, D.J.: A comparison of the cell phone driver and the drunk driver. Hum. Factors **48**(2), 381–391 (2006)
13. Teichner, W.H., Krebs, M.J.: Laws of visual choice reaction time. Psychol. Rev. **81**(1), 75–98 (1974)
14. Wickens, C.D., Sandry, D.L., Vidulich, M.: Compatibility and resource competition between modalities of input, central processing, and output. Hum. Factors **25**(2), 227–248 (1983)
15. Yankelovich, N.: How do users know what to say? Interactions **3**(6), 32–43 (1996)

Design Principles and Practices

Time Off: Designing Lively Representations as Imaginative Triggers for Healthy Smartphone Use

Kenny K. N. Chow[✉]

School of Design, The Hong Kong Polytechnic University,
Hung Hom, Hong Kong
sdknchow@polyu.edu.hk

Abstract. This paper describes the approach employed in an ongoing project aiming to foster healthy smartphone use via Time Off, a mobile application presenting an animated genie on the screen together with a physical jacket for the phone. The genie becomes tired and ill, when one spends prolonged time on the phone. Time Off demonstrates application of the liveliness framework, grounded in concepts from cognitive science including animacy and blending, to designing dynamic representations of behavioral data that stimulate users' imagination of possible outcomes and reflection on the causes, highlighting the motivators for a change. We conduct a field trial with 14 participants for two to six weeks. Qualitative findings show that participants having intention to change expressed more levels of imagination and reflection. Their logged data also show reduction in length or frequency of use sessions, suggesting that lively representations can project a kind of imaginative trigger that motivates people.

Keywords: Internet or mobile addiction · Liveliness · Behavior change

1 Introduction

Use of smartphones and similar mobile devices in everyday life has become almost inevitable in urban societies. According to reports [1, 2] issued by the Yahoo!-owned company, Flurry, Americans' average daily time spent on mobile devices has shown significant growth from 162 min in 2014 Q1 to 220 min in 2015 Q2, and lately reached a record of 300 min in 2016 Q4. The app categories mostly used range from social media, messaging, entertainment media, to games, which imply the variety of digital activities enabled by mobile devices. This mobile pervasiveness poses a threat of possible addiction globally. The findings of a survey [3] done in Hong Kong (by the Department of Health) among 4,300 children and youngsters as well as their parents and teachers between 2013 and 2014 echo the concerns, showing that over half of the primary school students (aged from 6 to 12) and over 90% of the secondary school students (aged from 12 to 18) possessed smartphones. Around 50% of parents considered their children had spent excessive amount of time on the Internet and affected their daily lives. We have been working with an NGO in Hong Kong, Integrated Centre on Addiction Prevention and Treatment (ICAPT) of Tung Wah Group of Hospitals

© Springer International Publishing AG, part of Springer Nature 2018
J. Ham et al. (Eds.): PERSUASIVE 2018, LNCS 10809, pp. 135–146, 2018.
https://doi.org/10.1007/978-3-319-78978-1_11

(TWGHs), on this issue and exploring possibilities of intervening the problematic use through technology. This paper describes the approach in one of our ongoing projects, Time Off, which includes a mobile app presenting an animated genie as a widget on the home screen together with a physical jacket for the phone (Fig. 1 shows different styled genies with the jackets). The genie feels tired, becomes ill, and wants to put on the jacket, when one spends too much time on the mobile device and the screen. Starting from shivering, sneezing, to coughing (in terms of short animations, phone vibrations, and notification messages), the genie incrementally prompts the user to switch off the screen. It might seem like a Tamagotchi digital pet (that can be familiar to youngsters) with reverse logic, requiring one to pay less attention on the device. Yet, it can be more stimulating if one ignores the genie. It contingently "disappears" and leaves messages (e.g., "I take a shower") as indirect suggestions of alternatives to focusing on the phone. The main goal of Time Off is to insert breaks in users' continuous, long sessions of smartphone use.

Fig. 1. Four different styled genies installed on four participants' phones, together with the jackets, some of which are like a pocket while the other like a cover.

2   Related Work

The idea of using technology to track, log, or even restrict smartphone and app usage can be commonly seen in a dozen of similar apps in the market [4]. These apps allow users to set time limit on devices or particular apps, send warnings on overuse, and even cut the Internet access. Among them *AppDetox* let users set usage restriction on particular apps according to specific time of day or the accumulated duration of use, and its large-scale quantitative analysis after field deployment shows that people most often break their rules they set on messaging and social media applications [5]. Besides, studies with field trials of more experimental interventions, usually mixing quantitative with qualitative methods, have been flourishing in HCI with varied topics including energy consumption [6–8], physical activity [9–11], use of digital devices [12–14], and other daily habits [15–18]. Rooksby et al. [12], by logging a user's screen time across multiple devices and presenting data back to the user, reveal that representation of "raw" data is required for user reflection. Lin et al.'s *Fish 'n' Steps* [9] tracks a user's physical activity via a pedometer and displays a virtual fish tank wherein user progress is mapped to the growth and facial expressions of the fish. The findings include not only participants' changes in exercise habits but also their emotional attachments to the fish. Consolvo et al.'s *UbiFit Garden* [11] displays a virtual garden on the wallpaper of the user's mobile phone, with flowers representing exercise events and butterflies indicating goals achieved. Consolve et al. [19] summarize the advantages of stylized representations of behavioral data.

Our Time Off project employs the liveliness framework [20] in designing dynamic metaphorical representations of users' mobile screen time (i.e., time spent on mobile devices) that stimulate one's imagination of possible outcomes for reflection on the mobile use. The notion of liveliness, grounded in concepts from cognitive science including blending and animacy, suggests designing indirect yet understandable representations by blending concepts from seemingly unrelated domains, which shows contingent changes over time prompting reinterpretation and re-imagination [17]. The genie in Time Off shivers, sneezes, and coughs, which evoke experiences of feeling unwell in the user. One blends the genie's responses with remembered cases of being sick, inferring that continuously using the phone makes the genie sick and switching off the screen can give it time to rest. If the user ignores, the genie becomes more ill and suddenly leaves. The genie's disappearing from the phone causes one to become curious, reinterpreting and reimagining that it may feel unbearable. One may take the genie's perspective to self-review the excessive use. The imaginative blends and contingent changes trigger self-reflection and hopefully behavior change.

3 The Liveliness Framework

Liveliness refers to the dynamic phenomena that echo life, including autonomous transformation, reaction, and contingent behavior [21] (pp. 11–12). People experience and interpret lively phenomena via blends. For example, we understand the reaction of a cat by blending our own behavior with the perceived cat action [22] (p. 21). We might also use life-reminiscent blends to understand behavior of an interactive system. For instance, one might see a slowly, repeatedly glowing and dimming light (that found in some versions of Apple MacBook) as something (not only humans) sleeping with a steady breathing rate and understand the computer is just "sleeping". Lively phenomena often include contingent changes [23], causing observers to become curious and reason them out by reframing the situation, what Coulson calls "frame-shifting" [24] (pp. 35–36), and elaborating successive blends. The liveliness framework includes a protocol of cognitive processes for designers or researchers to analyze or predict the user experiences [20]. At the initial stage of use, immediate understanding is achieved:

1.1 Knowing action possibilities – The user perceives possible motor actions on the interface by recognition or exploration.

1.2 Receiving quick feedback – The user receives quick sensory feedback based on the action taken, forming an experience at the sensorimotor level.

1.3 Triggering immediate blends – The sensorimotor experience echoes scenarios from another domain, triggering immediate blends between the two experiences and yielding imaginative effects of the operation.

1.4 Becoming second nature – After repeated use, the operation becomes second nature. Gaps between action and feedback are bridged by the blends and become unnoticed.

At later stages of use, changes prompt reinterpretation:

2.1 Noticing contingent changes – The user perceives changes over time, and becomes curious about the causes in accordance with the blended concept in 1.3.
2.2 Invoking interpretive frames – The user invokes a frame from memory, which structures a remembered or imagined scenario with similar changes, to reason out the changes in 2.1.
2.3 Elaborating successive blends – The remembered or imagined scenario is ana-logically mapped with the blended concept in 1.3 plus the changes. Both become inputs to the next blend, yielding an imaginative narrative elaborated from the scenarios, the changes, and the causes.
2.4 Reflecting on the situation – Through invoking different frames, the user reviews possible explanations for the situation, which invite one to see from different perspectives.

4   Time off

Time Off applies liveliness to designing intervention for healthy mobile use via metaphorical representations with contingent changes, the genie and its different states, that trigger successive imaginative blends in users during different stages. Time Off consists of a mobile app (implemented on the Android operating system for the trial), which polls the screen status (i.e., on or off) of the user's smartphone for every five minutes, together with a widget, which displays an animated genie on the wallpaper. A tailor-made phone jacket is also provided to enhance the multimodal experience. Following the liveliness framework, the use of Time Off has at least two stages.

When consecutive polls are positive (i.e., the screen is on), which is a heuristic indicator of spending much time on the phone, the genie starts to be incrementally ill in five different states. At each state, the widget displays the genie in different short animations, coming with phone vibrations in different patterns and notification alerts with different messages. The vibrations become longer and longer with escalating states. To stop a vibration, the user needs to turn off the screen. The user can imme-diately switch the screen back on and continue to use the phone, yet the genie does not recover and the phone will vibrate again at the next polling time. For the genie to recover, the user has to turn off the screen for a time longer than one polling interval in order to break the consecutive positive polls. The metaphorical meaning of the action is to give the genie time to rest, as well as giving the user a break from mobile use. This is Stage 1.

If the user neglects the genie or gets around the vibrations, the consecutive positive polls continue to grow. The genie finally disappears from the screen and only leaves messages (i.e., notifications) to the user in every polling time without any phone vibration. The user may become curious where the genie has gone. In fact, the messages

Table 1. Subsequent states of the genie representation.

States	Animations	Sample messages	Vibrations (in sec.)	Sample images of "Chicken"	Samples images of "Typical"
0	Relieved	-	-		
1	Shivering Uncomforting	-	3-4		
2	Chilly Tired	"It's chilly"	8-10		
3	Freezing	"It's freezing"	12-15		
4	Sneezing Running nose	"Achoo!"	Non-stop		
5	Coughing	"Cough…"	Non-stop		
6	Leaving for cure (no animation)	"I go to the clinic" "I go to the doctor"	No vibration		
7	Leaving for other activities (no animation)	"I take a shower" "I go to bed" "I go to bookstore" "I go hiking" "I go to cinema" "I go get something to eat"	No vibration		

tell the user that the genie is doing other activities elsewhere, which are intended to be indirect suggestions of alternatives for the user to consider other than just using the phone. This is Stage 2.

The following Table 1 lists the subsequent states of the genie with the corresponding sample notification messages and the approximate length of the vibrations. The genie has five "incarnations" (i.e., Chicken, Anime-styled, Superhero, Strange, and Typical) for individual user selection. Sample state images of two incarnations are also included in Table 1. After State 5, the genie cannot be seen on the screen, at times leaving a note.

5 Field Trial

5.1 Participants

A trial of Time Off has been started in Summer 2016. This paper presents the study and findings of 14 participants (11 male, 3 female). Eleven participants were recruited through ICAPT of TWGHs, the local NGO, from a pool of their cases of potential addiction, and the others were volunteers recruited in the campus of a university in Hong Kong. All participants voluntarily used Time Off for at least three weeks up to six weeks or more, except three of them using it for two weeks. Each of them selected one favorite "incarnation" of the genie (see Table 2).

Table 2. Trial participants, their profiles, choices of genie, and respective length of trial.

ID	Gender	Age	Recruitment	Selected genie	Weeks of trial
1	M	18–25	NGO	Chicken	5
2	M	18–25	NGO	Chicken	6
3	M	26–35	NGO	Chicken	4
4	M	18–25	NGO	Anime	5
5	M	18–25	NGO	Superhero	6
6	M	12–17	NGO	Chicken	6
7	M	12–17	NGO	Superhero	2
8	M	12–17	NGO	Chicken	6
9	M	12–17	NGO	Superhero	6
10	M	12–17	NGO	Typical	5
11	M	12–17	NGO	Superhero	3
12	F	26–35	Campus	Chicken	2
13	F	18–25	Campus	Chicken	2
14	F	18–25	Campus	Chicken	3

5.2 Surveys for Personalization

Each participant was first surveyed with a questionnaire, which asked about general usage of mobile phones, including self-estimated daily total time spent on the phone and usual length of a continuous session of use. Responses informed the customization of Time Off for each participant. One setting was the time scale for the genie's various states (i.e., how many minutes for each state), which ensured each participant experience most of the states (0–5) often times, which corresponded to Stage 1 of the protocol, and higher states (6–7) sometimes, which corresponded to Stage 2. The goal was to let the genie's contingent changes intervene the participant.

The survey also probed each participant's suspended or latent interests other than the digital. This information provided personalized contents for the genie's leaving messages in Stage 2 as more relevant suggestions.

Another important question in the survey: "Is there anything you would like to change about the way you use your phone?" This checked one's intention to change. The survey lastly allowed the participant to choose the favorite genie incarnation.

5.3 Logs and Interviews

The personalized app was then installed on the participant's smartphone, and the genie was put on the wallpaper. The phone jacket was given and the participant was strongly encouraged to use it. The participant was told that if the phone was used too long, the genie might feel unwell. The screen status data was logged and stored in the participant's phone, and the participant was asked to send us the daily log file by email.

We conducted multiple interviews with each participant, respectively after the first week of use (also for tuning the customization if necessary), after the second week, and as a conclusion after the final week. The interview outline followed the protocol of cognitive processes from the liveliness framework. To probe users' imagination and reflection retrospectively, the questions were crafted carefully. The first-level questions were kept open to avoid directing the participant, as follows:

1.1 Have you tried anything with your genie? How about the jacket?
1.2 Did you notice anything with your genie? (e.g., notifications and animations)
1.3 When your genie shivered, what did you think?
1.4 How often did your genie shiver? How did you usually deal with this?
2.1 Did you notice that your genie disappeared? What did you see then?
2.2 Did you think why your genie disappeared? What do you think now?
2.3 Have you thought of how to get it back? Have you tried? Did you make it?
2.4 How did you think about your genie's behavior?

The interviews were semi-structured, and the questioning was agile. For instance, a participant might elaborate 1.2 that automatically covered 2.1, which would not be asked directly then.

5.4 Data Analyses

All interviews were transcribed and coded according to a scheme informed by the protocol, including keywords "motor action" in Stage 1.1, "sensory feedback" in Stage 1.2, scenarios from "another domain" in Stage 1.3, scenarios with "similar changes" in Stage 2.1 and 2.2, "imaginary scenario" with "causes" in Stage 2.3, and "different perspectives" in Stage 2.4. Each set of coded data, for instance those of "another domain", was then clustered into different groups, which imply different frames invoked among the participants.

The app logged a participant's screen status by polling. A series of positive polls resulted in escalation of the genie's states, until the participant switched off the screen to give a negative poll. The last state reached at the end of each session of use indicated the session length. The higher the state, the longer the session is. The total number of each state marking the session length was summarized weekly for each participant, which showed one's usual continuous time spent on the phone.

The app also kept track of the "running difference" between positive and negative polls on a day. A user-defined threshold of this difference functioned like a daily quota of mobile use for the participant. The number of days the participant exceeded the quota indirectly indicated one's overall achievement in controlling the behavior.

5.5 Findings

From the logs, P2, P3, and P4 showed a drop in sessions of various lengths and the number of days exceeding the threshold (see Figure P2, a visualization of P2's logged data, for example). P8 and P14 showed obvious shifts from long to short sessions. P9 showed a boost in longer sessions first and then dramatically cut down to shorter sessions (see Fig. P9, a visualization of P9's logged data). For P7, P12, and P13, their 2-week data were too short to show patterns. Others (P1, P5, P6, P10, P11) did not show any obvious change.

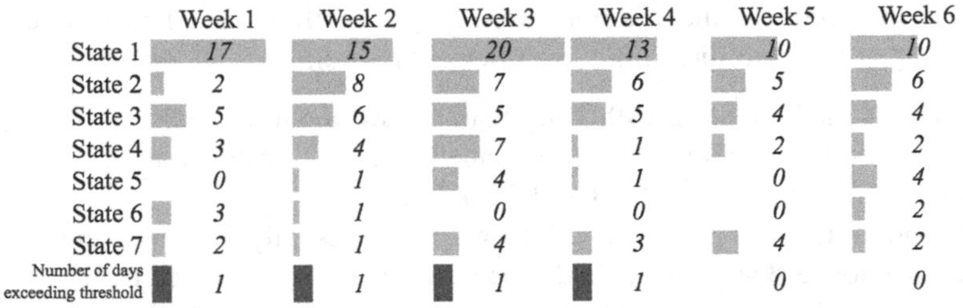

	Week 1	Week 2	Week 3	Week 4	Week 5	Week 6
State 1	17	15	20	13	10	10
State 2	2	8	7	6	5	6
State 3	5	6	5	5	4	4
State 4	3	4	7	1	2	2
State 5	0	1	4	1	0	4
State 6	3	1	0	0	0	2
State 7	2	1	4	3	4	2
Number of days exceeding threshold	1	1	1	1	0	0

Fig. P2. Visualization of P2's logged data in six weeks

	Week 1	Week 2	Week 3	Week 4	Week 5	Week 6
State 1	10	10	10	9	6	11
State 2	2	3	8	8	4	7
State 3	2	4	2	2	1	3
State 4	1	2	2	2	2	0
State 5	1	0	3	1	0	0
State 6	2	0	4	2	0	2
State 7	0	1	5	2	2	1
Number of days exceeding threshold	0	1	3	4	1	0

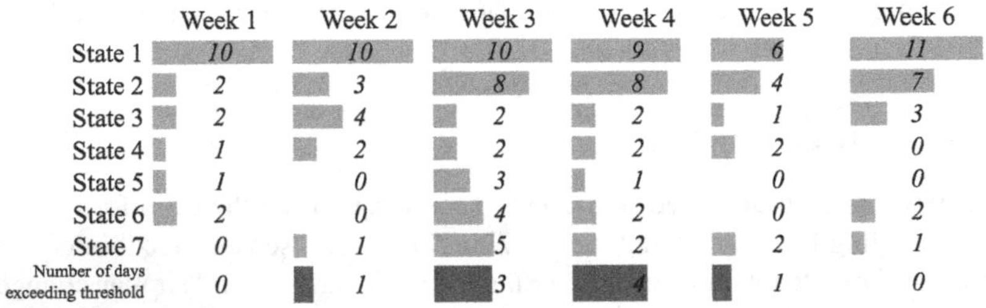

Fig. P9. Visualization of P9's logged data in six weeks

From the interviews, the clustering of coded data, mainly the codes "another domain" and "different perspectives" among others, is summarized as follows, with sample quotes (informative words in italics) from the participants.

Another domain. When participants spoke about the initial changes of the genie, their wordings revealed that most of them unconsciously drew concepts from different domains to describe the genie, which implied the immediate blends in their minds. Two main clusters formed were both anthropomorphizing the genie, namely someone being overloaded, and someone responsible for reminding others.

Someone needs rest

P2: "Switching off the screen, *leaving it alone* for a while"

P4: "Just switched off the phone and let it *rest* a bit."

P14: "The genie *couldn't rest* because I kept using the phone, just like giving it too much work."

Someone reminds you

P5: "It is similar to humans … like *somebody being with* you, reminding you."

P6: "It *asked me* to stop."

P10: "It was *asking me to turn off* the screen but I just ignored it."

Different perspectives. Half of the participants showed in their verbal responses reinterpretation of the genie's contingent disappearing, elaboration of the imagined link with the genie, and reflection on their own behaviors. Some became aware of other possible activities to do. Five participants took the genie's perspective, attributing its emotions to their behavior. Three of these five further challenged and questioned their phone usage.

I have other options

P5: "It's like suggesting me let's go to *do something else* instead of using the phone."

P9: "It asked me to follow it to *do the activities*."

P13: "It's telling me I can *use the time to do other things*."

Unbearable with me

P2: "It *could not take me anymore* because I played games for too long … like a *girlfriend* could not take anymore and leave."

P4: "It felt *disappointed*."

P5: "It may be *angry* and leave." "It has a character. If *I ignore* its messages, it will leave; if I stop using the phone, it will come back. I'm interacting with it."

P14: "It was *angry at me* because I didn't give it the jacket, I didn't take care of it."

Self-evaluation

P2: "I'm *wasting my time*."

P8: "*Should I* need to stop a while?"

P14: "*I did reflect* on my own usage, asking myself is it necessary to spend so much time on the phone?"

6 Discussion

Half of the participants (P2, P4, P5, P8, P12, P13, P14) showed traces of imaginative blends at the immediate level, and then elaborated successive blends with frame-shifting due to the genie's disappearing, resulting in reflection. Four out of the seven did show evidence of change. Most importantly, six out of these seven participants (except P8) expressed in surveys their intention to control or reduce the usage of smartphones. Conversely, the other half of the participants without showing much evidence of blends all said nothing that needed to be changed. These results suggest that users with intention to change are more ready for imagination and reflection, and also more likely to make a change. Some might argue to attribute this observation to the so-called Hawthorne effect [25] wherein participants adjusted their behavior because of being observed. We think that it was hard for our participants to make the change over several weeks of the trial period solely due to this effect. Moreover, those showed both intention and evidence of change did reimagine and develop the relationship with the genie (e.g., becoming unbearable, angry with the user). These cognitive responses could not be purposely "adjusted" by the participants. We believe that for those who contemplate to change, lively representations can effectively stimulate their imagination of possible consequences of a behavior, which functions like a spark in the Fogg's behavior model [26], motivating them to take action.

The study has limitations. The app polls the phone's screen every five minutes, which is a heuristic measure of the screen time. Many brief interactions between consecutive polls might be missed, given that the average duration of mobile use can be very short [27, 28]. Increasing the polling frequency might improve the accuracy, yet that would come with extra battery power cost. As mentioned, this system aims to introduce breaks in prolonged use. Short sessions of use are relatively tolerable so long as the cumulative screen time remains below the threshold, which is also monitored and responded by the system.

The phone jacket given to each participant was intended to serve two purposes. It makes the phone kept inside less accessible to the user and becomes a physical barrier preventing one from using the phone so easily. The jacket also adds physicality to the user's imaginative blends between physical actions ("putting on" the jacket) and virtual responses ("shivering" and "asking for" the jacket). It is believed that multimodal experience makes imagination more vivid. Yet, most participants did not use the jackets because of the perceived inconvenience of use or simply without the habit of using phone cases. Although the jackets were not physically used, a few participants were aware of the non-use and felt sorry to the genie. We believe that physical objects can project psychological presence in one's imagination and strengthen the triggers. Our future work will enhance users' cognitive link between the virtual genie and the physical elements, for example, by stressing the latter in the messages or responses from the former.

Acknowledgements. We thank all the participants. We gratefully acknowledge the grant from The Hong Kong Polytechnic University and the assistance from Tung Wah Group of Hospitals.

References

1. http://flurrymobile.tumblr.com/post/127638842745/seven-years-into-the-mobile-revolution-content-is
2. http://flurrymobile.tumblr.com/post/157921590345/us-consumers-time-spent-on-mobile-crosses-5
3. Chan, C.: Report of advisory group on health effects of use of internet and electronic screen products. Department of Health (2014)
4. http://igamemom.com/smartphone-addiction-apps-to-control-screen-time/
5. Löchtefeld, M., Böhmer, M., Ganev, L.: AppDetox: helping users with mobile app addiction. In: 12th International Conference on Mobile and Ubiquitous Multimedia. ACM Press (2013)
6. Ferreira, D., Ferreira, E., Goncalves, J., Kostakos, V., Dey, A.K.: Revisiting human-battery interaction with an interactive battery interface. In: UbiComp 2013. ACM Press (2013)
7. Atzl, C., Meschtscherjakov, A., Vikoler, S., Tscheligi, M.: Bet4EcoDrive: In: MacTavish, T., Basapur, S. (eds.) PERSUASIVE 2015. LNCS, vol. 9072, pp. 71–82. Springer, Cham (2015). https://doi.org/10.1007/978-3-319-20306-5_7
8. Lu, S., Ham, J., Midden, C.: Persuasive technology based on bodily comfort experiences: the effect of color temperature of room lighting on user motivation to change room temperature. In: MacTavish, T., Basapur, S. (eds.) PERSUASIVE 2015. LNCS, vol. 9072, pp. 83–94. Springer, Cham (2015). https://doi.org/10.1007/978-3-319-20306-5_8
9. Lin, J.J., Mamykina, L., Lindtner, S., Delajoux, G., Strub, H.B.: Fish'n'Steps: encouraging physical activity with an interactive computer game. In: Dourish, P., Friday, A. (eds.) UbiComp 2006. LNCS, vol. 4206, pp. 261–278. Springer, Heidelberg (2006). https://doi.org/10.1007/11853565_16
10. Maitland, J., Sherwood, S., Barkhuus, L., Anderson, I., Hall, M., Brown, B., Chalmers, M., Muller, H.: Increasing the awareness of daily activity levels with pervasive computing. In: Pervasive Health Conference and Workshops, 2006. IEEE (2006)
11. Consolvo, S., McDonald, D.W., Toscos, T., Chen, M.Y., Froehlich, J., Harrison, B., Klasnja, P., LaMarca, A., LeGrand, L., Libby, R., Smith, I., Landay, J.A.: Activity sensing in the wild: a field trial of UbiFit garden. In: CHI 2008 Proceedings of the SIGCHI Conference on Human Factors in Computing Systems, pp. 1797–1806. ACM Press (2008)
12. Rooksby, J., Asadzadeh, P., Rost, M., Morrison, A., Chalmers, M.: Personal tracking of screen time on digital devices. In: CHI 2016 Proceedings of the 2016 CHI Conference on Human Factors in Computing Systems, pp. 284–296. ACM Press (2016)
13. Ko, M., Choi, S., Yatani, K., Lee, U.: Lock n'LoL: group-based limiting assistance app to mitigate smartphone distractions in group activities. In: CHI 2016 Proceedings of the SIGCHI Conference on Human Factors in Computing Systems, pp. 998–1010. ACM Press (2016)
14. Alrobai, A., McAlaney, J., Phalp, K., Ali, R.: Online peer groups as a persuasive tool to combat digital addiction. In: Meschtscherjakov, A., De Ruyter, B., Fuchsberger, V., Murer, M., Tscheligi, M. (eds.) PERSUASIVE 2016. LNCS, vol. 9638, pp. 288–300. Springer, Cham (2016). https://doi.org/10.1007/978-3-319-31510-2_25
15. Vacca, R., Hoadley, C.: Self-reflecting and mindfulness: cultivating curiosity and decentering situated in everyday life. In: Meschtscherjakov, A., De Ruyter, B., Fuchsberger, V., Murer, M., Tscheligi, M. (eds.) PERSUASIVE 2016. LNCS, vol. 9638, pp. 87–98. Springer, Cham (2016). https://doi.org/10.1007/978-3-319-31510-2_8

16. Ilhan, E., Sener, B., Hacihabiboğlu, H.: Creating awareness of sleep-wake hours by gamification. In: Meschtscherjakov, A., De Ruyter, B., Fuchsberger, V., Murer, M., Tscheligi, M. (eds.) PERSUASIVE 2016. LNCS, vol. 9638, pp. 122–133. Springer, Cham (2016). https://doi.org/10.1007/978-3-319-31510-2_11

17. Chow, K.K.N.: Lock up the lighter: experience prototyping of a lively reflective design for smoking habit control. In: Meschtscherjakov, A., De Ruyter, B., Fuchsberger, V., Murer, M., Tscheligi, M. (eds.) PERSUASIVE 2016. LNCS, vol. 9638, pp. 352–364. Springer, Cham (2016). https://doi.org/10.1007/978-3-319-31510-2_30

18. Wunsch, M., Stibe, A., Millonig, A., Seer, S., Dai, C., Schechtner, K., Chin, Ryan C.C.: What makes you bike? exploring persuasive strategies to encourage low-energy mobility. In: MacTavish, T., Basapur, S. (eds.) PERSUASIVE 2015. LNCS, vol. 9072, pp. 53–64. Springer, Cham (2015). https://doi.org/10.1007/978-3-319-20306-5_5

19. Consolvo, S., Klasnja, P., McDonald, D.W., Landay, J.A.: Designing for healthy lifestyles: design considerations for mobile technologies to encourage consumer health and wellness. Found. Trends Hum. -Comput. Inter. 6, 167–315 (2014)

20. Chow, K.K.N.: Investigating user interpretation of dynamic metaphorical interfaces. In: Marcus, A., Wang, W. (eds.) DUXU 2017. LNCS, vol. 10288, pp. 45–59. Springer, Cham (2017). https://doi.org/10.1007/978-3-319-58634-2_4

21. Chow, K.K.N.: Animation, Embodiment, and Digital Media Human Experience of Technological Liveliness. Palgrave Macmillan, Basingstoke (2013)

22. Turner, M.: The Literary Mind. Oxford University Press, New York (1996)

23. Mandler, J.M.: How to build a baby: II. Conceptual primitives. Psychol. Rev. 99, 587–604 (1992)

24. Coulson, S.: Semantic Leaps: Frame-Shifting and Conceptual Blending in Meaning Construction. Cambridge University Press, Cambridge (2001)

25. McCarney, R., Warner, J., Iliffe, S., Haselen, R.V., Griffin, M., Fisher, P.: The Hawthorne effect: a randomised, controlled trial. BMC Med. Res. Methodol. 7, 30 (2007)

26. Fogg, B.J.: A behavior model for persuasive design. In: Persuasive 2009 (2009)

27. Böhmer, M., Hecht, B., Schöning, J.: Falling asleep with Angry Birds, Facebook and Kindle – a large scale study on mobile application usage. In: MobileHCI 2011. ACM Press (2011)

28. Falaki, H., Mahajan, R., Kandula, S., Lymberopoulos, D., Govindan, R., Estrin, D.: Diversity in smartphone usage. In: MobiSys 2010, pp. 179–194. ACM Press (2010)

Rationale Behind Socially Influencing Design Choices for Health Behavior Change

Vasiliki Mylonopoulou[1]([✉])(iD), Karin Väyrynen[1](iD), Agnis Stibe[2](iD), and Minna Isomursu[1,3]

[1] University of Oulu, Pentti Kaiteran Katu 1, 90014 Oulu, Finland
{vasiliki.mylo, karin.vayrynen}@oulu.fi, miis@itu.dk
[2] Paris ESLSCA Business School, 1 Rue Bougainville, 75007 Paris, France
a.stibe@eslsca.fr
[3] IT University of Copenhagen, Rued Langgaards Vej 7,
2300 København S, Denmark

Abstract. Persuasive technologies for health behavior change often include social influence features. Social influence in the design of persuasive technology has been described as a black box. This case study sheds light on design practices by identifying factors that affect the design of social influence features in health behavior change applications and the designers' understanding of the social influence aspects. Our findings are twofold: First, the two most positively inclined social influence features, namely cooperation and normative influence, were missing from the reviewed applications. Second, the medical condition - the persuasive technology targets - has a major influence on consideration and integration of social influence features in health behavior change applications. Our findings should be taken into account when frameworks and guidelines are created for the design of social influence features in health behavior change applications.

Keywords: Health behavior change · Social influence · Design factors

1 Introduction

Different kinds of persuasive technology applications have been designed in recent years to support health behavior change facilitating social features. Different theories of persuasive technology give basis for designing, among others, the social features of these technologies [1–3]. However, it is unclear how designers take these theories into account and how they actually decide about the inclusion and design of social influence features. In previous research, social influence features have often been viewed as a black box [3–5], and their designs seem to be popped out without any particular explanation of why this particular feature was chosen and why it was designed in a specific way. In this paper, we address this gap through the research question: "*What are the designers' rationales for the inclusion and design of social influence features in health behavior change applications?*" We aim to understand and describe the designers' rationale behind their decisions on these features and the relevant design process.

© Springer International Publishing AG, part of Springer Nature 2018
J. Ham et al. (Eds.): PERSUASIVE 2018, LNCS 10809, pp. 147–159, 2018.
https://doi.org/10.1007/978-3-319-78978-1_12

2 Related Research

2.1 Factors Affecting the Design Process

Design process is characterized as a messy process, difficult to be described, or even taught [6, 7]. The published methods and knowledge are not always used [8], and even if they are used, it is unsure if they will be perceived and used as intended [9]. More particularly, education is perceived as a way to gain knowledge, while methods are perceived as a check list or tools to help designers remember [10]. As such, the theories are used in the design as a guide, but they are not followed to the letter.

Despite the theories influencing the design through the designer's interpretations, the designer's own culture, values, and experience influence the design as well [11]. Research [12] on the design practice has described the design process as structured - after the ideation phase is completed - even though there are variations on user involvement and prototype creation. The design practice has also been characterized as qualitative, subjective, and sometimes based on a gut feeling [8]. This underlines the influence of the designer's personal interpretations on the design.

According to Stolterman [13], the decisions on the design process are taken by reflecting on the theories (scientific), the practices, and the intrinsic knowledge of the designer, but also by the client – the one served by the designer. Stolterman [6] supports that the result of the design is the result of the resources, knowledge, and involvement of the different stakeholders/clients and their desires at the particular time and place. The result of the design process (the real) is influenced by the science (the true), and the desires and wishes of the stakeholders that describe what "it ought to be" if there were no limitations (the ideal) [6]. Stolterman includes in the design process the clients and different constrains that exist in the real world to create the designed product. In addition, a focus on the stakeholders and users becomes more and more common in design thinking [14]. User-center design – where the design is based on the users, their perspectives and needs, and where in many cases the users participate in the design - [15, 16] has been also used in healthcare for the development of applications and prototypes [17–19].

2.2 Social Influence as a Black Box

In the design of behavior change applications it is common to include social features. The influence of other people on our behavior has been well established in psychology [20–22] and it has been moved to the design of technology supporting behavior change. Fogg [23] describes this technology as persuasive, because through means of persuasion and social influence the behavior change is supported. However, social influence in the design of persuasive technology oftentimes is described as a black box that needs to be opened [3–5]. Designers understand the importance to implement social influence features in behavior change technologies, but they often do not discriminate between the different social influence aspects. In fact, social influence is multifaceted, having such distinct sub-dimensions as social learning, social comparison, normative influence, social facilitation, cooperation, competition, and recognition [3], so it should be designed with care.

We focus on the design of social influence features (which we refer to also as social features in the text for brevity) on the health related applications and we try to understand and describe the designers' rational behind their decisions regarding these features in healthcare related applications. The aim is to understand and study the practice in order to have a better image of the design process and see if the different social aspects can be seen in the designs.

3 Research Setting and Methodology

The research question of this study is "What are the designers' rationales for the inclusion and design of social features in health behavior change applications". In order to get in-depth insight into this question, we conducted a qualitative case study in one Spanish company that develops health behavior change applications.

The case company (Alpha) is a Spanish start-up in the area of health and IT which has close connections to academia and academic research. This increased the possibilities of the company's designers to be aware of the relevant literature/theories in addition to the commercial products, and the designers were accustomed to rationalize over their decisions also based on theory. Moreover, as it is a small company, projects were running at the same time, but in a way that the investigator could participate in and observe more than one project during the visit. The company consisted of four employees (medical advisor/PhD candidate, programmer, chief financial officer, CEO) and several co-operators. During the investigator's visit, one more PhD candidate was hired for the prostate cancer project. Apart from the employees, two co-operators from the local university (PhD candidate, senior lecturer) were working closely with the company. The three PhD candidates, the programmer and the senior lecturer participated in the design of the projects described below.

Data was collected in three phases in the years 2016 and 2017. During the pre-visit period before the actual visit in Alpha (two months), two 30-min informal-conversation interviews were conducted with the co-operators who were responsible for the smoking cessation (D) and prostate cancer (A) application, and interview notes were taken. Participant observation started in this phase, when the investigator acted as advisor (by distance) in the breast cancer app (B), and was getting informed on the App D evaluation. During the visit (three months), the investigator acted as interaction designer in Alpha's projects (A, D) and additionally observed App B. She conducted four semi-structured interviews (average length: 45 min) with the employees and Alpha's cooperators. Interviews were recorded and anonymized during transcription. In the post-visit period, the investigator acted as interaction design counselor to follow the progress of the projects. The medical advisor moved to the investigator's place of work for three months, allowing the investigator to observe and participate in the design of the multiple scleroses app (C). During participant observations, notes were taken and transferred to the investigator's digital diary. Overall, data was collected on 10 technological applications (see Table 1). E–G were Alpha's past planned or implemented projects, and H–J were projects in the employees' past before they started to work in Alpha. Data on A–D was collected through both observation and interviews, data on E–J was collected through interviews. A–E and G–H targeted health behavior change –

which is the focus of this paper. However, applications related to general behavior change within the healthcare field (F, I, J) were also included, because it helped us to gain a more general understanding of designers' rationales regarding social features. It also underlined the difference between designing for patients and non-patients - users of A–E, G, and H are perceived as patients by the designers while users of F, I, and J were not perceived as patients.

Table 1. Summary of health behavior change applications

Application description	Social features
Prostate cancer app: supporting patients in being physically active (A)	Mentoring, sharing with family, community (incl. blogs and discussions), patients' paring and communication
Breast cancer app: supporting patients in being physically active (B)	Messaging (pre-determent), activity company
Multiple Sclerosis app: supporting patients on managing their stamina (C)	Feeds feature, comparison to others (on an action indirectly connected with their condition)
Smoking cessation app: supporting people on the smoking cessation (D)	Messaging (one-way communication), Facebook group, block feature
Goat disease – trivial like game: awareness on goat disease (E)	Level ranking on Facebook (the patients were grouped in levels)
Doctor's IT knowledge – trivial like game: awareness on healthcare technology (F)	Ranking on Facebook
Quiz and education on male sexual health: awareness and support on diagnosis (G)	Application's specifications sharing on social media
Diabetes app: supporting diabetic adolescence through gamification (H)	Messaging/emoticons, and creation of teams
Medical records' completion: motivate patients to fill in their records though gamification elements (I)	Compared a user with the average
Quiz on myths in healthcare targeting education and awareness (J)	Facebook game on myths in healthcare, ranking and comparison with friends

The data was analyzed using thematic analysis [24] and the cutting and shorting technique [25]. From the data, we extracted the rationales/justifications the designers gave for their design choices concerning social features in behavior change applications related to health issues. We identified four categories of rationales (Theories and Practices, Medical Condition, Designer's perspective, and External factors), and several sub-categories for each of them. These categories, which we will describe in more detailed in Sect. 4.2, arose from the data.

4 Results and Analysis

In this section, we first describe our results from a micro-level view, focusing on the social features implemented in different applications as well as the designer's rationales. Then, we describe our results from a macro-level view, introducing the four categories of designers' rationales for social influence design choices in health behavior change applications.

4.1 Rationales for Consideration and Implementation of Specific Social Features

In Table 2, we present the rationales behind different types of social features (micro level view). In Column 1, we present the social features that were either implemented or considered for implementation in the applications, together with a classification of the seven types of social features/aspects (see Legend below Table 2). In Column 2, we present the options of how that feature was (discussed to be) implemented, together with a reference to the application (A–I) within which the implementation was discussed or executed. In Column 3, we present representative interview quotations together with a reference to the application (A–I). Statements from the investigator's diary are marked with "-inv" after the application code (e.g., "A-Inv" to indicate that information concerning application A was from the diary).

In general, opinions about the social aspect were controversial. They all underline the importance of the social factor in influencing people's behavior and motivation but they also reveal that some conditions are taboos and some people may be unwilling to share health information with others: *"dependent on the group of the user I see social is very important in e-health."* and *"Well the social part in the health application is, [...] controversial part, because... not all the people want to share something [...] related to the disease"*. Moreover, the comments have confirmed that designers used social influence as a black box without differentiating between any of the different aspects such as social comparison, cooperation, social learning etc.: *"We should really have some social aspects in this application."*

The reasoning behind the different variations on features can demonstrate in a micro level the different factors influencing the designer's decisions. **Messaging** was included as a way to support and motivate others (see quotes at Table 2). In one case (H), the designer thought that the theory applied needed something social, so he just chose messaging and emoticons. In another case (B), the messaging was predetermined text, as the free text was perceived potentially harmful: *"ok, how do I stop someone who's having a really really bad day to get into a new patient -that is a new user for the app- and starts telling -this new user – all the bad things awaited for her in the breast cancer permeation"*. In a third case (D), the rationale behind the different types of messaging were influenced by the interviews with patients and the designers' interpretation. Patients who wanted to quit smoking were perceived to want to support others, but to be unwilling to have conversations. The designers decided to have one way communication, i.e., to send messages to support other patients, but the recipients were unable to respond: *"We saw that they were happy to help others, but they didn't*

Table 2. Reasoning around specific social features

Social feature	Possible implementation	Reasoning (representative quotes)
Messaging/chat [SL, SF]	Free text (H) Predetermined messages (B) One – way communication with Free text and predetermined messages (D)	"the first one [of the theory] – relatedness- builds with social aspects I was thinking 'hm we should really have some social aspects in this application" (H), "what if I could create a tribal group of breast cancer patients that could exert their group pressure to be healthy" (B), "how do I stop someone who's having a really really bad day to get into a new patient" (B) "to provide encouragement between members of the group" (D), "We saw that they were happy to help others," (D)
Grouping [CR]	Gamification elements like group targets and obligations (H)	"So when you have this friends you all have group goal to achieve and so for example if you and three friends all stick to the treatment for a week, you got a bonus price and then were specific challenges that were only available if you had a group of friend that were keeping you in check and you are checking on them" (H)
Social media [SF, RE]	Share only the application characteristics (G) Share your achievements in the application (F) Closed groups as a common space to connect with other patients and doctor(s) (D)	"Because we wanted to make it viral." (G), "you have to have a player base" (E, F), "there are a lot of different type of patients [...] so we did this FB group especially for them, for those who are more open" (D), "they can cheer other people" (D)
Ranking [CT, SC, RE]	Ranking between friends in social media and between all players/medical doctors trivial (F) and patients trivial (E) Ranking between friends who played the game (J)	"we know doctors are [...] competitive [...] It was a tool to motivate them, to poke them" (F), "The client wants a similar app" (E), "since they were patients, we couldn't say: 'okay, you are the best patient!' (E)" And in Facebook you would compare that to your friends so it's like all of your friends have 55 correct than you have 70 you are wining and there was a ranking of that" (J)

(continued)

Table 2. (*continued*)

Social feature	Possible implementation	Reasoning (representative quotes)
Comparison to the AVG [SC, CT]	Progress bar that shows how much the user had progressed in relation to others (I)	"Because we wanted to see [...] If I can drive your behaviour with something as simple as that" (I)
Comparison tool [SC, CT]	In the ideation phase (C)	"Social comparison between the MS patients regarding how accurate they are when they estimate their energy for the activities (AB test)" (C-inv)
Following/sharing [SL]	In the ideation phase (C)	"was sharing data with family in the sense that patients will not feel alone and they will have the support of someone", "he wants to implement a 'following' feature" (C-inv)
Community [SL]	In the ideation phase (A)	"with motivational experiences from PCa survivors" (A-inv)
Sharing [SF]	In the ideation phase (A)	"sharing data with family in the sense that patients will not feel alone and they will have the support of someone" (A-inv)
Mentoring [SL, SF]	In the ideation phase (A)	"one user that feels healthy can help motivating another one" (A-inv)

Legend: SL = Social Learning; SC = Social Comparison; SF = Social Facilitation; CR = Cooperation; CT = Competition; RE = Recognition

want to have more friends, or, they didn't want to have a new relation with someone just because they stopped smoking."

Grouping feature was implemented (I) as part of gamification of the application. The users had to create or be in groups, and when that happened they received group challenges and rewards. The people in the groups were also prompted by the application to check on inactive group members through messaging.

Social media had three variations connected to them: share, closed groups, and games. The share option was used to make the applications viral and open (G and J). The users could share only the details of the application in cases the disease was considered to be a taboo (G) and they could share their achievements in a gamified app (E, F). However, there was a design difference between apps of which the target users were perceived to be patients and those of which the target users were not perceived as patients, described in detail in ranking and comparisons sections.

Ranking and comparisons were used in applications that target healthy individuals or applications indirectly connected to the patients and their health such as: how complete was their electronic record in comparison to others (I), the knowledge on a subsect (patient oriented: E, non-patient oriented: F, J), and compare an activity that is indirectly connected with the condition (C). Comparisons targeting knowledge on a disease (E) were designed with the thought that the user is a patient. The individual ranking was used in the application targeting medical doctors and their knowledge on technology (F) in order to "poke them". Later, the client asked to tweak the application and target the knowledge regarding a disease (E). The designers perceived and treated the users of the application E as patients and they rationalized accordingly: *"If you tell someone that 'you are the one that is at the bottom of the ranking about IT things in healthcare', that's fine, but if you tell a patient that 'you are the worst patient because you are the bottom of the ranking', that's very disappointing for the patient"*. The suggested design was to group the individual ranking into categories, so if the user answered mostly right, then he/she is in the category "expert" or if he/she answered mostly wrong, he/she gets in the category "newbies" together with others. In that way, the users would not feel that they are the "worst patient". Even though the application was targeting everyone regardless of having the disease (the app was about awareness), the designers perceived the users as patients of the disease.

Not yet implemented social features are those discussed about getting implemented, but not at the first stage of the application's development (A and C quotes Table 2). These features were decided to get implemented later, because they were perceived as unrelated to the main focus of the applications, to the minimum viable product, or to the promised deliverable. For example, in the prostate cancer application (A), the social part was recognized and social feature suggestions (see Table 2) were made, but never implemented in the first stage, because it was perceived as unrelated to the promotion of physical activity (main target of the application as it was ordered) and the promised deliverables, and because of the lack of time and budget.

Social influence. After reviewing the collected reasoning around social influence features (Table 2), it is easy to realize that several social influence features were present (multiple times), such as social learning and social facilitation (4 times each), social comparison and competition (3 time each), and recognition (2 times). We found one sign of cooperation (H) (tied to peer pressure). However, this was from the past experience of an employee and was not applied in any of the other applications developed in the company. This makes cooperation and normative influence completely absent from the Alpha's health behavior change applications.

4.2   Factors Influencing the Decisions

Looking at the data in the bigger picture (macro level), we found that the decision making process of the designers implementing a social feature is complicated and influenced by more than one factor. These factors are presented in Fig. 1.

The first factor is **the theories**. Theories from the design field such as user-centered design have been applied in the design of the applications as methodologies that influence also the design of the social features. Users/patients were in the center of the design. Psychological theories focused on behavior change and motivation were used in the overall design of applications and also in the decisions regarding the inclusion or exclusion of a social feature: *"the self-determination theory [...] says that usually we do things because of relatedness, autonomy, mastery, and purpose. And since the first one –relatedness- builds with social aspects"*.

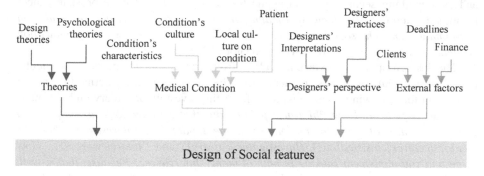

Fig. 1. Factors influencing the inclusion and design of social features

The second factor is the **medical condition**. All the interviews show that the designers perceived the users and the users' needs first and foremost based on their condition. Namely, seeing the users through the lens of the medical condition and transforming them from users to patients. One of the sub-factors in the medical condition is the *condition's characteristics*. In the interviews there were references to the stages of the condition (and how that can influence the patient), on the type of stages the condition has, or whether it has stages or it is random: *"the progression of multiple scleroses it's not linear [...].you could be completely without symptoms for 20 years, or you can [have a symptom attack] and then you [recover], or you can stay there"*. Another sub factor is the effect of the *local culture on the condition* that can have an impact on the inclusion of social features. For example, if the condition is socially unacceptable in a certain culture, then it would be tricky for the patients to share that they have the condition: *"I think that's a problem - I do not know is a global problem – [...]. In prostate cancer people are men, and one of the frequently disease... or commonality is ehh sexual problem [...] and I think that is a problem with mentality, because if I say that 'I am a patient with prostate cancer' people will say 'ok you are not completely man because you are sexual impotence' or something like that."*. Apart from the local culture's effect on the condition, *the condition itself has a culture* which may affect the inclusion of social features: *"Now the cause of the whole tendency aimed at breast cancer women survivors, men -with breast cancer- feel completely inadequate and they are completely ashamed"*. Namely, this tendency in the breast cancer community can influence the design of application in inclusion of social features, e.g., applications for female patients may have social features whereas applications for male patients may not. The last subfactor influences the design is the *patient*. The interviewees came in contact with patients, patients' families, medical professionals etc. to understand the patients who have a condition and their needs. As they base their design philosophy mainly on user-centered design, they apply different techniques to understand the patients.

The third factor influences the design and inclusion of social features is the **designer's perspective and practices**. Each designer has his/her own reflection on the theories and his/her own interpretation on the data collected from patients 'relevant studies. For example, social comparison has been perceived as gamification technique and as something secondary in an application that was to motivate prostate cancer patients to exercise: *"The focus was mainly in the physical activity and secondary on self-management. The social aspect gets into the discussion mainly as a gamification element on the physical activity"*. (Investogator's diary).

The last group is the **external factors** from the design team, such as clients' demands, financial constraints and deadlines. The influence of the external factors can be seen in the following comments taken from the investigator's diary and the interview transcripts: *"He [new PhD] also pointed out that we have to focus on physical activity, because of practical reasons (e.g., the funder was interested in that, the [senior lecturer] insisted etc.). (Investigator's diary)"* and *"Interviewer: Er... How come and you implement ranking in both of them? Interviewee: Because, that's, well, er... The client wants a similar app because it was very successful with the healthcare professionals, so they said: 'ok, we want something very very similar, keep the same structure, and we introduced this little change to tweak it for patient."*

Table 3 summaries our findings and presents in which of the applications A–J we found examples for the different categories of rationales. Applications which did not perceive the user as patient (F, I, J) are absent in the medical condition factor.

Table 3. Categories of rationales for the design of social features

Theories:	Medical condition	External factors	Designer's perspective
- Design theories: A, B, C, D, F - Behaviour change and psychological theories: A, B, C, D, E	- Medical perspective: A, B, C, D, H - Condition's culture: A, B, D - Local culture on condition : A, B, G, - Patient : A, B, C, D, E	- Clients: C, E, F - Finance: A, B - Deadlines: A, C -Collaborators: B	- Personal practice : A, B, C, H, I - Personal believes/interpretations: A, B, C, D, E, F, G, H, J

5 Discussion

Theory [3, 4], but also practice, show that social influence features are oftentimes treated as a black box. In the previous section, we shed light on this black box by presenting our results regarding the designers' rationales for the inclusion and design of social influence features in health behavior change applications. We will briefly discuss our two main findings: First, the designer's rationales for including specific social influence features, and second, the role of the medical condition.

The designers quite often did refer to social support. However, such mindset is too generic for the creation and designing of specific social influence features [3]. In fact, social influence is more than just social support, which usually is implemented just as a possibility to connect and network. This finding informs that designers should be better equipped with deeper understanding of the multifaceted nature of social influence to succeed in designing effective health behavior change technologies. Moreover, the results of this study revealed that only five (social learning, social comparison, social facilitation, competition, and recognition) out of seven social influence features were present in the designers' rationales to some extent. Thus, normative influence and cooperation were absent. By their nature, the two missing features actually are some of the most positive inclined out of the seven social influence features [3].

The literature characterize the design process as messy and difficult to describe [6]. However, understanding the practice is the main step to change or support the practice by proposing a theory, framework, or method [10]. Our findings regarding three of the four categories of designers' rationales we identified in the data – Theories and Practices, Designer's perspective, and External factors – are supported by previous research. The design practice is influenced by the theories, even though they are not followed to the letter by the practice [8, 10]. The individual characteristics of each designer (such as experience, practices, interpretations etc.) are also part of the design, as well as the constraints related to factors usually external to the design team (such as clients, funding, time limitations etc.) [6, 8, 9]. However, our study adds to previous research by identifying an additional important category in the design practices of social features in health persuasive technologies: the medical condition. In this case, the designers saw the user through the lens of a particular medical condition. They took into account the particularities of each condition (e.g., that multiple scleroses has unpredictable symptoms and the patients may feel tired most of the time). The designers took into account how the patients of this condition currently interact with each other based on the condition's culture (e.g., breast cancer patients have their communities which are mainly focused on the females). They also took into account the influence of the local culture on the condition (e.g., prostate cancer patients can be stigmatized because it is related to sexual health, and males with relevant problems are consider less of males in the local culture). Finally, the designers focus on the particular patient/user through interviews and workshops, as is the case also in the user centered design [15]. The difference is that the users are perceived through the particular lens of their condition. Thus, in the designers' vocabulary and perception "the users" become "the patients" which carry with them all the pre-referred subcategories of the medical condition.

6 Conclusion

In this paper, we studied the designers' rationales for including social features in applications supporting health behavior change. Our contribution is twofold: first, we revealed that the designers often have a limited view on social influence that may lead to less effective designs and implementations of health behavior change technologies. This finding can help practitioners (i.e., designers of health behavior change applications) in realizing the need for acquiring more refined understanding about various social influence principles that exist and can be purposefully used for designing persuasive technologies in health domain, and possibly the need of relevant design guidelines. Second, we contribute to research by showing that the medical condition plays a significant role on the design of social features together with the scientific theories, designer's interpretation, and external factors [13]. Our results can be used to underline the importance of the medical condition and its sub factors in the design practice in the field of health behavior change, and give a better understanding of the current practice for creating relevant frameworks and guidelines for better supporting the practitioners in the design of the social features [3–5, 10].

In the future, more research of practice will be needed in order to inform the theory on the design practice of social influence features in persuasive technologies [3] as it is vital to know the practice before changing the relevant theory [10].

Acknowledgments. We thank all the designers contributing to this research by sharing their experiences. This publication has received funding from the European Union's Horizon 2020 research and innovation programme - Marie Sklodowska-Curie Actions grant agreement no. 676201 - CHESS - Connected Health Early Stage Researcher Support System.

References

1. Fogg, B.J.: Creating persuasive technologies: an eight-step design process. Technology **91**, 1–6 (2009). https://doi.org/10.1145/1541948.1542005
2. Oinas-Kukkonen, H., Harjumaa, M.: Persuasive systems design: key issues, process model, and system features. Commun. Assoc. Inf. Syst. **24**, 485–500 (2009)
3. Stibe, A.: Towards a framework for socially influencing systems: meta-analysis of four PLS-SEM based studies. In: MacTavish, T., Basapur, S. (eds.) PERSUASIVE 2015. LNCS, vol. 9072, pp. 172–183. Springer, Cham (2015). https://doi.org/10.1007/978-3-319-20306-5_16
4. Oduor, M., Alahäivälä, T., Oinas-Kukkonen, H.: Persuasive software design patterns for social influence. Pers. Ubiquitous Comput. **18**, 1689–1704 (2014)
5. Mylonopoulou, V., Väyrynen, K., Isomursu, M.: Designing for behavior change - 6 dimensions of social comparison features. In: 51st Hawaii International Conference on System Sciences. IEEE (2018)
6. Nelson, H.G., Stolterman, E.: The Design Way: Intentional Change in an Unpredictable World. The MIT Press, Cambridge (2012)
7. Boland, R.J., Collopy, F.: Managing as Designing. Stanford University Press, Palo Alto (2004)
8. Zannier, C., Chiasson, M., Maurer, F.: A model of design decision making based on empirical results of interviews with software designers. Inf. Softw. Technol. **49**, 637–653 (2007)
9. Gould, J.D., Lewis, C.: Designing for usability: key principles and what designers think. Commun. ACM **28**, 300–311 (1985)
10. Stolterman, E.: How system designers think about design and methods: some reflections based on an interview study. Scand. J. Inf. Syst. **4**, 7 (1992)
11. Razzaghi, M., Ramirez Jr., R.: The influence of the designers' own culture on the design aspects of products. Eur. Acad. Des. 1–15 (2005)
12. Rosson, M.B., Maass, S., Kellogg, W.A.: Designing for designers: an analysis of design practice in the real world. In: Proceedings of SIGCHI/GI Conference on Human Factors in Computing Systems and Graphics Interface - CHI 1987, pp. 137–142 (1987)

13. Harold, G.N., Stolterman, E.: Design judgement: decision-making in the real world. Des. J 6, 21–31 (2003)
14. Goldschmidt, G., Planning, T., City, T., Rodgers, P.A.: The design thinking approaches of three different groups of designers based on self- reports. Des. Stud. 34, 454–471 (2013)
15. Norman, D.A., Draper, S.W.: User Centered System Design; New Perspectives on Human-Computer Interaction (1986)
16. Abras, C., Maloney-Krichmar, D., Preece, J.: User-centered design, p. 154 (2013)
17. Monteiro-Guerra, F., Rivera-Romero, O., Mylonopoulou, V., et al.: The design of a mobile app for promotion of physical activity and self-management in prostate cancer survivors : personas, feature ideation and low-fidelity prototyping. In: 30th IEEE International Symposium on Computer-Based Medical Systems. IEEE, Thessaloniki (2017)
18. Johnson, C.M., Johnson, T.R., Zhang, J.: A user-centered framework for redesigning health care interfaces. J. Biomed. Inform. 38, 75–87 (2005)
19. Clemensen, J., Larsen, S.B., Kyng, M., Kirkevold, M.: Participatory design in health sciences: using cooperative experimental methods in developing health services and computer technology. Qual. Health Res. 17, 122–130 (2007)
20. Aronson, E.: The Social Animal. Macmillan, New York (2003)
21. Festinger, L.: A theory of social comparison processes. Hum. Relat. 7, 117–140 (1954)
22. Buunk, B., Gibbons, F.X.: Health, Coping, and Well-Being: Perspectives from Social Comparison Theory. Routledge, London (2016)
23. Fogg, B.J.: Persuasive Technology: Using Computers to Change What We Think and Do (2003)
24. Guest, G., MacQueen, K.M., Namey, E.E.: Applied Thematic Analysis. Sage Publications, Thousand Oaks (2012)
25. Lincoln, Y.S., Guba, E.G.: Naturalistic inquiry. Sage Publications, Thousand Oaks (1985)

The Values of Self-tracking and Persuasive eCoaching According to Employees and Human Resource Advisors for a Workplace Stress Management Application: A Qualitative Study

Aniek Lentferink[1,2,3](✉) ⓘ, Louis Polstra[1] ⓘ, Martijn de Groot[2] ⓘ,
Hilbrand Oldenhuis[1] ⓘ, Hugo Velthuijsen[1] ⓘ,
and Lisette van Gemert-Pijnen[3] ⓘ

[1] Marian van Os Centre for Entrepreneurship,
Hanze University of Applied Sciences, Groningen, The Netherlands
{a.j.lentferink,l.polstra,h.k.e.oldenhuis,
h.velthuijsen}@pl.hanze.nl
[2] Quantified Self Institute, Hanze University of Applied Sciences, Groningen,
The Netherlands
ma.de.groot@pl.hanze.nl
[3] Department of Psychology, Health & Technology,
Centre for eHealth and Wellbeing Research, University of Twente,
Enschede, The Netherlands
j.vangemert-pijnen@utwente.nl

Abstract. Self-tracking and automated persuasive eCoaching combined in a smartphone application may enhance stress management among employees at an early stage. For the application to be persuasive and create impact, we need to achieve a fit between the design and end-users' and important stakeholders' values. Semi-structured interviews were conducted among 8 employees and 8 human resource advisors to identify values of self-tracking, persuasive eCoaching, and preconditions (e.g., privacy and implementation) for a stress management application, using the value proposition design by Osterwalder et al. Results suggest essential features and functionalities that the application should possess. In general, respondents see potential in combining self-tracking and persuasive eCoaching for stress management via a smartphone application. Future design of the application should mainly focus on gaining awareness about the level of stress and causes of stress. In addition, the application should possess a positive approach besides solely the focus on negative aspects of stress.

Keywords: User-centred design · eHealth · Mobile phone
Remote sensing technology · Stress Physiological · Stress Psychological
Workplace · Health promotion

© Springer International Publishing AG, part of Springer Nature 2018
J. Ham et al. (Eds.): PERSUASIVE 2018, LNCS 10809, pp. 160–171, 2018.
https://doi.org/10.1007/978-3-319-78978-1_13

1 Introduction

1.1 Stress and Employees

It is widely recognized that prolonged stress is a major burden for employees as well as for organizations and society. Stress is related to several health and wellbeing related issues, such as depression, anxiety, and cardiovascular diseases [1]. The last two decades, a trend is observed in the rise of stress risks in Europe. One of the explanations in this is the increasing use of information and communication technology [2], which resulted into a working culture characterized by increased work intensification and possibilities to work everywhere, making employees working with digital screen equipment (DSE) at risk for stress.

Many different psychological theories exist on stress among employees. Most of these theories include an overarching component: balance [3]. Being able to mobilize enough personal and social resources to overrule the demands, a positive response to stress occurs (i.e., eustress). Being unable to mobilize enough personal and social resources to overrule the demands, a negative response occurs (i.e., distress) [3, 4]. Distress might result in poor health and low performance, whereas eustress might result in good health and high performance [5].

1.2 Smartphone Stress Management Application for Prevention

The EU compass for action on mental health and well-being advocates for taking preventive measure to reduce negative responses to stress and enhance positive responses to stress [6]. However, many interventions are labour-intensive which limits the ability for all DSE employees to opt-in an intervention targeting stress at an early stage [7]. To target stress at an early stage, a smartphone stress management application that focusses on self-management might be an effective approach. Two important components for self-management via a smartphone application are self-tracking and persuasive eCoaching [8]. Self-tracking can create awareness among individuals about their current level of stress and their personal demands and resources in relation to stress. Where traditional interventions mostly gain insights into such information by means of recall [9], smartphones can capture real-time information as the smartphone is usually kept in close proximity to the user. This can result into the identification of vulnerable moments for adverse behaviour and can be used by an eCoach to send personally relevant feedback to (re)gain balance in the personal demands and resources at times when it is most needed (i.e., just-in-time suggestions [10]).

1.3 The Identification of Values for eHealth Design

We see a potential in the combination of self-tracking and persuasive eCoaching in a smartphone stress management application to target DSE employees at an early stage. However, this approach is rather new [8]. As impact and uptake of new eHealth technologies are highly dependent on the fit between design and end-users' and stakeholders' values, it is important to involve the end-users and other important stakeholders in the development process [11, 12]. Besides the identification of values for design elements, such as self-tracking and persuasive eCoaching, it is also needed to have insights into the preconditions for the design, such as privacy and implementation [12].

This study is part of an overarching project into the development of a workplace stress management application for DSE employees and builds upon results from a previously performed scoping review [8]. This scoping review identified key components for self-tracking and persuasive eCoaching in healthy lifestyle interventions. To increase the chance of creating a fit between the design and end-users' and stakeholders' values, this study aims to answer the following research question: "What are the values according to DSE employees and human resource advisors (HR advisors) for self-tracking, persuasive eCoaching, and preconditions of a workplace stress management application?".

2 Methods

2.1 Study Design

General procedure. Qualitative, semi-structured interviews [13] were conducted with 8 DSE employees and 8 HR advisors in 2017 in different organizations in the Netherlands. DSE employees and HR advisors were recruited because of their important role in the development and uptake process with DSE employees being the end-users of the design and HR advisors for having a key role in the decision-making process concerning the organizational implementation of interventions that benefit employees' vitality. In addition, HR advisors can both place emphasis on the employees' perspective and the employers' perspective.

During interviews, the value proposition design [11] was used as a basis to identify values from DSE employees and HR advisors. In addition, a persona and low-fi prototype were presented to the participants.

Value proposition design. The value proposition design is two-sided: (1) *the customer profile,* which aims at creating customer understanding, (2) *the value map,* which aims at the way the product creates value for the customer [11]. A fit between the two is believed to improve successful development and implementation of a product. The interviews were solely focused on the customer profile; creating customers understanding and identify values by mapping out *customer jobs*, *pains*, and *gains*. Customer jobs relate to the tasks users want to complete, the problems users experience, and the users' needs. Pains focus on the undesired aspects and outcomes and on expected risks and obstacles. Gains focus on the desired and expected aspects and outcomes and on expected benefits and stimulators [11].

Persona. A persona is a lively representative of possible end-users [14]. The persona was used to enable the respondent to better understand the situation of a person suffering from stress or to speak form the situation of the persona instead of their own situation, as stress is subject to stigmatization [7]. Via literature, general characteristics of DSE employees experiencing high levels of stress and general causes and symptoms of stress were identified. Then, a female and male persona were created that represented a typical DSE employee suffering from stress, respectively for male and female respondents.

Low-fi prototype. A low-fi prototype was used as experience shows that respondents often find it difficult to formulate values without them having a concrete idea of what the technology might look like [15]. A preliminary idea for the low-fi prototype was based on the results of a scoping review performed by the researchers of this study. This scoping review identified key components of self-tracking and persuasive eCoaching in eHealth design and the way the components can be best designed [8] (e.g., from the persuasive system design (PSD) model [16] (*in italic*)). In short, the *self-tracking* element was based on the Sense-IT app, a product from the University of Twente, Scelta/GGNet, VUmc, Arkin, and Pluryn [17]. Their goal is to develop a scientifically informed, ambulatory biofeedback eCoaching app that supports its users in learning to better recognize changes in emotional arousal. The Sense-IT app collects heart rate measurements as a proxy for changes in physiological arousal due to emotional events. When a significant increase in heart rate is detected and, to a certain extent, adjusted for increases in physical activity of the subject, it is presumed that the increase in heart rate is the result of emotional arousal. Myrtek and colleagues developed and tested this concept as a proxy for emotional arousal [18]. As to find out which type of emotion caused physiological arousal, two questions followed based on the circumplex model of affect [19]: (1) "Do you experience a positive or negative emotion?", (2) "How strong is the emotion you are experiencing on a scale from 1–10?". The different types of measurements can be seen in a graph (*simulation*). The eCoaching components consist of helping to find out causes of stress by combining data (*reduction*) and provision of *suggestions* to reduce stress. The suggestions were based on the coping strategies by Lazarus and Folkman: emotion-focused coping strategies and problem-focused coping strategies [4]. Additional, persuasive eCoaching components were *goal-setting* and *rewards*. Also, the user is able to *personalize* settings (e.g., to set timing and frequency of messages) and to share self-tracking data with others (*social support*). The low-fi prototype was created via balsamiq.com and resulted in a clickable prototype in a PDF-document.

2.2   Participant Selection

A systematic, non-probabilistic sampling method was applied to ensure inclusion of different types of DSE employees and HR advisors. We aimed to include an equal number of male (n = 7) and female (n = 9) participants and participants from commercial (n = 5), semi-commercial (n = 6), and non-commercial settings (n = 5). Ages ranged from 27–61. Inclusion criteria were: (1) employees needed to be open for future use of a stress management application and HR advisors needed to be open to advise a stress management application to their organization, in order to involve only potential (end-)users; (2) employees needed to perform continuous periods of DSE work for an hour or more at a time on a more or less daily basis, to be labelled a DSE employee [20].

Respondents were recruited via representatives of suitable organizations from the personal network of the research team. Potential respondents were first contacted by email providing them with initial information about the interviews. When they agreed to participate, they were contacted by telephone to provide additional information and to set a date. During one interview with an HR advisor, a company nurse was present and her comments were included in the data.

2.3   Data Collection

Semi-structured, in-depth interviews took place one-on-one by one researcher (AL) in the original work setting of the participants. After obtaining informed consent from participants, interviews were audiotaped and resulted in recordings of 42–82 min.

A topic list was used to guide the interviews. Participants were first presented with the persona. Then, they were questioned about their *perception of stress* to better understand their perspective on stress due to its complexity. The body of the interview consisted of topics from the value proposition design [11]: *customer jobs, pains,* and *gains.* Customer jobs (e.g., problems and needs) were questioned in relation to stress and stress management in general. After gaining insights into the customer jobs, the low-fi prototype was shown. Thereafter, pains and gains were questioned in relation to *self-tracking* (e.g., device and validity [8]), *persuasive eCoaching* (e.g., elements from the PSD model such as personalisation and reminders [16] and existing literature on (e)coaching methods for stress [4, 21]), and *preconditions* of a stress management application (e.g., privacy and implementation [8]). A topic of interest was also to gain insights into the level of importance of the mentioned values. A final question asked them about willingness to *using* such an intervention in the *future* for DSE employees and willingness to *advising* such an intervention to implement in the organization in the *future* for HR advisors. The topic list for HR advisors differed from the topic list for DSE employees in that HR advisors were asked to provide answers from both the employees' and employers' perspective.

2.4   Data Analysis

The transcribed interviews were rendered anonymously and uploaded in the qualitative analysis software package Atlas.ti version 8.0 (Scientific Software Development GmbH, Berlin). We analysed the data separately for DSE employees and HR advisors as the authors of the value proposition design advice to create a customer profile per stakeholder group. Initial analysis included selecting relevant fragments and coding these fragments using a coding scheme based on the topic list, which included constructs from the value proposition design [11], the earlier mentioned scoping review [8], the PSD model [16], and existing literature on (e)Coaching for stress management [4, 21]. Most fragments could be coded using the initial coding scheme. For fragments that remained, we used new codes that emerged from the data. To assess and intensively discuss the consistency of coding and reliability of the codebook, two researchers (AL and LP) independently coded 2 interviews (one from a DSE employee and one from an HR advisor). This resulted in minor adjustments in the interpretation of certain codes.

After several rounds of coding, values were extracted per code. Values emerged that could be organized under the main themes *self-tracking, persuasive eCoaching, preconditions*, *awareness*, and *future use*. Subthemes were created by means of the most significant values under the main themes considering the level of importance mentioned by respondents. Further analysis focused on searching for defiant cases and searching for relations between what has been said.

3 Results

3.1 Self-tracking

Self-tracking of stress. Self-tracking of both physical reactions to stress (e.g., heart rate) and psychological reactions to stress (e.g., perceived emotions) is seen as helpful for creating awareness about stress. Respondents especially perceived it useful to become aware of variables that they could hardly make an estimation about when recalling results on the variable, such as sleep or emotions. Although some respondents doubted if users need a wearable device to create awareness about stress. Another DSE employee elaborated on the added value of measuring physical stress factors: "Well, I would find it interesting, because I believe that you could signal the physical discomfort earlier than the mental discomfort. [..] So actually a sort of signal function would seem quite interesting to me" (DSE employee #8).

Both groups, especially female respondents, liked the idea of tracking positive emotions due to increases in heart rate besides negative emotions to effectuate a positive approach. In addition, the focus on solely negative emotions was expected to be a burden for use. Also, a few DSE employees mentioned that they liked the idea of receiving biofeedback after an exercise to see if their physiological reactions to stress are diminished. In addition, DSE employees and an HR advisor believed that having objective measurements about stress may encourage to start a conversation with the employer about stress. "Maybe it can help for an employer to see that it are not just complaints of the employee but that there is an actual problem. I hope that it will start a dialogue between employer and employee [..]" (DSE employee #5).

Self-tracking the causes of stress. Respondents saw the potential in combining different types of data (e.g., sleep, physical activity, connection with the planning) in order for the system to provide suggestions on possible causes of stress. Although most DSE employees believed that they are able to observe patterns themselves, they also believe that self-tracking of causes could help them in this process. Especially respondents who were more focused on the possibilities of the technology, instead of the challenges, saw the potential in discovering causes by collecting more personal data. Respondents' opinions differed about the expected openness of DSE employees to collect more personal data due to privacy concerns. This is described in more detail below. In addition, some respondents had mixed feelings about the effectiveness of the system to suggest causes based on self-tracking data as stress is complex or the system's analysis may lead to false conclusions.

The validity of the measurements. DSE Employees and HR advisors believed that the poor validity of physical stress measurements negatively affect usage. Though, some margin of error is accepted by most employees. Of special importance according to employees and HR advisors was to provide proper information about what the user can expect from the validity when measuring stress.

Although respondents saw the validity as a barrier to use, some believed that inaccurate measurements might still have added value for the user as it still creates a moment of reflection, even when the increase in heart rate is not the result of stress.

3.2   Persuasive eCoaching

Guidance. After obtaining insights into the level and stress and causes of stress via self-tracking, some HR advisors believed employees are able to take the first steps by themselves. They believed that awareness stimulates action, i.e. to actually do something about stress. Other HR advisors believed that some form of guidance is necessary to effectively do something about stress. The form of guidance may be automated eCoaching via the application whereas others expect that a human coach is needed due to the complexity of stress. An advantage that was appointed for automated eCoaching was that the application could be consulted anonymously. It was expected that some employees might experience a burden to take actions on stress due to feelings of failure.

The tasks for the eCoach were mostly seen in the provision of guidance throughout the awareness process and the provision of short and practical suggestions. An important step in the awareness process was to, together with the eCoach, reflect on the moments of stress experienced to better understand their own situation. "It goes on and on, so it would be appropriate to build in time for reflection. Just to stand still with what I was up to the past few hours and what effect did that have on me? Also to find out what you could do differently in the future. [...] I think that this could have a substantial effect on the reduction of work-related stress" (DSE employee #5). Some employees said that the eCoach could help them throughout this process by asking open and reflective questions.

Timing and frequency of messages. Opinions of respondents on the appropriate timing and frequency of messages was depended upon the type of message: (1) messages for self-tracking or (2) messages to perform exercises or reflection. According to some employees, it is acceptable to respond to simple questions for self-tracking during the stress moment (e.g., when the heart rate is increased) that will cost as much time as checking new messages on the smartphone. DSE employees and HR advisors expected both negative and positive effects of providing messages in the stress moment based on self-tracking data. Negative effects were that providing a message in the stress moment might lead to annoyance and it might distract users from work. A positive effect was that sending a message during the stress moment was perceived as essential for creating awareness. In addition, respondents expected positive effects for the validity of measurements as there are no recall problems. Older respondents (46–65 years) were more positive about sending a message during the stress moment than younger respondents (25–45 years).

Asking to perform reflection or an exercise may cost more effort and might, therefore, be less appropriate during the stress moment. One HR advisor expected users to be incapable of performing reflection during the stress moment as stress narrows your mind. "Reflection asks time and space, but there is no time and space because stress narrows. So there is no point in sending a message in my opinion" (HR advisor #8).

Natural breaks during the day are often mentioned as convenient times for sending messages, such as at the end of the morning, end of the afternoon, or evening. Especially a moment of reflection seemed appropriate during these moments.

Opinions differed between respondents about users having the ability to adjust when to receive messages or to mute the system. Being able to choose settings increases feelings of control over the system, which was found important for usability. In contrast, some employees mentioned that it may not be ideal to set messages on personally chosen moments as it interferes with the awareness function of the system. In the past, a light obtrusive form (e.g., not with sound but lights) of sending messages was experienced as somewhat annoying but effective for behaviour change.

Goals and rewards. DSE employees and HR advisors had different opinions about the usefulness of setting goals and receiving rewards in relation to stress. Some believed that goals and rewards can increase motivation to change behaviour, which was more often mentioned by male respondents. One HR advisors and one employee saw the goal setting feature as an essential element: "If you do not know where to go, you will not get there of course" (HR advisor #7). Other respondents mentioned that it seems strange to motivate people to reduce stress by setting goals and providing rewards as is it is not fully in their ability to control the stress reactions. In addition, a few HR advisors mentioned that it is preferable to set a goal in the form of a personal value (e.g., I want to take a break every day).

3.3   Awareness

Awareness emerged to be a desired value for stress management. Before the low-fi prototype was shown, respondents mentioned that a first necessity for effective stress management is to obtain awareness about the employee's stress level and causes of stress. "Everything starts or coincides with some degree of awareness. As long as you do not have that, you keep on going" (HR advisor #6). Both groups believed that creating awareness should be the main focus of the intervention and believed that this is an achievable goal for a stress management application using self-tracking and persuasive eCoaching. "I think that it would be mostly a tool for the employee himself. As to find out 'hey' what are my moments of stress, how is that so, and during which moments do I suffer from stress, in order to obtain insights into the patterns" (HR advisor #7).

3.4   Preconditions

Privacy. Respondents had differing expectations about privacy concerns for the collection of additional personal data. Some employees expected no issues as the collection of personal data already happens on a large scale via the internet or smartphones. Others believed that not all employees would feel comfortable to collect more personal data. Also, some types of data are expected to raise more privacy concerns (e.g., location) than other types of data.

Respondents' opinions differed about the willingness of sharing data with others. Half of the respondents felt that the application would be something for the user self, which was more often perceived in this way by female respondents. Sharing of data with others is something that they only want to do on a voluntary basis. Furthermore, it is seen as helpful by some and dubious by others when the organization has access to the data on an aggregated level.

Some respondents believed that it might withhold potential users to use the system due to privacy concerns. According to HR advisors, conditions concerning privacy that should be met were to inform intensively about data security, the user should agree with conditions, and data may not be deduced by others at the individual level. According to employees, conditions concerning privacy were that they want to have control over who has insights into their data and what kind of data the system is allowed to collect.

Implementation and embedding. A negative atmosphere in the organization to do something about stress was perceived as a burden for successful implementation. Respondents believed that starting the implementation with a pilot to collect and represent first positive reactions might lead to quick adoption throughout the organization.

According to HR advisors, it is important to have a clear vision about how the application would fit into the health and safety policy of the organization. "I think that you should carefully look into why would you implement it? What is the goal of this in the overall plan? How do we want to deal with employability and how can we support employees in this? I think you need a good story about this, a proper vision [..]" (HR advisor #3).

Respondents believed that the application should not be stand-alone but should be part of a complete programme. With some employees, especially older employees, seeing potential in a broader application that also focuses on other health aspects relevant for the employee. Other employees and HR advisors said this in relation to embedding the application in a total programme of measures for improving employees' vitality in the organization, with the app being one step in the total programme.

3.5 Future Use

All DSE employees were willing to use such an application in the future, or at least try the intervention. Most HR advisors hesitate whether to advise the design to their organization although nobody refused the idea. The most mentioned argumentation for hesitation was that the intervention should be part of a whole and the design should be further developed before making a final call.

4 Discussion and Conclusion

In this study, we identified values related to self-tracking, persuasive eCoaching, and preconditions to inform future development of a workplace stress management application for DSE employees. In general, DSE employees and HR advisors see potential in a stress management app combining self-tracking and persuasive eCoaching.

Respondents mention that an initial need for stress management is to obtain awareness about the stress level and causes of stress and believe that the application could play a part in the process of gaining awareness. Earlier research also emphasizes that self-tracking using wearables can create awareness [8]. However, Patel et al. argue that more is needed [22]. Self-tracking is only one of the persuasive strategies that can be deployed for health behaviour change [16]. Other strategies can be offered via persuasive (e)Coaching, such as personalized suggestions for behaviour change [16], and may be necessary to bridge the gap between awareness and real behaviour change.

Specifically for the eCoach, respondents see potential in receiving guidance throughout the awareness process via reflection on moments of stress. In relation to technologies for behaviour change, reflection is one of the stages in the model of personal informatics systems and precedes the action stage for behaviour change [23]. This model indicates that reflection is necessary to activate the participants.

Furthermore, it is important during design and implementation to emphasize expected gains whereas avoiding pains [11]. First, the future design should include tracking of positive emotions to avoid the risk of setting the focus too much on negative emotions. In addition, focusing both on positive and negative emotions can help (re)gaining balance in personal demands and resources. Positive emotions can be seen as a resource. From the positive psychology theory, setting the focus on positive emotions increases resilience in moments when negative emotions are experienced [24]. In addition, collecting and reminding the user real-time about negative emotions enables the provision of just-in-time suggestions [10]. Just-in-time suggestions increase the resources of a DSE employee to deal with negative emotions at an early stage when it is most needed. Second, another important aspect mentioned was appropriate timing and frequency of sending messages to the users. Discrepancies exist among respondents for sending messages during the stress moment. Positive expectations are creating a moment of awareness of the experienced emotions and negative expectations are annoyance and distraction from work. Future research could focus on finding the appropriate balance for timing and frequency of sending messages. Third, respondents in this study consider it important, but not a prerequisite, that the design entails a proper validity and data safety of collected data about stress. Respondents want to be informed extensively about what to expect from the design on these aspects. According to the expectations-confirmation model, users will form their level of satisfaction with a product based on their prior expectations and the extent to which these expectations are met [25]. By communicating to the user what they can expect from the design with respect to validity and privacy, it may be less likely that they will be disappointed [25]. Also, the persuasive power of the system could be enhanced by providing trustworthy and unbiased information about these aspects [16]. Furthermore, it might be worthwhile to further study the necessity of validity in light of relevance of the data for the user. This study found that self-tracking of physical measures of stress might still have added value although the physical measures do not always reflect a moment of stress. Fourth, as the culture within the organization towards stress management is of importance for the adoption of use, a positive approach for implementation should be deployed and should focus not just on individuals but on the organization as a whole.

Identification of values before actual design is advocated by many to be important for successful eHealth design [11, 12, 15]. However, it should be kept in mind that our findings are in reference to expectations based on a low-fi prototype shown during the interviews. These expectations might not reflect values based on user experience.

We conclude that DSE employees and HR advisors see potential in combining self-tracking and persuasive eCoaching for stress management via a smartphone application. Future design of the application should mainly focus on gaining awareness about positive and negative emotions and personal demands and resources in order to (re)gain balance.

Acknowledgements. This study is partly funded by Menzis. Menzis had no involvement in the study's design, execution, or reporting. We would like to thank all respondents who participated in this study.

References

1. Brosschot, J.F., Gerin, W., Thayer, J.F.: The perseverative cognition hypothesis: a review of worry, prolonged stress-related physiological activation, and health. J. Psychosom. Res. **60** (2), 113–124 (2006). https://doi.org/10.1016/j.jpsychores.2005.06.074
2. Milczarek, M., Brun, E., Houtman, I., et al.: Expert Forecast on Emerging Psychosocial Risks Related to Occupational Safety and Health. European Agency for Safety and Health at Work, Luxembourg (2007)
3. De Jonge, J., Le Blanc, P., Schaufeli, W.: Theoretische modellen over werkstress. In: Schaufeli, W., Bakker, A.B. (eds.) De psychologie van arbeid en gezondheid, 3rd edn, pp. 23–45. Bohn Stafleu van Loghum, Houten (2013). (in Dutch)
4. Lazarus, R.S., Folkman, S.: Transactional theory and research on emotions and coping. Eur. J. Pers. **1**(3), 141–169 (1987)
5. Nelson, D.L., Simmons, B.L.: Health psychology and work stress: a more positive approach. In: Quick, J.C.E., Tetrick, L.E. (eds.) Handbook of Occupational Health Psychology, pp. 97–119. American Psychological Association, Washington (2003). https://doi.org/10.1037/10474-000
6. Cuijpers, P., Shields-Zeeman, L., Walters, B.H., et al.: Prevention of depression and promotion of resilience – consensus paper. The European Commission (2016)
7. Ebert, D.D., Heber, E., Berking, M., et al.: Self-guided internet-based and mobile-based stress management for employees: results of a randomised controlled trial. Occup. Environ. Med. **73**(5), 315–323 (2016). https://doi.org/10.1136/oemed-2015-103269
8. Lentferink, A.J., Oldenhuis, H.K.E., De Groot, M., et al.: Key components in eHealth interventions combining self-tracking and persuasive eCoaching to promote a healthier lifestyle: a scoping review. J Med. Internet Res. **19**(8), e277 (2017). https://doi.org/10.2196/jmir.7288
9. Shiffman, S., Stone, A.A., Hufford, M.R.: Ecological momentary assessment. Annu. Rev. Clin. Psychol. **4**, 1–32 (2008). https://doi.org/10.1146/annurev.clinpsy.3.022806.091415
10. Nahum-Shani, I., Hekler, E.B., Spruijt-Metz, D.: Building health behavior models to guide the development of just-in-time adaptive interventions: a pragmatic framework. Health Psychol. **34**(S), 1209–1219 (2015). https://doi.org/10.1037/hea0000306
11. Osterwalder, A., Pigneur, Y., Bernarda, G., et al.: Value Proposition Design: How to Create Products and Services Customers Want, 1st edn. Wiley, Hoboken (2014)
12. Van Gemert-Pijnen, J.E.W.C., Nijland, N., Van Limburg, M., et al.: A holistic framework to improve the uptake and impact of eHealth technologies. J. Med. Internet Res. **13**(4), e111 (2011). https://doi.org/10.2196/jmir.1672

13. Flick, U.: An Introduction to Qualitative Research, 5th edn. Sage, Thousand Oaks (2014)
14. LeRouge, C., Ma, J., Sneha, S., et al.: User profiles and personas in the design and development of consumer health technologies. Int. J. Med. Inform. **82**(11), e251–e268 (2013). https://doi.org/10.1016/j.ijmedinf.2011.03.006
15. Van Limburg, M., Wentzel, J., Sanderman, R., et al.: Business modeling to implement an eHealth portal for infection control: a reflection on co-creation with stakeholders. JMIR Res. Protoc. **4**(3), e104 (2015). https://doi.org/10.2196/resprot.4519
16. Oinas-Kukkonen, H., Harjumaa, M.: Persuasive systems design: key issues, process model, and system features. Commun. Assoc. Inf. Syst. **24**(1), 485–500 (2009)
17. Derks, Y.P., Visser, T.D., Bohlmeijer, E.T., et al.: mHealth in Mental Health: how to efficiently and scientifically create an ambulatory biofeedback e-coaching app for patients with borderline personality disorder. Int. J. Hum. Fact. Ergon. **5**(1), 61–92 (2017). https://doi.org/10.1504/IJHFE.2017.088418
18. Myrtek, M., Aschenbrenner, E., Brügner, G.: Emotions in everyday life: an ambulatory monitoring study with female students. Biol. Psychol. **68**(3), 237–255 (2005). https://doi.org/10.1016/j.biopsycho.2004.06.001
19. Posner, J., Russell, J.A., Peterson, B.S.: The circumplex model of affect: an integrative approach to affective neuroscience, cognitive development, and psychopathology. Dev. Psychopathol. **17**(3), 715–734 (2005). https://doi.org/10.1017/S0954579405050340
20. Executive HaS: Work with Display Screen Equipment. HSE Books, Sudbury (2003) http://www.hse.gov.uk/pubns/books/l26.htm. Cited 7 July 2017
21. Richardson, K.M., Rothstein, H.R.: Effects of occupational stress management intervention programs: a meta-analysis. J. Occup. Health Psychol. **13**(1), 69–93 (2008). https://doi.org/10.1037/1076-8998.13.1.69
22. Patel, M.S., Asch, D.A., Volpp, K.G.: Wearable devices as facilitators, not drivers, of health behavior change. JAMA **313**(5), 459–460 (2015). https://doi.org/10.1001/jama.2014.14781
23. Li, I., Dey, A., Forlizzi, J.: A stage-based model of personal informatics systems. In: Proceedings of SIGCHI Conference on Human Factors in Computing Systems - CHI 2010, pp. 557–566. ACM, New York (2010). https://doi.org/10.1145/1753326.1753409
24. Seligman, M.E., Csikszentmihalyi, M.: Positive psychology: an introduction. In: Csikszentmihalyi, M. (ed.) Flow and the Foundations of Positive Psychology, pp. 279–298. Springer, Dordrecht (2014). https://doi.org/10.1007/978-94-017-9088-8_18
25. Oliver, R.L.: A cognitive model of the antecedents and consequences of satisfaction decisions. J. Mark. Res. **17**(4), 460–469 (1980)

Participatory Design of a Persuasive Mobile Application for Helping Entrepreneurs to Recover from Work

Markku Kekkonen[1]([⊠]), Harri Oinas-Kukkonen[1], Piiastiina Tikka[1],
Janne Jaako[1], Anna-Mari Simunaniemi[2], and Matti Muhos[2]

[1] Faculty of Information Technology and Electrical Engineering,
Oulu Advanced Research on Service and Information Systems,
University of Oulu, 90570 Oulu, Finland
{markku.kekkonen, harri.oinas-kukkonen,
piiastiina.tikka, janne.jaako}@oulu.fi
[2] Micro-Entrepreneurship Research Group (MicroENTRE),
Kerttu Saalasti Institute, University of Oulu, Pajatie 5, 85500 Nivala, Finland
{anna-mari.simunaniemi, matti.muhos}@oulu.fi

Abstract. Involving end-users in a participatory design process may help researchers and developers to gain better understanding of the end users' views about the target system. In this study, we utilized participatory design approach with focus group meetings and participatory design workshops to figure out requirements for persuasive features of a mobile application for entrepreneurs to recover from work related strain and stress. In many cases, end-user participation in the design process may lead into building more efficient persuasive technology solutions and at least avoidance of many of the design pitfalls, but setting up meetings and organizing workshops can be time-consuming.

Keywords: Persuasive Systems Design · PSD · Focus groups
Participatory design · Inspiration cards · Micro-entrepreneurs
Recovery from work · Mobile app

1 Introduction

Web-based health promotion can be very effective for health behavior interventions [1] and at times being much better than printed material for problem domains such as dietary practices [2]. Mobile applications can reach people for large-scale population level interventions similarly to web-based approaches, but with seemingly better adherence rates [3]. For health interventions, smartphone technology also offers sensors such as accelerometers for health problem measurement [4] and internal applications such as sound measurement for occupational noise [5].

We as a persuasive systems development team worked as a part of a research consortium that was trying to make a difference with evidence-based health promotion for micro-entrepreneurs. Our aim was to build a mobile behavior change support system [6] based on Persuasive Systems Design model [7] targeting micro-entrepreneurs' health behavior change as regards recovery from work. Because of the assumption of the

© Springer International Publishing AG, part of Springer Nature 2018
J. Ham et al. (Eds.): PERSUASIVE 2018, LNCS 10809, pp. 172–183, 2018.
https://doi.org/10.1007/978-3-319-78978-1_14

heterogeneous nature of micro-entrepreneurs, our end-user representatives, we decided to involve them in the participatory design process. We sought out for valuable insights from the entrepreneurs via focus group meetings and participatory design workshops in order to develop the target system. Our research question for this paper is the following: What persuasive system features for a mobile application do end-users view as valuable within the health problem domain at hand?

2 Work-Life Balance of Micro-entrepreneurs

In the European Union, microenterprise is defined as an enterprise which employs fewer than 10 persons and whose annual turnover and/or annual balance sheet total does not exceed EUR 2 million [8]. 93% of all companies in the EU-28 countries are microenterprises [9]. Their importance for European economies is notable as microenterprises accounted for 30% of employment and 37% of the growth in total employment in 2015 [10]. However, as entrepreneurs are personally responsible for the success and survival of their firms, work tends to dominate entrepreneurs' lives. A clear division between work and family or social lives is often lacking [11]. Thus, entrepreneurship is often stressful and demanding with lots of financial and other kinds of stress. In spite of this, entrepreneurs in general are still satisfied with their work or, in other words, entrepreneurs seem to be energized and fatigued at the same time [11]. Entrepreneurs can achieve an important competitive advantage over their competitors if they can learn to deal effectively with job demands and work-related strain [12].

Owing to the size of the companies, microenterprises by nature have limited human resources: from self-employed to only a few employees in size, there is little opportunity for delegating work during illness or holiday time. Micro-entrepreneurs tend to take fewer sick days [13] and fewer holidays than people employed by others [14]. Factors both at work and outside of work influence recovery. For example how work is organized, what are the requirements and demands, available resources and a person's ability to commit to work are all factors in work that affect recovery; Outside of work factors such as age, family, amount and quality of free time, and amount and quality of sleep affect recovery from work [15]. Sufficient recovery from work is a key factor in anyone's work ability and quality of life [16]. Different types of recovery experiences, namely psychological detachment, relaxation, high control and mastery during off time from work are beneficial [17].

3 Persuasive Design of Mobile Applications

Persuasive Systems Design (PSD) is a framework for designing and evaluating persuasive software solutions, offering a set of postulates to describe the core characteristics of persuasive systems, ways to analyze the persuasion context, and design principles for persuasive system content and functionality [7]. Persuasive systems enable affecting end-users' behavior even in situations where their attitude is not favorable towards the behavior, as attitudes do not necessarily predict or determine behavior. The end-users may know the proper behaviors or may have the right attitudes, but may not act according to them. Understanding the goal of the end-users is important, including past performance and current progress. When considering persuasion, the message and the route direct and/or indirect should be defined or analyzed. In the PSD model, there are four categories of persuasive system principles: primary task support e.g. self-monitoring tools, dialogue support e.g. reminders, system credibility support e.g. third-party endorsements, and social support e.g. social comparison. [7]

In our study, we were developing a health behavior change support system [6] for helping micro-entrepreneurs to recover from work. The team had previously worked on a web information system targeting obesity and weight loss with preventing metabolic syndrome at the core [18], whereas the Android-based mobile application here was targeting several health problem domains such as stress and nutrition with recovery from work at the core.

4 Study Setting

Involving end-users, or their representatives, in the participatory design process can potentially lead to effective persuasive technologies [19]. In doing so, the user involvement needs to be structured, facilitated and interpreted accordingly for true enhancement of a target system to be possible, as one can easily be overly fascinated to the extent that results become superficial or one is lead astray by the end-user views [20].

In order to learn which persuasive system features end-users view as valuable, we organized exploratory focus groups [21] and arranged participatory design workshops [19, 20, 22]. See Fig. 1. Additionally, we also wanted the whole research consortium to be involved in the design process of the mobile application. Three focus group (FG) meetings with the end-user representatives were organized before moving into arranging three participatory design (PD) workshops. Obtaining feedback from the end-user representatives in exploratory FGs may help improve the design of the target system incrementally and rapidly [21]. With the help of the exploratory FG meetings based on paper prototypes, we implemented rapid iteration cycles. The iteration cycles also helped us to refine the semi-structured questions for the second and third exploratory FG meetings, and we were able to present smartphone versions of the target system mockup in the PD workshops.

We arranged the first and second PD workshops in a more conventional participatory design manner, whereas the third PD workshop was arranged as an inspiration card

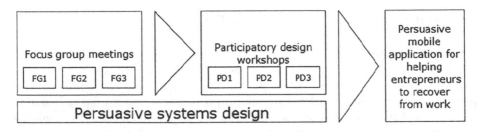

Fig. 1. Persuasive systems design process in our case.

workshop, following the example of Davis [19]. Two categories of inspiration cards were utilized: Technology cards that represent a specific application of technology with a description, and domain cards that represent the information of domains [22].

4.1 Study Participants

The end-user representatives were contacted through the micro-entrepreneurship research group, who sent an invitation for groups of micro-entrepreneurs who had previously attended their networking and peer support meetings. The topics and health problem domains of our FG meetings and PD workshops were advertised for the micro-entrepreneurs, who then decided whether they wanted to participate or not. Each of the first four meetings and workshops took place in a local company and the end-user representatives came from nearby areas. The average distance to the local companies was 68 km from the university.

The entire research consortium was involved in the development process through three-week iteration cycles. A total of 19 end-user representatives participated in the focus group meetings (FG1 = 9, FG2 = 4, FG3 = 6). We did not explicitly inquire the participants' line of businesses in the exploratory FGs, but the following enterprises rose up during discussions: web design, car part dealership, cleaning, video editing, studio work, digger operating, and web application design.

A total of 20 people participated in the participatory design workshops (PD1 = 5, PD2 = 9, PD3 = 6). We asked the participants of the first PD workshop to fill in their basic personal data information. The participants' ages differed from 29 to 63 and the level of education from elementary school to university (Ph.D.). The participants reported photography, research, gym and massage, kindergarten and arts, clocks and jewelry as their line of business with an average of 16 years of experience as entrepreneurs (variation from 6 to 31 years).

The participants of the second workshop consisted of the research consortium (9 researchers), which included research assistants, doctoral students, post-doctoral researchers, principal investigators and professors. All participants had an academic degree, ranging from bachelor's degree to Ph.D.

For the third workshop, the participants were again end-user representatives. The participants' ages differed from 30 to 51 and the level of education from vocational training/school to university (Master's degree). The participants reported financial administration and accounting, arts and wellness, real estate agency, wellness, video services as their line of business with an average of 6 years of experience as entrepreneurs (variation from less than a year to 17 years).

All end-users participated in only one meeting or workshop, with the exception of PD3, which had two participants from FG3. Therefore, we had a total of 37 individuals to participate in the process, including 28 individual end-user representatives in the FG meetings and PD workshops. No monetary fee was paid for the participants, but they gained a small tax-free kilometer-based allowance for travel costs.

4.2 Focus Group Meetings

The working agenda of the explorative FGs consisted of semi-structured questions prepared together with the research consortium. Discussion and end-user representatives' opinions or ideas about the usage of persuasive system features followed the questions. We presented mockup versions of the target system in all the meetings. We extracted the data from observer notes and audio files.

In FG1, the end-user representatives expressed their opinions of paper mockups presented. The issues tackled included the use of a slide bar versus typing for inputting numerical feedback, user's personal selection of a goal versus having the system set a goal, and receiving feedback with or without *social comparison*. Also the questions whether to give *praise* with or without *rewards* and if with rewards what type of rewards (trophy icon with or without rich graphic details) were addressed.

In FG2, we brought up the issue of using praise, reward or a combination of both. The participants were also shown icons ('trophy', 'checkmark', 'medal', 'smiley', 'thumps up') of which they could choose their preferred ones. We asked the participants about their preferences for the frequency of reminders (push notifications) and willingness to input feedback through self-monitoring tools.

As for FG3, we asked the participants whether we should consider some kind of *normative influence* function or not and what would be suitable factors as points for social comparison. We also inquired the user preferences for reminders and sought additional ideas for tools for self-monitoring and preferred usage frequency for these tools and reminders.

4.3 Participatory Design Workshops

In PD1, we gave the participants an assignment to sketch an additional feature into the mobile application: to design a way for the users to *cooperate* for recovering from work by exercising e.g. jogging. For inspiration, we showed them our prototype version available at that moment. We then divided them into two teams and handed out sticky notes, color pencils and A1 size papers. Both teams sketched a rough model of their perception of the given assignment. The second task was to draw a mind-map of issues they would associate with recovery from work, physically straining work and cooperation.

PD2 did not involve end-user representatives, but the research consortium. Researchers were split into four teams and they were given blank papers, sticky notes and color pencils while tasked to generate ideas about tools for self-monitoring.

PD3 was implemented as inspiration card workshop [19, 22]. We divided the participants into two teams and handed out the card decks. One side of a card gave the name of a PSD principle or health problem domain (sleep, stress, nutrition, sedentary work, recovery from work, physically straining work, working hours efficiency), and the other side had a brief explanation. We instructed them to proceed by choosing one health problem domain and to discuss which PSD principles would be suitable for the domain. Occasionally we had to remind the end-user representatives to read the brief explanations from the backside of the cards. We also encouraged them to discuss the relevance of all the cards placed around a health problem domain. Occasionally the end-user representatives removed cards after a discussion. When necessary, we gave either examples or details about the PSD principles. For collecting data, we photographed all card sets from both teams.

4.4   Target System Mockups

The first version of the target system mockup presented in FG1 was a crude paper prototype, containing simplified examples about the functions, tasks and feedback. The paper prototype had two options for each presented persuasive feature e.g. goal setting (choosing the goal versus having the goal set by the system). We discussed the collected data with the research consortium and the discussions guided the next iteration of the target system mockup. The process remained similar during the three-week cycles. We made a second version by using PowerPoint, which allowed participants in FG2 to navigate inside the mockup with 'hyperlinks' in the slides, which imitated target system functionalities e.g. pressing a radio button changed slide. The mockup in FG3 had an upgraded graphical layout. Fourth version of the target system mockup was made with Android Studio for PD1. From this point onwards, we presented a crude demo version of the target system in PD2 and PD3.

4.5   Study Setting and Timeline

The three meetings and the first workshop followed a three-week cycle timeline (from March to May 2017). In the first week of each cycle, the development team held design meetings. The planned participatory design materials for participants were presented for the research consortium in the following week. The third week of each cycle consisted of us traveling to meet the end-user representatives. See Fig. 2.

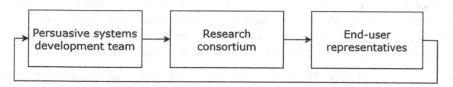

Fig. 2. Three week-cycle of the design process between three parties involved.

The second workshop took place at June at the university campus, right after the first one. The results of the previous research steps were discussed and a participatory design workshop with the researchers was held. The third workshop was arranged at September in the premises of a shopping center, during a two-day event for entrepreneurs. We invited the end-user representatives to join our workshop as a warm-up to the main event.

A small number of other interested parties (researchers or colleagues of end-user representatives) were present in the meetings and workshops, with the exception of PD2, which was only for the research consortium. However, we carefully instructed that only end-user representatives could comment verbally on the issues presented. The end-user representatives formed their own teams consisting solely of micro-entrepreneurs, and the additional participants present at meetings and workshops had their own teams. The contribution of the additional participants was explicitly marked, for example by giving pencils of different colors, and excluded from the final data analyzed.

4.6   Data Gathering

We sought out to gather data, both qualitative and quantitative, from the focus group meetings and participatory design workshops. On the one hand, we expected that qualitative data in the form of ideas, opinions and preferences would help us to understand our target group. On the other hand, we expected that quantitative data would help us to reach decisions about which PSD principles we should implement into the target system.

We had at least one moderator or facilitator per team and at least one observer making notes present in all the meetings and workshops. We recorded all the workshops and meetings that involved end-user representatives. The audio files were helpful for backfilling observer notes.

5   Results

In our study, we received valuable data about persuasive system features and their categories as well as subareas of health and well-being.

5.1   Persuasive System Features

As *goal setting* is a core element of PSD, we sought to learn about the end-user representatives' views about goal setting in FG1. Seven participants wanted to choose their own goal and two wanted a goal chosen for them by the system. All participants in the FG meetings expressed their opinions quickly and with no hesitation.

Primary task support. The participants expressed their willingness to monitor self-perceived recovery from work by regularly answering timed inquiries. They also ended-up discussing ideas about *self-monitoring tools* independently (in FG2 and FG3), and came up with ideas such as linking heart rate monitoring and a health diary with the application. The concept of brainstorming self-monitoring tools was the core of PD2 (Table 1). Some of the ideas presented at PD2 were actually *reminders* rather than self-monitoring tools (and therefore did not qualify as ones), e.g. alarms that inform the users to go to sleep or push notifications that remind the users to eat at appropriate times.

In PD3, we also gave end-user representatives a quick chance to brainstorm ideas about self-monitoring tools. They came up with two categories: giving input for self-perceived situation e.g. stress can be associated with different colors or different animal icons; different sensors or external devices for detecting health problems e.g. blood pressure monitor, decibel measurement, muscle tightness measurement et cetera.

Table 1. Self-monitoring tool ideas from PD2

Tools for self-monitoring	Health problem domain
Input for reflecting sleep (quality and quantity)	Sleep
A sensor for measuring sleep quality (rolling around in bed)	Sleep
Input for describing stressful situations (when and why)	Stress
Photos of meals and a diary (what and when)	Nutrition
Input for answering questions about recovery from work	Recovery from work
A sensor for detecting user stillness	Physically straining work
Input for dividing the hours between actions during the day	Working hours efficiency
Diary and/or calendar (time used and for what)	Working hours efficiency

Dialogue support. The participants in FG2 and FG3 came up with the same average number for *reminders*, three per week, and thought that more than four weekly reminders would be irritating. Some of the participants also commented that if they had a busy or stressful week, having to deal with reminders might be irritating, even if there was less than three per week. Both groups preferred an option to set the time and day of the reminders themselves. In overall, the end-user representatives thought that reminders can be helpful, but they would have to be relevant. For example, a timed reminder that informs the user about coffee breaks was considered useful. Another example was a reminder for an external wearable activity tracker connected to a mobile application, which would remind the user to start exercising e.g. go to a walk.

As for the PSD principles of *praise* and *reward*, we wanted to know if the participants in the exploratory FGs would prefer both or just one of them (and which one). The participants preferred praise as a standalone feature, whereas reward or a combination of both were not preferred. The participants commented that trophies, medals and other similar virtual reward icons could be associated with competition, which they would like to avoid in mobile applications meant to relieve stress (health problem domain presented in FG1 and FG2). Because of the comments from FG1, we presented different images of virtual reward icons in FG2. Three out of four participants deemed the 'thumps up' icon as encouraging and positive therefore being best from the presented options. The end-user representatives did not prefer 'trophy' and 'checkmark' icons, whereas they thought that 'medal' and 'smiley' icons are moderately good as virtual rewards.

Social support. We brought up *social comparison* in all the focus group meetings. Most participants liked the idea of social comparison and came up with such factors as age, gender and geographical area as comparison points. Interestingly enough, they thought that line of businesses might not be a suitable factor for social comparison because of the heterogeneous nature of micro-entrepreneurs. Additionally one team of participants in PD1 ended up ideating about the possibility of having a geographical social comparison function in a mobile application. As for *normative influence*, the participants in FG3 thought that it was a good idea, but did not discuss it in detail.

Interestingly, the FG participants came up with some system feature ideas occasionally even without prior discussion. *Cooperation* was one of the persuasive features that arouse in the free form discussions during the exploratory FG meetings. We did not introduce cooperation in the focus groups, but as the participants brought it up by themselves, we decided to have cooperation as a theme for PD1. We asked the end-user representatives to design ideas about cooperation for recovering from work through exercising e.g. jogging. The ideas were two different matchmaking functionalities that enabled cooperation between different micro-entrepreneurs. The user could choose a geographical area and sport e.g. tennis, after which the application would suggest someone interested in the same sport from the same area; the application would support gathering a group of people and the user could choose to join the group. The participants also came up with ideas of relaxing exercises and small exercising acts of everyday life e.g. walking the dog or going to swimming together with a colleague.

5.2 Subareas of Health and Well-Being

We presented seven health problem domains (domain cards) and twenty-eight PSD principles (technology cards) for the participants in PD3. The participants proceeded by picking one domain card and discussing which technology cards to place next to the domain card. After the participants were finished discussing and had placed the cards, we photographed the result and the participants were free to pick the next domain card. The inspiration card workshop was finished when all the domain cards had been discussed by both teams. The number of principle category cards is presented in Table 2.

Table 2. PSD principle card placement by categories and health problem domains

	Primary task support	Dialogue support	Credibility support	Social support	Total
Sleep	2	3	2	1	8
Stress	8	1	2	0	11
Nutrition	3	5	1	0	9
Sedentary work	3	3	0	1	7
Recovery from work	5	7	1	2	15
Physically straining work	5	6	0	0	11
Working hours efficiency	5	3	2	4	14
Total	31	28	8	8	75

It is noteworthy that the participants held primary task support and dialogue support categories in much greater value than system credibility or social support. Credibility support was somewhat overlooked and for instance *real-world feel, authority and surface credibility* were not deemed as important. Neither team placed cards of the aforementioned principles next to a domain card. The end-user representatives from earlier meetings and workshops had brought up *social comparison* from social support category. Therefore, it was a bit surprising to find out that the participants of PD3 did not consider social comparison very valuable for the presented health domains, since neither team placed social comparison card next to any domain card. The other social support features were not popular for the given problem domains either, with the exception of *social learning*, which both teams emphasized for 'recovery from work'.

Another surprise was that *praise* was considered a key feature by one team (working hours efficiency), whereas *reward* for four other domains (one card per domain from all teams). This contradicts our findings in the exploratory FGs, since praise was deemed better than rewards. In addition to praise, both *similarity* and *liking* from the dialogue support category were suggested only once for one domain (similarity for physically straining work and liking for nutrition). From the primary support category, both *simulation* and *tunneling* were chosen twice with one principle card per domain from either team (simulation for stress, recovery from work and tunneling for stress, nutrition). All the other PSD principle cards from the primary support and dialogue support categories were considered suitable either for several domains and/or by both teams. Nevertheless, this indicates that for the given context, both primary support and dialogue support categories were seen as especially valuable, which can also be seen from the total amount of PSD cards chosen by both teams: 31 for primary support, 28 for dialogue support.

6 Discussion

We succeeded to recruit 28 individual micro-entrepreneurs to join our meetings and workshops. All the focus group meetings and participatory design workshops were successful as we gained valuable data about the end-user representatives' preferences and views. We suggest that the participatory design process described here helped us to reach a seemingly effective design specification, yet we noticed that setting up meetings and workshops is time consuming. Recruiting participants, planning and communicating with other researchers, traveling, organizing meeting places, coffee, snacks and helping participants in travel arrangement while at the same time developing the actual target system took a tremendous amount of resources and time.

In order to avoid becoming too fascinated with the views of the involved users [20], we decided to arrange an inspiration card workshop [19, 22] in PD3, so the end-user representatives could discuss and justify their persuasive technology preferences. The popularity of primary task support and dialogue support feature categories in this workshop might be because they offer direct hands-on ways to persuade e.g. tools for *self-monitoring* and *rehearsal* as well as *reminders* and *suggestion*. Some other PSD principles are more abstract and perhaps more difficult to be understood by non-experts during single short workshop. It might also be that the participants could have been unsure about the differences between the concepts of *social comparison*, *social learning* and *social facilitation*, since the concepts are so close to each other and had to be explained more than once to the participants.

One could speculate that as system credibility support features are more or less default in professional websites and applications, they might not stand out in this setting. Nevertheless, absence of system credibility support features, such as surface credibility, e.g. competent look and feel, might lead into situations where users might be less willing to use such systems. Additionally, one of the expressed challenges regarding self-monitoring tools was that if the end-user representatives are shown self-perceived input, they might not have interpreted their own situation properly when they were inputting the feedback, e.g. self-perceived stress level could be either too low or too high.

There are also limitations for this study. We advertised the meetings and workshops for the local micro-entrepreneurs, but only those supposedly interested about health topics and mobile application development joined the meetings and workshops. All the end-user representatives also came from a relatively limited geographical area.

7 Conclusions

This paper offers insight into the views of micro-entrepreneurs for persuasive system features in mobile health applications. Helping system developers to understand the needs and preferences of end-users is important in order to make the system practical. Exploratory focus group meetings and participatory design workshops help involving the end-users into design processes and collecting data. Additionally, this paper discusses the methodology of how to carry out such processes. With good planning and when in conjunction with a research project, valuable research data can be acquired. In sum, participatory design is a fruitful approach albeit laborious approach for developing persuasive systems.

Acknowledgements. We wish to thank our colleagues at Promo@Work. This study is part of Promo@Work research project, funded by the Strategic Research Council at the Academy of Finland, contract no. 303430 (Finnish Institute of Occupational Health), contract no. 303431 (University of Oulu, OASIS) and contract no. 303434 (University of Oulu, MicroENTRE).

Harri Oinas-Kukkonen wishes to thank the Finnish Cultural Foundation for supporting this research.

References

1. Marshall, A.L., Leslie, E.R., Bauman, A.E., Marcus, B.H., Owen, N.: Print versus website physical activity programs: a randomized trial. Am. J. Prevent. Med. **25**(2) (2003). https://doi.org/10.1016/s0749-3797(03)00111-9
2. Cook, R.F., Billings, D.W., Hersch, R.K., Back, A.S., Hendrickson, A.: A field test of a web-based workplace health promotion program to improve dietary practices, reduce stress, and increase physical activity: randomized controlled trial. J. Med. Internet Res. **9**(2) (2007). https://doi.org/10.2196/jmir.9.2.e17
3. Stroulia, E., Fairbairn, S., Bazelli, B., Gibbs, D., Lederer, R., Faulkner, R., Ferguson-Roberts, J., Mullen, B.: Smart-phone application design for lasting behavioral changes. In: Proceedings of 26th IEEE International Symposium on Computer-Based Medical Systems, pp. 291–296. Curran Associates Inc., Red Hook (2013). https://doi.org/10.1109/cbms.2013.6627804
4. Garcia-Ceja, E., Osmani, V., Mayora, O.: Automatic stress detection in working environments from smartphones' accelerometer data: a first step. IEEE J. Biomed. Health Inform. **20**(4) (2016). https://doi.org/10.1109/JBHI.2015.2446195

5. Kardous, C.A., Shaw, P.B.: Evaluation of smartphone sound measurement applications. J. Acoust. Soc. Am. **135**(4) (2014). https://doi.org/10.1121/1.4865269
6. Oinas-Kukkonen, H.: A foundation for the study of behavior change support systems. Pers. Ubiquit. Comput. **17**(6), 1223–1235 (2013)
7. Oinas-Kukkonen, H., Harjumaa, M.: Persuasive systems design: key issues, process model, and system features. Commun. Assoc. Inf. Syst. **24**, 28 (2009)
8. European Commission: Commission Recommendation of 6 May 2003 concerning the definition of micro, small and medium-sized enterprises. Off. J. Eur. Union **46**, 36–41 (2003)
9. Eurostat. http://ec.europa.eu/eurostat/statistics-explained/index.php/Archive:Business_economy_%E2%80%93_size_class_analysis. Accessed 13 Oct 2017
10. Muller, P., Devnani, S., Julius, J., Gagliardi, D., Marzocchi, C.: Annual Report on European SMEs 2015/2016 - SME Recovery Continues. European Union (2016)
11. Parasuraman, S., Simmers, C.A.: Type of employment, work-family conflict and well-being: a comparative study. J. Org. Behav. **22**(5), 551–568 (2001)
12. Dijkhuizen, J., van Veldhoven, M., Schalk, R.: Four types of well-being among entrepreneurs and their relationships with business performance. J. Entrep. **25**(2), 184–210 (2016)
13. Pärnänen, A., Sutela, H.: Itsensätyöllistäjät Suomessa 2013. Tilastokeskus, Helsinki (2014)
14. Lundell, S., Visuri, S., Luukkonen, R.: Hyvinvointibarometri 2014 - Suomen Yrittäjät. Euroopan sosiaalirahasto, European Union (2014)
15. Kinnunen, U., Mauno, S.: Irtiottoja Työstä: työkuormituksesta palautumisen psykologia. Tampereen yliopistopaino Oy, Tampere (2009)
16. Zijlstra, F.R.H., Sonnentag, S.: After work is done: psychological perspectives on recovery from work. Eur. J. Work Org. Psychol. **15** (2006). https://doi.org/10.1080/13594320500513855
17. Bennett, A.A., Bakker, A.B., Field, J.G.: Recovery from work-related effort: a meta-analysis. J. Org. Behav. (2017). https://doi.org/10.1002/job.2217
18. Karppinen, P., Oinas-Kukkonen, H., Alahäivälä, T., Jokelainen, T., Keränen, A.-M., Salonurmi, T., Savolainen, M.: Persuasive user experience in health behavior change support system: a 12-month study for prevention of metabolic syndrome. Int. J. Med. Inform. **96**, 51–61 (2016)
19. Davis, J.: Generating directions for persuasive technology design with the inspiration card workshop. In: Ploug, T., Hasle, P., Oinas-Kukkonen, H. (eds.) PERSUASIVE 2010. LNCS, vol. 6137, pp. 262–273. Springer, Heidelberg (2010). https://doi.org/10.1007/978-3-642-13226-1_26
20. Bødker, S., Iversen, O.S.: Staging a professional participatory design practice: moving PD beyond the initial fascination of user involvement. In: Proceedings of 2nd Nordic Conference on Human-Computer Interaction, NordiCHI 2002, pp. 11–18. ACM, New York (2002)
21. Tremblay, M.C., Hevner, A.R., Berndt, D.J.: Focus groups for artifact refinement and evaluation in design research. Commun. Assoc. Inf. Syst. **26**, 27 (2010)
22. Halskov, K., Dalsgård, P.: Inspiration card workshops. In: Proceedings of 6th Conference on Designing Interactive systems, DIS 2006, pp. 2–11. ACM, New York (2006)

Might We Learn from Learning?

Sandra Burri Gram-Hansen[(✉)]

Department of Communication and Psychology,
Aalborg University, Aalborg, Denmark
burri@hum.aau.dk

Abstract. Theories on learning are vast, however constructivist learning in particular holds potential to strengthen designer's ability to tailor design solutions, by directing specific attention towards the user's ability to process the persuasive intent as mediated through technology. In this paper, we provide a brief introduction to Piaget's learning theory, and argue towards the potential of considering learning a theoretical benchmark for persuasive design practitioners.

Keywords: Persuasive technology · Persuasive design
Learning · Constructive learning · Persuasive designs for learning

1 Introduction

For more than a decade, persuasive technologies have been widely applied in various domains, out of which health and sustainability constitute the predominant application areas referenced within the persuasive technology community. A distinct characteristic of these domains, is that they require the attitude and behaviour change to be continuous rather than momentary. E.g. within health, patients must remember to take their medicine or perform their exercises, even when technology fails to remind them, and similarly, when striving to lead a more sustainable lifestyle, the desirable outcome is for users to be able to sort their waste or save energy, even when there is no mobile app to assist or remind them. In other words, as argued by Spahn; "Ideally, the aim of persuasion is to end persuasion" [1].

Alongside developments in persuasive technology, the field of technology enhanced learning has developed progressively, as digital solutions are being applied in broad variety through all steps of educational systems. None the less, learning remains a domain which has scarcely been explored or discussed within the persuasive technology field. In spite that a brief overlook indicates that learning and persuasion share many fundamental perspectives in the sense that both fields strive to intentionally influence the user. None the less, within the first decade of persuasive technology conferences, only 3 full papers discussing persuasive technology in learning, have been presented. [2–4], and the main focus of the papers have been in the potential of applying persuasive principles in learning technologies, rather than on the potential of considering theories and methods from learning in the development of persuasive technology and persuasive design.

Persuasive technologies were initially defined by Fogg, as interactive technologies designed with the intent to change user's attitudes, behaviours or both (without using

© Springer International Publishing AG, part of Springer Nature 2018
J. Ham et al. (Eds.): PERSUASIVE 2018, LNCS 10809, pp. 184–189, 2018.
https://doi.org/10.1007/978-3-319-78978-1_15

coercion or deception) [5]. While remaining the most often referenced definition of persuasive technology, the notion of persuasion is generally understood to hold far more complexity.

In an attempt to broaden the perspective on "being persuaded", reference is often made to Miller state of the art of persuasion in a social psychological perspective [6]. Persuasion is described as a more ethical approach to influencing others, and extended from to include not only behaviour change, but also shape and reinforcement. It is furthermore specified that persuasion is a process, and that it requires a deeper understanding of the given situation and the active decision [6].

In this paper, some overall perspectives from learning, and particularly constructivist learning, are introduced, and suggested to hold potential in relation to a further development of the persuasive technology field.

2 On the Concept of Learning

The term learning is generally broad, and often used with different meaning. However, according to Illeris, the most often applied perceptions of the word refers to outcomes of a learning process, mental processes within an individual, and interaction processes between individuals, their material and their social environment [7]. The particular importance of these distinctions is that learning is something which takes place within the individual, and that the overall intention of any learning design is to facilitate the learning process. As such, it must also be acknowledged that learning does not necessarily take place during the interaction with a learning technology, but that the technology may be one of several factors facilitating the learning process.

By reference to Miller [6], persuasion shares similarity with learning in the sense that persuasion also constitutes a process during which a person is influenced by one or more persuasive initiatives. Moreover, when also considering persuasion in a rhetorical perspective, persuasive design may be seen as highly context dependent, in the sense that persuasive technologies only meet their full potential if applied within the intended use context [8]. This particular distinction is often explained by reference to the rhetorical notion of Kairos, which constitutes the opportune moment when a persuasive initiative may be successful [9]. Kairos is general understood as three dimensional, combining the opportune time, place and manner. However, whilst a designer may be able to explore and identify the opportune time and place for a persuasive initiative to be executed, the appropriate manner is to some extent dependant on the user's perception of the situation and the context.

Consequently, persuasive design also calls for careful reflections regarding the user's ability to process whatever persuasive initiative is being mediated. It is with this in mind that theories of learning and knowledge processing, such as Piaget's conceptualisation of *assimilation* and *accommodation* holds much potential with regards to strengthening the theoretical foundation of persuasive design.

Piaget's theory of learning may be considered centred on the process of equilibration, by which the learning individual strives to maintain a balanced perception of the surrounding worlds, through continuously adapting to the surroundings and making the surroundings adapt to the needs of the individual [7]. This adaptation process is suggested to take place by continuously adjusting the cognitive schemas of the individual, referred to as the assimilative and accommodative processes. Assimilation refers to including new input in already existing schemas, while accommodation refers to adapting new input which does not comply with any existing schemas. Out of the two, assimilation is considered the easiest way of learning, where accommodative learning requires a higher cognitive effort by the learner [10]. In practice, it is not untypical for education professionals to develop learning designs that enable the students to build new knowledge on existing understandings, in order to ease the learning process, however, occasionally new schemas must be created, for instance when taking on an entirely new topic. Piaget's approach to learning is known as constructivist, thus excluding any forms of waterfall approaches to learning, where knowledge is simply transferred from the teacher to the student. In contrast, learning is constructed through interaction with the learning material and with the surrounding world [7]. As such, the constructivist approach to learning shares a fundamental commonality not only with Miller's understanding of persuasion as a process [6], but also with Fogg's claim that computer mediated persuasion occurs during the interaction between the computer and the user [5].

The relevance of considering Piaget becomes even more accentuated when considering similar perspectives already touched upon within behaviour design. Within the social psychological approach to persuasion, The Elaboration Likelihood Model refers to a "dual process" approach to information processing [11], and also in Nudging, Dual Process Theory argues that users process input either reflectively or automatically [12]. As such, Piaget's theory on learning and knowledge processing appears to be somewhat in line with already applied perspectives on persuasion and behaviour design. We find this as an indication that besides from considering the potential of applying persuasive principles in learning designs, there may also be a significant potential in considering learning theories when designing persuasive technologies.

3   What We Might Learn from Learning

Although developed in relation to behaviour design, the relationship between ability and motivation may be considered by reference to Fogg's behaviour model (Figs. 1 and 2):

According to Fogg's behaviour model, difficult tasks, such as processing complex information, requires a high level of motivation. When complexity is high and motivation is low, behaviour change, or in this case knowledge processing, is likely to fail [13]. While the behaviour model may lead to the understanding that a primary feature of persuasive design is to increase ability by making things easier to do, Piaget's concepts of assimilation and accommodation provide an important gradation to this approach. Processing of knowledge which does not fit into existing schemas require more cognitive effort and are as such not easy. Nor is breaking habits in order to establish a continuous change in behaviour. As such, the role of a persuasive technology, may be seen as a facilitator of knowledge processing, rather than simply a tool which makes a task easier to do. Consequently, theories on learning (in term of knowledge processing) plausibly holds much potential in relation to persuasive design,

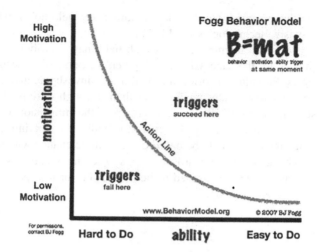

Fig. 1. Fogg's behaviour model

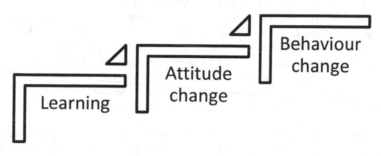

Fig. 2. Steps towards continuous behaviour change [4]

however not as a comparable approach to behaviour design but as a theoretical foundation for the persuasion process.

In order for a person to change attitude towards a given subject, he or she must obtain and process new information. Either by experience, by knowledge being provided and processed, or preferably by a combination of the two. Therefore, as theories of learning, such as Piaget's constructivist approach, provide insights regarding this process, learning may be seen as a fundamental step towards continuous behaviour change. Once having processed new input, the user may change attitude towards a subject, and subsequently become endogenously motivated to change behaviour [4].

4 Summing Up

In Fogg's original definition of persuasive technologies, he presented Captology as the cross-field between interactive technologies and social psychology [5]. Fogg did reference classical rhetoric, and with the establishment of an international research field, several researchers have argued that this classic humanistic field holds much potential in relation to persuasive technologies [8, 14–17].

This paper suggests that learning as a research field may contribute as yet another theoretical benchmark for the successful development of persuasive designs and persuasive technologies. Providing theories and methods to investigate and consider how users process the persuasive intent mediated to them through design, thereby facilitating a more substantial consideration of Kairos and the dimension of appropriate manner. If the intent of a persuasive design is to facilitate a continuous behaviour change, such change must inevitably be based on an attitude change within the user. In order for a user to change attitude towards a given subject, he or she must process new insights and thus learning may be argued to be a requisite for transparent and ethical persuasion.

References

1. Spahn, A.: And lead us (not) into persuasion...? Persuasive technology and the ethics of communication. Sci. Eng. Ethics **18**(4), 633–650 (2011)
2. Lucero, A., Zuloaga, R., Mota, S., Muñoz, F.: Persuasive technologies in education: improving motivation to read and write for children. In: IJsselsteijn, W.A., de Kort, Y.A.W., Midden, C., Eggen, B., van den Hoven, E. (eds.) PERSUASIVE 2006. LNCS, vol. 3962, pp. 142–153. Springer, Heidelberg (2006). https://doi.org/10.1007/11755494_20
3. Müller, L., Rivera-Pelayo, V., Heuer, S.: Persuasion and reflective learning: closing the feedback loop. In: Bang, M., Ragnemalm, E.L. (eds.) PERSUASIVE 2012. LNCS, vol. 7284, pp. 133–144. Springer, Heidelberg (2012). https://doi.org/10.1007/978-3-642-31037-9_12
4. Gram-Hansen, S.B., Ryberg, T.: Acttention – influencing communities of practice with persuasive learning designs. In: MacTavish, T., Basapur, S. (eds.) PERSUASIVE 2015. LNCS, vol. 9072, pp. 184–195. Springer, Cham (2015). https://doi.org/10.1007/978-3-319-20306-5_17
5. Fogg, B.: Persuasive Technology Using Computers to Change What We Think and Do. Kaufmann Publishers, Morgan (2003)
6. Miller, G.R.: On Being Persuaded, Some Basic Distinctions. In: Dillard, J.P., Pfau, M. (eds.) The Persuasion Handbook, Developments in Theory and Practice. Saga Publications, London (2002)
7. Illeris, K.: How We Learn - Learning and Non-learning in School and Beyond. Routledge, Abingdon (2007)
8. Gram-Hansen, S.B., Ryberg, T.: Persuasion, learning and context adaptation. Spec. Issue Int. J. Concept. Struct. Smart Appl. **1**, 28–37 (2013)
9. Kinneavy, J.L.: Kairos in classical and modern rhetorical theory. In: Sipiora, P., Baumlin, J. S. (eds.) Rhetoric and Kairos, Essays in History, Theory and Practice. State University of New York Press, Albany (2002)
10. Piaget, J.: The Psychology of Intelligence. Routledge, London, GBR (1999)
11. O'Keefe, D.J.: The elaboration likelihood model. In: Dillard, J.P., Shen, L. (eds.) The Persuasion Handbook. SAGE, Thousand Oaks (2013)
12. Johnson, E.J., et al.: Beyond nudges: tools of a choice architecture. Mark. Lett. **23**(2), 487–504 (2012)
13. Fogg, B.: A behaviour model for persuasive design. In: Persuasive 2009. ACM (2009)

14. Kjær Christensen, A.K., Hasle, P.F.V.: Classical rhetoric and a limit to persuasion. In: de Kort, Y., IJsselsteijn, W., Midden, C., Eggen, B., Fogg, B.J. (eds.) PERSUASIVE 2007. LNCS, vol. 4744, pp. 307–310. Springer, Heidelberg (2007). https://doi.org/10.1007/978-3-540-77006-0_36

15. Pertou, M., Iversen, S.D.: Persuasive Design i Retorisk Perspektiv. Rhetor. Scand. **46**, 15 (2009)

16. Ehninger, D.: Contemporary Rhetoric: A Reader's Coursebook. Scott Foresman and Company, Glenview (1972)

17. Glud, L.N., Jespersen, J.L.: Conceptual analysis of Kairos for location-based mobile devices. Series A, Research Papers. Department of Information Processing Science, University of Oulu, pp. 17–21 (2008)

Persuasive Games

Shock Tactics: Perceived Controversy in Molleindustria Persuasive Games

Katja Rogers[✉] and Michael Weber

Institute of Media Informatics, Ulm University, Ulm, Germany
{katja.rogers,michael.weber}@uni-ulm.de

Abstract. Shock tactics in the form of controversial messages are used in advertising to solicit viewer attention and as a persuasive tactic. Persuasive games are becoming increasingly popular, however the use of shock tactics in games have not been explored in much detail. This paper discusses how three Molleindustria games use potentially controversial mechanics and messages for persuasion. In a user study, we explored how the perceived controversy of these games influenced their efficacy. Overall, the results show that perceived controversy correlates significantly with the percentage of their study compensation participants were willing to donate. The findings point towards shock tactics as a potential tool for the design and evaluation of persuasive games.

Keywords: Persuasive games · Molleindustria · Attitude change
Controversy · Donation

1 Introduction and Background

In marketing, the use of shock tactics has a long history in commercial advertising, with the goal of catching viewers' attention, increasing brand recall, and influencing purchase decisions [1]. It has also been used in the context of social non-profit advertising, for example to raise public awareness for topics such as safe sex, health screenings, and fair and sustainable labour practices [2]. Many persuasive games have similar goals of increasing awareness and influencing behaviour. Research on persuasive games has long pointed to their potential for changing players' attitudes and behaviour compared to more passive media (such as videos or flyers), as interactivity has a significant effect on effectiveness of communicating messages and influencing behaviour [3]. This could potentially also increase the effects of shock advertising through controversial content or game mechanics (we use the term shock tactics to describe a game design approach, and controversy for players' perception thereof). Results from exploring this research question could lead to both an improved understanding of how shocking content is processed in the context of player-game interaction, and guidelines on how to use shock tactics for more effective persuasive games. To our knowledge, the use of shock tactics has not yet been explored in the context of persuasive games.

© Springer International Publishing AG, part of Springer Nature 2018
J. Ham et al. (Eds.): PERSUASIVE 2018, LNCS 10809, pp. 193–199, 2018.
https://doi.org/10.1007/978-3-319-78978-1_16

Shock advertising is said to work through distinctive or ambiguous content, and transgression of social or moral norms, although its efficacy differs based on demographic and cultural factors [4]. Some research has declared it obsolete [5], pointed out potential fatigue effects [1], adverse effects (e.g., defensive reactions, avoidance) [2], and ethical issues [6]. Nevertheless it has been and continues to be used extensively, and often yields results [6]. Further, there is a difference between the effects of shock in commercial and social advertising [2]: viewers tolerate shock advertising more from social non-profit organizations than commercial companies. Controversy does not lead to brand fallout, but rather increases public awareness even through negative discussion [6]. There is however a danger of compassion fatigue [7].

Dahl et al. [8] explained the cognitive response in viewers as shock working to increase attention, thus leading to additional cognitive processing. This in turn facilitates message comprehension and retention, and can yield behavioural effects. Notably, Dahl et al. showed that shocking advertisements increase attention, memory, and positive behaviour, while a more recent study has showed that shock advertising has a significantly greater emotional impact than positive or neutral content [7].

This paper explores the use of controversial messages in three existing games by Molleindustria. In a user study, we investigate the link between perceived controversy surrounding persuasive games, and their efficacy. The results show that perceived controversy correlates with increased donating behaviour. Finally, we discuss these findings in relation to guidelines for the design and evaluation of persuasive games.

(a) *Unmanned* [9].   (b) *McDonald's Video Game* [10].

Fig. 1: Players in these Molleindustria games (a) pilot an unmanned military drone or (b) can corrupt a politician.

2   Molleindustria Games

Since 2003, games by developer Molleindustria have been attracting attention for their satirical and often provocative underlying messages and presentation [11]. The games criticize subjects such as non-sustainable and non-ethical business practises in various industries, abuse cases in the Catholic church, trademark abuse, or gun laws. The games employ simple graphics and controversial gameplay mechanisms to provoke players and convey a message. Due to their controversial and sometimes crass game mechanics (e.g. requiring the player to cover up sexual abuse in *Operation: Pedopriest*), they have received notable media attention [11].

The **McDonald's Video Game** [10] was discussed regarding its implementation of procedural rhetoric by Bogost [12], and has been called an anti-advergame. The game consists of a simulation targeting sustainable development in the fast food industry; players have to control agriculture, operate a feedlot, manage a fast food restaurant, and choose marketing strategies. In the name of avoiding bankruptcy, the game drives players to chop down the rain forest for more farmland, inject harmful substances into livestock fodder, and bribe politicians (see Fig. 1b); "ethical" gameplay leads to failure.

Phone Story [13] is a mobile application consisting of four mini-games, each focusing on a different stage of smartphone manufacture. It received media attention when it was banned from the Apple App Store in the wake of the Foxconn suicide scandal [14]. Player are tasked with enforcing child labour, catching suicidal factory workers, throwing phones at consumers so intent on rushing the store that they would otherwise smash into the store's doors, and recycling unused phones in environmentally harmful ways (see Fig. 2). Its use of satirical and persuasive rhetoric is discussed in detail by Ferri [15].

The winner of multiple awards, **Unmanned** [9] is stylistically different to the two previous games, showing the everyday life of an unmanned drone pilot. Players have to complete mundane tasks such as shaving or driving to work, but also choose dialogue options that drive the narrative development of the main character's relationships with his son, wife, and potential workplace romance. The game features a scene wherein players take over the character's remote drone piloting job (Fig. 1a), or participate in a shooter game with his son. The drone piloting allows for the player to launch a missile, to the shock of his partner—who then merely complains about the forms they will have to fill in. The game is nonlinear; each play-through differs based on player choices.

3   Exploratory Study

We conducted an exploratory within-subjects user study to explore potential links between how persuasive a game is, and how controversial it is perceived to be. The three Molleindustria games *McDonald's Video Game* (*MCD*), *Phone Story* (*PS*), and *Unmanned*[1] (*UNM*) were used as the stimuli of this study.

We formulated two research questions (RQs) for this study: ***RQ1: Can gameplay of the Molleindustria persuasive games cause a difference in player attitude towards the underlying messages (i.e., criticism of the fast food industry, phone manufacture, and military unmanned drone piloting)?*** Further, what is the role of perceived controversy in these effects: ***RQ2: Does perceived controversy of the game and/or message correlate with the games' efficacy?***

---

[1] http://unmanned.molleindustria.org/.

We used questionnaires to investigate the efficacy of the Molleindustria games: custom-designed as there are no standardized scales for these topics. Due to space limits and the Cronbach's alpha of the attitude survey, we only discuss two of the used measures, both of which were administered at the end of the session: self-reported game influence, and their donating behaviour at the end of the study.

To measure participants' self-reported influence of each game, we asked them about their perception of the *game influence* (*"The game influenced me in my opinion of the game's topic"* rated on a 5-point Likert scale from *strongly agree* to *strongly disagree*), and how it influenced them (single choice question *"How did the game influence your opinion of the underlying topic?* with the choices of *"changed my opinion"*, *"did not influence my opinion"* and *"strengthened my opinion"*). At the end of the study, their *donating behaviour* was measured in a final question on how much of their compensation they wanted to donate to three different non-profit organizations engaged in causes relating to the games, and how much they wanted to keep. The organizations' names were faked to avoid bias through pre-existing impressions, and accompanied by descriptions of the corresponding cause. Perceived controversy was also measured via 5-point Likert scales, and divided insofar as it related to the game itself, or the game's message.

Fig. 2: The four *Phone Story* [13] mini-games in sequence: (1) child labour, (2) factory worker suicides, (3) consumer injuries, and (4) environmentally harmful substances.

3.1   Participants

We recruited 20 participants (15 male) with a mean age of 26.9 ($SD = 2.53$) via mailing lists and word of mouth in a university setting. Most participants (80%) had a gaming background in the form of playing at least once a month. The final questionnaire asked participants if they were familiar with the games prior to the study; 4 had heard of one of them before (2 for *PS* and *MCD* each), but only one had previously played one (*MCD*).

3.2   Study Procedure

Participants were given a consent form followed by a brief questionnaire on demographics and a pre-test survey on their beliefs about various topics, including the games' themes (not reported here, see above). They then played the three Molleindustria games (in counterbalanced order) and filled out a questionnaire on the game experience (also not reported here). Based on preliminary gameplay tests by the authors and colleagues, gameplay durations were set for each game to allow for complete game experiences while keeping the overall study duration at a total of approximately one hour. This led to 14 (*UNM*), 10 (*MCD*), and 6 m (*PS*) of gameplay, respectively. As test sessions with *MCD* often resulted in early bankruptcy, participants were allowed to restart this game; the other game sessions finished after a single play-through.

After all three gameplay sessions, participants were asked to complete a final questionnaire that included the measure of perceived controversy of each game and its message. Finally, they were asked how much of their reward they wanted to donate to three different (non-existent) charities corresponding to each game's topic. Afterwards, the participants were informed that the charities did not exist, and were handed their full compensation of 5 €.

3.3   Results

For this paper, we discuss only findings regarding participants' donating behaviour and the perceived controversy.

Donation Behaviour. Participants kept a total of 2000 cents (20%) on average, and donated the rest. Three participants did not donate; of the remainder, ten participants distributed their donation across all three organizations. *MCD* amassed 3110 cents, followed by *PS* with 2710 and *UNM* with 2180 cents. A Friedman's ANOVA showed that this difference in amounts donated to each cause was not significant, $\chi^2 = 6.43$, $p = .09$.

Effect of Perceived Controversy. Overall, the *MCD* game was perceived as slightly controversial ($M = 3.1$, $SD = 1.29$), as was its message ($M = 3.45$, $SD = 1.15$). We used proportional odds logistic regression (`polr` from the *MASS* R package) to explore whether the Likert responses for perceived controversy were able to predict percentage donated. A likelihood ratio test showed that a model using the perceived controversy of *MCD* and its message was a significant predictor of the percentage donated compared to the null model, $X^2(2) = 6.82$, $p < 0.05$.

The *PS* game ($M = 3.35$, $SD = 1.23$) and its message ($M = 3.35$, $SD = 1.09$) were also perceived as somewhat controversial. Here too, a likelihood ratio test showed that a model using perceived controversy of game and message was a significant predictor of percentage donated compared to the null model, $X^2(1) = 9.47$, $p < 0.01$.

Similarly, *UNM* was perceived as slightly controversial on average ($M = 3.15$, $SD = 1.18$), as was its message ($M = 3.00$, $SD = 1.08$). In this case, the likelihood ratio test also yielded a significant result for the perceived controversy of game and message as a predictor of percentage donated compared to the null model, $X^2(1) = 20.84$, $p < 0.001$.

4   Discussion and Conclusion

The study has some limitations that should be noted, particularly the sample size and homogeneous sample background, given that previous research has indicated differences in learning effects through games based on socio-economic status [16]. Further, as with many studies on persuasive games, participants tended to have a positive view of the topics *a priori*; strengthening an existing attitude is likely much easier than eliciting or changing one [17]. It also remains to be seen whether the effect translates to behaviour change.

Nevertheless, we have demonstrated that perceived controversy surrounding a game influences players' subsequent donation behaviour. This raises questions on how this effect can be leveraged in the design of persuasive games. Can persuasive effects be leveraged more effectively by adding or increasing content that is perceived controversially? In this study, perceived controversy of content and message correlated, but effects may differ if only one of these is perceived as controversial. Further, we point towards research opportunities on whether the use of shock tactics may be more acceptable for some kinds of topics than others. Banyte et al. [2] have described different types of emotional appeals that can be used in shock advertising; a comparison of these tactics in the context of a persuasive game would be highly valuable for game designers and researchers. Finally, much like shock advertising raises ethical issues, so the use of shock tactics in games should also be used with caution. Game designers and researchers should consider their ethical responsibilities towards players carefully before using shock tactics, to decide whether benefits outweigh potential harm.

In summary, as in advertising, shock tactics and controversy may also be an effective strategy in persuasive game design. As such, it should be considered as a tool by designers and researchers designing games for social change. Further explorations are needed to study how efficient this tool can be in creating optimally persuasive games.

References

1. Skorupa, P.: Shocking contents in social and commercial advertising. Creat. Stud. **7**(2), 69–81 (2014)
2. Banyte, J., Paskeviciute, K., Rutelione, A.: Features of shocking advertising impact on consumers in commercial and social context. Innov. Mark. **10**(2), 35–46 (2014)
3. Steinemann, S.T., Mekler, E.D., Opwis, K.: Increasing donating behavior through a game for change: the role of interactivity and appreciation. In: Proceedings of the 2015 Annual Symposium on Computer-Human Interaction in Play, pp. 319–329. ACM (2015)
4. Virvilaite, R., Matuleviciene, M.: The impact of shocking advertising to consumer buying behavior. Econ. Manage. **18**(1), 134–141 (2013)
5. Urwin, B., Venter, M.: Shock advertising: not so shocking anymore. An investigation among generation Y. Mediterr. J. Soc. Sci. **5**(21), 203 (2014)
6. Pflaumbaum, C.G.: Shock advertising-a sensationalised media construct? Ph.D. thesis, Curtin University (2013)

7. Cockrill, A., Parsonage, I.: Shocking people into action: does it still work? J. Advert. Res. **56**(4), 401–413 (2016)
8. Dahl, D.W., Frankenberger, K.D., Manchanda, R.V.: Does it pay to shock? reactions to shocking and nonshocking advertising content among university students. J. Advert. Res. **43**(3), 268–280 (2003)
9. Molleindustria: Unmanned. Game, Molleindustria, Pittsburgh (2012). http://www.phonestory.org/game.html
10. Molleindustria: McDonald's Video Game. Game Molleindustria, Pittsburgh (2006). http://www.mcvideogame.com/
11. Molleindustria: Press listing (2016). http://www.molleindustria.org/blog/press/. Accessed 20 Sept 2016
12. Bogost, I.: Persuasive Games: The Expressive Power of Videogames. MIT Press, Cambridge (2007)
13. Molleindustria: Phone Story. Game, Molleindustria, Pittsburgh (2012)
14. Bilton, R.: Apple 'failing to protect Chinese factory workers'. BBC News, December 2014. http://www.bbc.com/news/business-30532463. Accessed 20 Sept 2016
15. Ferri, G.: Rhetorics, simulations and games: the ludic and satirical discourse of molleindustria. Int. J. Gaming Comput. Mediat. Simul. (IJGCMS) **5**(1), 32–49 (2013)
16. Paperny, D.M., Starn, J.R.: Adolescent pregnancy prevention by health education computer games: computer-assisted instruction of knowledge and attitudes. Pediatrics **83**(5), 742–752 (1989)
17. Oinas-Kukkonen, H., Harjumaa, M.: A systematic framework for designing and evaluating persuasive systems. In: Oinas-Kukkonen, H., Hasle, P., Harjumaa, M., Segerståhl, K., Øhrstrøm, P. (eds.) PERSUASIVE 2008. LNCS, vol. 5033, pp. 164–176. Springer, Heidelberg (2008). https://doi.org/10.1007/978-3-540-68504-3_15

Reflection Through Gaming: Reinforcing Health Message Response Through Gamified Rehearsal

Piiastiina Tikka$^{(\boxtimes)}$, Miia Laitinen, Iikka Manninen,
and Harri Oinas-Kukkonen

University of Oulu, Pentti-Kaiteran katu 1, Oulu, Finland
`piiastiina.tikka@oulu.fi`

Abstract. Reflection is generally considered an effective means of achieving behavior change. A gamified approach to promoting rehearsal and reflection in a healthy eating context was studied. The game was based on the principles of the Implicit Attitude Test: by categorizing food items under positive or negative associations the players would gain points according to how fast they categorized foods under positive or negative associations. Game scores constituted feedback for reflection, and repeated playing constituted rehearsal of target responses. Experiment participants (N = 58) played the game over a five-day period. Constructs of Rehearsal (REH), self-reported questionnaire responses on Reflection (REFL) and Perceived Persuasiveness (PEPE), and self-reported Perceived Health Behavior Change (PHBC) were analyzed using PLS-SEM. The results show that PLAY moderates the REFL-PEPE relationship, and there are also significant relationships between REH and PEPE, PEPE and PHBC, and REFL and PHBC.

Keywords: Persuasive technology · Behavior change · Gamification
Self-reflection · Perceived Persuasiveness · PSD · PLS-SEM

1 Introduction

The role of reflection in behavior change is well established [1–3] and typically the approach is to allow system users to monitor their own behavior – a common device for such self-monitoring being activity bracelets or smart watches. A plethora of sensors carried by modern information technology products ensures that there is no shortage of means for monitoring what people do physically, but how can technology support turning that monitoring into actual reflection and, in turn, potential for behavior change? What mechanisms are required in order to help turn reflection into action?

In health behavior, monitoring behavior provides a good view of whether a person is doing what he or she is meant to do: a food diary (provided it is accurate) will reveal if the diet is what it should be, or an activity record from a bracelet will show if there has been enough activity and exercise in a day. It is also known that the attrition rates with systems for behavior change is rather high [4]. To even start using such a system a person first needs to become aware of a problem. Further to that, acknowledging a

© Springer International Publishing AG, part of Springer Nature 2018
J. Ham et al. (Eds.): PERSUASIVE 2018, LNCS 10809, pp. 200–212, 2018.
https://doi.org/10.1007/978-3-319-78978-1_17

problem is only the first step, while learning and developing ways of addressing it is quite another. Activity monitoring or food diaries are good methods for tracking behavior and a source for feedback, which a person can use as the basis for reflection. They can be, however, overwhelming in the active effort required.

In the present study we wanted to explore the potential of gamifying a method of feedback provision on decision-making and even implicit attitudes as means of supporting a change in existing thinking. Gaming has been associated with rehearsal [5, 6] and combining a rehearsal with an immediate feedback through the engagement in a game offers an appealing environment for learning and reinforcing target behaviors. We developed a mobile game 'Implicity' based on the principles of the Implicit Association Test (IAT) [7] where the prevailing implicit associations and attitudes are presumed to be automatic and reactions to relevant stimuli are faster than to stimuli opposite to the automatic attitudes. We hypothesized that by playing a game where the player has to quickly categorize food items into positive and negative categories would (a) expose the player to a possible attitude bias in their thinking, and (b) through repetition the player would be rehearsing responses to types of food as if learning by rote. For example, when the player is consistently slower in placing vegetables into the positive category than placing bacon in the negative category, the message to the player would be that they need to be aware of their automatic choices and preferences, and by playing the game more the player can rehearse and learn the target response. The reflection that takes place can teach the player to observe his or her own thinking as regards target behavior. Health behavior in the present study is vegetable and fruit consumption.

In the present study we then ask (1) does a gamified process of drawing attention to implicit attitudes evoke self-reflection, (2) does gamification of response rehearsal contribute positively to behavior change?

2 Background

The theoretical cornerstones for the present study are found in the Behavior Change Support System (BCSS) framework and the Persuasive Systems Design (PSD) model [8, 9]. Building on this base we used gamification principles [10] and the Implicit Association Test (IAT) [7] to create a game mechanism, feedback provisioning (for reflection) and engagement elements in the form of a highly gamified BCSS.

2.1 Persuasive Systems Design and Behavior Change Support Systems

A system that from the onset aims at behavioral and psychological outcomes, but does this openly and without coercion or deception is, by definition, a Behavior Change Support System (BCSS) [8]. The aims and goals to be defined when developing a behavior change support system involve the type and expected outcome of the system: should the system form, reinforce or change a user's compliance, behavior or attitude? Further to that, the Persuasive Systems Design (PSD) model is a tool for analyzing and implementing those goals through system features [9].

The development of the game and the selection of persuasive system features was guided by a PSD analysis of the goals, intentions and persuasion context. The main goals of the system were identified as changing behavior and/or attitude, or reinforcing behavior and/or attitude where change was not necessary. Gamification aspects of the system used Dialogue Support features *praise* and *rewards*. More at the core of the persuasiveness were Primary Task Support features of *rehearsal*, *self-monitoring* and *reduction*. System credibility support features included reliable sources for health information, transparency in sources, and use of authorities. Of the core persuasive features the role of rehearsal should be highlighted: playing a game can involve numerous repetitions of the set tasks, which in the present case means numerous repetitions of quick decision-making as regards food items. Such repetition means that the target response is rehearsed at a quick pace in volumes that a person would not readily encounter in real life. A player of such a game also rehearses the target response.

Many persuasive systems are built to encourage reflection (cf. especially self-monitoring in the PSD model) that is expected to lead to change in behaviors while others engage in a more prescriptive approach [1]. Open-ended reflection can, perhaps, be seen as a less obtrusive means to an end than a purposefully prescriptive one. The PSD model [9] postulates that one of the key elements of a persuasive system is that it is unobtrusive: it does not get in the way of a system user's primary task. Reflection, when a by-product of an activity, can be seen as a subtle approach to paying attention to behaviors and to changing them. The feedback from the game allows the player to observe his or her own thinking in a game context.

2.2 Gamification

Using core characteristics of gaming (self-purposefulness and hedonistic use) with an ultimately utilitarian goal such as behavior change or learning is the essence of gamification [10]. Gamification repurposes the intrinsic motivation that goes with game play as a tool for utilitarian use by using typical game elements of points, badges, leaderboards, goals, narratives, feedback and achievements in the system design [10, 11]. At the highly gamified end the utilitarian benefits come almost as a side product of a pleasurable activity. Just as in BCSS development, gamifying a system or a service involves definitions of goals [12]. Target behavior is analyzed and the system is set to monitor the defined performance, then features supporting engagement and fun (a key part of any game) are developed [12]. On the one hand, gamification of behavior change could be seen as a form of "sugaring the pill", but on the other hand the appeal of the gamification approach may be more closely related to the pursuit of unobtrusiveness. Using gamification as an element of a BCSS is not unheard of, and it can be done successfully [13–17]. Further to that, cognitive tests have also been used before as the basis of a gamified system [18].

2.3 Implicit Association Test

The IAT [7] was developed to test implicit attitudes by revealing automatic associations. In the test subjects' response times to test objects are used to determine automatic associations. While in the present study the developed game does not follow the IAT concept fully so that it could be used to determine a player's implicit associations as such, the concept of reaction times as an indicator of automatic associations is used as the basic mechanism for scoring and game progression. In research IAT has been used also in healthy eating and diet related studies. For example, people who actively avoided high-calorie foods also showed an implicit association with low-calorie foods [19], and obese people showed stronger negative implicit associations towards high-fat foods than a control group [20]. In the present paper the focus is on the effect of rehearsal, and the IAT scores over the test period are not included. This selection was necessary in order to limit the scope of the present paper.

3   Method

3.1   Model, Hypotheses, and Measurement Instruments

The research model (Fig. 1) illustrates the constructs of Reflection (REFL), Rehearsal (REH), Perceived Persuasiveness (PEPE), and Perceived Health Behavior Change (PHBC) and their relationships, as hypothesized. In addition, a further hypothesis (H8) is presented regarding the effect of the study on reported fruit and vegetable consumption. Measurement instruments used in the study are described in Table 5.

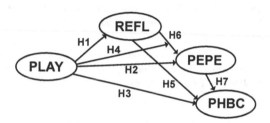

Fig. 1. Research model and hypotheses.

Rehearsal (REH) is the number of game sets played by each participant. The PSD model [9] presents rehearsal as a means in a system for a user to rehearse a behavior. Participants were asked to play a minimum of three sets per day on five consecutive days, and they were told that they were free to play as much as they wished. The more an individual plays the game the more he or she is exposed to the underlying health message and the feedback (score) on his or her (implicit) associations. We hypothesize that the exposure will lead to reflection, higher perceived persuasiveness of the system, as well as have a positive effect on post-experiment health behavior. We also hypothesize that REH has a moderating effect on the relationship between REFL and PEPE (Table 1).

Reflection (REFL) construct indicates engagement in reflection [21], how individuals inspect and evaluate their own thoughts, feelings and behaviors [22]. While H1 supposes that playing a game would trigger users to think about their thinking more, it is

Table 1. Hypotheses regarding REH construct.

H1	*Higher number of game sets played means a higher level of exposure to the health message, leading to a positive effect on Reflection*
H2	*Higher number of game sets played offers a higher level of repetition of the target response and it directs a player to associate healthier foods with positive words (or vice versa). Such exposure will have a positive effect of Rehearsal on Perceived Persuasiveness of the system*
H3	*Higher number of game sets will directly enforce the concept of healthier food choices in a repeated way as the player is expected to categorize foods and words. The volume of game play will thus have a positive effect on the Perceived Health Behavior Change*
H4	*The higher exposure to the health message and reinforced target response (correct choices) will have a moderating effect on the relationship between Reflection and Perceived Persuasiveness*

likely this tendency is already present in some degree in the participants. However, regardless of its origin, reflection is a component in measuring an individual's readiness for purposeful behavior change [21] (Table 2).

Table 2. Hypotheses regarding REFL construct.

H5	*Reflection on one's behavior and choices in the game is directly connected to evaluating the qualities of various foods, and high engagement (more games played) in the game will lead to higher reflection and thus have a positive effect on Perceived Health Behavior Change*
H6	*Reflection on one's own behavior and choices in the game is directly connected to evaluating one's own responses to an openly influencing system and will have a positive effect on Perceived Persuasiveness*

Perceived Persuasiveness (PEPE) is a construct combining system user's perception of the system itself and its message into an attitude item that consists of cognitions and affect [23, 24]. A favorable attitude and a person's assessment of the system and its effect on his or her own behavior or thinking is a factor in a system's ability to support behavior change [24, 25] (Table 3).

Table 3. Hypotheses regarding Perceived Persuasiveness construct.

H7	*Perceived Persuasiveness of a system has a positive effect on the readiness of an individual to immediately evaluate the direct impact of the system on his or her behavior, and supports system users in engaging in target behavior*

Perceived Health Behavior Change (PHBC) is a construct made of open-ended evaluations by participants on the actual changes they may have noticed after the experiment. The construct is close to PEPE in that it is based on an individual's perception of behavior change impact as regards the system. However, PHBC assesses the direct result of system use, in the present case increased use of fruit and vegetables or contemplation of existing dietary habits with a view to engage in behavior change. Where PEPE as an instrument focuses on evaluating how the user relates to the system and on the respondent's view of the role of the system in any change and personal relevance, the PHBC instrument asks the participants in an open-ended question to describe the exact and actual change (or lack of it). In addition to the PHBC as a measure of behavioral outcome, we collect a one-day food diary at the start and finish of the study period (Table 4).

Table 4. Hypothesis regarding Perceived Health Behavior Change construct.

H8	*The gameplay and the increased reflection triggered by gameplay will result in an increase in actual fruit and vegetable intake after the study period*

Table 5. Measurement instruments in the study.

Measurement	Instruments
Reflection (REFL)	The experiment used a previously validated and published self-assessment scale [21], which was further studied by [22]. The original scale included three components: need for reflection, engagement in reflection, and insight. Relevant questions from the scale on engagement in reflection were included in the post-test questionnaire
Perceived persuasiveness (PEPE)	The perceived persuasiveness scale used in this experiment has been developed specifically for assessing BCSSs [24] and as such is a validated scale. I is a self-assessment scale for assessing the impact a persuasive system
Perceived Health Behavior Change (PHBC)	The instrument is based on an open-ended question presented at the end of the experiment asking participants what (if any) changes they have noticed in their food choices. The scale is then formed by two researchers individually categorizing all the statements into five categories based on the strength and type of effect from no impact to raised awareness, contemplation of change and actual behavioral impact. The ground-up approach of the scale allows users to freely describe their experience rather than having to evaluate their responses against a ready-set frame. The scale has been used earlier in [27]
Rehearsal (REH)	Collected from the game
Food intake (1-day food diary)	The present study used a self-administered fruit and vegetable portion estimation form [26] The questionnaire instruction included guidance for estimating a portion of vegetables and fruit. After guidance, portion-based estimations have been found to be realistic and reliable [26]. The guidance given in this study is not directly comparable to [26], but it provides a basis for comparable variables for pre- and post-test assessments

3.2   Sample Selection and Study Procedure

Sample selection. The sample, N = 58, is one of opportunity, largely made up of university students. The participants were recruited by distributing fliers at university campus and in two shopping centers. In addition, the researchers distributed a simple advert for the experiment online in social media platforms Facebook and Twitter. Participants were offered a cinema ticket for completing the full experiment. To take part in this study participants had to be over 18 years old.

Procedure. The study consisted of starting questionnaires (background, one-day food diary), gameplay period (5 days) and final questionnaires (Reflection, Perceived Persuasiveness, Perceived Health Behavior Change and another one-day food diary). Upon sign-up participants were informed about the test setup and asked to indicate they agreed to participate. They were also informed that they could stop at any point and ask for their data to be removed. The experiment information also explained data and information security and protection of identity. A unique user ID, obtained from the mobile game, was used in all the forms in order to maintain anonymity.

The participants were instructed to play the game on five consecutive days, a minimum three sets per day, and then finally send their gaming data to the researchers by using a send button in the application. 2–3 days after sending the data, participants received the post-test questionnaire. The flexibility in sending the instruction for the final questionnaire aimed at allowing the users at least one full day after completing the game period before filling in the food diary but also at avoiding the reporting landing on weekend days. By encouraging working days for reporting the intention was to collect the food diaries under as similar conditions as possible.

3.3   Materials: The Game

The game (example screens in Fig. 2) in the present study was developed from the start as a highly gamified BCSS with persuasive features selected based on a Persuasive Systems Design (PSD) analysis [9]. As a means of producing the selected PSD features the game adapted the Implicit Association Test (IAT) [7] as a mechanism for (a) producing feedback for the users and (b) as the basis for scoring logic. The game is not intended to be an IAT in itself, but rather uses the mechanism as a means of providing instant feedback that is entirely based on the player's own reactions and responses. In other words, the score is not based on any game-originating random factors, surprises or obstacles that are not under a player's control.

The game contains two categorization tasks. In the first task, the user has to associate healthy foods with a positive word and unhealthy foods with negative words. In the second task, positive words are associated with a healthy food and negative words with an unhealthy food. Reaction times from the point of presenting the food/word are measured. After each set of ten items a score screen is shown. Scoring was based on reaction thresholds described in [7, 28]. Gamification elements included points, levels, and content unlocking [10].

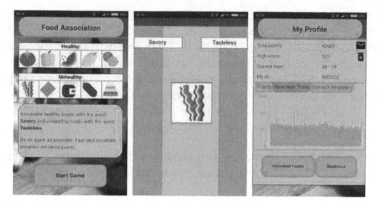

Fig. 2. 'Implicity the Food Game' start screen (left), categorization task item (center) where left and right margins are the touch target, and score screen (right).

4   Data Analysis and Results

4.1   Sample Characteristics

Of the total sample of 58 participants 33 were female, 25 male. Average age for the whole sample was 24 years (median 23), average for females being 24 (18–35 min/max, median 22) and for males 23 (18–33 min/max, median 23). Eight participants reported that they do not usually play any computerized games, 19 used a computer as their main gaming platform, 20 used a gaming console, and 11 reported a mobile device as their primary gaming platform. The sample size satisfies the general rule of thumb of ten times the largest number of paths directed at a particular construct [29].

4.2   Measurement Model

Using PLS-SEM analysis the relationships between latent variables were examined. The analysis demonstrates the explained variance (R^2 values) in the latent variables, and indicates the strength (β-values) and their statistical significance of the relationships in the model [29, 30]. See Fig. 3 for the R^2-values and β-values.

Table 6. Internal consistency and indicator reliability assessment.

	CA	CR	AVE	1	2	3	4	5
1. REH	1.000	1.000	1.000	*1.000*				
2. Moderator (REH on REFL > PEPE)	1.000	1.000	1.000	−0.272	*1.000*			
3. PEPE	0.692	0.868	0.692	0.179	0.325	*0.832*		
4. PHBC	1.000	1.000	1.000	−0.009	0.080	0.835	*1.000*	
5. REFL	0.668	0.923	0.668	−0.161	0.191	0.281	0.338	*0.817*

Convergent reliability is indicated with average variance extracted (AVE) and Fornell-Larcker analysis.
Square root of AVE and inner-construct correlations are shown in italics.

In terms of internal consistency, the reliability of the indicators, the convergent validity of the indicators, and the discriminant validity the measurement model adheres to recommended guidelines [29, 31, 32] (see Table 6). REH and PHBC were single indicator constructs, and while generally speaking single item constructs are not encouraged with PLS-SEM practical considerations are acceptable for example when the single items measure an observable characteristic [29].

4.3 Structural Model

The research model (Fig. 1) presented the hypotheses regarding the relationships in the model. The results of the PLS analysis are illustrated in Fig. 3.

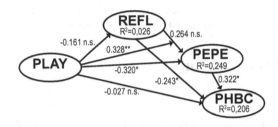

Fig. 3. Structural model. ***p < .01; **p < .02; *p < .05, n.s. for non-significant paths.

The path coefficients for the research model were obtained using parametric bootstrapping with 5000 subsamples (parallel processing, no sign changes). The constructs in the model were reflective. In the complete model we see that 21% of the variance in PHBC was explained by REFL and PEPE (supporting H5 and H7), and 25% of the variance in PEPE was explained by REH (supporting H2 and H4); REH was a significant moderator in the relationship between REFL and PEPE. Hypotheses H1, H3 and H6 were not supported.

4.4 Total Effects and Effect Sizes, and Predictive Validity of the Model

Practical relevance of the model was determined by assessing the total effects and effect sizes (Cohen f^2), assessing an exogenous construct's contribution to the R^2 value of an endogenous latent variable (Table 7). Assessment guide values were 0.02 (small), 0.15

Table 7. Total effects and effect sizes (non-significant not reported).

	PEPE	PHBC	REFL
REH	−0.320 (0.125)	n.s.	n.s.
Moderator (REH on REFL > PEPE)	0.328 (0.157)		
PEPE		0.322 (0.113)	
PHBC			
REFL	n.s.	0.243 (0.065)	

(medium), and 0.35 (large). In the present model there were five small, one non-relevant and one medium f^2, indicating that on the whole there is some practical relevance in the model. The non-relevant f^2 was REH to PHBC, and the medium f^2 was REH as a moderator for REFL and PEPE.

A blindfolding procedure was used to observe the predictive validity of the model (Table 8). The Stone-Geisser cross-validated redundancy value (Q^2) above 0 is considered to indicate predictive validity of endogenous constructs. All endogenous constructs (PEPE, PHBC and REFL) demonstrate $Q^2 > 0$, and thus indicate the path model's predictive relevance to each of the constructs [29].

Table 8. Predictive validity of the model: Q^2 values for endogenous constructs.

Construct	Q^2
PEPE	0.108
PHBC	0.122
REFL	0.011

4.5 Fruit and Vegetable Consumption Before and After the Study Period

A one-way repeated measures ANOVA was conducted to compare the effect of timing of self-reported fruit and vegetable consumption before the game play period and immediately after it (Table 9). At α-level of .05 there was a significant effect of timing, Wilks' Lambda = .860, $F(1,57) = 9.316$, $p = .003$. The result provides indirect support for the use of PEPE and PHBC constructs in assessing the effect of system use on behavior through showing that the self-reported behavior observations are in line with the food diaries. The result supports H8.

Table 9. Descriptive statistics for one-way repeated measures ANOVA.

	N	Mean	Std.Dev.
Pre-study vegetable consumption	58	4.06	3.182
Post-study vegetable consumption	58	5.10	2.732

5 Discussion and Conclusions

Successful design of Behavior Change Support Systems involves selecting the right persuasive tools for the purpose [9, 34]. The forms of BCSSs are various from simple information sharing websites to interactive mobile applications to, as in the present paper, gamified systems. Whatever the format, the basic persuasive design principles can be applied. In the game presented in this paper the selected persuasive design principles [9] were built on top of a cognitive test concept and they were implemented as gaming features, following game development principles [10].

In our study the game provided the users with an opportunity to rehearse a target behavior and also to reflect upon the rehearsal results with the help of immediate feedback. The main interest in the paper was in the effect of rehearsal on reflection leading on to perceived persuasiveness and health behavior change. Research into reflection suggests that unless the reflection leads to insight, behavior change is less likely to take place [34–36], and dysfunctional attitudes can hinder the path from insight to personal well-being [37]. A review into use of digital games in cancer management found potential (and also challenges) in both treatment training but more notably for example when active participation or behavioral rehearsal for physical and psychosocial activity are needed [6]. The moderating role of rehearsal on the relationship between reflection and perceived persuasiveness would appear to be an element persuasive systems should consider utilizing when intending to facilitate behavior change through reflection.

What we can learn from the results is that rehearsal can amplify the effect of reflection as regards a user's perception of the persuasiveness of a system. We can also see that rehearsal alone may not be enough to result in positive behavioral outcomes: volume of game play did not affect the immediate health behavior directly in the way it did Perceived Persuasiveness. In turn, Perceived Persuasiveness had an impact on the immediate health behavior, as did Reflection. In other words, for a change to take place, both reflection and perceived persuasiveness are necessary and they can be made more effective through rehearsal. The perceived outcomes were supported in the study with the actual fruit and vegetable consumption estimates, as seen in the ANOVA on the consumption of vegetable and fruit before and after the test period.

The study naturally does not provide insights into long-term effects. The gameplay period was also relatively short (5 days) and game content was limited (only 34 levels). Further insights into the direct role of various persuasive features (such as rewards and praise) would have made for an even richer study set-up, but owing to the necessity to have participants commit to play the game for five days it was necessary to be parsimonious as regards the extent of the questionnaire batteries and demands on participant time. As existing research shows, for example [20], we can see that the relationship between implicit attitudes and behavior can be complicated. Therefore, future research directions leading on from the present study should involve the actual implicit association directions and strengths and their development after reflection.

Acknowledgement. Harri Oinas-Kukkonen wishes to thank the Finnish Cultural Foundation for supporting this research.

References

1. Ploderer, B., Reitberger, W., Oinas-Kukkonen, H., et al.: Social interaction and reflection for behaviour change. Pers. Ubiquit. Comput. **18**, 1667–1676 (2014)
2. Li, I., Dey, A.K., Forlizzi, J.: Understanding my data, myself: supporting selfreflection with ubicomp technologies. In: Proceedings of UbiComp 2011 International Conference on Ubiquitous Computing. ACM, New York (2011)
3. Rogers, R.R.: Reflection in higher education: a concept analysis. Innov. High. Educ. **26**, 37–57 (2001)

4. Kelders, S.M., Kok, R.N., Ossebaard, H.C., Van Gemert-Pijnen, J.E.: Persuasive system design does matter: a systematic review of adherence to web-based interventions. J. Med. Internet Res. **14**(6), 2–25 (2012)
5. Liboriussen, B.: Craft, creativity, computer games: the fusion of play and material consciousness. Philos. Technol. **26**(3), 273–282 (2013)
6. Ghazisaeidi, M., Safdari, R., Goodini, A., Mirzaiee, M., Farzi, J.: Digital games as an effective approach for cancer management: opportunities and challenges. J. Educ. Health Promot. **6**, 30 (2017)
7. Greenwald, A.G., McGhee, D.E., Schwartz, J.: Measuring individual differences in implicit cognition: the implicit association test. J. Pers. Soc. Psychol. **74**(6), 1464 (1998)
8. Oinas-Kukkonen, H.: A foundation for the study of behavior change support systems. Pers. Ubiquit. Comput. **17**(6), 1223–1235 (2013)
9. Oinas-Kukkonen, H., Harjumaa, M.: Persuasive systems design: key issues, process model, and system features. Commun. Assoc. Inf. Syst. **24**, 28 (2009)
10. Hamari, J., Koivisto, J.: Social motivations to use gamification: an empirical study of gamifying exercise. In: Proceedings of ECIS 2013 European Conference on Information Systems (2013)
11. Huotari, K., Hamari, J.: Defining gamification – a service marketing perspective. In: Proceedings of MindTrek 2012, 3–5 October 2012
12. Werbach, K., Hunter, D.: For the Win: How Game Thinking can Revolutionize Your Business. Wharton Digital Press, Philadelphia (2012)
13. Alahäivälä, T., Oinas-Kukkonen, H.: Understanding persuasion contexts in health gamification: a systematic analysis of gamified health behavior change support systems literature. Int. J. Med. Inform. **96**, 62–70 (2016)
14. Kawachi, I.: It's all in the game – the uses of gamification to motivate behavior change. JAMA Intern. Med. **177**(11), 1593–1594 (2017)
15. Schoech, D., Boyas, J.F., Black, B.M., Elias-Lambert, N.: Gamification for behavior change: lesons from developing a social, multiuser, web-tablet based prevention game for youths. J. Technol. Hum. Serv. **31**(2), 197–217 (2013)
16. King, D., Greaves, F., Exeter, C., Darzi, A.: "Gamification": influencing health behaviours with games. J. Roy. Soc. Med. **106**(3), 76–78 (2013)
17. Kappen, D.L., Orji, R.: Gamified and persuasive systems as behavior change agents for health and wellness. XRDS: Crossroads, ACM Mag. Stud. **24**(1), 52–55 (2017). ACM
18. Lumsden, J., Edwards, E.A., Lawrence, N.S., Coyle, D., Munafò, M.R.: Gamification of cognitive assessment and cognitive training: a systematic review of applications and efficacy. JMIR Ser. Games **4**(2), e11 (2016)
19. Maison, D., Greenwald, A.G., Bruin, R.: The implicit association test as a measure of implicit consumer attitudes. Pol. Psycholog. Bull. **32**, 1–9 (2001)
20. Roefs, A., Jansen, A.: Implicit and explicit attitudes toward high-fat foods in obesity. J. Abnorm. Psychol. **111**(3), 517–521 (2002)
21. Grant, A.M., Fraklin, J., Langford, P.: The self-reflection and insight scale: a new measure of private self-consciousness. Int. J. Soc. Behav. Person. **30**, 821–835(15) (2002)
22. Roberts, C., Stark, P.: Readiness for self-directed change in professional behaviours: factorial validation of the self-reflection and insight scale. Med. Educ. **42**, 1054–1063 (2008)
23. Crano, W.D., Prislin, R.: Attitudes and persuasion. Annu. Rev. Psychol. **57**, 345–374 (2006)
24. Lehto, T., Oinas-Kukkonen, H., Drozd, F.: Factors affecting perceived persuasiveness of a behavior change support system. In: Proceedings of International Conference on Information Systems (ICIS 2012) (2012)
25. Petty, R.E., Cacioppo, J.T.: The elaboration likelihood model of persuasion. Adv. Exp. Soc. Psychol. **19**, 123–205 (1986)

26. Cox, D.N., Anderson, A.S., Reynolds, J., McKellar, S., Lean, M.E.J., Mela, D.J.: Take five, a nutrition education intervention to increase fruit and vegetable intakes: impact on consumer choice and nutrient intakes. Br. J. Nutr. **80**(2), 123–131 (1998)

27. Tikka, P., Oinas-Kukkonen, H.: Contributing or receiving – the role of social interaction styles in persuasion over a social networking platform. Pers. Ubiquit. Comput. **21**, 705–721 (2017)

28. Nosek, B.A., Banaji, M.R.: The go/no-go association task. Soc. Cogn. **19**(6), 625–666 (2001)

29. Hair, J.F., Hult, G.T.M., Ringle, C.M., Sarstedt, M.: A Primer on partial Least Squares Structural Equation Modeling (PLS-SEM). SAGE Publications, Thousand Oaks (2014)

30. Hair, J.F., Ringle, C.M., Sarstedt, M.: PLS-SEM: indeed a silver bullet. J. Mark. Theory Pract. **19**(2), 139–152 (2011)

31. Gefen, D., Ringdon, E.E., Straub, D.W.: Editor's comment: an update and extension to SEM guidelines for administrative and social science research. MIS Q. **35**(2), 3–14 (2011)

32. Fornell, C., Larker, D.: Evaluating structural equation models with unobservable variables and measurement error. J. Mark. Res. **1**(18), 39–50 (1981)

33. Nunally, J.C., Bernstein, I.: Psychometric Theory. McGraw-Hill, New York (1994)

34. Fogg, B.J.: Persuasive Technology: Using Computers to Change What We Think and Do. Morgan Kaufmann, San Francisco (2003)

35. Lyke, J.A.: Insight, but not self-reflection, is related to subjective well-being. Person. Ind. Differ. **46**, 66–70 (2009)

36. Halttu, K., Oinas-Kukkonen, H.: Persuading to reflect: role of reflection and insight in persuasive systems design for physical health. Hum.-Comput. Interact. **32**, 1–32 (2017)

37. Stein, D., Grant, A.M.: Disentangling the relationships among self-reflection, insight, and subjective well-being: the role of dysfunctional attitudes and core self-evaluations. J. Psychol. **148**, 505–522 (2014)

Designing and Testing Credibility: The Case of a Serious Game on Nightlife Risks

Luciano Gamberini[1,3]($\boxtimes$), Massimo Nucci[1,3], Luca Zamboni[1,3], Giovanni DeGiuli[2,3], Sabrina Cipolletta[1,3], Claudia Villa[2,3], Valeria Monarca[2,3], Mafalda Candigliota[1,3], Giuseppe Pirotto[1,3], Stephane Leclerq[2,3], and Anna Spagnolli[1,3]

[1] Department of General Psychology, University of Padova, Padova, Italy
luciano.gamberini@unipd.it
[2] Psicologi Senza Frontiere ONLUS, Padova, Italy
[3] ABD - Energy Control, Barcelona, Spain

Abstract. This paper describes a game directed to young adults and aimed at sensitizing them about potential risks of psychoactive substance abuse during nightlife events. Of interest here is that this game targets a domain in which the credibility of a persuasive intervention is particularly fragile. The design decisions and the recommendations inspiring them are described first, characterized by an effort to fit the context in which the game was going to be used. In addition, a field study with real users during nightlife events is reported (N = 136), in which several dimensions of the game credibility are evaluated and compared with the credibility of a serious information tool (leaflets) in a between-participant design. By describing this case, the opportunity is taken to emphasize the importance of serious games credibility, and to enumerate some of the occasions to improve its strength that can be found during its design to evaluation.

Keywords: Short intervention · Serious games · Nightlife well-being
Credibility

1 Introduction

Clubs, festivals, and parties represent recreational scenarios for thousands of young adults in Europe. Popular music festivals such as Tomorrowland in Belgium or the Outlook festival in Croatia have attracted audiences of 180,000 and 15,000 attendees, respectively. Within these contexts, the use legal and illegal psychoactive substances, such as alcohol, ecstasy, cocaine, amphetamines ('speed'), and ketamine is very frequent [6]. The possible health, legal and safety risks connected to recreational drug consumption and abuse motivates campaigns and interventions addressing young adults to increase their awareness. Frequently found in this context are 'short interventions', which take place during nightlife events and aim at sensitizing potential users about the need for acquiring more information [20]. The advantage of these interventions is that they take place where and when risky behaviours are likely to

© Springer International Publishing AG, part of Springer Nature 2018
J. Ham et al. (Eds.): PERSUASIVE 2018, LNCS 10809, pp. 213–226, 2018.
https://doi.org/10.1007/978-3-319-78978-1_18

occur; the main problem instead resides in the very environment in which they take place, whose mood and noise prevent any serious information exchange to occur.

For this reason we thought of designing a game to accompany field interventions to and convey information about risks and precautions in a format more consistent with the nature of the context. Existing games that target substance consumption are mostly gamified programs for prevention [34] or for identifying craving triggers [21]; our game instead aims to provide information in clubs and festivals, where recreational drug consumption occurs [6, 7]. While doing so we had to take into account the peculiarity of the target users. Differently from drug addicts, nightlife consumers of recreational drugs see psychoactive substances as just one part of their repertoire of life experiences and can rely on meaningful social roles that grant them a positive identity outside nightlife 'transgression' [5, 14]. Moreover, they are likely not to be considered as deviants by their peers [24], with whom the use of recreational drugs is shared in stories that become a sort of "epic genre" [33], often constructing the narrator as a responsible drug user [4, 25]. Finally, in nightlife events music, space, and outfits follow some specific aesthetics (e.g., [22]), establishing what (and who) is appropriate or not and helping the transition inside the recreations dimension [13]. Specific music events and types fit specific drugs and viceversa [17, 36]. The result of all these peculiarities expose persuasion attempts to the risk of looking patently inappropriate if based on mainstream notions of what would be safe, health and correct nightlife behaviour. Target users are sceptical of persuaders with different cultural background holding "an anti-drug agenda" and "likely to focus on the adverse effects of the drug" [10] [30]. They trust expert peers [8] who are seen as unbiased by moral prejudice, and knowledgeable.

We could summarize all these issues by saying that nightlife interventions risk of appearing poorly credible, if by credibility we mean not only the extent to which the source of the intervention is perceived as a well-informed, trustworthy and consistent [12, 15, 16, 18] but also the extent to which the content, format, and protocol of the intervention fit the target's culture, environment, and expectations. The role of credibility as a key factor in persuasion is well known in social psychology [15] and has been also acknowledged very early in the field of persuasive technology [31, 32]. However, empirical research and design have mostly focused on improving the perceived credibility of the source in itself (e.g. [3, 32]), and not the appropriateness of the persuasive intervention to the context in which it is received, despite some explicit solicitations [19, 28]. Trying to be credible also represents an effort to carefully comprehend and sympathize with the context targeted by a persuasive intervention thereby avoiding the risk of patronizing the user, which has been one point of criticism towards persuasive technologies [29].

In this paper we would like to take the opportunity of this nightlife game to emphasize the importance of credibility in serious games and persuasive technology, and to offer at the same time some examples of the ways in which it can be improved.

We will describe first how we tried to achieve credibility in designing our serious game and then how we evaluated the success of our effort in a field study with target users. We will discuss about the relevance of credibility to serious games in the last section.

2   Designing the Serious Game

The game we designed to provide information during nightlife interventions was a quiz (a screenshot is visible in Fig. 1). Questions covered several types of drugs[1] and addressed the possible aftermaths and complications deriving from consumption[2]. The full version of the game contained 4,032 questions (of which 1,193 were multiple choice, and 2,839 were true/false questions) in five different languages (English, Italian, German, French, and Spanish). Each question included explanations based on psychological, physical, or legal information. Each individual player received scores based on the correctness of his/her answers and was ranked in a leader-board.

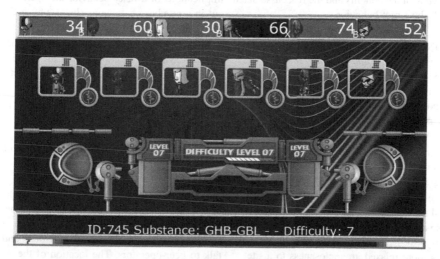

Fig. 1. A screenshot from the game to show its graphics and aesthetics. The highest portion of the screen shows each player's score. Difficulty level of the last quiz question, substance it relates to and correctness of each players' answer (a green/red circle close to each avatar). (Color figure online)

---

[1] Alcohol, cannabis, ecstasy and methamphetamine, hallucinogenic substances, amphetamines and other stimulants, ketamine, GHB/GBL, poppers and other solvents, cocaine, heroin, mix of drugs.

[2] Desired effects; undesirable acute psychological effects; undesirable long-term psychological effects; undesirable physical/medical effects; legal issues, history, politics, and geography; curiosities, myths, and urban legends; gender specificities and pregnancy; driving; sexually transmitted diseases; violence, bullying and micro-interethnic conflicts; first aid, precautions, and context; other).

Table 1. Credibility recommendations from literature and stakeholders and related design decisions for the field intervention.

Recommendations	Our intervention
GETTING FAMILIAR WITH THE TARGET's ... *habits*	A participatory, user-centered approach was adopted to design the game
... *values and language*	Graphics and music reflect those used in nightlife parties and advertising. Narrative storyboards and pictures were developed by target users during dedicated workshops
... *profiles* and information needs	The difficulty of the questions and the type of risky behaviors can be selected in advance to fit each specific event
... *relevant others*, who influence the targeted habits	Group sessions were created to imagine scenarios. A category on the quiz was devoted to friendship and relationships
... *view* of the benefits and the risks associated with the target behavior	Implications of a risky behavior are spelled out in a number of domains (legal, physical, social)
CONTEXTUALIZING TO... ... a family of *communication media*; avoid conceiving the interventions as a stand-alone event: It is more effective if it allows opportunities for integration with other intervention modalities (e.g., leaflets, websites, and workshops)	A peer-operator supervised the game session and was available to complement the game with other information material (e.g., leaflets)
... *stakeholders'*, to facilitate the access to certain events and advise about possible obstacles to implementing the intervention	Access to summer events was negotiated with the event organizers in order to have an official space for the intervention
... *physical setting* in which the intervention will take place and its constraints; this will also allow for the selection of the right area to carry out the intervention (e.g., chill-out zones in a more relaxed area, closeness to a site where other safe nightlife interventions are carried out, and areas where water and food are available)	Questions are short, contextualized by visual narratives, and followed by short explanations facilitating comprehension. Players interested in deeper information can collect leaflets and talk to peer-operators. The location of the gazebo should be central enough to reach as many players as possible, but it should also be quiet and away from crowded areas to allow gameplay and some verbal exchanges
... *the social interaction* between players, and between players and bystanders	Multi-player game, large screen, high-resolution graphics. All players solve the same quiz in parallel and their scores are displayed. The game is projected on a wall to attract bystanders who can learn passively
INFORMING ABOUT ... ... healthier/safer *alternatives* to the target behaviors	Questions and related explanations include practical advice about safer alternatives to risky substance consumption practices

(continued)

Table 1. (*continued*)

Recommendations	Our intervention
... resistance skills necessary to *recognize and face* risky situations and social pressure	Narratives highlight choices that might have undesirable effects. Questions and related explanations include information about how to face risky situations while they are at their incipit
... *scientific results*, presented neutrally in terms of value judgment	Scientific material and prevention material (e.g., flyers, Web portals) from reliable sources were collected and examined to extract the quiz content and its related explanations; all content was then double-checked for correctness by experts. Urban legends and myths are addressed and unveiled (e.g., "Alcohol always has inhibitory effects.")
... *short-term* consequences of the target behavior that are immediately relevant for the night out (and its preparation and aftermaths)	Questions about short-term effects were included in the quiz database (e.g., "One of the effects of inhalers is that it increases one's aggressiveness, and consequently the probability of violent behaviors.")

We included experts and target users in the design process since its early stage. Initially we had a brainstorming session with 21 European peer operators and experienced nightlife operators to collect recommendations about nightlife interventions [1]; we also interviewed about 60 young adults (20 women and 46 men, aged 25.5 on average, SD = 3.6) during festivals to collect their opinion about credibility of drug prevention campaigns in general. The credibility recommendations we collected from the literature and from stakeholders and the related design decisions are listed in Table 1.

3   Field Evaluation

3.1   Evaluation Rationale and Material

Design efforts are obviously not a sufficient warrant that the wanted effects are achieved. Their achievement needs to be evaluated with users. The game described here underwent several tests that evaluated its effectiveness from several points of view, including usability and increase of players' knowledge and awareness of risks, as reported in another paper [11]. In the present paper, we report the evaluation of its credibility to the target users.

The evaluation rationale adopted here consisted not only of collecting credibility rates at the end of a game session played in the field during night events by real target users, in order to see whether the evaluations were positive or negative. We wanted to ground the evaluations by comparing them with an established, serious tool that has the qualities of a trusted information source in the target context, since it is non-judgmental, practical and peer-based. This term of comparison was for us represented by safety leaflets, i.e., information brochures produced and printed by peer associations providing practical advice. Leaflets provide our validation criterion within a validation rationale according to which the new tool (the game) must perform as the one already accepted (peer-produced leaflets). The hypotheses can be expressed as follows: the credibility scores received by the game were positive (H1) and they did not differ from those obtained by leaflets (H2).

We used leaflets (10 cm × 15 cm) produced by a department of the municipality in which the study took place related to one of six psychoactive substances: cannabis, speed, ecstasy, LSD, ketamine, and cocaine. The leaflets adopted the graphics of nightlife events cards and provided information about the substance appearance, its active principle, its consumption modality and effects, the physical and legal consequences of the consumption; some advice to avoid health risks and first aid notions; and contact information. An example is provided in Fig. 2, translated in the footnote[3].

The design of the study was between-participants: participants either played the game or read the leaflets. A subset of the game database was activated for the study, only using 321 questions covering the same information as the leaflets. One game session offered 9 subsequent quiz questions that were randomly selected from that database. Thirty seconds were allocated to answer each question.

---

[3] DEFINITION. Cocaine is a stimulant alkaloid extracted and refined from the coca plant, typically appearing as a white, odorless powder, with a bitter, numbing taste. It is also possible to find freebase crystals or crack obtained by chemically manipulating the power, which can resist the decomposition caused by heat and allow users to inhale the active compound through glass or plastic pipes. Given its high price, cocaine is often mixed with amphetamines, anesthetics, or laxatives. TIME TO TAKE EFFECT. A line of cocaine can contains 10 to 40 mgs of coke, depending on the amount and purity of the powder. The strongest effects of blowing it last 20 to 40 min. Crack smoke has its highest effects in about 10 s and lasting 3 to 4 min. EFFECTS. Coke results in tachycardia and increases blood pressure, temperature, and breathing. It acts upon the brain, increasing the production of dopamine, a pleasure neurotransmitter. It improves mood, increases self-confidence, and boosts egocentrism. Physical and sexual performance is perceived as better and more satisfying; hunger and fatigue are not perceived. It is also a local anesthetic and restricts the blood vessels. PRECAUTIONS. If you blow or inject cocaine, use clean tools; do not trade them or reuse them. Banknotes are frequently responsible for conveying diseases such as hepatitis. Washing teeth and nostrils after a line can reduce the damage to mucosa. If your mouth numbs too much, it might be because coke is mixed with lidocaine, an anesthetic that can be dangerous to your heart. Mixing cocaine and alcohol produces cocaethylene in the blood, which engenders a high dependence (the need for continuously using the substance to prevent abstinence crisis) and can lead to problems. LAW. It is an illegal substance. Administrative penalties are foreseen in the case of personal use (suspension of driving license, passport, or other documents). In addition, a socio-rehabilitation program is proposed at the local social service for drug addiction. For distribution, criminal penalties are foreseen (imprisonment). In case of sickness, call 118. It is important to avoid driving or activities requiring attention.

Fig. 2. A picture of one of the leaflets used in the study (courtesy of U.O.C. Riduzione del Danno della Direzione Politiche Sociali, Partecipative e dell'Accoglienza del Comune di Venezia e dall'Associazione Tipsina di venezia).

3.2 Method

Procedure. The data collection took place during music events hosted in two clubs in northeast Italy; the clubs made us available a large room, separated from the main dancing room and divided into two areas, one for the game and one for the leaflets. Club guests were asked for their availability to participate in a study to evaluate our information material about the risks of drug abuse. Game and leaflet participants were recruited separately, and signed an informed consent. Then they either choose one of the 6 leaflets on display, if recruited for the leaflet condition, or participated in a game session, if they were recruited for the game condition. Given that it was a field study, the individual game session could include any number of players ready to start, up to six. The two conditions varied between participants. Immediately after the leaflet was read or the game session completed, each participant filled in the questionnaire individually.

Participants and design. Participants were 136 young adults (aged 23.53 on average; DS = 4.17, 85 men and 51 women); between them, 67 participants used the game (M = 24.34, DS = 4.96, 47 men and 20 women) and 69 read the leaflets (M = 22.74 DS = 3.06, 38 men and 31 women).

Questionnaire. The comparative evaluation of the perceived credibility was assessed via a paper and pencil questionnaire. During a field study taking place in a club, participants cannot be expected to respond to long and articulated questionnaires; thus our questionnaire consisted of 12 statements with which participants were asked to express their agreement on a Likert scale ranging from 1 to 5, where 1 meant total disagreement. The questionnaire also collected information about the respondents' age, gender, education, and game expertise (in the game condition).

Item 1.1 ("The information provided by the game/leaflet is the same that I could get from an experienced friend") measured the perceived expertise of the source [15, 16], compared with what is the usual source of information for recreational matters, namely friends [8, 10, 27]. Items 1.2 ("I think that the goal of the game/leaflets can be agreed upon"), 1.3 ("The game/leaflet deals with the matter objectively"), and 1.4 ("I trust the information provided by the game/leaflet") measured source trustworthiness [12, 16, 18, 23], namely whether the game goal was acceptable to them, and its information unbiased and trustworthy. Items 1.5 and 1.6 measured the extent to which users found the intervention format appropriate to the context (1.6, "I believe that a game/leaflet is a good method to provide this information during a night out") and the content as relevant (1.5, "People attending events such as this can find in the game/leaflet some relevant content"). The perceived accuracy of the information[30] was investigated by Item 1.7 ("Although brief, explanations are accurate"). Finally, five items measured the perceived effectiveness of the intervention: items 1.8 ("By reading the leaflet/playing with the game I learnt something new about the substances"), 1.9 ("By reading the leaflet/playing with the game I felt the wish to get better informed about substances"), 1.10 ("I'd like to read the information in a quieter moment"), 1.11 ("I appreciated the presence of an operator to clarify some doubts") and 1.12 ("The advice in the leaflet/game can be put into practice"). The overall Cronbach alpha of the items was 0.74.

Data analysis. An exploratory factor analysis with oblique rotation (oblimin) was conducted on the questionnaire items to reduce redundancy in the evaluation dimensions. One Sample Wilcoxon Signed-Rank tests were run to compare each measurement dimension with the central value of the scale and then define whether the evaluation was significantly positive or negative (H1). Mann–Whitney U tests for Independent Samples were then run to compare the two conditions, game and leaflet, on each evaluation dimension (H2). We also controlled the effect of conditions, gender, education, and expertise with a Mann–Whitney U test for Independent Samples and Kruskal-Wallis test. The statistic analysis was performed with R software (version i386 3.4.3) and an SPSS package (IBM SPSS Statistics 20).[4]

---

[4] In the analysis, the scores of each player - even though part of a multiplayer session - was considered individually. There are no reasons to believe that co-players might have affected each other' evaluation of game credibility. The scores gained in the game were gained on an individual basis, so the individual performance was difference than the performance of other group members. Credibility scores were collected individually immediately after the end of the game session, with paper and pencil questionnaires. During the game, players were focused on responding quickly to the quiz than by sharing comments on the game.

Ethics. The study followed the declaration of Helsinki. All participants were of age, and volunteered to take part in the study, which provided trusted information for their wellbeing (as described above) and was then beneficial to them in both study conditions. Nothing in the research instruments was invasive or inductive of any kind of harm, and no sensitive data about individuals' behaviour was collected. All data was collected anonymously. Permission to carry out the intervention was obtained from the venue manager. Informed consents (including study goal, contact information, data collected, funding institution) were collected as printed forms including both the information and the declaration part, before starting the data collection.

3.3   Results

Before testing the hypotheses, an exploratory factor analysis with oblique rotation (oblimin) was conducted in order to identify the dimensions underlying the 12 items of the questionnaire and to facilitate the interpretation of the subsequent analyses by working on fewer dimensions. Based on the saturation values (Table 2), the items meant to measure effectiveness were split into effectiveness and informativeness and the items measuring expertise and trustworthiness were grouped into one dimension named 'reliability'. The remaining items kept their original interpretation (accuracy and appropriateness). These five evaluation dimensions were considered in the subsequent analyses.

Table 2. Summary of exploratory factor analysis loadings (N = 136). Factor loadings grouped in dimensions appear in bold.

Item	Effectiveness	Accuracy	Appropriateness	Informativeness	Reliability
1.1	−0.02	−0.04	0.05	0.19	**0.25**
1.2	−0.05	0.24	0.41	0.04	**0.35**
1.3	−0.19	0.21	0.17	0.06	**0.32**
1.4	−0.11	0.27	0.27	−0.08	**0.34**
1.5	0.13	−0.08	**0.70**	0.10	−0.03
1.6	0.22	0.06	**0.41**	−0.05	0.03
1.7	0.04	**0.97**	−0.03	0.01	−0.01
1.8	**0.55**	0.11	0.13	−0.02	−0.07
1.9	**0.73**	0.08	0.11	−0.01	0.01
1.10	**0.38**	−0.20	−0.06	−0.08	0.39
1.11	0.36	0.08	−0.16	**0.36**	0.30
1.12	−0.05	0.01	0.06	**0.78**	−0.04

To address the first hypothesis, the participants' evaluations of the game were considered in order to determine if they were positive or negative. The results are displayed in Table 3 below. Overall, the evaluations of the game credibility and effectiveness were positive in each evaluation dimension, their score significantly differing from the central value of the response scale ("3").

Table 3. Frequencies distribution in the game condition for each evaluation dimension and results of the One Sample Wilcoxon Signed-Rank test for difference from the central value of the scale

Dimension	Scores					Wilcoxon signed rank test	
	1	2	3	4	5	V	P
Effectiveness	33	24	47	51	46	7228	0.02
Reliability	15	25	71	77	80	15965.5	p < .001
Appropriateness	11	10	23	53	37	4933.5	p < .001
Accuracy	3	2	12	28	22	1380	p < .001
Informativeness	9	9	40	33	43	3655	p < .001
General score	71	70	193	242	228	143209	p < .001

To address the second hypothesis, the evaluations of the game were compared with the evaluations of the leaflets. Figure 3 below shows the results on each evaluation dimension and overall. No significant difference was found between game and leaflets, except for informativeness, on which leaflets performed better than the game (Fig. 3).

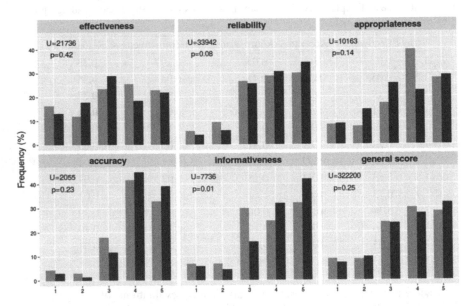

Fig. 3. Frequencies and results of the Mann–Whitney U test for independent samples in the two conditions (red = game, blue = leaflet) in each five dimensions and overall. (Color figure online)

4   Discussion and Conclusions

The results of the field study reported above suggest that participants' evaluations were mostly positive (H1) and did not significantly differ from those obtained by the leaflet-based intervention used as a comparative criterion (H2). The hypotheses are then confirmed, suggesting not only that the credibility evaluation from target users was positive but also that it was in line with the credibility attributed to a serious information tool well-established as fitting these kinds of events. We can then conclude that a game such as ours can be adopted in support of nightlife interventions without any risk of being inconsistent or detrimental to the serious purpose of the intervention itself. The only weakness of the game was its informativeness, probably because the game is designed to provide piecemeal information to players and passers-by. This is actually the reason that our intervention foresees to use the game side by side to a peer-managed booth where more information can be provided to interesting partygoers. Wellbeing interventions during nightlife events commonly include such information booths, sometimes close to first-aid stations.

To the community of researchers and practitioners interested in designing wellbeing interventions, this paper describes the case of an intervention domain much at risk of provoking users' sarcastic dismissal as untrustworthy or inappropriate because of a friction between the values conveyed by the intervention and those cherished by the targeted subculture. The case described here adopts a user-centred design approach that is sensitive to the context of use and is corroborated by a field test with target users as a strategy to maximize the credibility of the game. It contributes an articulated set of recommendations to improve credibility in a broad sense, including a sense of appropriateness to the context of use, which can easily be generalized to other domains than nightlife. It also provides a possible a rationale for the field test, which grounds the users' evaluation to a criterion that is already deemed reliable in the context targeted by the intervention. This is applicable to several domains, if the persuasive system or serious game derives from the addition of game elements to a pre-existing task, procedure, or activity that has a serious goal and is often well established, as is the case with treatment protocols [21] or with training protocols [35]. The purpose of the comparison might be to show that the performance of the serious game matches the performance of the criterion.

Via the case described in this paper, we also hoped to emphasize to the persuasive technology community the importance of covering credibility during the design and evaluation process of a serious game or persuasive intervention mediated by a technology. Although credibility is present in the most popular persuasive technology models, empirical research seldom recognize how crucial yet fragile credibility is. In a game, credibility is fragile because players might respond only to the entertaining aspects of the game and prove less committed than to a serious program, as was already highlighted in the educational domain [26]. In a persuasive technology in general, credibility is particularly fragile when the game addresses behaviour that is regulated by very specific, peculiar subcultures. When the target context is unfamiliar and when recipients have peculiar views of the target behaviour, proposing a solution that is perceived as inappropriate to the target context would make the intervention look ridiculous. This was the risk for recreational drugs consumption in our study but could be the case in health interventions targeting other conducts, such as eating disorders, where the view of health and control cultivated in the targeted community can be at odds with the values defended by the treatment attempts [2, 9]. Our approach to design was to get familiar with the target users, to take into account the physical and social context in which the persuasive technology is used, and to provide information that is unbiased by moral judgment and authoritative. We think that in addition of strengthening credibility, the genuine attentiveness to the target users' values leads to a more respectful persuasion attempt.

Acknowledgements. The study described here was partially supported by the European Commission, via the Nightlife, Empowerment and Well-being Implementation (NEW-IP, no. 29299) project. The funding body did not affect the authors' decisions about the study design, collection, analysis and interpretation of data, the writing of the report, or the decision to submit the article for publication.

References

1. Zamboni, L., Gamberini, L., Spagnolli, A., Cipolletta, S., De Giuli, G., Tion, I.: Serious games in social intervention: designing technologies to promote safe and healthy behaviors. In: Proceedings of the 9th ACM SIGCHI Italian Chapter International Conference on Computer-Human Interaction: Facing Complexity, pp. 139–142. ACM, September 2011
2. Bates, C.F.: "I am a waste of breath, of space, of time" metaphors of self in a pro-anorexia group. Qual. Health Res. **25**(2), 189–204 (2014). https://doi.org/10.1177/1049732314550004
3. Choi, M., Rifon, N.: Antecedents and consequences of web advertising credibility: a study of consumer response to banner ads. J. Interact. Advert. **3**(1), 12–24 (2002). http://jiad.org/article26.html. Accessed Nov 2013
4. Dahl, S.L., Heggen, K.: Negotiating identities patterns of self-presentations among socially integrated cannabis users. Young **22**(4), 381–398 (2014)
5. Decorte, T.: Drug users perceptions of controlled and uncontrolled use. Int. J. Drug Policy **12**, 297–320 (2001)
6. European Monitoring Centre for Drugs and Drug Addiction: Responding to drug use and related problems in recreational settings. Document no. TDXA12003ENN (2012a). http://www.emcdda.europa.eu/attachements.cfm/att_184673_EN_Recreational_settings_WEB.pdf
7. European Monitoring Centre for Drugs and Drug Addiction: Travel and drug use in Europe: a short review. Document no. TD-XA-12-004-EN-N (2012b). http://www.emcdda.europa.eu/attachements.cfm/att_185273_EN_Travel%20and%20drug%20use.pdf
8. Falck, R.S., Carlson, R.G., Wang, J., Siegal, H.A.: Sources of information about MDMA (3, 4-methylenedioxymethamphetamine): perceived accuracy, importance, and implications for prevention among young adult users. Drug Alcohol Depend. **74**(1), 45–54 (2004)
9. Fox, N., Ward, K., O'Rourke, A.: Pro-anorexia, weight-loss drugs and the internet: an 'anti-recovery' explanatory model of anorexia. Sociol. Health Illn. **27**(7), 944–971 (2005)
10. Gascoigne, M., Dillon, P., Copeland, J.: Sources of ecstasy information: their use and perceived credibility. Technical report No. 202, National Drug and Alcohol Research Centre, University of New South Wales, Sydney (2004). http://www.ndarc.med.unsw.edu.au/sites/ndarc.cms.med.unsw.edu.au/files/ndarc/resources/TR.202.pdf

11. Gamberini, L., et al.: A gamified solution to brief interventions for nightlife well-being. In: Meschtscherjakov, A., De Ruyter, B., Fuchsberger, V., Murer, M., Tscheligi, M. (eds.) PERSUASIVE 2016. LNCS, vol. 9638, pp. 230–241. Springer, Cham (2016). https://doi.org/10.1007/978-3-319-31510-2_20

12. Gaziano, C., McGrath, K.: Measuring the concept of credibility. Journal. Q. **63**(3), 451–462 (1986)

13. Gregory, J.: Too young to drink, too old to dance: the influences of age and gender on (non) rave participation. Dancecult **1**(1), 65–80 (2009)

14. Grund, J.P.C.: Drug Use as a Social Ritual: Functionality, Symbolism and Determinants of Self-Regulation. Instituut voor Verslavingsonderzoek, Rotterdam (1993)

15. Hovland, C.I., Janis, I.L., Kelley, H.H.: Communication and Persuasion: Psychological Studies of Opinion Change. Yale University Press, New Haven (1953)

16. Hovland, C.I., Weiss, W.: The influence of source credibility on communication effectiveness. Public Opinion Q. **15**, 635–650 (1951). https://doi.org/10.3233/978-1-61499-282-0-70. ISBN 978-1-61499-281-3

17. Maxwell, J.C.: Party drugs: properties, prevalence, patterns, and problems. Subst. Use Misuse **40**, 1203–1240 (2005)

18. McCroskey, J.C., Teven, J.J.: Goodwill: a reexamination of the construct and its measurement. Commun. Monogr. **66**, 90–103 (1999)

19. Mitgutsch, K., Alvarado, N.: Purposeful by design? A serious game design assessment framework. In: Proceedings of the International Conference on the Foundations of Digital Games, pp. 121–128. ACM, New York (2012)

20. Moyer, A., Finney, J.W.: Brief interventions for alcohol problems: factors that facilitate implementation. Alcohol Res. Health **28**(1), 44–50 (2004)

21. North, L., Robinson, C., Haffegee, A., Sharkey, P.M., Hwang, F.: Using virtual environments for trigger identification in addiction treatment. In: Proceedings of the 9th International Conference on Disability, Virtual Reality & Associated Technologies, Laval, France, 10–12 September 2012, pp. 345–353 (2012)

22. O'Grady, A.: Spaces of play the spatial dimensions of underground club culture and locating the subjunctive. Dancecult **4**(1), 86–106 (2012)

23. Ohanian, R.: Construction and validation of a scale to measure celebrity endorser's perceived expertise, trustworthiness, and attractiveness. J. Advert. **19**(3), 39–52 (1990)

24. Parker, H., Williams, L., Aldridge, J.: The normalization of "sensible" recreational drug use. Sociology **36**(4), 941–964 (2002)

25. Ravn, S.: Contested identities: identity constructions in a youth recreational drug culture. Eur. J. Cult. Stud. **15**(4), 513–527 (2012)

26. Rice, J.W.: New media resistance: barriers to implementation of computer video games in the classroom. J. Educ. Multimedia Hypermedia **16**(3), 249 (2007)

27. Roberts, G., McCall, D., Stevens-Lavigne, A., Anderson, J., Paglia, A., Bollenbach, S., et al.: Preventing substance use problems among young people: a compendium of best practices. Report no. Cat. No. H39-580/2001E, produced by Canadian Centre on Substance Abuse, Office of Canada's Drug Strategy. Health Canada, Ottawa, Canada (2001). http://www.hc-sc.gc.ca/hc-ps/alt_formats/hecs-sesc/pdf/pubs/adp-apd/prevent/young-jeune-eng.pdf

28. Sillince, J.A.A.: A model of the strength and appropriateness of argumentation in organizational contexts. J. Manag. Stud. **39**(5), 585–618 (2002)

29. Spagnolli, A., Chittaro, L., Gamberini, L.: Interactive persuasive systems: a perspective on theory and evaluation. Int. J. Hum.-Comput. Interact. **32**(3), 177–189 (2016)

30. Spencer, R.: "It's not what i expected": a qualitative study of youth mentoring relationship failures. J. Adolesc. Res. **22**(4), 331–354 (2007)

31. Torning, K., Oinas-Kukkonen, H.: Persuasive system design: state of the art and future directions. In: Proceedings of the 4th International Conference on Persuasive Technology (Persuasive 2009), Article 30, 8 p. ACM, New York, April 2009
32. Tseng, S., Fogg, B.J.: Credibility and computing technology. Commun. ACM **42**(5), 39–44 (1999)
33. Tutenges, S., Rod, M.H.: 'We got incredibly drunk … it was damned fun': drinking stories among Danish youth. J. Youth Stud. **12**(4), 355–370 (2009)
34. Vogl, L.E., Teesson, M., Newton, N.C., Andrews, G.: Developing a school-based drug prevention program to overcome barriers to effective program implementation: the CLIMATE schools: alcohol module. Open J. Prev. Med. **2**(3), 410–422 (2012)
35. Williams-Bell, F.M., Kapralos, B., Hogue, A., Murphy, B.M., Weckman, E.J.: Using serious games and virtual simulation for training in the fire service: a review. Fire Technol. **51**, 1–32 (2015)
36. Yacoubian, G.S., Miller, S., Pianim, S., Kinz, M., Orrick, E., Link, T., Palacios, W.R., Peters, R.J.: Toward an ecstasy and other club drug (EOCD) prevention intervention for rave attendees. J. Drug Educ. **34**(1), 41–59 (2004)

Personalization and Tailoring

Persuasive Interventions for Sustainable Travel Choices Leveraging Users' Personality and Mobility Type

Evangelia Anagnostopoulou[1]([⊠]), Efthimios Bothos[1],
Babis Magoutas[1], Johann Schrammel[2], and Gregoris Mentzas[1]

[1] ICCS - Institute of Communication and Computer Systems,
NTUA - National Technical University of Athens, Athens, Greece
{eanagn, mpthim, elbabmag, gmentzas}@mail.ntua.gr
[2] AIT – Austrian Institute of Technology, Vienna, Austria
Johann.Schrammel@ait.ac.at

Abstract. Sustainable mobility has received significant attention over the recent years due to the negative impact of peoples' transportation habits on the environment and the society, especially in congested urban areas. In this paper, we present our approach for personalized persuasion aiming to nudge travelers to opt for sustainable mode choices. Our approach leverages persuadability profiles comprising of users' personality and mobility type in order to identify the persuasive strategy that fits best to the user's profile, and supports transportation decisions towards more environmental friendly routes, by providing targeted interventions in the form of persuasive messages integrated in a route planning application. A pilot study in the city of Vienna showed evidence that the application affects users' mobility choices.

Keywords: Persuasion · Mobility · Behavioural change · Personalization

1 Introduction

The impact of transport systems on the environment is becoming increasingly higher, accounting for between 20% and 25% of world energy consumption and carbon-dioxide emissions [1] while transport related greenhouse gas emissions are increasing faster than other energy sectors. A major contributor to the above situation is road transport, resulting to high local air pollution and smog, especially in urban areas. Thus, it is crucial for people to consider the impact of their mobility choices on the environment and change unsustainable transportation habits and choices.

The available strategies for improving the sustainability of mobility vary. One way that does not require significant infrastructure investments is nudging travellers to shift to greener transportation modes. To achieve this, it is important to design and implement approaches that increase travellers' awareness of the environmental impact of their travel mode choices, and provide persuasive interventions that support green travel choices and eventually lead to transportation habits that rely more on the use of public transportation, bicycles and walking and less on private cars.

© Springer International Publishing AG, part of Springer Nature 2018
J. Ham et al. (Eds.): PERSUASIVE 2018, LNCS 10809, pp. 229–241, 2018.
https://doi.org/10.1007/978-3-319-78978-1_19

Past research has shown that people differ in their susceptibility to different persuasive strategies [2] which means that personalized persuasive approaches can be more successful than "one size fits all" approaches. The majority of persuasive applications for transport sustainability have been implemented for a general audience using persuasive strategies such as self-monitoring or rewards. Thus, it is necessary to create services that address the specific needs of individual users. Some first results are encouraging, e.g. Jylhä et al. [3] reached better results by personalizing persuasive challenges, however further exploration of personalized persuasive strategies for behavioural change towards sustainable modes of transportation is required.

In this paper, we present a personalized persuasive approach which aims to motivate users on a personal level to change their mobility behavior and make more sustainable choices. To achieve this, we leverage user persuadability profiles comprising of user personality and mobility type in order to select the persuasive strategy that best fits to the individual user [10]. A set of selected persuasive strategies (suggestion, self-monitoring and comparison) are implemented in persuasive messages which are displayed to users, aiming to nudge them to adopt sustainable transportation habits. More specifically, we have implemented our personalized persuasion approach as a set of services integrated into a mobile route planning application. The services receive as input a list of alternative routes for travelling from A to B provided by a routing engine, combine the personality and mobility type of users in order to select the most appropriate persuasive strategy and generates persuasive messages which are displayed in the route selection screen of the application. The routing engine generates a variety of multimodal (i.e. routes which involve the use of more than one transportation means such as combinations of private car and public transportation or bicycle and public transportation) and unimodal routes. The displayed message aims to affect user choices towards selecting environmentally friendly routes. A pilot study has been conducted in order to evaluate the effectiveness of our approach.

The rest of this paper is organized as follows. Section 2 presents related work for sustainable mobility and message based persuasion; Sect. 3 describes our approach for personalized selection of persuasive strategies, while Sect. 4 presents the evaluation results of a pilot study; Finally, Sect. 5 concludes the paper with our final remarks and plan for the next steps.

2 Related Work

Persuasive systems addressing behaviour change in the context of personal mobility in urban environments is an active area of research, and numerous systems and implementations exist, aiming to motivate users towards making more eco-friendly choices; e.g. adopting transportation habits that rely more on the use of public transportation, bicycles and walking and less on private cars. Some of the existing applications display personalized information, such as the decrease in emissions, saved money and burnt calories, to persuade users to make more sustainable choices [3, 4]. Another way that existing systems use to nudge users is by providing visual feedback in the form of adapting the background graphics of the smartphone when making sustainable choices [5].

Message based persuasive technologies have been implemented in various domains with promising results. Indicative application includes motivating adherence to insulin therapy in adolescent diabetics [6], smoking cessation [7], increasing physical activity [8] and nudging users to shift to less polluting transportation modes [9]. A main drawback of existing applications is the limited use or lack of personalization aspects that consider differences in users' susceptibility to persuasive strategies. Moreover, none of the existing applications for sustainable mobility take into account the personality and the mobility type of users.

3   Our Approach for Sustainable Travel Choices

In our previous study [10], we explored two user traits that can be used for personalizing the selection of persuasive strategies applied to end users: personality and mobility type. Using the results of that study, in this paper we implemented a personalized persuasive approach aiming to motivate users to make more environmentally friendly choices considering their preferences, personality and mobility type. Figure 1 provides an overview of our approach, which is based on two complementary services: the route recommendation service, and the personalized persuasion service.

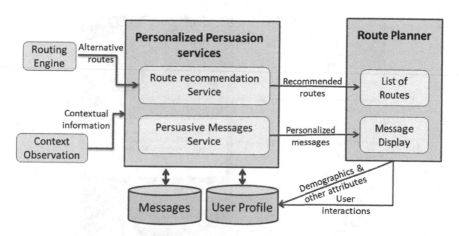

Fig. 1. Architecture of personalized persuasive framework.

The route recommendation service receives as input a list of alternative routes for travelling from origin A to destination B. The list is generated by a routing engine and contains an extended set of unimodal (e.g. taking a car or a bus) and multimodal (e.g. park and ride) options for reaching the destination. The service integrates functionalities for filtering and structuring the available routes, and returns a personalized list of recommended routes. Filtering concerns the exclusion of routes based on preferences set by the user in her profile and other pre-defined restrictions. More specifically users set if they own a car or bicycle and the maximum walking and biking distance they are willing to travel. System defined restrictions include the filtering of routes that commonly do not make sense (e.g. taking a car for 100 m).

Structuring involves ranking of the filtered routes in a personalized manner, and highlighting one route that is environmentally friendly and adheres to user preferences as well as the current context. A utility function has been defined for ranking the routes. It captures the effect of psychometric and demographic parameters on travel time and cost, user stated preferences, past user behaviour, active context variables and the environmental friendliness of the routes in terms of the emissions caused. The highlighted route is selected based on the mobility type of the user, trying to nudge him/her towards more environmentally modes of transportation than the one s/he is currently using the most. The highlighted route is displayed in a prominent position in the route planning application and is considered as the target for the persuasive attempts (see part 1 of Fig. 2 for an indicative capture of the routes presentation screen of the application).

Given a route with a transportation mode as the target for user persuasion, the role of the personalized persuasion service is to provide personalized persuasive features that aim to persuade the user to take that particular route. The personalized persuasion service is called by the route recommendation service with the aim to attach a personalized persuasive message to the route selected by the former as the target for user persuasion, as shown in see part 1 of Fig. 2.

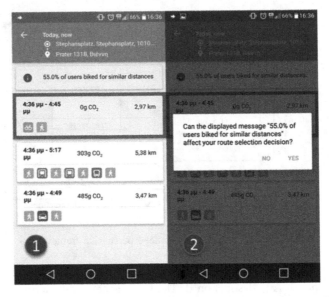

Fig. 2. Example of route results in the route planning app (part 1). A "popup" asks users to provide feedback (part 2).

The personalized persuasion service specifically addresses different users and tailors the persuasive messages to the individual, with the aim to maximize the impact of the persuasive attempts. The service selects from a set of persuasive messages corresponding to different persuasive strategies, the message that each individual user is more susceptible to, by also considering the current user, trip and environmental context. More specifically, the provision of the personalized persuasive messages is enabled through a four-step methodology as shown in Fig. 3. In the following we describe each step of the methodology.

1. <u>Selection of persuasive strategies</u>: The persuasive strategies of self-monitoring, comparison and suggestion were selected among the 10 persuasive strategies suggested by [11], by taking into account strategy appropriateness for message-based persuasion and the suitability of the strategy to the overall scope of our approach.
2. <u>Identification of user persuadability</u>. The user persuadability, i.e. the user susceptibility to the persuasive strategies of self-monitoring, comparison and suggestion is identified implicitly, i.e. without the need of explicit user involvement, and dynamically, i.e. after some attempts to persuade the user with the same strategy. The approach is based on previous successful persuasive interactions of that particular user and other similar users and builds upon the work proposed by [12]. More specifically, the effectiveness of a message implementing a single persuasive strategy for a particular user is estimated by considering the specific user's previous responses to that same message and the known effectiveness of the message for other users. Note that a persuasive interaction is considered to be successful when the user declares that the message affects her/his route choice through a small "popup" that is presented in the application under the message as shown in part 2 of Fig. 2.

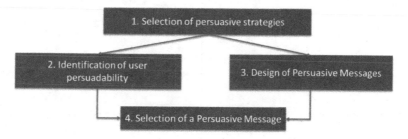

Fig. 3. Methodological steps enabling the provision of personalized persuasive messages.

The probability of a user selecting the recommended route on multiple occasions is regarded as a binomial random variable $B(n, p)$ where n denotes the number of attempts to persuade the user using a specific strategy and p denotes the probability of success i.e. the probability of taking the route on which the message it attached to. Given S different strategies, we compute for each individual and each strategy, the probability $p = k/n$ where k is the number of observed successes after presenting the message implementing this strategy n times to a specific user. Every time the system displays a message to an individual, the probabilities of success of each strategy are updated and the user is considered more susceptible to the strategy that has the highest p value for her. The higher the number of users receiving persuasive interventions and the number of persuasive attempts per user, the faster this approach converges.

However, this approach suffers from the so-called cold start problem, according to which the system cannot draw any inferences for users until it has gathered sufficient information for them. To address this problem and enable faster convergence of the algorithm, we have implemented a persuadability model that is used to explicitly identify user susceptibility to the different persuasive strategies on the basis of user personality and mobility type. Data from this model are used as prior information in the aforementioned binomial random process to kick start the calculation of probabilities of success for all the strategies. The persuadability model has been developed as part of our previous work [10] and is applied during user registration in the application. The personality of each user is identified with ten relevant questions as shown in Fig. 4. User responses are used to estimate her/his five personality traits (i.e. openness, con-scientiousness, extraversion, agreeableness and neuroticism - often listed under the acronym OCEAN). The calculations are based on the Big Five personality traits model defined in [13] and provide a score per personality trait. The trait with the highest score is the one that characterizes the user the most. The mobility type of a user is determined by explicitly asking which transport modes he/she uses the most. That personality trait characterizing the user the most, along with the user mobility type, in turn feed our persuadability model with the aim to derive the individual user's persuadability.

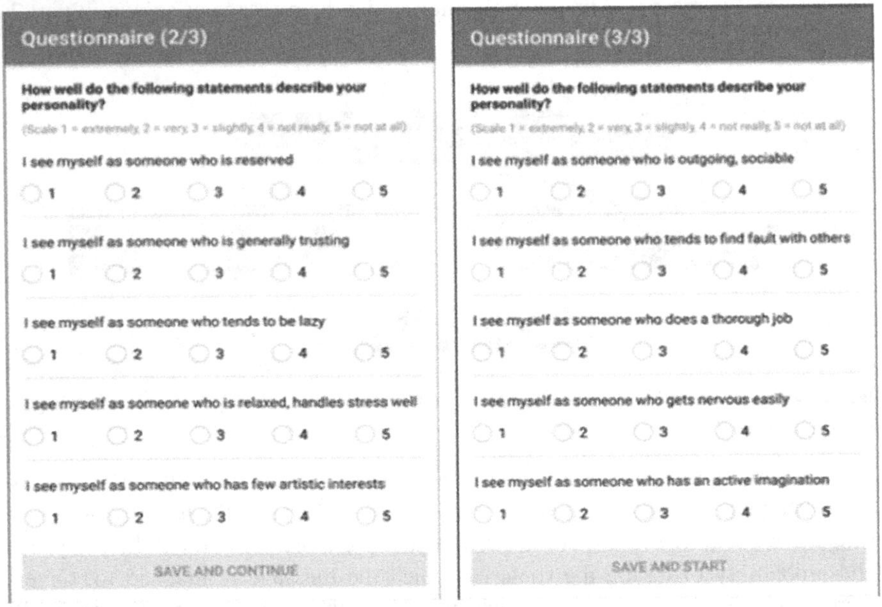

Fig. 4. The ten questions which are used to identify users' personality. The questions are answered upon user registration and are based on the Big Five inventory proposed in [13]. Their analysis provides a measure of the user's personality over five dimensions: Openness, Conscientiousness, Extroversion, Agreeableness and Neuroticism (OCEAN).

3. <u>Design of persuasive messages.</u> We have defined ninety-eight (98) persuasive messages with each one implementing a single persuasive strategy. Multiple messages have been designed per persuasive strategy, while all of them are context-aware, in the sense that they are valid for specific contexts. The contextual elements used in our pool of messages capture the context in which the travel behaviour takes place. We have defined seven binary contextual variables (i.e. their value can be true or false) as follows: (i) three variables based on personal travel behaviour characteristics (increased car usage in terms of distance travelled over the previous period, increased public transportation usage in terms of distance travelled over the previous period, caused emissions increasing compared to other users); (ii) three variables based on trip-related characteristics (the destination is in a biking or walking distance, the duration of the route is similar to driving); (iii) one variable based on weather status (nice or bad weather). Note that for the calculation of trip related context variables, users provide their preferences, including the maximum walking and bike distance with which they feel comfortable as well the ownership of a bicycle, during registration.

Making the messages context-aware enhances the ability of the personalized message generation service to provide tailored messages. Only messages with a context that is valid for a particular user with a particular profile, who is planning for a particular trip made under specific environmental conditions, are selected. Each context-aware persuasive message is associated to one or more transportation modes which the particular message tries to persuade the user to follow. Table 1 provides indicative examples of defined persuasive messages.

Table 1. Indicative persuasive messages. The associated transportation modes that each message tries to persuade the user to follow is shown in brackets.

Context	Persuasive strategy		
	Suggestion	Comparison	Self-monitoring
Walking distance	You are near to your destination. It's an opportunity to walk. [Walk]	**PWalkSD** % of users walked for similar distances [Walk]	Last week you caused **C02Em** g of CO2 emissions. Try to reduce it by walking [Walk]
Too many car routes	If you can drive less, you'll be doing a lot to help save the planet. [Public Transport], [Bike&ride], [Bike], [Walk]	Take public transport. **PReduceDriving** % of users have already reduced driving [Public Transport]	You have been using a car a lot the past days. Take public transportation [Public Transport]
Nice weather	Nice weather for bike&ride [Bike&ride]	**PPtGW** % of users used public transport when the weather was as good as today! [Public Transport]	When the weather was good you used bike sharing **MinBikeSharing** minutes per day on average [Bike Sharing]

The messages may contain percentages or numbers as placeholders in the text of the message (bolded in Table 1). The actual values of the placeholders are calculated in the runtime through a number of functions that have been developed for that purpose. Examples of functions include PWalkSD that calculates the percentage of other users that walked for similar distances and PReduceDriving that calculates the percentage of users who have already reduced driving. The calculation is based on the detection of user activities through GPS monitoring. A specific module embedded in the application, tracks user activities and infers their mode, duration and length.

4. <u>Selection of a persuasive messages</u>. Given a pair of user and route as the target for user persuasion, one persuasive message is selected among those designed in the previous step. The persuasive message selection method, which is outlined in Fig. 5, takes into account the user susceptibility to the different persuasive strategies and the current context. User persuadability defines the selection space, since the message to be selected belongs to the set of messages that implement the persuasive strategy that works best with the particular user.

To select among the messages corresponding to a specific persuasive strategy, we consider the current status of the various binary contextual variables for which context-aware messages have been defined, along with the primary transportation mode of the route that each message tries to persuade the user to follow. Since some primary transportation modes are only targeted by messages in particular contexts but not in others, some contextual variables may be irrelevant for a given primary mode (e.g. 'walking distance' context variable is irrelevant for all primary modes but walking).

The message selection method identifies the relevant contextual variables for a given primary mode (see also Fig. 5). There are two possibilities depending on the

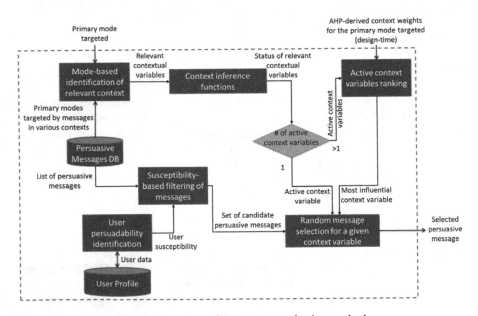

Fig. 5. Overview of the message selection method

number of the relevant contextual variables that are active (i.e. their status is true): a) if only one contextual variable is true, a message targeting the given transportation mode is randomly selected among the one(s) defined for that context variable; b) if more than one contextual variables are true at the same time, there is a need to select a message defined for the context variable that is considered more influential.

In order to rank context variables according to their potential for influencing users, we developed a model based on the Analytic Hierarchy Process (AHP), multi criteria decision making method [14]. More specifically, we asked three domain experts in Intelligent Transportation Systems to evaluate by pairwise comparisons the relative influence that the contextual variables have on the user choice of the corresponding mode. Experts were asked to rate the relative influence of each contextual variable compared to its pair on a nine-point Likert scale, while their responses were used to derive the context weights for the seven conflicting cases identified (i.e. for cases where two or more context variables can be active at the same time).

4 Evaluation

To evaluate our approach, identify the user acceptance of the messages and it's effectiveness, we setup a pilot study. During the pilot study, users from the city of Vienna in Austria installed and used the route planning application for their everyday urban trips. Vienna offers a variety of mode choices including advanced public transportation networks as well as bike and car sharing options. The duration of the pilot study was 6 weeks, beginning on April 2017 and ending on May 2017. In total 27 participants took part in the pilot study, 13 female, 14 male, between 21 and 70 years (mean = 39.5; SD = 12.04). Mean age of female users were 35.73 years (SD = 9.40) and of male users 43.27 (SD = 13.17).

The participants filled in a set of questionnaires before and after the study and were interviewed at the end. The pre-trial questionnaire asked for participants' travel preferences and past travel behaviour. The post-trial questionnaire contained questions regarding the usefulness of the persuasive interventions as well as their influence on participants' actual travel behaviour and environmental awareness. Finally, four semi-structured interviews were carried via telephone after 7 weeks and lasted for about 30 min each. Topics covered during the interviews include the user opinions about persuasive messages and their influence on travel mode choices and personal environmental awareness.

Both quantitative and qualitative data were collected to gather as much insight as possible. For the data analysis, we took into account logged interactions of users using the app, the mobility and the personality type of participants and responses to the questionnaires.

During the pilot study, 142 routing requests were sent by the users and 105 messages were displayed (matching corresponding context activations). The effectiveness of the messages was measured by considering two cases as having a positive effect: (i) "popup only": the user provided a positive reply in the related "popup" displayed in the route selection screen (see part 2 of Fig. 2) and (ii) "popup and viewed routes": the user provided a positive reply in the "popup" as in case (i) or the user checked the details screen of the recommended route to which the message referred (the route details appear when the users selects a route and provides details regarding the itinerary). Note that we report case (ii) because there were cases where users skipped the "popup" and didn't provide any feedback (by e.g. pressing the "home" button of their smartphone).

In more details, we received feedback from the "popup" for 51 requests. The positive feedback was for 15 messages or 30% of the total messages for which we received feedback. When considering also the viewed routes (as described in case (ii) above) the positive feedback was 34%. These results are "inline" with previous studies (see e.g. [15, 16]), although we cannot be certain that users who provided positive feedback actually followed the more environmentally friendly route.

Moreover, we analysed the collected questionnaire responses and interview data in order to identify the effect of the persuasive interventions on user mobility choices. Subjects stated that they found the messages useful. Most of them reported that the ranking of routes influences their decision regarding the transport choice (see part 1 of Fig. 6). Participants reported that the messages are easy to understand and clear (see part 2 of Fig. 6). Moreover, the willingness to see persuasive messages in their daily mobile applications was high as participants stated that they would like to receive persuasive messages in route planning applications (see part 3 of Fig. 6), while the persuasiveness of the personalized messages was perceived as somewhat convincing as shown in part 4 of Fig. 6.

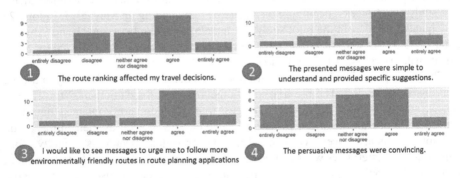

Fig. 6. Questionnaire responses.

The perceived quality and ease of understanding of interventions followed the same patterns in the interviews. Two participants recalled an example of transport modes that they were persuaded by the app to follow "Received the better option to take the bus instead of the tramway" - "Received better route to go the doctor". Moreover, a participant stated "I received the message: Nice weather, others have been walking. At that moment, I changed my mind and walked down the Mariahiflerstraße instead of taking the underground (U3) to the station Volkstheater". In the phone interview, one participant shared her thoughts that she personally had become more aware of the possibility to use the bike (although preferably not in city traffic). As a consequence, she used the bike two times to reach the train station instead of using public transport.

Another interesting finding came out of users who stated that the suitability of a suggested mode would strongly depend on the given situation such as trip purpose and social context of the trip. Accordingly, the assumption holds that individual trip purpose has a strong influence on transport mode choice. This means that the personalization of messages can be improved by taking into account the trip purpose.

5 Conclusions

In this paper, we presented our personalized persuasive approach for sustainable urban mobility. Our approach identifies user persuadability profiles based on users' personality and mobility type, and selects the persuasive strategy that fits best to the specific user. This information is used to personalize persuasive interventions in the form of messages in a route planning application. A pilot study involving users from Vienna provided evaluation results which show that users perceived the messages as useful and we encountered cases of behavioural change. One limitation of our evaluation is the fact that a high number of users were already following environmentally friendly modes. Due to this, there was a bias in the results. We plan to extend our evaluation with more users who use their car a lot but recognize that it would be good if they reduced car use. Another limitation of our work is making people aware of persuasive attempts may increase the bias. This may affect their behavior in positive or negative manner. Either they might do their best while they feel they are tracked or they might not want to admit that they were persuaded by a message. This may influence the persuasiveness of the system.

Currently, we are examining ways which could extend the proposed persuasive services. These include the implementation of visual (in addition to verbal) presentation of persuasive strategies (e.g. through graphs), that will allow us to examine the combined effect of visual and verbal presentations on users' behaviour and compare it to that of solely visual or verbal presentations. Examples include graphs that provide visual cues of the CO_2 emissions caused by a user's activities compared to those of the other users (comparison strategy) and graphs that show the CO_2 emissions caused by the user in different time periods (self-monitoring strategy). Furthermore, we are looking into ways of extending the contextual variables and integrate knowledge that concerns users' trip purpose. Towards this direction, a mode detection module is being extended with a set of rules, to derive the trip purpose from Foursquare categories classifications (e.g. shopping mall, restaurant) and frequently visited locations (e.g. work, home). For example, if destination is a shopping mall there is a high probability that the user is travelling for leisure, information that can be used in order to intensify the persuasive attempts.

Acknowledgements. Research reported in this paper has been partially funded by the European Commission project OPTIMUM (H2020 grant agreement no. 636160-2).

References

1. Birch, E.: A review of "climate change 2014: impacts, adaptation, and vulnerability" and "climate change 2014: mitigation of climate change". J. Am. Plann. Assoc. **80**(2), 184–185 (2014)
2. Kaptein, M., Markopoulos, P., de Ruyter, B., Aarts, E.: Can you be persuaded? Individual differences in susceptibility to persuasion. In: Gross, T., Gulliksen, J., Kotzé, P., Oestreicher, L., Palanque, P., Prates, R.O., Winckler, M. (eds.) INTERACT 2009. LNCS, vol. 5726, pp. 115–118. Springer, Heidelberg (2009). https://doi.org/10.1007/978-3-642-03655-2_13
3. Jylhä, A., Nurmi, P., Sirén, M., Hemminki, S., Jacucci, G.: MatkaHupi: a persuasive mobile application for sustainable mobility. In: UbiComp 2013, Zurich, Switzerland (2013)
4. Reitberger, W., Ploderer, B., Obermair, C., Tscheligi, M.: The PerCues framework and its application for sustainable mobility. In: de Kort, Y., IJsselsteijn, W., Midden, C., Eggen, B., Fogg, B.J. (eds.) PERSUASIVE 2007. LNCS, vol. 4744, pp. 92–95. Springer, Heidelberg (2007). https://doi.org/10.1007/978-3-540-77006-0_11
5. Froehlich, J., Dillahunt, T., Klasnja, P., Mankoff, J., Consolvo, S., Harrison, B., Landay, J.A.: UbiGreen: investigating a mobile tool for tracking and supporting green transportation habits. In: Proceedings of the SIGCHI Conference on Human Factors in Computing Systems, pp. 1043–1052. ACM, New York (2009)
6. Franklin, V.L., Waller, A., Pagliari, C., Greene, S.A.: A randomized controlled trial of sweet talk, a text-messaging system to support young people with diabetes. Diabet. Med. **23**(12), 1332–1338 (2006)
7. Rodgers, A., Corbett, T., Bramley, D., Riddell, T., Wills, M., Lin, R.B., Jones, M.: Do u smoke after txt? Results of a randomised trial of smoking cessation using mobile phone text messaging. Tobacco Control **14**(4), 255–261 (2005)
8. Purpura, S., Schwanda, V., Williams, K., Stubler, W., Sengers, P.: Fit4life: the design of a persuasive technology promoting healthy behavior and ideal weight. In: Proceedings of the SIGCHI Conference on Human Factors in Computing Systems, pp. 423–432. ACM, May 2011
9. Bothos, E., Prost, S., Schrammel, J., Röderer, K., Mentzas, G.: Watch your emissions: persuasive strategies and choice architecture for sustainable decisions in urban mobility. PsychNology J. **12**(3), 107–126 (2014)
10. Anagnostopoulou, E., Magoutas, B., Bothos, E., Schrammel, J., Orji, R., Mentzas, G.: Exploring the links between persuasion, personality and mobility types in personalized mobility applications. In: de Vries, P.W., Oinas-Kukkonen, H., Siemons, L., Beerlage-de Jong, N., van Gemert-Pijnen, L. (eds.) PERSUASIVE 2017. LNCS, vol. 10171, pp. 107–118. Springer, Cham (2017). https://doi.org/10.1007/978-3-319-55134-0_9
11. Halko, S., Kientz, J.A.: Personality and persuasive technology: an exploratory study on health-promoting mobile applications. In: Ploug, T., Hasle, P., Oinas-Kukkonen, H. (eds.) PERSUASIVE 2010. LNCS, vol. 6137, pp. 150–161. Springer, Heidelberg (2010). https://doi.org/10.1007/978-3-642-13226-1_16
12. Kaptein, M., van Halteren, A.: Adaptive persuasive messaging to increase service retention: using persuasion profiles to increase the effectiveness of email reminders. Pers. Ubiquit. Comput. **17**(6), 1173–1185 (2013)
13. Rammstedt, B., Goldberg, L.R., Borg, I.: The measurement equivalence of big-five factor markers for persons with different levels of education. J. Res. Pers. **44**(1), 53–61 (2010)
14. Tayali, H.A., Timor, M.: Ranking with Statistical Variance Procedure Based Analytic Hierarchy Process (2017)

15. Gabrielli, S., Maimone, R.: Digital interventions for sustainable urban mobility: a pilot study. In: UbiComp 2013, Zurich, Switzerland (2013)
16. Kaptein, M., Markopoulos, P., De Ruyter, B., Aarts, E.: Personalizing persuasive technologies: Explicit and implicit personalization using persuasion profiles. Int. J. Hum. Comput. Stud. **77**, 38–51 (2015)

Building Website Certificate Mental Models

Milica Stojmenović[(⊠)] (iD), Temitayo Oyelowo, Alisa Tkaczyk,
and Robert Biddle (iD)

Carleton University, Ottawa, ON K1S 5B6, Canada
milica.stojmenovic@carleton.ca

Abstract. Expert security users make safer online decisions. However, average users do not have mental models for browser security and web certificates. Thus, they may make unsafe decisions online, putting their sensitive information at risk. Users can learn about browser security and their mental models can be developed using information visualization. We introduce an interactive interface designed for building mental models of web certificates for the average user, through visualization and interaction. This model was implemented to facilitate learning with a Mental Model Builder (MMB). The interface underwent a cognitive walkthrough usability inspection to evaluate the learnability and efficacy of the program. We found that there were unique and useful elements to our visualization of browser certificates. Thus, a 2nd generation interface was created and user-tested. Results show that it was successful in building mental models, and users made safer decisions about trusting websites.

Keywords: Online security · Website identity · Mental model builder
Persuasive interaction · Usable security

1 Introduction

Users that are unaware of dangerous online situations can find themselves victim of identity theft, phishing scams, and other spoofing related network attacks [2]. To help users make better online decisions, this paper focuses on the design and implementation of an interface to educate a non-expert computer user of basic browser security concepts related to certificates.

A web certificate is a cryptographic data structure that can provide website identity information. Such certificates establish an encrypted link between a client (e.g. your computer) and server (e.g. a powerful computer holding all information from the website you are interacting with), and can provide information on website identity. However, not many people know about them. Advanced users are more likely to make safer decisions online since developed mental models are positively correlated with expertise in computer security [1]. Developing mental models allowing users to make safer online decisions, and helps avoid danger online [2].

Our research question was: *Can we persuade users to use web certificates when making online decisions, by building their mental models?* Fogg suggests that media can be used to educate and persuade user behaviour, by simulating cause-and-effect relationships, providing people with experiences and motivations, and helping people

© Springer International Publishing AG, part of Springer Nature 2018
J. Ham et al. (Eds.): PERSUASIVE 2018, LNCS 10809, pp. 242–254, 2018.
https://doi.org/10.1007/978-3-319-78978-1_20

rehearse behaviours [4]. Thus, we speculate that people *can* understand certificates. It has been proposed that information visualizations can help users construct mental models [7]. This approach has been used for other issues in computer security [14].

Moreover, persuasive authentication techniques encourage users to make more secure passwords [5]. However, there are very few papers on the influence of persuasive technology in instructional web security [14]. Thus, we developed a teaching aid to explore this issue.

Our interface aims to build mental models for online certificate security, using persuasive technology principles. In particular, our goal was to educate users and assist in the building of mental models of network security, including the explanation of website identity through browser certificates, in an easy and persuasive way. The interface aims to influence users to avoid sharing their personal information online with unknown/unidentifiable websites, by teaching basic computer security concepts including encryption and identity, through persuasive interaction.

This paper is structured as follows. The next section defines certificates and presents a summary of work done in the area. The following section illustrates a certificate mental model that we suggest and encourage. Next, we discuss the 1st Generation Interface we created based on our mental model, and tested with Human-Computer Interaction (HCI) experts. This is followed by a description of the testing of the 2nd Generation Interface. We conclude with an interface results and implications discussion.

2   Certificates

Encryption is the encoding of data before sending it to the intended recipient, so that only they have the key to decrypt it. There are two types of encryption: symmetric and asymmetric. In symmetric encryption, the same key encrypts and decrypts the data. In asymmetric, one key encrypts and another decrypts (i.e. private and public keys). The underlying principle of asymmetric encryption is mathematical factoring using large prime numbers. Certificate Authorities (CAs) create and issue website certificates, which use asymmetric cryptography to support both in-transit encryption and some assurance of identity using X.509 certificates. The CA confirms the identity of the organization requesting the certificate.

Domain Validation (DV) certificates offer an encrypted connection, assuring users that an eavesdropper will not intercept the information they are sending. The lock symbol and the green colour are current browser indicators of DVs. The website of CIBC, a bank, was chosen as an example of a DV indicator (Fig. 1). DVs are free and issued very quickly, allowing an encrypted connection between the browser and the domain.

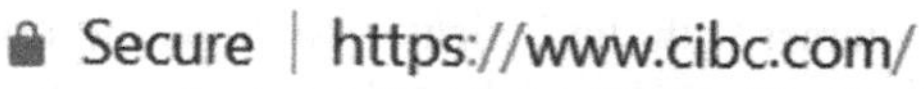

🔒 Secure | https://www.cibc.com/

Fig. 1. Example of a DV on Google's Chrome: green padlock and "https" (Color figure online)

While an encrypted connection means that data sent is inaccessible to eavesdroppers, it offers no assurances that the destination is the expected one. A trustworthy destination is one with a verified identity. An Organization Validation (OV) certificate provides encryption and also has a field in the certificate about the organization behind the website (identity). In Google's Chrome, OV and DV appear the same (Fig. 1). OVs are not examined in this study.

The highest level of identity verification available is an Extended Validation (EV) certificate. EV secures the connection with encryption but includes a thorough background check done by a CA (more rigorous than for an OV), to ensure the website's identity. Once the check is passed, the EV is granted and browsers portray them by adding the organization name before the URL, seen in Fig. 2. In the browser, the name of the organization and its country of origin appear in green text next to the encryption lock. Twitter was chosen as an example of a website with an EV.

🔒 **Twitter, Inc. [US]** | https://twitter.com/?lang=en

Fig. 2. EV in Chrome: green padlock, company name, country of origin, and "https," (Color figure online)

Certificate interfaces differ between browsers and operating systems. The wording in the interfaces is usually very brief, often with technical details, making it hard for the user to understand. Moreover, there are constant updates to the interfaces. This leads to user confusion and out-of-date help guides. Our goal is to aid the typical user to distinguish between different certificate verification levels by displaying information in a meaningful way.

2.1 Previous Work on Certificate User Studies

An influential early study [9] showed that most users do not notice or interact with certificate indicators on the browser. More recently, a study at Google [8] investigated how to improve the indicators, and then implemented the findings in Google's Chrome browser. An important aspect of these studies is that there was no specific focus on *identity*. In particular, the recent study emphasized the importance of having some certificate, thereby offering an encrypted connection, but there was little mention of identity to help users avoid fraudulent sites.

There have been studies that did address identity, especially since the introduction of EV certificates. One study [10] compared the security indicators of certificate interfaces used by Mozilla Firefox with their own proposed redesign with users. The results showed that the then current indicator was too subtle: none of the participants noticed it. Only fifteen (out of 28) participants did claim to notice the indicator on the proposed redesign and three included the indicator in their decision making. No participants attempted to interact with the indicator and thus did not see the explanatory popup. Twenty-two participants preferred the redesign since it was more noticeable and provided information without interaction. Those that preferred the existing design liked that it took up less space in the browser, but needed a prompt to see it in the first place.

Another study [3] compared the usability of the authors' proposed new interface for the EV certificate interface to the existing one. The purpose of the study was to discover which features of the certificate interface the users could understand: whether the different levels of authentication were clear and if the users could distinguish between website identity and encryption. They found that the existing interface used technical terms, unfamiliar to the typical user. Technical information should be available through deeper levels for advanced users but hidden at the first level from the typical user, to avoid confusion. Moreover, the statement "this website is secure" for DV did not accurately portray that encryption is not enough to determine that a website is really secure: it may simply support an encrypted connection for a fraudulent site.

Their proposed certificate interface separated identity from privacy protection. The identity confidence was provided by the presence and authentication level of the certificate, where low confidence meant no certificate was provided, medium confidence meant a DV, and high confidence was achieved through an EV. Privacy protection was determined by whether encryption was used by the website, and the researchers employed an eavesdropping metaphor instead of using the term 'encrypted'. The results showed that participants made safer decisions using the alternative design. They correctly determined the ownership of the website and the privacy of transmitted data. Participants were also more certain about their decisions using the alternative design.

One limitation with these studies is that none of them examined participants' prior knowledge and understanding of certificates and of CAs. Are users aware that CAs exist and that their purpose is to regulate website certificates? Can a new interface be developed to help deliver the certificate information? The next section outlines the different theoretical frameworks used in our paper.

The most relevant paper to our work is one on the use of persuasive images and software updates in antivirus software. Zhang-Kennedy et al. [14] created and tested infographics that persuaded users update their computer antivirus software. Their results showed that their persuasive visualizations were more successful in influencing users to update their antivirus software than mainstream textual security advice.

Since visualizations were found to be influential with antivirus software updates [14], our work focused on creating interactive software to build mental models of web certificates. The aim was to persuade users to actively check for web identity in an effort to reduce the risk of sharing personal details with fraudulent websites.

3 Mental Models

Mental Models are a combination of our perceptions and ideas [11]. They are used to help us understand an individual's comprehension of concepts in the environment.

We suggest and encourage the use of the mental model for certificates shown in Fig. 3. Users interact with the Internet through the browser of their choice. They load a website that appears to belong to the intended organization – but how can they be sure? The certificate, issued by trusted CAs and shown by browsers, can confirm this.

When a user accesses a website with a certificate, the browser retrieves it and determines if it was issued by a recognized CA (itself a cryptographic process). If not, the browser will disallow access or require the user to confirm an exception. If the CA is recognized, the browser then uses the certificate to establish encrypted access to the website, and if the certificate has identity information, then it is presented to the user.

Most participants fail to notice the existence of the security indicator, or deem it unimportant in decision making [12]. If users had stronger mental models of EV certificates, they would more readily notice and properly interpret security indicators to make safer online decisions [12]. To encourage users to seek out browser cues, we aim to show them the various levels of certification and how the information is displayed in browsers. By developing their understanding of web certificates, we can increase the ability to determine website identity, and have a greater understanding of its importance. This mental model was used as a theoretical framework to structure our work.

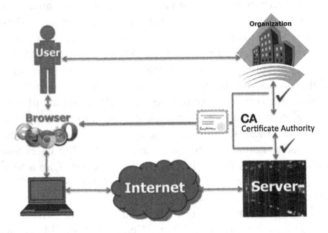

Fig. 3. Key players and process of website identity determination.

4   1st Generation Mental Model Builder (MMB): Pipeline Model

Our 1st Generation Interface was meant to encourage interaction and exploration of the interface in order for the user to understand the grouping of images. The first interface we created is shown in Fig. 4. The numbers correspond to the following sections:

1. Houses the textual descriptions of the security aspects
2. The network box: shows if encrypted or not
3. Describes what the level of encryption means
4. Displays identity information: Not validated (criminal) or validated (police)
5. Displays identity information
6. Encryption/identity summary
7. Displays information when elements are hovered over

As users clicked on security levels in (2), field (3) updated. Selecting identity in (4) populated the relevant information in (5). The combination of security and identity auto-populated (6). More information showed in (7) when elements were hovered over.

4.1 Cognitive Walkthrough

We tested the interface with a cognitive walkthrough [6, 12], while a facilitator and two usability experts inspected the program's learnability and efficacy. The tasks were: to create a secure connection, create an insecure connection, reset the interface, display the information regarding http, and display the unverified destination information.

For each task, the evaluators asked themselves: (1) Will users attempt to achieve the correct outcome? (2) Will they be aware that the correct action is available? (3) Will they be able to connect the correct action with their expected outcome? (4) Will they recognize that they have made progress towards their intended outcome when they perform a correct action?

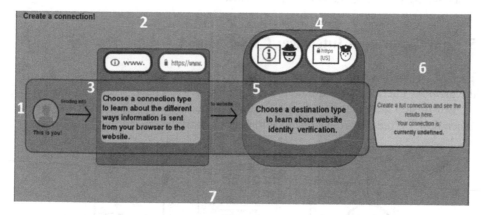

Fig. 4. Browser certificate learning: interface upon opening up the screen.

Cognitive Walkthrough Result Summary. For the first task, a potential problem was that 'https' was mentioned twice in the interface: under security and again in the identity box. To create a secure connection, one needed to select the Police Officer, which was unclear since it was not labeled. The "[US]" label also did not intuitively stand for country code, according to the evaluators. The company name was never mentioned and is the main component in the identity verification process associated with EV.

The next task was to create an insecure connection. These components were also unlabeled so the next step was not intuitive for the evaluators. Thus, the interface should have used labels. For example, 'browser security status' should be used, because a 'status' implies more than one level. Evaluators were unable to answer all four sub questions positively and they were unable to reset the interface.

To display information about http and unknown identity, the user needed to hover over the appropriate areas. These were not clear interactions since none of the options seemed clickable, thus uninviting for a hover. One evaluator did notice 'https' and proceeded to click on it. This resulted in failure to notice that hovering was available. This is a result of icon and images used, as they do not suggest possible interactions.

Adding an option to reset, cancel or undo changes may encourage users to play with the interface without fear of making mistakes. Also, it may not be obvious to the user that this interface is designed to be a learning tool. Users would benefit from an introduction or instruction screen, ensuring that they would know the interface options. Users may be goal-oriented and providing scenarios may encourage directed interactions.

Summary. To our knowledge we were the first to create an interactive interface to build mental models that assist in understanding browser security concepts, to persuade users to make safer online decisions. Educating users would effectively improve their mental model and improve their ability to make safe online decisions [2]. We found that the interface could develop mental models and would help users obtain a better understanding of browser certificates, but improvements were necessary and were addressed by the 2nd Generation MMB, below.

5   2nd Generation Interface: Cyclic Model

The 2nd Generation web certificate MMB (Fig. 5) corrected all of the issues found in the previous interface. In addition, the first interface was linear, where the interaction seemed to stop after the user interpreted the certificate security level. For the second generation, we redesigned it to include a more cyclical model, starting with the user's

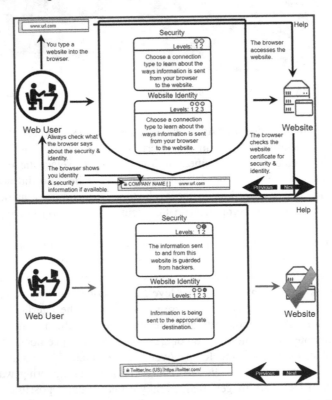

Fig. 5. 2nd generation certificate MMB; tutorial above, EV connection below.

interaction with the web browser, and ending with the user's decision on whether or not to proceed interacting with a website, depending on the certificate. The MMB showed the user interaction with the web browser, the browser's role in checking the certificates, and how the certificate indicators are portrayed in the Chrome browser.

At first, the MMB displayed a tutorial, illustrating the cyclical model of the website identification process. This simulated the relationship between users, websites, and browsers. Users were then directed to an interactive mode in which they navigated through the MMB at their own pace. This interaction simulated the cause-and-effect relationships between browser indicators and web security and identity levels. The MMB also provided users with examples of each certificate indicator in Chrome. Summaries of what each security and identity level meant were shown to users, with more detailed information available when hovering over the identity and encryption boxes.

5.1   Method: User Testing the MMB

Our research question was: Can we persuade users to use web certificates when making online decisions, by building their mental models? To test this, we designed a within-group study that asked users to judge the identity and safety of websites, before and after using our 2nd Generation MMB.

Participants. There were 21 participants (9 male, 12 female). Of these, 16 were aged 18–19, four 20–19, and one 30–39. Twenty were undergraduates and one was a master's student. Four studied computer science, three studied psychology, three engineering, two studied biology, one HCI, two studied business/commerce, two political science, one environmental science, and one undeclared. All participants were daily mobile, internet, and computer/laptop users. None had taken a course in computer security. Each participant did the study separately and each session lasted about 30 min. Our research studies were cleared by our Research Ethics Board.

Materials. A sample of 20 website login/home pages was collected for this study. Eight of these were modified in Photoshop to alter the website's URL (henceforth referred to as 'fake'). This was done in an effort to simulate phishing attacks. Ten were shown to participants pre-MMB, and the other half was shown after.

Pre-MMB, the websites and their certificates were: Toronto-Dominion Bank (EV), Amazon (OV), Carleton University (OV), Twitter (EV), Banana Republic (OV), Best Buy (EV), The Source (real has OV, ours had a fake URL and DV), Fido (real has OV, ours had a fake DV), Rogers (real has OV, ours had a fake DV), and Royal Bank of Canada RBC (real has OV, ours had a fake DV). Post-MMB, the ten websites were: Gmail (OV), Canadian Imperial Bank of Commerce (OV), Facebook (OV), Yahoo mail (OV), Paypal (EV), Scotiabank (EV on login page), Instagram (real has OV, ours had fake DV), Cineplex (real has OV, ours is a fake DV), Bank of Montreal (fake, no cert), and Bell (real has OV, ours had a fake DV). These were well known in our environment.

After seeing each website, participants were asked to rate ten website homepage screenshots, based on identity, using 5-point Likert scale questions. The identity questions were: "the website in the image is the real one", "hackers can intercept the information I send to this website", and "I'm willing to enter my personal information (e.g. phone number, address, credit card number, etc.) on this website".

Procedure. After the consent form was signed, the online study began with the participants reading the welcome screen. They proceeded to fill in the online demographic questionnaires. Then, they were asked to rate ten website homepage screenshots, based on authenticity. Four (/10) websites had fake URLs (Photoshopped), the rest were real.

This was followed by the interaction with our MMB. The interaction started with a tutorial mode to allow participants the opportunity to learn how to use the interface. Next, the interaction included exploring different security.

After the interaction with the MMB, the participants filled in the post-tutorial questionnaire. They then repeated the rating of ten different website homepage screenshots on visual appeal and identity. Finally, they filled out an online post-task questionnaire.

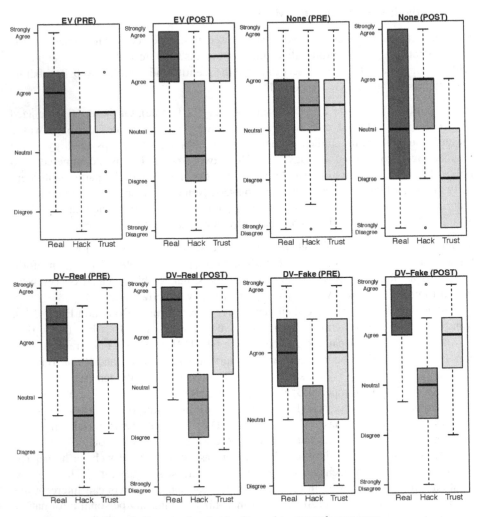

Fig. 6. Perceived web identity and trust result summary.

5.2   Results

When participants were asked if they knew what a web certificate was, *most, 61.90%, said that they did not, while the rest said that they did.* Those who stated that they knew what certificates were, were asked four more questions. Of these, 12.5% agreed that they looked at them when interacting with a website, while 62.5% said that they did not, and the rest did not know. When asked if they find the web certificate indicators easy to understand, 25% agreed, 62.5% disagreed, and the remaining 12.5% did not know. When asked if they felt that learning how to use web certificates is relatively easy, 12.5% agreed, 50% disagreed, and 37.5% remained neutral. 87.5% of the participants who stated that they knew what certificates were also stated that they were confident in their ability to distinguish real websites from fake websites, and 12.5% disagreed. In sum, most people were unfamiliar with certificates.

They proceeded to rate the first ten website screenshots, interact with the MMB and then rated a different set of ten website screenshots. The average MMB use was 2.4 min, with interactions ranging between 1–4.5 min.

In Fig. 6, the bars represent the answers to the website identity questions: 'Real' refers to the 'is it the real website' question, 'Hack' summarizes the 'can hackers intercept the information' question, and 'Trust' refers to the 'willingness to enter personal information into the website' question. The answers were aggregated across certificate types, pre and post-MMB use. 'None' refers to websites that had no certificates, 'EV' refers to the aggregated websites with EV certificates, and 'DV' refers to the set of websites with DV or OV certificates. Only the DV category had fake and websites because they are free and more likely to be used for fraud.

Table 1. Result summary and Wilcoxon test results

Cert	Scale	Pre			Post			Pre vs Post	
		M0	Md0	SD0	M1	Md1	SD1	W	p
EV	Real	3.9	4	0.8	4.5	4.5	0.6	18	**0.00599**
EV	Hack	3.1	3.3	0.7	2.7	2.5	1.4	142.5	0.16611
EV	Trust	3.5	3.7	0.6	4.3	4.5	0.6	15	**0.00049**
None	Real	3.5	4	1.2	3.1	3	1.6	83.5	0.18902
None	Hack	3.4	3.5	1.1	3.4	4	1.3	67	0.97923
None	Trust	3.3	3.5	1.2	2.2	2	1.1	157.5	**0.00175**
DV-Real	Real	4.2	4.3	0.7	4.5	4.8	0.7	32.5	0.06976
DV-Real	Hack	2.9	2.7	0.9	2.7	2.8	1.1	128.5	0.39033
DV-Real	Trust	3.8	4	0.7	3.8	4	0.9	101	0.62622
DV-Fake	Real	4	4	0.7	4.3	4.3	0.7	35	**0.02892**
DV-Fake	Hack	2.9	3	0.8	2.9	3	1.1	89	0.8245
DV-Fake	Trust	3.7	4	0.8	3.7	4	0.9	97	0.77918

In Table 1, 'Cert' stands for web certificate type. 'None' refers to websites that had no certificates, 'EV' refers to the aggregated websites with EV certificates, and 'DV-real' refers to the set of websites with real DV or OV certificates. 'DV-fake' is made up of websites with URLs that we altered in Photoshop. 'DV-both' refers to the aggregation of both real and fake DV/OV websites, since the browser indicator is the same for these certificate types. 'Real' refers to the 'is it the real website' question, 'Hack' summarizes the 'can hackers intercept the information' question (so lower is better), and 'Trust' refers to the 'willingness to enter personal information into the website' question. 'M' is the mean, 'Md' is the median, and 'SD' is the standard deviation. The '0' and '1' are the pre and post-MMB data. The 'W' is the Wilcoxon paired test statistic for non-parametric data (the three questions participants filled in for 10 websites pre- and 10 websites post-MMB). The 'p' represents the p-value from the Wilcoxon tests.

Results show that after a very brief exposure to the persuasive MMB (i.e. just over two minutes, on average), participant sentiment changed towards web certificates. Specifically, as seen in Table 1, *willingness to enter personal information into the website went down 2 points on the Likert scale after the MMB, for websites without certificates*. For *EV*, the answers for *both the authenticity and willingness to enter personal information into the website questions were more favourable after the MMB* (i.e. participants went from 'agreeing' to 'strongly agreeing' to trust EV certificates). The fake DV websites saw a 0.3 increase in the authenticity rating, discussed in the next section.

6   Discussion and Conclusion

The 2nd Generation MMB was successful in persuading users to trust EV certificates more, and websites without certificates less. For no certificate, this was expected since participants previously may not have known how vulnerable an unencrypted connection was. Their post-MMB responses show that they would avoid sharing their details with websites without certificates.

For EV, the answers for both the authenticity and willingness to enter personal information into the website questions were more favourable after the MMB. This was expected since EV certificates are the highest level of online security available for users. EVs provide evidence of identity and confirm encryption. The brief exposure to the MMB was enough for participants to recognize and understand EV. This confirms that participants did understand the MMB, and that after only a brief interaction with it (i.e. on average 2.4 min), it worked in developing their mental models for EV and no certificates. Participants made safer online decisions. Therefore, we conclude that for both websites without certificates and for websites with EV, our intervention led to safer results. Based on the results, we can also propose that their understanding of web certificates was improved, thus developing relevant mental models. However, given that mental models are not tangible, we cannot be certain without a longitudinal study.

For DV, the message is mixed since it signifies safe communication but the destination of the commutation is not verified. While this offers more security than an unencrypted website, it is not as safe as a website with an EV certificate where the website owners have been verified by the Certificate Authorities. The confusion becomes even greater when OV is taken into consideration, since the browser indicator is the same for OV and DV, yet OV does offer a hint about the website owners. Thus, perceived and actual safety of DVs may need to be examined in more detail in a future study.

6.1 Future Work

Future work could extend the work done in this paper to evaluate the impact of visual appeal on trustworthiness and understandability of browser indicators of web certificates. It can also include the creation, evaluation of a video version of the MMB. It may also examine the perceived difference in DV and OV certs with users, where their expectations of the appearance and purpose of each is examined more thoroughly.

Current browser interfaces provide terse indicators or complex technical details: neither is well understood by users. Future work could focus on creating standardized browser indicators to help users more readily recognize and understand web security.

One limitation in this study is that we asked for their subjective opinions on identity, hackability, and willingness to share personal information with the websites. A future study could examine the actual behaviour of users, and not just their intentions.

The results in this paper show that even a brief interaction with a persuasive Mental Model Builder was successful in improving safe behaviour online. Users with these mental models were then correctly persuaded in being more cautious when interacting with websites without certificates. Participants were also more trusting of websites with EV certificates, where the identity of website owners and encrypted communication offered the highest security online to users.

References

1. Asgharpour, F., Liu, D., Camp, L.J.: Mental models of security risks. In: Dietrich, S., Dhamija, R. (eds.) FC 2007. LNCS, vol. 4886, pp. 367–377. Springer, Heidelberg (2007). https://doi.org/10.1007/978-3-540-77366-5_34
2. Bravo-Lillo, C., Cranor, L.F., Downs, J., Komanduri, S.: Bridging the gap in computer security warnings: a mental model approach. IEEE Secur. Privacy Mag. 9(2), 18–26 (2011)
3. Biddle, R., Sobey, J., Whalen, T., Oorschot P.V., Patrick, A.: Browser interfaces and extended validation SSL certificates: an empirical study. In: Proceedings of ACM Workshop on Cloud Computing Security (2009)
4. Fogg, B.J.: Persuasive Technology: Using Computers to Change What We Think and Do. Morgan Kaufmann, Burlington (2002)
5. Forget, A., Chiasson, S., van Oorschot, P.C., Biddle, R.: Persuasion for stronger passwords: motivation and pilot study. In: Oinas-Kukkonen, H., Hasle, P., Harjumaa, M., Segerståhl, K., Øhrstrøm, P. (eds.) PERSUASIVE 2008. LNCS, vol. 5033, pp. 140–150. Springer, Heidelberg (2008). https://doi.org/10.1007/978-3-540-68504-3_13
6. Jaspers, M.W.: A comparison of usability methods for testing interactive health technologies: methodological aspects and empirical evidence. Int. J. Med. Inf. 78(5), 340–353 (2009)
7. Liu, Z., Stasko, J.T.: Mental models, visual reasoning and interaction in information visualization: a top-down perspective. IEEE Trans. Vis. Comput. Graph. 16(6), 999–1008 (2010)
8. Felt, A.P., Reeder, R.W., Ainslie, A., Harris, H., Walker, M., et al.: Rethinking connection security indicators. In: SOUPS, pp. 1–14 (2016)
9. Schechter, S.E., Dhamija, R., Ozment, A., Fischer, I.: The emperor's new security indicators. In: Proceedings of IEEE Symposium on Security and Privacy, pp. 51–65. IEEE Computer Society, Washington, D.C. (2007)

10. Sheng, S., Magnien, B., Kumaraguru, P., Acquisti, A., Cranor, L.F., et al.: Anti-phishing phil: the design and evaluation of a game that teaches people not to fall for phish. In: Proceedings of SOUPS, NY, USA, pp. 88–99 (2007)
11. Sinreich, D., Gopher, D., Ben-Barak, S., Marmor, Y., Lahat, R.: Mental models as a practical tool in the engineer's toolbox. Int. J. Prod. Res. 43(14), 2977–2996 (2005)
12. Sobey, J., Biddle, R., van Oorschot, P.C., Patrick, A.S.: Exploring user reactions to new browser cues for extended validation certificates. In: Jajodia, S., Lopez, J. (eds.) ESORICS 2008. LNCS, vol. 5283, pp. 411–427. Springer, Heidelberg (2008). https://doi.org/10.1007/978-3-540-88313-5_27
13. Wharton, C., Rieman, J., Lewis, C., Polson, P.: The cognitive walkthrough method: a practitioner's guide. In: Usability Inspection Methods, pp. 105–140. Wiley, Hoboken (1994)
14. Zhang-Kennedy, L., Chiasson, S., Biddle, R.: Stop clicking on "update later": persuading users they need up-to-date antivirus protection. In: Spagnolli, A., Chittaro, L., Gamberini, L. (eds.) PERSUASIVE 2014. LNCS, vol. 8462, pp. 302–322. Springer, Cham (2014). https://doi.org/10.1007/978-3-319-07127-5_27

Persuasive Technology to Support Chronic Health Conditions: Investigating the Optimal Persuasive Strategies for Persons with COPD

Beatrix Wais-Zechmann[1(✉)], Valentin Gattol[1], Katja Neureiter[1],
Rita Orji[2], and Manfred Tscheligi[1,3]

[1] AIT Austrian Institute of Technology, Vienna, Austria
{beatrix.wais-zechmann, valentin.gattol,
katja.neureiter, manfred.tscheligi}@ait.ac.at
[2] Faculty of Computer Science, Dalhousie University, Halifax, NS, Canada
rita.orji@dal.ca
[3] University of Salzburg, Salzburg, Austria
manfred.tscheligi@sbg.ac.at

Abstract. Persuasive technology can support persons with chronic conditions to comply with their treatment plan. For persons with chronic obstructive pulmonary disease (COPD), staying physically active is crucial to prevent deteriorations of their health status. However, most persons with COPD do not reach and maintain recommended levels of physical activity goals. Although COPD is expected to become the third most common cause of death worldwide, research on how to design persuasive systems for motivating specifically persons with COPD to engage in regular physical activity is still scarce. To bridge this gap, we conducted a study involving persons with COPD ($n = 115$) to investigate the *perceived persuasiveness* of 17 strategies (i.e., ratings of their concrete implementation) and *individual susceptibility to persuasion* (i.e., an underlying disposition to be more receptive to certain persuasive strategies). Based on our analysis, the following strategies were perceived as most persuasive: *personalization, reminder, commitment, self-monitoring, rewards, customization, authority,* and *scarcity.* Interestingly, the data revealed differences between *perceived persuasiveness* and *individual susceptibility to persuasion*, indicating that both constructs measure distinct aspects of persuasiveness. Our results are relevant to designers and developers of persuasive systems by providing valuable insights about the most promising persuasive strategies and their practical implementation when designing for persons with COPD.

Keywords: Chronic obstructive pulmonary disease (COPD)
Persuasive strategies · Perceived persuasiveness
Individual susceptibility to persuasion

1 Introduction

Chronic obstructive pulmonary disease (COPD) is a chronic progressive lung disease with symptoms like breathlessness, muscle weakness, and chronic cough that leads (in severe stages) to the dependence on external oxygen supply. About 10% of adults

© Springer International Publishing AG, part of Springer Nature 2018
J. Ham et al. (Eds.): PERSUASIVE 2018, LNCS 10809, pp. 255–266, 2018.
https://doi.org/10.1007/978-3-319-78978-1_21

above the age of 40 are affected [1] and COPD is expected to become the third most common cause of death worldwide in 2030 [2]. Within the European Union, health care costs of COPD are estimated to be about 23.3 billion Euro [3]. COPD is not curable, thus, patients have to deal with it throughout their lifetime and there is no getting around without a successful self-management process. Mitigating the disease progression significantly is possible through lifestyle changes [4, 5]. In particular, frequent physical activity is considered to be one of the most effective measures to prevent decline [6]. However, many patients lack motivation and do not reach the recommended physical activity level leading to increased hospitalizations, mortality, reduced quality of life and loss of productivity [6, 7]. Thus, a solution is required that motivates persons with COPD (PwCOPD) to engage in frequent physical activity as a preventive measure. While the use of persuasive technology has been broadly investigated in training applications for the general population [8], little work has been done regarding the use of persuasive technology to motivate PwCOPD to exercise more [9].

The aim of our research is to investigate how persuasive systems should be designed for PwCOPD. In this paper, we contribute to the existing research by answering the following research question: *Which persuasive strategies (PS) are most effective in motivating PwCOPD to engage in more physical activity?*

Findings of this research allow for a more effective design and adaptation of persuasive systems for PwCOPD. The paper is structured as follows: we start with reviewing the related work, followed by a description of the methods, the analysis of the results, their discussion including implications and conclusions for designers and developers of persuasive systems for PwCOPD.

2   Related Work

Persuasive technologies have been successfully applied in a wide range of contexts to trigger behavior change, such as increased physical activity [10]. However, the applications focus mainly on the general population without considering disease-related circumstances of PwCOPD. In those few applications that focus on motivating PwCOPD for physical activities, only little work has been done to investigate the use of persuasive design strategies and principles for this target group [9]. Thus, the scientific literature in the context of PS in COPD treatment reveals knowledge gaps. Behavioral interventions that aim at increasing physical activity in PwCOPD mainly use conventional approaches such as counselling and education [11]. However, the effectiveness of individual PS has not been evaluated specifically for PwCOPD.

Voncken-Brewster et al. [12] evaluated the usability of an online self-management intervention for COPD patients in a lab setting that included eight behavioural change techniques (based on the I-Change Model [13]). However, they provide few insights on how PwCOPD experience behavioral change strategies. Instead, the paper focuses chiefly on usability aspects of the overall intervention and does not investigate the effectiveness of the strategies. Similarly, other studies include various PS in their interventions but do not evaluate the comparative effectiveness of the individual strategies per se (e.g. [14]).

Bartlett et al. [9] investigated the acceptance of different persuasive design principles for technologies that aim at encouraging physical activity among PwCOPD. They investigated three different prototypes using the three design principles *dialogue support, primary task support, and social support* and investigated acceptance and persuasiveness of the technologies. Although the authors account for design principles, each of them incorporating several PS, their work does not assess the persuasiveness of the individual strategies.

It is essential to evaluate the effectiveness of various PS before implementing them in an intervention. In a review involving 17 randomized controlled trials, four techniques were associated with significantly larger effect sizes related to smoking cessation in COPD patients: *facilitate action planning/develop treatment plan, prompt self-recording, advise on methods of weight control*, and *advise on/facilitate use of social support* [15]. This review also points out that the most frequently used strategy (*boost motivation and self-efficacy*; used in 70.6% of interventions) was associated with very low effectiveness.

To develop suitable persuasive systems for PwCOPD, our paper investigates which of the PS are perceived as most persuasive by PwCOPD to increase their physical activity.

3   Method

To answer the research question, we conducted an online survey involving 118 PwCOPD. The goals of the survey were to assess whether the participants differed in their *perceived persuasiveness* towards the 17 implemented strategies and in their *individual susceptibility to persuasion* as measured by the STPS scale [16]. The detailed methodology is described in this chapter.

3.1   Persuasive Strategies and Storyboards

We chose to employ ten widely-used strategies by Oinas-Kukkonen and Fogg in our study, which have been used in the health context earlier [17–19]: *comparison, competition, cooperation, customization, personalization, punishment, rewards, self-monitoring, simulation*, and *suggestion*. In addition, we employed the strategy *reminder*, which is an important strategy in fitness applications to increase physical activity [10].

To allow for a comparison with the STPS scale, we employed the six well-established strategies by Cialdini: *reciprocity, scarcity, authority, commitment, consensus, and liking* [20].

To communicate the PS in a visually appealing way, we created storyboards for all 17 PS, each consisting of three individual illustrations that represent the strategy as a scripted interaction between the user and the smartphone application (see Fig. 1 as an example of the storyboard representing the competition strategy). The storyboards were based on those used in the work of Orji et al. [17, 19].

We validated our storyboards prior to the main study to make sure that the visualizations accurately represented each of the PS as intended. We first made two internal rounds of evaluation and adaptation of the storyboards. After that we sent out the storyboards to seven researchers in the field of human–computer interaction familiar with persuasive technology and asked them to allocate the correct storyboard to the 17 strategies. Additionally, we asked the experts to provide further feedback about the storyboards. Following this procedure, the storyboards were further refined and finalized.

Fig. 1. Example storyboard of the PS *competition* translated to English.

3.2   Questionnaire Measures

Perceived Persuasiveness. To measure the *perceived persuasiveness* of the 17 strategies, each storyboard was followed by four questions of the perceived persuasiveness scale by Drozd et al. [21], as also used in the work of Orji et al. [19]. The participants were asked to indicate on a 7-point Likert scale to which degree the strategy (a) would influence them, (b) would be convincing, (c) would be personally relevant for them, and (d) would make them reconsider their physical activity habits.

Individual Susceptibility to Persuasion. In addition to *perceived persuasiveness*, which represents the participants' ratings of external stimuli (i.e., the storyboards), we assessed also their *individual susceptibility to persuasion*. The key distinction between the two constructs is that the former is a person's evaluation of external stimuli, whereas the latter can be understood as a trait that resides within the person. In other words, *individual susceptibility to persuasion* describes a person's underlying disposition to be more or less receptive to certain PS. To measure the individual susceptibility of participants, we included the *Susceptibility to Persuasion Scale* (STPS) [16]. The scale measures the participant's susceptibility towards Cialdini's six strategies [20]: *reciprocity, scarcity, authority, commitment, consensus* and *liking*.

3.3   Procedure of the Online Survey

Recruitment of potential participants in Austria and Germany was first done through asking COPD self-support groups to distribute the survey in their network of PwCOPD. As an incentive, participants who finalized the survey could win an Amazon voucher. The survey was additionally distributed via a recruiting panel based in Austria. Participants who completed the survey received credit points via the panel that could be exchanged for money or vouchers. After the potential participants opened the survey link that they received either via mail or the recruiting panel, they first read a short introduction about the aims of the study. Two screening questions assessed the presence or absence of COPD and the age of the person. Each of the subsequent pages showed in randomized order one of the 17 PS, presented as storyboards, followed by four questions assessing the participant's *perceived persuasiveness* of the respective strategies [21]. The next part of the survey contained the STPS items in randomized order followed by sociodemographic questions such as gender, education, height, weight, the presence of other diseases, their physical activity level as well as their stage of change towards doing more physical activity. The entire survey was conducted in German.

3.4   Participants

Given that PwCOPD are typically older, the majority of participants recruited for the study were above the age of 40 (97%). The survey was completed by a total of 118 participants. Three participants were excluded from the analysis because they completed the survey in a time that we deemed unrealistic (i.e., below 5 min); for comparison, participants took 18.77 min on average ($SD = 12.99$). The remaining 115 participants included 30 women and 85 men. More details on sociodemographic data is shown in Table 1.

Table 1. Sociodemographic data of participants

Sample size	115
Gender	30 women/85 men (26%/74%)
Age	<40 (3%), 40–49 (11%), 55–59 (28%), 60–69 (36%), >69 (23%)
Education	Compulsory school (3%), Professional school (16%), Vocational training (24%), High school (36%), University (or similar) (21%)
Other diseases	no other (35%), 1 other (37%), 2 other (18%), 3–5 other diseases (10%)

3.5   Data Analysis

The data analysis was conducted with SPSS version 22. Boxplot figures were created with the statistics software Wessa.net (Wessa, 2017). To assess which of the 17 PS are most effective for PwCOPD, we first calculated an average score per participant across the four items measuring the *perceived persuasiveness* for each strategy. Similarly, we calculated an average score per participant for the items measuring *individual susceptibility to persuasion*, separately for Cialidini's six strategies: five items were averaged for the strategy of *reciprocity*, another five for *scarcity*, four items for *authority*, another five for *commitment*, another four for *consensus*, and three items for *liking*. We conducted altogether two repeated-measures ANOVAs (analysis of variance), separately for the two within-subject factors *perceived persuasiveness* (i.e., the 17 strategies implemented as storyboards) and *individual susceptibility to persuasion* (i.e., an underlying disposition to be more receptive to certain PS). Comparing the average values of the study sample per strategy allows gaining insights specifically for the target group of PwCOPD in terms of their underlying dispositions (*individual susceptibility to persuasion*) and their perceptions of implemented strategies (*perceived persuasiveness*). Moreover, we generated notched boxplots that depict the data descriptively and provide a visual gauge of potentially significant differences for each of the 17 strategies with the neutral mid-point of the perceived persuasiveness scale [18].

4   Results

4.1   Perceived Persuasiveness of the 17 Strategies

In order to identify the most suitable PS for PwCOPD, we compared the means of the perceived persuasiveness scores of the 17 strategies. Results from the repeated-measures ANOVA revealed a significant effect for the within-subjects factor PS, ($F(16, 1824) = 16.15$, $p < .001$, partial eta squared = .124). This indicates that there is a significant difference in the *perceived persuasiveness* between the PS. Figure 2 below shows notched boxplots of the *perceived persuasiveness* for all 17 strategies. Notches indicate the 95% confidence interval of the median and allow estimating significant differences between the strategy and the neutral mid-point of the persuasiveness scale [18]. The neutral mid-point for *perceived persuasiveness* (i.e., the value '4' on the 7-point Likert scale) indicates that a strategy is perceived as rather neutral (i.e., neither persuasive nor unpersuasive). Out of the 17 strategies, PwCOPD perceived eight strategies as significantly more persuasive than the neutral mid-point—in the following listed from highest (most persuasive) to lowest (least persuasive): *personalization, reminder, commitment, self-monitoring, rewards, customization, authority,* and *scarcity* (see Fig. 2 and Table 2). Interestingly, two PS were perceived as significantly less persuasive than the neutral mid-point, namely *liking* and *reciprocity*.

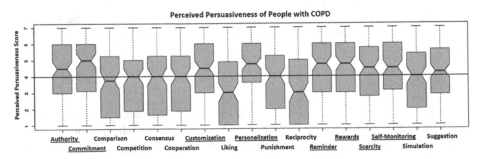

Fig. 2. Perceived persuasiveness (y-axis) of the 17 PS (x-axis) on a Likert-type scale ranging from 1 to 7 (higher scores indicate a higher persuasiveness; the horizontal line at 4 indicates the neutral mid-point, the eight underlined strategies are perceived as significantly more persuasive than the neutral mid-point).

Table 2. Means and standard deviations of perceived persuasiveness towards the 17 strategies

Strategy	M(SD)	Strategy	M(SD)	Strategy	M(SD)
Authority	4.3 (±1.9)	Customization	4.3 (±1.9)	Rewards	4.4 (±2.0)
Commitment	4.4 (±1.9)	Liking	3.2 (±2.0)	Scarcity	4.1 (±1.9)
Comparison	3.6 (±2.1)	Personalization	4.6 (±1.9)	Self-monitoring	4.4 (±1.8)
Competition	3.7 (±2.1)	Punishment	3.7 (±2.1)	Simulation	3.8 (±1.9)
Consensus	3.7 (±2.0)	Reciprocity	3.3 (±2.0)	Suggestion	4.1 (±1.9)
Cooperation	3.7 (±2.0)	Reminder	4.4 (±2.0)		

Note. M = mean, *SD* = standard deviation.

4.2   Individual Susceptibility to Persuasion

In order to examine the *individual susceptibility to persuasion* of PwCOPD to different strategies, we compared the mean scores for each of the strategies that we calculated from the *Susceptibility to Persuasion Scale* (STPS).

Results from the repeated-measures ANOVA revealed a significant effect for the within-subjects factor *individual susceptibility to persuasion*, ($F(5, 545) = 89.00$, $p < .001$, partial eta squared = .449), indicating that people's self-assessment of individual susceptibility differed for Cialidini's six PS.

As illustrated in Fig. 3 and Table 3 below, PwCOPD had a significantly higher individual susceptibility towards *reciprocity, commitment* and *liking*, than to *scarcity, authority* and *consensus.*

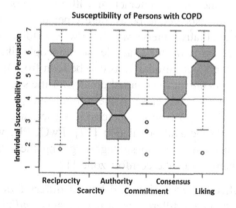

Fig. 3. Individual susceptibility (y-axis) towards Cialdini's six strategies (x-axis) on a Likert-type scale ranging from 1 to 7 (higher scores indicate a higher susceptibility; the horizontal line at 4 indicates the neutral mid-point).

Table 3. Means and standard deviation of individual susceptibility to persuasion

Strategy	M(SD)	Strategy	M(SD)	Strategy	M(SD)
Reciprocity	5.4(±1.3)	Authority	3.6 (±1.5)	Consensus	4.2 (±1.3)
Scarcity	3.9 (±1.5)	Commitment	5.6 (±1.1)	Liking	5.4 (±1.2)

Note. M = mean, *SD* = standard deviation.

5 Discussion

In the following section, we first discuss the *perceived persuasiveness* of the 17 strategies by elaborating on the most interesting strategies (i.e., the most and least PS as well as a group of strategies that rely on social interaction). We follow up by addressing *individual susceptibility to persuasion* and how it differs from participants' *perceived persuasiveness*.

Perceived persuasiveness of the 17 strategies. The analysis of our online survey data revealed a significant difference in the *perceived persuasiveness* of the 17 PS. *Personalization* was perceived as the most PS for PwCOPD. This could suggest a need to account for individual requirements due to individual-specific disease conditions. This highlights the need to establish an appropriate activity plan in line with each person's physical abilities. *Liking*, on the other hand, was perceived as the least PS for PwCOPD. This strategy rests on the principle that people like people, who are familiar and similar to them [22]. Therefore, the strategy might work only for PwCOPD when the other person understands what it means to be living with this disease and be physically active (e.g., when the other person is also affected by the disease or familiar with COPD). Hence, further investigations are required to see if the social context might have an influence on the PS *liking*. Moreover, a worsening of the disease can make it difficult to maintain, let alone surpass past activity levels for which they might have previously received acknowledgement in the form of likes from others. Getting likes for underperforming could be perceived as demotivating for them. Thus, relying on 'social gratification' might put them on the spot what they rather like to avoid. Those PS that rely on some kind of interaction with other persons (i.e., *comparison*, *competition* or *cooperation*) showed to be averagely persuasive for PwCOPD. Bartlett et al. [9] found in their qualitative interviews, that PwCOPD had very diverse opinions about those social strategies with, for example, some people liking the idea of competitive activities and others not. Similarly, as can be seen from our own data (Fig. 2), the ratings of *perceived persuasiveness* varied greatly for the social strategies, resulting in an overall persuasiveness score close to the neutral mid-point of the scale. Interestingly, *competition* and *comparison* are increasingly used and widely appreciated in persuasive systems for the general population [17]. PwCOPD, who feel stressed by their symptoms, may disfavor the two strategies, giving them the feeling of losing control and drawing them out of the comfort zone [17].

Individual susceptibility to persuasion and how it differs from perceived persuasiveness. We found significant differences in participants' *individual susceptibility to persuasion*. PwCOPD showed high susceptibility to *reciprocity* ($M = 5.4$) and *liking* ($M = 5.4$). These two strategies, however, were the least persuasive ones when evaluating the respective storyboard implementations in terms of their *perceived persuasiveness* ($M = 3.3$ and $M = 3.2$, for *reciprocity* and *liking* respectively). Similarly, *authority* had the lowest susceptibility score ($M = 3.6$) but was perceived as slightly above average persuasive in the storyboard implementation ($M = 4.3$). It appears that the *perceived persuasiveness*, as measured by the scale of Drozd et al. [21], and *individual susceptibility to persuasion*, as measured by the STPS [16], both assess distinct aspects of persuasiveness and are more diverse as expected.

5.1 Implications for Designing Persuasive Systems for PwCOPD

Based on the results from our study in which we investigated the *perceived persuasiveness* and *individual susceptibility to persuasion* of PwCOPD, we can derive several implications for the future development of persuasive systems targeting specifically PwCOPD. In the following we provide examples of how the strategies could be implemented. These are based on our experiences from working with PwCOPD. Our analysis shows which PS were perceived as significantly above (below) average with respect to their persuasiveness by PwCOPD and are thus most (least) suitable in the design of persuasive systems targeting the group. Based on the experience from running the study and the evaluation results, we provide the following suggestions:

(1) A physical activity plan and suggestions for physical activity that are personalized to the individual needs of PwCOPD are more effective than generic recommendations. Physical activity recommendations should especially account for each person's health status as this hugely affects their motivation to engage in physical activity (*personalization*).

(2) In addition, the persuasive technology should be designed to allow the PwCOPD to adapt the suggested physical activity plan to her/his individual needs (*customization*). A defined daily or weekly physical activity goal could be presented as a virtual contract by the persuasive system. Our findings reveal that there is a higher motivation to comply to the plan when the person committed herself/himself to a goal (*commitment*). However, additional reminders to meet their physical activity goals are useful (*reminder*). Ideally, those reminders should account for the person's current symptoms, which could vary on a day-to-day basis. Specifically, exacerbations, which are acute deteriorations of the disease, have to be considered when giving recommendations or reminders. The detection of an exacerbation in clinical practice relies on the patient's self-reporting of symptoms, such as dyspnea, cough and increased sputum. Assessing those indicators allows a technology to recognize upcoming exacerbations, thus, give recommendations and reminders accordingly [23].

(3) Setting time limits to achieve goals is further motivating for PwCOPD. This could be implemented by informing them about how much time they have left to achieve this goal (*scarcity*). This strategy is suited to be combined with reminders or rewards, which both showed to motivate PwCOPD (*reminder*, *reward*).

(4) A persuasive system that provides the person's activity data and feedback in a visually appealing and understandable way is further motivating. For PwCOPD, not only their activity data but also their subjectively indicated symptoms and physiological data (e.g., oxygen saturation, pulse) could be presented. Overviews and retrospectives as well as correlations of data (e.g., the more you walk, the better you feel) could help them to understand the importance of regular physical activity (*self-monitoring*).

(5) Information and suggestions coming from an authority figure are more persuasive for PwCOPD (compared to information that is not provided by an authority figure). In case of COPD, recommendations could be presented in a persuasive system not only from physicians but also from acknowledged COPD institutions such as the Global Initiative for Chronic Obstructive Pulmonary Disease (GOLD) [24], the European Respiratory Society or the American Thoracic Society [25] (*authority*).
(6) Two of the 17 PS were perceived as below average in persuasiveness by PwCOPD and are thus not suitable for this target group: *liking* and *reciprocity*. Thus, we would recommend avoiding these two strategies when designing persuasive systems for PwCOPD.

6 Conclusions

With this research, we extend the existing literature of persuasive technology in healthcare by presenting findings from an online study that investigated *perceived persuasiveness* of widely-used PS for PwCOPD (who have been majorly neglected by researchers), with the goal of increasing their physical activity level. To the best of our knowledge, this study is the first research in the domain of persuasion that is focused on PwCOPD.

Our results have several implications for the future development of persuasive systems for PwCOPD. Our research shows that PwCOPD perceive the individual strategies to be significantly different in their persuasiveness. Thus, it is beneficial to employ only those strategies that were rated above average in *perceived persuasiveness*. Based on our findings, we offer some suggestions on how the strategies can be implemented to motivate PwCOPD.

Further research is necessary to see if those findings apply only to the target behavior of increasing physical activity or if the outcomes can be generalized to other target behaviors. Our findings additionally need to be verified in the real-life context of PwCOPD to investigate their validity and reliability and to gather more details on the impact of persuasive systems for PwCOPD. Further research should investigate if the ascertained differences in *perceived persuasiveness* and *individual susceptibility to persuasion* pertain also to people without COPD. A limitation is that the results are based on implementations of PS in the form of storyboards, which differ from real-world implementations in the form of applications for mobile devices.

Acknowledgements. This research has partly been funded by the Vienna Business Agency under contract no. ID 1605387 (SmartCOPDTrainer).

References

1. Buist, A.S., McBurnie, M.A., Vollmer, W.M., Gillespie, S., Burney, P., Mannino, D.M., Menezes, A.M.B., Sullivan, S.D., Lee, T.A., Weiss, K.B., Jensen, R.L., Marks, G.B., Gulsvik, A., Nizankowska-Mogilnicka, E.: International variation in the prevalence of COPD (the BOLD Study): a population-based prevalence study. Lancet **370**(9589), 741–750 (2007)
2. World Health Organization (WHO): Burden of COPD. http://www.who.int/respiratory/copd/burden/en/. Accessed 31 Jan 2018

3. Gibson, G.J., Loddenkemper, R., Lundbäck, B., Sibille, Y.: Respiratory health and disease in Europe: the new European lung white book. Eur. Respir. J. **42**(3), 559–563 (2013)
4. Wilkinson, T.M.A., Donaldson, G.C., Hurst, J.R., Seemungal, T.A.R., Wedzicha, J.A.: Early therapy improves outcomes of exacerbations of chronic obstructive pulmonary disease. Am. J. Respir. Crit. Care Med. **169**, 1298–1303 (2004)
5. Halpin, D.M.G., Laing-Morton, T., Spedding, S., Levy, M.L., Coyle, P., Lewis, J., Newbold, P., Marno, P.: A randomised controlled trial of the effect of automated interactive calling combined with a health risk forecast on COPD using EXACT PRO. Prim. Care Respir. J. **20** (3), 324–331 (2011)
6. Watz, H., Pitta, F., Rochester, C.L., Garcia-Aymerich, J., ZuWallack, R., Troosters, T., Vaes, A.W., Puhan, M.A., Jehn, M., Polkey, M.I., Vogiatzis, I., Clini, E.M., Toth, M., Gimeno-Santos, E., Waschki, B., Esteban, C., Hayot, M., Casaburi, R., Porszasz, J., McAuley, E., Singh, S.J., Langer, D., Wouters, E.F., Magnussen, H., Spruit, M.A.: An official European respiratory society statement on physical activity in COPD. Eur. Respir. J. **44**, 1521–1537 (2014)
7. van Boven, J.F.M., Chavannes, N.H., van Der Molen, T., Rutten-van Mölken, M.P.M.H., Postma, M.J., Vegter, S.: Clinical and economic impact of non-adherence in COPD: a systematic review. Respir. Med. **108**(1), 103–113 (2014)
8. Matthews, J., Win, K.T., Oinas-Kukkonen, H., Freeman, M.: Persuasive technology in mobile applications promoting physical activity: a systematic review. J. Med. Syst. **40**(3), 1–13 (2016)
9. Bartlett, Y.K., Webb, T.L., Hawley, M.S.: Using persuasive technology to increase physical activity in people with chronic obstructive pulmonary disease by encouraging regular walking: a mixed-methods study exploring opinions and preferences. JMIR **19**(4), e124 (2017)
10. Yoganathan, D., Kajanan, S.: Persuasive technology for smartphone fitness. In: PACIS 2013 Proceedings, Paper 185 (2013)
11. Leidy, N.K., Kimel, M., Ajagbe, L., Kim, K., Hamilton, A., Becker, K.: Designing trials of behavioral interventions to increase physical activity in patients with COPD: insights from the chronic disease literature. Respir. Med. **108**, 472–481 (2014)
12. Voncken-Brewster, V., Moser, A., van der Weijden, T., Nagykaldi, Z., De Vries, H., Tange, H.: Usability evaluation of an online, tailored self-management intervention for chronic obstructive pulmonary disease patients incorporating behavior change techniques. JMIR Res. Protoc. **2**(1), e3 (2013)
13. De Vries, H., Mesters, I., Van De Steeg, H., Honing, C.: The general public's information needs and perceptions regarding hereditary cancer: an application of the integrated change model. Patient Educ. Couns. **56**, 154–165 (2005)
14. Van Der Weegen, S., Verwey, R., Spreeuwenberg, M., Tange, H., Van Der Weijden, T., De Witte, L.: The development of a mobile monitoring and feedback tool to stimulate physical activity of people with a chronic disease in primary care: a user-centered design. JMIR Mhealth Uhealth **1**(2), e8 (2013)
15. Bartlett, Y.K., Sheeran, P., Hawley, M.S.: Effective behaviour change techniques in smoking cessation interventions for people with chronic obstructive pulmonary disease: a meta-analysis. Br. J. Health. Psychol. **19**, 181–203 (2014)
16. Kaptein, M., De Ruyter, B., Markopoulos, P., Aarts, E.: Adaptive persuasive systems. ACM Trans. Interact. Intell. Syst. **2**(2), 25p (2012). Article 10
17. Orji, R., Vassileva, J., Mandryk, R.L.: Modeling the efficacy of persuasive strategies for different gamer types in serious games for health. User Model. User-Adap. Inter. **24**, 453–498 (2014)

18. Busch, M., Mattheiss, E., Reisinger, M., Orji, R., Fröhlich, P., Tscheligi, M.: More than sex: the role of femininity and masculinity in the design of personalized persuasive games. In: Meschtscherjakov, A., De Ruyter, B., Fuchsberger, V., Murer, M., Tscheligi, M. (eds.) PERSUASIVE 2016. LNCS, vol. 9638, pp. 219–229. Springer, Cham (2016). https://doi.org/10.1007/978-3-319-31510-2_19

19. Orji, R., Nacke, L.E., DiMarco, C.: Towards personality-driven persuasive health games and gamified systems. In: Proceedings SIGCHI Conference on Human Factors Computer System (2017)

20. Cialdini, R.B.: Harnessing the science of persuasion. Harv. Bus. Rev. **79**(9), 72–81 (2001)

21. Drozd, F., Lehto, T., Oinas-Kukkonen, H.: Exploring perceived persuasiveness of a behavior change support system: a structural model. In: Bang, M., Ragnemalm, E.L. (eds.) PERSUASIVE 2012. LNCS, vol. 7284, pp. 157–168. Springer, Heidelberg (2012). https://doi.org/10.1007/978-3-642-31037-9_14

22. Cialdini, R.B.: The science of persuasion. Sci. Am. **284**(2), 76–81 (2004)

23. Leidy, N.K., Wilcox, T.K., Jones, P.W., Jones, P., Roberts, L., Powers, J.H., Sethi, S., Donohue, J., Eremenco, S., Erickson, P., Martinez, F., Patrick, D., Rennard, S., Rodriguez-Roisin, R., Schünemann, H.: Standardizing measurement of chronic obstructive pulmonary disease exacerbations: reliability and validity of a patient-reported diary. Am. J. Respir. Crit. Care Med. **183**(3), 323–329 (2011)

24. Vestbo, J., Hurd, S.S., Agustí, A.G., Jones, P.W., Vogelmeier, C., Anzueto, A., Barnes, P.J., Fabbri, L.M., Martinez, F.J., Nishimura, M., Stockley, R.A., Sin, D.D., Rodriguez-Roisin, R.: Global strategy for the diagnosis, management, and prevention of chronic obstructive pulmonary disease GOLD executive summary. Am. J. Respir. Crit. Care Med. **187**(4), 347–365 (2013)

25. Celli, B.R., Decramer, M., Wedzicha, J.A, Wilson, K.C., Agustí, A., Criner, G.J., MacNee, W., Make, B.J., Rennard, S.I., Stockley, R.A., Vogelmeier, C., Anzueto, A., Au, D.H., Barnes, P.J., Burgel, P.R., Calverley, P.M., Casanova, C., Clini, E.M., Cooper, C.B., Coxson, H.O., Dusser, D.J., Fabbri, L.M., Fahy, B., Ferguson, G.T., Fisher, A., Fletcher, M.J., Hayot, M., Hurst, J.R., Jones, P.W., Mahler, D.A., Maltais, F., Mannino, D.M., Martinez, F.J., Miravitlles, M., Meek, P.M., Papi, A., Rabe, K.F., Roche, N., Sciurba, F.C., Sethi, S., Siafakas, N., Sin, D.D., Soriano, J.B., Stoller, J.K., Tashkin, D.P., Troosters, T., Verleden, G.M., Verschakelen, J., Vestbo, J., Walsh, J.W., Washko, G.R., Wise, R.A., Wouters, E.F., ZuWallack, R.L.: An official American Thoracic Society/European Respiratory Society statement: research questions in COPD. Eur. Respir. J. **45**, 879–905 (2015)

Cardiovascular Reactions During Exposure to Persuasion Principles

Hanne Spelt[1,2]([⊠]) [iD], Joyce Westerink[1,2] [iD], Jaap Ham[2],
and Wijnand IJsselsteijn[2] [iD]

[1] Philips Research, 5656 AE Eindhoven, Netherlands
Hanne.Spelt@philips.com
[2] Eindhoven University of Technology, 5612 AZ Eindhoven, Netherlands

Abstract. To optimize effectiveness of persuasive technology, understanding also psychophysiological processes of persuasion is crucial. The current research explored cardiovascular reactions to persuasive messages using four persuasion principles proposed by Cialdini (authority, scarcity, consensus, and commitment) in a laboratory experiment. The study had a randomized within-subject design. Participants ($N = 56$) were presented with 4×14 persuasive messages while cardiovascular reactions were measured with electrocardiography. Findings showed significantly different cardiovascular arousal regarding inter-beat interval and standard deviations of normal-to-normal heart rate peaks during persuasive principles compared to baseline or startle reflex. Results show no relation between cardiovascular arousal and self-reported susceptibility to persuasion. However, during the presentation of authority-based persuasion messages, data of the first stimulus condition showed a negative correlation between self-reported susceptibility and inter-beat interval reactivity. This explorative study advances our knowledge of psychophysiological processes underlying persuasion and suggested that at least certain persuasive principles may relate to physiological changes.

Keywords: Psychophysiology · Persuasion profiling · Cardiovascular arousal

1 Introduction

Behavior change interventions are frequently used to influence various kinds of behavior, as for example unhealthy lifestyles [1]. Because many generic interventions have failed to accomplish effective and sustainable change [1], tailored interventions have received considerable attention in recent years. Understanding the psychological processes underlying persuasion is a key factor in the successful use of tailored interventions [2].

To investigate the effects of persuasion on human experience and behavior, self-report measures are commonly used. An additional way of gaining insight into the effects of persuasion is studying the relation between psychological and physiological events, because psychological events have a physiological substrate [3]. As self-report measures, psychophysiological measures also aim at explaining human experience and behavior, but are less subject to introspection and have a bigger focus on visceral

© Springer International Publishing AG, part of Springer Nature 2018
J. Ham et al. (Eds.): PERSUASIVE 2018, LNCS 10809, pp. 267–278, 2018.
https://doi.org/10.1007/978-3-319-78978-1_22

reactions as a function of the nervous system. Therefore, a psychophysiological approach could provide objective information on the extent to which persuasion principles impact human experience and behavior. This could prove to be useful in various ways, including physiology-contingent selection and tailoring of persuasive content, or unobtrusive optimization of persuasive interfaces. However, the link between persuasion and psychophysiological events is not sufficiently established, with only a few papers in the domain [4–6].

This paper contributes to current knowledge by giving an overview of the psychophysiology of persuasion and explores cardiac arousal during persuasion and its link to self-reported susceptibility to persuasion. In the pages that follow, we argue why exploring peripheral psychophysiology might create insight in persuasion. Doing so, we first outline the psychological processes of persuasion. Then we elaborate why we expect a psychophysiological relation in persuasion based on current literature. Next, we present a study exploring cardiovascular reactions to persuasive messages using four persuasion principles. The paper concludes with possible directions for future research.

2 Background

2.1 Psychological Processes of Persuasion

A long-established, process-based model of persuasion is the elaboration likelihood model (ELM). It questions how likely it is that the individual thinks about the communicated arguments [7]. The model specifies two routes that people use to process communications: the central route provides conscious evaluations of the messages, whereas in the peripheral route individuals quickly scan the messages and let peripheral cues help them decide whether to be persuaded [7]. Although both routes are active during information processing, the prevailing route depends upon the motivation and ability of the individual to process the information. If both are high, the central route is more likely than the peripheral route [7]. Which route predominates can be manipulated by realizing situations that lower the individuals' motivation and/or ability and thus increase the likelihood of the peripheral route. There is a risk in using peripheral cues for a decision, as essential contradictory information could be missed and lead to wrong decisions. Professional persuaders use this to their advantage, as described by the *persuasion principles* proposed by Cialdini [8].

Cialdini [8] stipulates six different strategies with average positive effects on compliance with persuasive requests. *Reciprocity* describes how everyone has the norm to repay the favor he or she has received, also known as tit-for-tat. *Authority* reveals that people tend to follow the lead of perceived experts. For *likeability*, people react more positively to what they know and/or like. *Scarcity* describes the fear of losing out, making products more valuable. According to the *commitment and consistency* principle, people tend to follow their pre-existing attitudes, values and actions explained by the cognitive dissonance theory [9]. If people are uncertain they tend to do as everyone else is doing, also known as the *social proof* or *consensus* principle [8]. As provided, none of these principles highlight argument quality or information; they merely focus on peripheral cues.

Although Cialdini's principles generally provide the desired effects, not every principle is equally effective for everyone. Presumably, these principles are subject to interpersonal diversity, such as *involvement* and *need for cognition* [2, 7]. For individuals high in involvement the arguments are consciously processed and argument quality is more decisive, whereas for individuals low in involvement peripheral cues become dominant [10]. *Need for cognition* is the tendency for an individual to engage in and enjoy thinking. People who score high in need for cognition are more likely to be persuaded by the central route rather than the peripheral route [10].

Besides differences in overall responses to persuasion, scholars have been interested in deviations in response to specific persuasion principles. Tailoring health interventions is receiving increasing attention since it enhances the chance of desired results, primarily by using the individual differences as an advantage instead of a liability. Kaptein et al. [13] developed the *susceptibility to persuasion scale* (STPS). This scale explicitly profiles the tendencies of individuals to adhere to specific influence principles. The questionnaire enables a priori measurements on susceptibility to different persuasion principles and can be used to individualize the content of an intervention, thereby increasing effectiveness. Nevertheless, other, and specifically implicit, means of establishing the impact of various types of persuasion might be a welcome addition, and deploying psychophysiological measurements is one of the options.

In other words, previous research focused on how to use and understand the different psychological aspects of persuasion. However, to date, the connection between mental states related to persuasion and their physiological underpinnings has remained largely unexplored. An investigation is needed into whether distinct psychophysiological profiles can be identified that are reliably related to susceptibility to persuasion. Such profiles, in turn, will extend our understanding of the psychological processes underlying various persuasive interventions, and may enable more effective persuasive interventions, e.g., in the area of personal health and wellbeing.

2.2 Psychophysiological Approach to Persuasion

Psychophysiological research can complement the psychological discipline in research to persuasion. Both disciplines aim at understanding and explaining human experience and behavior, but differ in their measurement methods. Where psychology uses observations and self-report measures, psychophysiology focusses on changes in bodily events. Doing so, psychophysiology is less subject to introspection and has a bigger focus on visceral reactions as a function of the nervous system.

Psychophysiological research builds upon the idea that physiological reactions are an integral part of our experiences and that people exhibit detectable physiological signs associated with emotion, experiences, or psychological states [3]. Thus, it is possible that a change in a psychological state due to persuasion relates to a change in physiological arousal. Perhaps an individual feels heavily impressed or guilty with a certain argument evoking emotions. Emotions are acute, intentional states, which exist in a relatively short period of time and are related to a particular event, object, or action and can be categorized by valence and arousal. The generation of short, intense emotions is often uncontrollable, fast and unconscious. This unconscious fast part of emotions is reflected in certain physiological responses [3]. To date, a few studies have indeed investigated the relationship between physiology and persuasion. Previous research indicates adherence to persuasive messages correlates with increased heart rate variability [4] and higher brain activity in the medial prefrontal cortex (mPFC) [5, 6]. Furthermore, persuasion induced behavior change is better predicted from brain activity than self-report [5, 6]. These findings illustrate it is possible to measure real-time physiological responses to persuasion.

In particular for the cardiovascular system (CVS), previous research has established a correlation between activity in the persuasion-related mPFC and cardiovascular arousal [11]. The CVS has a rich structure with several subsystems. These subsystems are subject to both central and pheripheral autonomic control as well as hormonal influences. Therefore, the CVS is highly sensitive to neurobehavioral processes and reflects arousal, i.e. state of activity and energization [3]. Important parameters of the CVS are heart rate (HR) and heart rate variability (HRV), reflecting the variation in time interval between successive heart beats. Arousal is positively correlated with HR and negatively with HRV. There are a few time-domain tools used to asses HRV.

In sum, previous research established a link between persuasion and brain activity, and between brain activity and cardiovascular arousal. Therefore, studying the link between persuasion and cardiovascular arousal is a research direction worth exploring.

2.3   Rationale

This study intends to advance our knowledge of psychological processes related to persuasion. By measuring parameters of the cardiovascular system, this study tries to find a coherent relationship between psychological and physiological aspects of persuasion. Parameters of the CVS are unobtrusively measurable with wearables. If it is clear how the body responds to different persuasion principles and what this means in terms of persuasion susceptibility, this information can be used to implicitly profile and personalize future persuasion interactions. Based on previous literature establishing a link between cardiovascular and mPFC activity [11] and between mPFC activity and persuasion [5, 6], we expect to find a relation between the cardiovascular arousal and susceptibility to different persuasion principles. Since physiological measurements are heavily subject to movement and dependent on timing, a non-interactive lab setting with pre-programmed manipulations is most suitable for a first exploration. In our study, we use four (out of six) of the principles of persuasion, as formulated by Cialdini [8]: authority, scarcity, commitment and social proof. The other two principles, liking and reciprocity, proved difficult to implement in our non-interactive setting, as they both evolved from and heavily depend on human social interaction. We measured participants' individual susceptibility to each of these persuasive strategies using the scale developed by Kaptein [4]. The target behavior we aimed to change was tooth brushing – an important factor in dental hygiene and associated with a number of general health indices, including cardiovascular health.

3   Method

3.1   Participants and Design

Participants. Sixty particpants were recruited through a recruitement agency (average age 48 years; 30 women). Exclusion criteria included a history of cardiovascular diseases and current pregnancy, as cardiovascular data might deviate from normal subjects. Participants were selected to participate in the study only if they indicated they normally brushed their teeth less than 2 min (per session). To enhance motivation for the study, participants were led to believe that they would participate in a 1-week behavior monitoring test to improve their oral care, starting with a lab study. Prior to participation, all participants were informed about the experiment and signed an informed consent. Participants received a participation fee if the experiment was successfully completed.

Design. This experiment has a within-subject design with six conditions: one baseline of physiological state, four randomized persuasion conditions each followed by a short resting period, and an acoustic startle. This design was chosen to be sure that the changes in physiology are due to the persuasion-principle manipulation rather than to individual differences between subjects. One complication might be carryover effects or temporal dependencies between conditions [3]. Hence, short resting periods after stimuli act as fade-out and recovery time. Dependent measures are self-reported susceptibility to persuasion and cardiovascular arousal during the experimental procedure. The study aims at finding a relation between scores on self-report susceptibility to persuasion and cardiovascular arousal during different persuasion strategies.

3.2   Materials

Self-report measures. Questions regarding demographics, past behavior and attitude provided insight into participants' relation to oral healthcare. To determine participants' attitude towards brushing two minutes per session, 5 items reflecting the instrumental nature and the experiential quality of the behavior were composed based on the theory of planned behavior [12]. The susceptibility to persuasion scale (STPS) was administered to measure susceptibility to the different persuasion principles authority, commitment, social proof, scarcity, reciprocity and liking [13]. The STPS characterized susceptibility to distinct influence strategies, via six subscales, and overall susceptibility to persuasion, by averaging scores on the subscales. The scale has 26 items fitting the underlying latent variables (7-pointscale ranging from "completely disagree" to "completely agree").

Physiological measures. Physiological arousal was measured using a Nexus-10, i.e. a channel ambulatory and stationary system with bipolar electrophysiological inputs and a maximum sample rate of 2048 Hz. Three Kendall H124SG ECG electrodes measured electrocardiography (ECG)[1], one electrode on the right side below the collarbone, a

---

[1] Other physiological recordings were done as well, and will be reported on elsewhere.

ground electrode on the left side below the collarbone, and one electrode on the left side of the torso underneath the ribs.

Persuasive messages. Based on four persuasion principles (authority, scarcity, commitment and social proof, see [8]), we constructed 14 arguments per principle (both equally action-oriented and passive), summing up to a total of 56 messages (for examples, see Table 1). Messages were based on previous research employing persuasion principles [2, 13]. Important parts of the sentences appeared in bold. Messages were presented in the native language of the participants (Dutch) to control for language biases.

Table 1. Subset of the persuasive messages based on persuasion principles, translated from Dutch.

Principle	Message	Words
Authority	*Try brushing your teeth good. According to **the College of Dental care,** this is an easy way to lead a healthy life*	22
Authority	***Doctors** say that dental health is related strongly to your overall health. Therefore, participate in this experiment*	17
Authority	***Experts in this area** advise the habit of brushing your teeth for two minutes twice a day. Seriously participating in this experiment is a way to achieve that*	28
Scarcity	*Changing your oral care habits in the future will not reverse teeth decay. **Now is your chance** to work on healthy teeth*	22
Scarcity	*This experiment is here **only now.** You have the unique opportunity to receive our help and improve your oral care*	20
Scarcity	*Your dentures gives you **a unique appearance.** Do not ruin this and brush your teeth twice a day for two minutes. Starting now*	23
Commitment	*Try to achieve your goal to live a healthier lifestyle by brushing your teeth twice a day for two minutes. **Stay committed!***	22
Commitment	*You participated in this study to improve your oral care. **Finish what you started** and give your teeth the care they need*	22
Commitment	*You have done a lot of effort to maintain your dentures. **Do not throw this effort away** and **keep taking care** by improving your oral health*	26
Social proof	***Everyone agrees:** Brushing your teeth twice a day for two minutes improves multiple aspects of your life in terms of health and appearance*	23
Social proof	*You are not on your own: **95% of the preceding participants of this study** have already increased their healthy brushing behavior*	21
Social proof	***100 s of others** have already changed their oral care habits. **Be like them** and start brushing at least two minutes per session*	22

3.3   Procedure

Prior to visiting the laboratory, participants were instructed to refrain from drinking caffeinated beverages in the 2 h preceding the experiments. To increase their engagement in the experiments, they were led to believe that their oral health care would be monitored in the successive week, and that the lab tasks would prepare them for this.

After arriving in the laboratory and signing the informed consent, they were seated in front of a computer screen and attached to the Nexus physiological recording device. The experiments were run using custom OpenSesame software with a Legacy-backend [14]. The experiment started with the administration of questionnaires, excluding the STPS. Prior to the series of persuasive messages, a 5-min recording of their cardio-vascular arousal in baseline was performed, during which the participants watched a neutral sea life video with classical music. Next, the computer display showed to participants the series of persuasive messages clustered in 4 conditions. One condition for each persuasion principle (authority, scarcity, social proof, commitment). Each condition contains 14 persuasive arguments framed according to the corresponding principles. Exposure to a single message lasted 8 s. Messages were alternated with fixation points lasting 3 s. Each condition lasted approximately 3 min, which is required for HRV analysis. The order of the conditions was randomized over participants. After each condition, different neutral sea life videos with classical music were shown to measure physiological state in rest. After the last condition participants heard a loud brown noise to evoke a startle response. The STPS was intentionally administered after the stimuli, to rule out the possibility that some questions influenced the participants' perception of the stimuli. Finally, participants were debriefed and thanked for their participation.

3.4 Analysis

All questionnaires in this study were validated in previous research and were analyzed as instructed [12, 13]. Cardiovascular arousal is obtained during baseline, stimulus exposure, rest between stimuli, and acoustic startle. To calculate HRV parameters, R onsets and inter-beat intervals (IBIs) in the ECG data were identified. After manual check of the R-peaks, an absolute and relative criterion filtered the IBIs: (1) IBI's smaller than 0.4 s and bigger than 1.4 s were inspected and treated as missing values if necessary. (2) Normality of IBI's was checked by plotting the first derivative of the IBI's on the first derivative of the normal distribution. Deviations between distributions were treated as outliers. This leads to relative cut-off points −0.6 and 0.6. In this study the Root Mean Square of the Successive Differences (RMSSD) and the Standard Deviation of Normal-to-Normal peaks (SDNN) were used as parameters of HRV. From IBI data RMSSD and SDNN – as well as the mean IBI - were calculated for each experimental condition. To quantify reactivity in mean IBI, RMSSD, and SDNN, we calculated the difference between the value during stimulus presentation and that in the preceding rest phase. The arousal difference between baseline and startle response provided the possible range of each participants. Multiple repeated measures ANOVA's were used to find differences in arousal between experimental parts. STPS scores and reactivity during stimuli were correlated to examine their relation. All analyses were be carried out using R [15] and SPSS [16].

4   Results

Self-report data. Data of four participants was discarded due to experiment error, leaving a dataset of 56 participants of which only the STPS scarcity subscale was not normally distributed. Participants appeared to have a relatively positive attitude towards brushing ($M = 5.11, SD = 1.21$) and reported normally brushing at home between 1 and 1.5 min per session. Since this research area is still in early phase [17] and the scales have proven to be internally consistent in previous research [13], the items are viewed to have sufficient internal consistency, with exception of likability ($\alpha = .32$). For each subject, the mean per subscale and a total score of the STPS were calculated. See group-level Descriptive Statistics in Table 2.

Table 2. Descriptive statistics susceptibility to persuasion scale

	Authority	Scarcity	Commitment	Liking	Reciprocity	Consensus	Overall STPS
Mean	3.82	3.91	5.49	5.17	4.90	4.21	4.58
SD	1.10	1.10	0.86	0.84	0.99	1.03	0.61
Alpha	0.76	0.67	0.74	0.32	0.77	0.61	0.82
# items	4	5	5	3	5	4	26

Cardiac data. A repeated measures ANOVA with a Greenhouse-Geisser correction on the absolute data determined that mean IBI ($F(2.87, 155.10) = 4.88$, $p = 0.003$) and SDNN ($F(3.31, 178.47) = 5.19$, $p < .001$) values differed statistically significantly between conditions. Mean IBI during baseline gave the highest values, and post-hoc tests using the Bonferroni correction revealed significant differences with authority, scarcity, and startle response. Average SDNN values were highest for startle response, and post-hoc tests using the Bonferroni correction revealed significant differences with commitment and social proof (Fig. 1). For RMSSD, no significant effects were found.

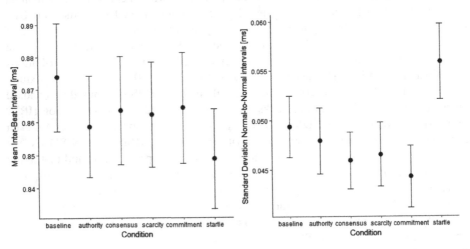

Fig. 1. Absolute mean inter-beat interval and standard deviation of the normal-to-normal intervals in milliseconds per condition with error bars representing standard errors

Shapiro-Wilk normality tests proved cardiac reactivity data was not normally distributed and sphericity was violated. Nevertheless, since the 56 participants constitute a reasonable sample size [18], a repeated measures ANOVA with a Greenhouse-Geisser correction determined that reactivity in IBI ($F(2.58, 139.07) = 2.82$, $p = 0.049$) and SDNN ($F(2.57, 138.51) = 7.16$, $p < 0.001$) differed statistically significantly among persuasion principles and startle response. IBI reactivity during startle response gave the lowest values, and post-hoc tests using the Bonferroni correction revealed significant differences with authority and scarcity. Average SDNN reactivity was highest for startle, and post-hoc tests using the Bonferroni correction revealed significant differences with commitment, scarcity, and social proof. There were no significant differences in reactivity for RMSSD among persuasion principles and startle response.

Relation between self-report and cardiac data. Multiple Spearman's correlations were run to determine the relationship between the self-report data, i.e. the different subscales and total score on the STPS, and cardiac arousal, i.e. absolute and reactivity data for mean IBI, SDNN and RMSSD, during presentation of the (corresponding) persuasive messages. There were no significant results. In addition, two Spearman's correlations were run to assess the relationship between cardiovascular arousal, i.e. absolute and reactivity data, and persuasion in only the first block of stimuli. There was a significant, negative correlation between reactivity in mean IBI and STPS subscale authority ($r_s = -.547, p = 0.043$), but not for other subscales or cardiovascular measures.

5 Discussion

This study explored the relation between psychological state of persuasion and cardiovascular arousal. Thereby, this work added to the growing literature on brain activity and persuasion. The results focus on cardiac responses gathered during persuasive messages deploying authority, commitment, scarcity and social proof persuasion principles. In addition to physiological data, we assessed each participants' persuasion profile (using the susceptibility to persuasion scale, STPS). It was expected that participants who are susceptible to a specific persuasion principle would show an increase in cardiovascular arousal when subjected to a message containing that principle. However, the results of this study provided no evidence for such a relationship, since the correlations of both components were not significant. The results do show that when exposed to persuasion, participants' cardiovascular arousal in inter-beat interval (IBI) and standard deviation of normal-to-normal intervals (SDNN) differ significantly compared to baseline and startle response. The study did not detect any differences in the other cardiac parameters during different persuasion principles.

Exploring the cardiac data, results indicate a difference in arousal during baseline and persuasive messages. This finding appears to support the hypothesis that persuasion has a psychophysiological nature. However, the change in heart beat pattern during persuasion might just as well be due to a more general orienting response [3] to the messages themselves. The fact that we did not find an association between a participant's average reactivity and his overall STPS susceptibility suggests that the latter of these two explanations is more likely.

Furthermore, results showed no significant differences in participants' cardiovascular arousal during different persuasion principles. This could mean that indeed on

average there is no difference in cardiovascular arousal in exposure to different persuasion principles. An alternative explanation is that the strength of our persuasive
manipulation might be relatively weak. Although message framing was inspired on and
very similar to previous research with successful persuasion [2], the stimuli were not
identical, especially since this study targets different health prevention behaviors.
Another reason for lower manipulation strength could come from the constraints
accompanying physiological measurement: Participants sat perfectly still and the
computer timed the experiment precisely. Although this improved quality of the
physiological data, it might have decreased the credibility of the persuasion stimuli, as
persuasion depends on human social interaction [8].

Another explanation for similar cardiovascular arousal during different persuasion
principles could be carryover effects between stimuli. Accordingly, there was a resting
period in between the conditions, and the order of stimuli and conditions was randomized. To check, the first manipulation received was analyzed as a between-subject
comparison: Results indicated no differences in cardiac data between different
manipulations, with exception of mean IBI values appearing to be lower during scarcity
than authority. Since these findings are comparable to our results, we discard the
possibility of carryover effects [3].

We did not find a relationship between self-reported and physiological measures for
specific persuasion principles, nor between total self-reported susceptibility to persuasion and average arousal during persuasion. One explanation for this finding might
be the above-mentioned passive set-up, potentially leading to participants' indifference
after a while. Therefore, an additional test analyzed the relationship between psychological and physiological events for only the first stimulus condition. In other words,
we transformed the experiment design to a between-subject design with four groups
defined by the persuasion principle they experienced first in the condition. Indeed, data
retrieved during the first authority condition show a negative correlation between
self-reported susceptibility to persuasion and inter-beat interval reactivity. This suggests that persuasion via the authority principle reflects in cardiovascular arousal.
However, the result of this last test should be interpreted with caution due to a small
number of participants in each group. Potentially though, individual differences in
susceptibility to the various persuasion principles would reflect in cardiovascular
arousal in a more active setting, since the ELM [7] contends that persuasion principles
operate at least partly via the peripheral route, which is especially relevant when people
are more engaged in active experiments.

Interestingly, the correlation direction between susceptibility for authority and IBI
reactivity was opposite of what we expected: Instead of being more aroused when more
susceptible, our participants were more aroused when they were less susceptible to
authority, as indicated by higher inter-beat intervals. This increase in heart rate might
suggest other psychological processes that become active when presented with
authority-based persuasion. Authority is often characterized by high controlling language and compelling wording, this could potentially lead to psychological reactance
[19]. Psychological reactance occurs when persuasion backfires and is best described
by an uncontrollable backlash when you are pushed too hard. Although reactance is
difficult to measure, perceived threat to autonomy, feelings of anger and restoration
intentions are often used [19]. These are components linked to authority. Therefore, it

might be a plausible idea that reactance is more likely to occur in people less susceptible to authority-based persuasion. In sum, further work is required to establish the link between low susceptibility to authority and psychological reactance, as well as the psychophysiology of reactance.

The lack of a correlation of cardiovascular arousal and self-reported susceptibility to persuasion principles in this non-interactive setting suggests that heart beat patterns cannot be used for profiling susceptibility to persuasion. This is underlined by the fact that no differences in participants' cardiovascular arousal between the different persuasion principles were found. However, the subject of psychophysiology in persuasion remains important for future development of persuasive technology, because of its potential to personalize the persuasive strategy in behavior change applications, and thus to enhance effectiveness. Future studies would benefit from a more active experiment setting, in which psychophysiological reactions to individual Cialdini principles remain worthy of exploring, especially for authority, as well as other, conflicting psychological processes such as reactance. In addition, alternative persuasion strategies as well as other physiological measures can be explored.

6 Conclusion

We investigated cardiovascular arousal during persuasive messages, and found it was higher than during baseline. However, results showed no differences in arousal between different persuasion principles, nor did we find a relation with susceptibly to persuasion principles. Thus, we have found no proof that cardiovascular arousal during persuasion can be used for profiling their susceptibility to persuasion principles. However, results did show that susceptibility to authority-based persuasion is correlated with cardiovascular arousal at first exposure, suggesting that psychophysiology of persuasion is worthy of further exploration. In sum, this explorative study advances our knowledge of psychophysiological processes underlying persuasion and suggested that at least certain persuasive principles may relate to physiological change.

Acknowledgment. This work was supported by INHERIT, and has received funding from the European Union's Horizon 2020 research and innovation programme under grant agreement No 667364.

References

1. Zhu, W.: Promoting physical activity through internet: a persuasive technology view. In: de Kort, Y., IJsselsteijn, W., Midden, C., Eggen, B., Fogg, B.J. (eds.) PERSUASIVE 2007. LNCS, vol. 4744, pp. 12–17. Springer, Heidelberg (2007). https://doi.org/10.1007/978-3-540-77006-0_2

2. Markopoulos, P., Kaptein, M.C., De Ruyter, B.E., Aarts, E.H.L.: Personalizing persuasive technologies: explicit and implicit personalization using persuasion profiles. Int. J. Hum. Comput. Stud. **77**, 38–51 (2015)

3. Cacioppo, J.T., Tassinary, L.G., Berntson, G.G.: The Handbook of Psychophysiology. Cambridge University Press, New York (2007)

4. Correa, K.A., Stone, B.T., Stikic, M., Johnson, R.R., Berka, C.: Characterizing donation behavior from psychophysiological indices of narrative experience. Front. Neurosci. **9**, 1–15 (2015)
5. Falk, E.B., Berkman, E.T., Mann, T., Harrison, B., Lieberman, M.D.: Predicting persuasion-induced behavior change from the brain. J. Neurosci. **30**, 8421–8424 (2010)
6. Vezich, S.I., Katzman, P.L., Ames, D.L., Falk, E.B., Lieberman, M.D.: Modulating the neural bases of persuasion: why/how, gain/loss, and users/non-users. Soc. Cogn. Affect. Neurosci. **12**, 283–297 (2016). nsw113
7. Cacioppo, J.T., Petty, R.E., Koa, C.F., Rodriquez, R.: Central and peripheral routes to persuasion: an individual difference perspective. J. Pers. Soc. Psychol. **51**, 1032–1043 (1986)
8. Cialdini, R.B.: Influence, The Psychology of Persuasion. Harper Collins, New York (2007)
9. Festinger, L.: Cognitive dissonance theory. In: Primary Prevention of HIV/AIDS: Psychological Approaches. Sage Publication, Newbury Park, California (1989)
10. Cacioppo, J.T., Petty, R.E., Kao, C.F.: The efficient assessment of need for cognition. J. Pers. Assess. **48**, 306–307 (1984)
11. Shoemaker, J.K., Goswami, R.: Forebrain neurocircuitry associated with human reflex cardiovascular control. Front. Physiol. **6**, 1–14 (2015)
12. Ajzen, I.: Constructing a TPB questionnaire: conceptual and methodological considerations (2006)
13. Kaptein, M.C., De Ruyter, B.E.R., Markopoulos, P., Aarts, E.H.L.: Adaptive persuasive systems: a study of tailored persuasive text messages to reduce snacking. ACM Trans. Interact. Intell. Syst. **2**, 1–25 (2012)
14. Mathôt, S., Schreij, D., Theeuwes, J.: OpenSesame: an open-source, graphical experiment builder for the social sciences. Behav. Res. Methods **44**, 314–324 (2012)
15. R Development Core Team: R: a language and environment for statistical computing. (2016). https://www.r-project.org/
16. IBM Corp.: IBM SPSS Statistics for Windows (2017)
17. Lance, C.E., Butts, M.M., Michels, L.C.: What did they really say? Organ. Res. Methods **9**, 202–220 (2006)
18. Norman, G.: Likert scales, levels of measurement and the "laws" of statistics. Adv. Heal. Sci. Educ. **15**, 625–632 (2010)
19. Dillard, J.P., Shen, L.: On the nature of reactance and its role in persuasive health communication. Commun. Monogr. **72**, 144–168 (2005)

Consumers' Need for Uniqueness and the Influence of Persuasive Strategies in E-commerce

Ifeoma Adaji$^{(\boxtimes)}$, Kiemute Oyibo, and Julita Vassileva

University of Saskatchewan, Saskatoon, SK, Canada
{ifeoma.adaji,kiemute.oyibo}@usask.ca,
jiv@cs.usask.ca

Abstract. We explore the use of persuasion and need for uniqueness in the continuance intention of e-commerce shoppers. In particular, we examine if Cialdini's six influence strategies have an effect on the three dimensions of need for uniqueness and if need for uniqueness further influences continuance intention of e-commerce shoppers. To achieve this, we carried out a study of 183 e-commerce shoppers. Using Partial Least Squares Structural Equation Modelling (PLS-SEM), we developed a hypothetical path model using the data from the study. Our results show that the three dimensions of need for uniqueness explain about 22% of the variance in continuance intention of e-commerce shoppers. In addition, scarcity had the highest influence on the three dimensions of need for uniqueness. We further carried out a multi group analysis based on gender. Our results suggest that scarcity influences the decision of females to buy products that are not only unique, but also socially acceptable, while commitment influences males to buy unique and socially acceptable products.

Keywords: Persuasive strategies · Need for uniqueness · E-commerce

1 Introduction

To contribute to the area of personalization in e-commerce, we explore the use of persuasive strategies and consumers' need for uniqueness in e-commerce. Persuasive strategies influence people to carry out a target behavior without the use of coercion [1]. Examples include Cialdini's six principles: *Authority, commitment, reciprocation, consensus, liking* and *scarcity* [1]. A consumer's need for uniqueness is the person's need to be different from others in terms of their purchase, use and disposition of consumer goods in order to boost their social or personal identity [2]. Need for uniqueness is commonly defined in three behavioral dimensions: *creative choice counter-conformity, unpopular choice counter-conformity* and *avoidance of similarity counter-conformity*. Consumers buy goods that make them feel different from others, thus, making them targets of various marketing ads that seek to increase their self-perception of uniqueness [2]. These ads could be personalized to the user by identifying which of the three behavioral dimensions the consumer is mostly influenced by and matching that dimension to an influence strategy that has the most effect on the behavioral dimension. For example, if a consumer is mostly influenced by the *avoidance of similarity counter-conformity* dimension of need for uniqueness, identifying what persuasive strategy has the most influence on *avoidance*

© Springer International Publishing AG, part of Springer Nature 2018
J. Ham et al. (Eds.): PERSUASIVE 2018, LNCS 10809, pp. 279–284, 2018.
https://doi.org/10.1007/978-3-319-78978-1_23

of similarity counter-conformity could lead to a more personalized shopping experience for the consumer if the e-commerce system adopts that persuasive strategy in presenting, adverts, products and in communicating with the user.

To identify what persuasive strategies have the greatest influence on the three dimensions of need for uniqueness, we develop a hypothetical path model using partial least squares structural equation modeling (PLS-SEM) and a sample size of 183 e-commerce shoppers. Our results show that scarcity has the greatest influence on the three dimensions: *creative choice counter-conformity, unpopular choice counter-conformity* and *avoidance of similarity counter-conformity* with almost equal magnitude. In addition, consensus has a positive influence on all three dimensions, with the strongest effect on *avoidance of similarity counter-conformity.* Reciprocity on the other hand has significant inverse effect on *creative choice counter-conformity, unpopular choice counter-conformity* but significant positive influence on *avoidance of similarity counter-conformity.* Furthermore, the three dimensions of need for uniqueness explain about 23% of the variance in the continuance intention of online shoppers with *avoidance of similarity counter-conformity* having the greatest influence.

To explore the difference in these results based on gender, we carried out multi-group analysis between females and males. The result of our analysis shows significant differences in the influence of the persuasive strategies on the dimensions of need for uniqueness between the genders.

This study is still work in progress. These findings suggest possible design guidelines in developing personalized e-commerce shopping experience for consumers using persuasive strategies and the consumers' need for uniqueness.

2   Related Work

2.1   Need for Uniqueness

A consumer's need for uniqueness is the person's need to be different from others in terms of their purchase, use and disposition of consumer goods in order to boost their social or personal identity [2]. Research shows that a high level of similarity with others is seen by individuals as unpleasant and could lead to a lower self-esteem in the individual [3]. This need to be different from others is tagged "counter-conformity motivation" [2]. Counter-conformity motivation improves people's self and social image [4] and is conceptualized by three behavioral dimensions: *creative choice counter-conformity, unpopular choice counter-conformity* and *avoidance of similarity counter-conformity. Creative choice counter-conformity* indicates that the consumer seeks social differentness from others through their choice of products. However, the products selected are likely to be approved by others. U*npopular choice counter-conformity* indicates that the consumer seeks products that are not only unique but are not accepted by others and deviate from group norms. People in this category risk social disapproval. *Avoidance of similarity counter-conformity* models consumers who have lost interest in and have stopped using particular products or brands (to re-establish their uniqueness) because these products are perceived to have become common. These dimensions of need for uniqueness have been used extensively in consumer studies, [4–6], thus, we adopted them in this study.

2.2   Persuasive Strategies

Persuasive strategies change peoples' attitude or behavior without coercion or deception [1]. Several persuasive principles exist such as Cialdini's six influence principles:
reciprocation, commitment, consensus, liking, authority and scarcity [1]. The principle
of reciprocation suggests that human societies subscribe to the rule of reciprocity,
hence, humans feel obligated to return a favor they have received in the past. The
principle of commitment suggests that humans tend to be consistent, therefore, it is
likely people honor things they have committed to. Consensus principle proposes that
people tend to manifest the same behavior and beliefs as others after observing several
people behaving in a similar manner. Authority principle suggests that because humans
are trained to believe in obedience of authority figures, hence in deciding what action to
take in any situation, information from people in authority could help humans make
decisions. Liking principle posits that people are more persuaded by something/
someone they like. Scarcity strategy suggest that, humans seemingly desire for things
that are scare, less readily available or limited in number.

These strategies have been used extensively in consumer studies and other
domains, thus, we adopted them in this study to measure persuasive strategies.

3   Research Design and Methodology

We developed a path model using PLS-SEM to measure the influence of persuasive
strategies on the dimensions of consumer need for uniqueness. Figure 1 describes this
model. Our model is made of six constructs that measure persuasion and three constructs
that measure need for uniqueness' three dimensions and one construct that measures
continuance intention. All constructs were measured with previously validated scales.

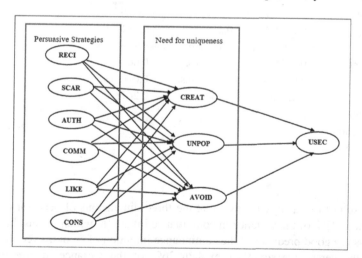

Fig. 1. Research model. All paths assumed positive. RECI = Reciprocity, SCAR = Scarcity,
AUTH = Authority, COMM = Commitment, LIKE = Liking, CONS = Consensus, CREAT =
creative choice counter-conformity, UNPOP = Unpopular choice counter-conformity, AVOID =
Avoidance of similarity counter-conformity, USEC = Continuance intention

We recruited 183 e-commerce shoppers for this study through Amazon's Mechanical Turk, online social media and news boards. This study was approved by the ethics board of our university. Our participants include 64% females and 36% males. In addition, 60% were less than 30 years old, 32% were between 30 and 50 years old, while 8% were over 50 years old.

4   Data Analysis and Results

We carried out Partial Least Squares Structural Equation Modelling (PLS-SEM) using SmartPLS. We determined the reliability and validity of our constructs and the relationships between the indicators and constructs as recommended in structural equation modelling [7]. Indicator reliability, composite reliability, convergent validity (using Average Variance Extracted - AVE) and discriminant validity were all met as required for structural equation modelling [7].

After establishing the reliability and validity of the constructs in our model, we examined the structural model. We computed the coefficients of determination (R^2 values) and the level and significance of the path coefficients. Table 1 shows the path coefficients between constructs. The number of asteriks represents the significance of each direct effect. The number of asteriks ranges from 1 to 4 which corresponds with the p-value of <0.05, <0.01, <0.001 and <0.0001 respectively.

Table 1. Path coefficient between constructs and their significance. $* = P < 0.05$, $** = p < 0.01$, $*** = p < 0.001$ and $**** = p < 0.0001$

	Creative choice	Unpopular choice	Avoidance of similarity	Continuance intention
Reciprocity	−0.152 n.s.	−0.273*	−0.197 n.s.	
Scarcity	0.272****	0.289****	0.332****	
Authority	−0.030 n.s.	−0.016 n.s.	−0.080 n.s.	
Commitment	0.197*	0.061 n.s.	0.065 n.s.	
Like	0.004 n.s.	−0.008 n.s.	0.046 n.s.	
Consensus	0.158 n.s.	0.180 n.s.	0.267*	
Creative choice				0.106 n.s.
Unpopular choice				0.126 n.s.
Avoidance of similarity				0.308**

The result of our analysis shows that the three dimensions of need for uniqueness explain about 22% of the variance in continuance intention, which means that need for uniqueness is a good predictor of the continuance intention of e-commerce shoppers. In addition, the persuasive strategies explain 26% of the variance in *creative choice counter-conformity* dimension of the need for uniqueness. Scarcity had the highest influence on the three dimensions of need for uniqueness with a path coefficient of 0.272****, 0.289****, 0.332**** for *creative choice counter-conformity, unpopular* *choice counter-conformity* and *avoidance of similarity counter-conformity* respectively. This suggests that scarce products are seen as being unique. This is line with other studies on scarcity and need for uniqueness [8].

To determine if there is any difference in our result between females and males, we carried out a multi-group analysis between both groups. The significant differences in our result is shown in Table 2.

Table 2. Path coefficients between constructs and their significance. RECI = Reciprocity, SCAR = Scarcity, AUTH = Authority, COMM = Commitment, LIKE = Liking, CONS = Consensus, CREAT = creative choice counter-conformity, UNPOP = Unpopular choice counter-conformity, AVOID = Avoidance of similarity counter-conformity, USEC = Continuance intention

	CREAT		UNPOP		AVOID		USEC	
	Female	Male	Female	Male	Female	Male	Female	Male
RECI								
SCAR	0.476****	0.091						
AUTH								
COMM	−0.155	0.376*	−0.118	0.539*				
LIKE								
CONS					0.152	0.561*		
CREAT							−0.289	0.379*

The result of the multi group analysis showed interesting findings. One of such is that scarcity influences the creative choice of females significantly while it is insignificant for males. This suggests that scarcity informs the decision of females to buy products that are not only unique but also socially acceptable. Another significant finding is that commitment significantly influences creative choice and unpopular choice for males and this influence is not significant for females. This suggests that males seek social approval in their choices of unique products and this need is influenced by their desire for commitment. Similarly, consensus influences avoidance of similarity in males with insignificant influence in females. This led us to conclude that men are more influenced by the need for uniqueness compared to females. Therefore, when shoppers are identified by their need for uniqueness, the influence strategies commitment and consensus could likely have more effect on males than females.

Our study has some limitations. The sample size is small compared to the number of e-commerce shoppers. We are still collecting data and we plan to repeat the study on a larger scale. In addition, the ratio of females to males is not equal. In the future, we plan to have a more equal number of males and females. Finally, the answer to the survey questions are self-reported by the participants and not based on observation. This is however common practice in the research community [9, 10].

This research is still work in progress and we are still collecting data. In the future, we plan to repeat the study on a larger scale with equal number of female and male participants. We also plan to test our results on an e-commerce platform to see what impact our result will have on the behavior of e-commerce shoppers.

5 Conclusion

We explored the influence of persuasive strategies on the need for uniqueness and the continuance intention of e-commerce shoppers. In particular, we examined if Cialdini's six influence strategies influence the three dimensions of need for uniqueness and if the need for uniqueness further influences continuance intention of e-commerce shoppers. We developed a hypothetical path model using Partial Least Squares Structural Equation Modelling (PLS-SEM) and data from a study of 183 e-commerce shoppers. Our results show that the three dimensions of need for uniqueness explain about 22% of the variance in continuance intention of e-commerce shoppers. In addition, scarcity had the highest influence on the three dimensions of need for uniqueness. We also carried out a multi group analysis based on gender. Our results suggest that scarcity influences the decision of females to buy products that are not only unique but also socially acceptable, while commitment influences males to buy unique and socially acceptable products. These findings suggest possible design guidelines in developing personalized e-commerce shopping experience for consumers using persuasive strategies and the consumers' need for uniqueness.

References

1. Cialdini, R.B.: Influence: Science and Practice, vol. 4. Pearson Education, Boston (2009)
2. Tian, K.T., Bearden, W.O., Hunter, G.L.: Consumers' need for uniqueness: scale development and validation. J. Consum. Res. **28**(1), 50–66 (2001)
3. Fromkin, H.L.: Effects of experimentally aroused feelings of undistinctiveness upon valuation of scarce and novel experiences. J. Pers. Soc. Psychol. **16**(3), 521–529 (1970)
4. Ruvio, A., Shoham, A., Makovec Brenčič, M.: Consumers' need for uniqueness: short-form scale development and cross-cultural validation. Int. Mark. Rev. **25**(1), 33–53 (2008)
5. Zimmer, M.R., Little, S.K., Griffiths, J.S.: The impact of nostalgia proneness and need for uniqueness on consumer perceptions of historical branding strategies. In: American Marketing Association Conference Proceedings, vol. 10, p. 259 (1999)
6. Tian, K.T., McKenzie, K.: The long-term predictive validity of the consumers' need for uniqueness scale. J. Consum. Psychol. **10**(3), 171–193 (2001)
7. Hair Jr., J., Hult, T., Ringle, C., Sarstedt, M.: A Primer on Partial Least Squares Structural Equation Modeling (PLS-SEM). Sage Publications, Thousand Oaks (2016)
8. Wu, W.-Y., Lu, H.-Y., Wu, Y.-Y., Fu, C.-S.: The effects of product scarcity and consumers' need for uniqueness on purchase intention. Int. J. Consum. Stud. **36**(3), 263–274 (2012)
9. Orji, R., Nacke, L.E., Di Marco, C.: Towards personality-driven persuasive health games and gamified systems. In: Proceedings of the 2017 CHI Conference on Human Factors in Computing Systems - CHI 2017, pp. 1015–1027 (2017)
10. Adaji, I., Vassileva, J.: Perceived effectiveness, credibility and continuance intention in E-commerce: a study of Amazon. In: de Vries, P.W., Oinas-Kukkonen, H., Siemons, L., Beerlage-de Jong, N., van Gemert-Pijnen, L. (eds.) PERSUASIVE 2017. LNCS, vol. 10171, pp. 293–306. Springer, Cham (2017). https://doi.org/10.1007/978-3-319-55134-0_23

Using an Artificial Agent as a Behavior Model to Promote Assistive Technology Acceptance

Sofia Fountoukidou[✉], Jaap Ham, Uwe Matzat, and Cees Midden

Human-Technology Interaction, Eindhoven University of Technology,
P.O. BOX 513, 5600 MB Eindhoven, The Netherlands
s.foutoukidou@tue.nl

Abstract. Despite technological advancements in assistive technologies, studies show high rates of non-use. Because of the rising numbers of people with disabilities, it is important to develop strategies to increase assistive technology acceptance. The current research investigated the use of an artificial agent (embedded into a system) as a persuasive behavior model to influence individuals' technology acceptance beliefs. Specifically, we examined the effect of agent-delivered behavior modeling vs. two non-modeling instructional methods (agent-delivered instructional narration and no agent, text-only instruction) on individuals' computer self-efficacy and perceived ease of use of an assistive technology. Overall, the results of the study confirmed our hypotheses, showing that the use of an artificial agent as a behavioral model leads to increased computer self-efficacy and perceived ease of use of a system. The implications for the inclusion of an artificial agent as a model in promoting technology acceptance are discussed.

Keywords: Persuasive technology · Artificial agents · Behavior modeling
Assistive technology acceptance

1 Introduction

Today's world runs on computers. It is difficult to imagine life without access to the internet or being able to communicate and share experiences with other people in electronic social media. However, individuals with physical disabilities face serious challenges in operating computers, which negatively affect their opportunities for employment, social inclusion, and independence. Although various Assistive Technologies (ATs) exist and are becoming more and more technologically advanced, the literature still warns about high rates of AT non-use [1]. Since the number of potential AT users is currently very high and is expected to continue growing during the years to come [2], strategies that aim at increasing AT acceptance are required.

Earlier research has shown that technology acceptance is dependent to a large extent on factors related to individual beliefs and attitudes towards a system [3, 4]. Persuasive Technologies (for an overview, see [5]) could be a key solution to AT acceptance. Though persuasive technology can take on many roles, findings suggest that it can be more persuasive when it takes on the form of a social agent [6]. This is, artificial agents (on-screen animated characters) might be very powerful technological

© Springer International Publishing AG, part of Springer Nature 2018
J. Ham et al. (Eds.): PERSUASIVE 2018, LNCS 10809, pp. 285–296, 2018.
https://doi.org/10.1007/978-3-319-78978-1_24

persuaders, due to their ability to simulate social interaction [7]. In the current study, we argue that an artificial agent, embedded into an AT, could promote AT acceptance by influencing its underlying constructs.

The identification of the constructs associated with technology acceptance has received much attention. A major construct that is linked to AT adoption, is computer self-efficacy (one's belief about his/her ability to perform a specific computer activity) [8]. This construct has its origins in Bandura's social cognitive theory [9], where self-efficacy is defined as "people's judgments of their capabilities to organize and execute courses of action required to attain designated types of performances" (p. 391). Due to the idiosyncratic nature of self-efficacy judgments to particular domains, a distinction has been drawn between general computer self-efficacy (one's judgments of efficacy across multiple computer application domains), and, specific computer self-efficacy (one's perceptions of ability to perform specific computer-related tasks) [10, 11]. Overall, the basic principle behind self-efficacy theory is that individuals are more likely to engage in activities for which they have high self-efficacy and less likely to engage in those they do not. Similarly, those with higher levels of computer self-efficacy would believe themselves capable of taking on a wide range of challenging computer tasks and successfully complete them.

Besides individuals' beliefs of their own abilities, an AT itself has unique features that could encourage or impede its acceptance. Indeed, it has been acknowledged that an AT could be fully used only if an easy and intuitive way of using is secured. However, technological advancements alone do not increase the easiness of AT usage. The Technology Acceptance Model (TAM), a widely used theoretical model examining individual reactions towards computing technology, recognized users' perceived ease of use of a specific system as one of the two beliefs (together with perceived usefulness) that drive individuals' intention to use a system [12]. Specifically, perceived ease of use has been defined as the degree to which the prospective user expects the target system to be free of effort. Computer self-efficacy has been found to be a major determinant of perceived ease of use (with specific computer self-efficacy to be a more proximal predictor [13]), especially in the absence of any direct experience with a system [12].

Training has been suggested as one of the most important interventions to enhance constructs of AT acceptance, during the early stage of an AT use (see e.g. [14, 15]). Behavior modeling has been found to be a very powerful instructional method across a diverse range of behavioral domains, including the adoption of technological innovations. This concept, originated from Bandura's social-cognitive theory, posits that much of our learning derives from vicarious experience and advocates the concept of modeling in which a person (the so-called 'model') demonstrates and explains how to solve a given problem [9, 10]. One of the principal mechanisms by which behavior modeling operates is self-efficacy. Research on behavior modeling in computer training indicated that behavior modeling yields higher scores of computer self-efficacy and subsequently better task performance, compared to other non-modeling instructional methods, such as a lecture-based instruction and self-manual [14, 16]. Though it is suggested that behavior modeling would be an effective method to influence perceived of ease of use (due to its impact on individuals' self-efficacy), this has not been empirically tested.

Despite the fact that human models have been found to strongly influence people's beliefs, human instructors are not always available [17]. In this study, we argue that artificial behavior models could be as effective as persuasive human models in enhancing individuals' computer self-efficacy and (subsequently) perceived ease of use of an AT, due to their ability to simulate human-human interaction [7]. The potential of replacing human models with artificial ones has received some attention [i.e., 18, 19]. Nonetheless, to our knowledge, earlier literature provides no direct evidence that behavior modeling by an artificial agent can enhance beliefs, such as computer self-efficacy and perceived ease of use.

1.1 Current Work

In the current study, we investigated whether an agent that models an AT-related behavior (i.e., demonstration and verbal instruction) can enhance individuals' computer self-efficacy and perceived ease of use of this AT, as compared to other non-modeling instructional methods. We further tested whether computer self-efficacy mediates the effect (if any) of the type of instructional method on perceived ease of use, as suggested by earlier literature [e.g., 12].

The test our hypotheses, we compare the agent-delivered behavior modeling condition to two, frequently used, non-modeling instructional methods: an agent-delivered instructional narration (behavior modeling absent) and a no-agent, text-only instruction (i.e., both behavior modeling and agent being absent). Specifically, the agent-delivered instructional narration condition (i.e., lecturing) contains an agent that only provides verbal instructions on how to use an AT, while the AT-related features are presented in a slideshow. The no-agent, text-only instruction condition (i.e., user manual) does not contain an on-screen agent. Instead, it includes the AT instructions in a written form, accompanied by a slideshow of the AT-related features.

We predicted that an agent-delivered behavior modeling will be more effective in enhancing individuals' computer self-efficacy beliefs (H1), and, perceptions of ease of use (H2), as compared to the non-modeling methods. Moreover, we expected computer self-efficacy to mediate the effect of the type of instructional method on perceived ease of use (H3).

In line with recommendations of earlier studies about self-efficacy beliefs being situation-specific, we examined the impact of agent-delivered behavior modeling on specific computer-self efficacy. Nonetheless, due to the fact that general computer self-efficacy has been found to impact specific computer self-efficacy, we examined our hypotheses, controlling for the effect of the general computer self-efficacy on both dependent variables.

2 Method

2.1 Participants and Design

A total of 197 individuals participated in the study. The participants were recruited using a local participant database, and most of them were students from Eindhoven

University of Technology. Of these participants, 122 (61.9%) were males and 74 (37.6%) were females (one person did not answer the question about gender). The age of the sample ranged from 19 to 29, with a mean age of 23 ($SD = 2.4$). One-hundred fifteen participants were educated to undergraduate level or higher, and 77 had completed high school (5 persons did not state their educational background). The vast majority of the participants (95.5%), reported using computers on a daily basis, with a computer use frequency for more than 12 h per week (82.5%). The average general computer self-efficacy of the population was high ($M = 5.5$, $SD = 0.7$), which is in line with the participants' stated extensive computer use. Nevertheless, more than half of the participants (63.5%) reported no previous experience with using assistive computer technologies (i.e., software and/or hardware).

The study employed a between-subjects design, with the participants being randomly assigned to one of the three experimental conditions: an agent-delivered modeling, an agent-delivered instructional narration and a no-agent, text-only instruction. We interviewed the first 10 participants after the debriefing to evaluate the success of our experimental manipulation, and we found support that the three instructional methods were successfully recognized as they were intended. The study's dependent variables were specific computer self-efficacy and perceived ease of use. Inclusion criteria were participants' fluency in English. Overall, the duration of the study was approximately 20 min, for which participants received 5€, as compensation for their participation.

2.2 Apparatus

The content of the instruction in the current study pertained to an eye-tracking software, called GazeTheWeb (GTW). GTW is a web-browser, developed to be controlled solely with the eyes, using an eye-tracking hardware (see [20]).

The 3D animated artificial agent, implemented in this study, was created using the CrazyTalk 8 software (https://www.reallusion.com/crazytalk/).

2.3 Artificial Agent

The agent was designed to resemble participants' characteristics in terms of appearance, according to the guidelines derived from earlier literature [18, 19]. Since the majority of the participants were young Dutch students, the agent was designed to be young (~ 25 years), attractive (as manipulated by the agent's facial features) and "cool" (as manipulated by the agent's clothing and hairstyle).

2.4 Materials

The main dependent variable for the first hypothesis was specific computer self-efficacy. Specific computer self-efficacy was assessed by asking participants to answer 5 self-constructed questions regarding their perceived ability to perform the necessary steps of the instructed computer task, using GTW. Specifically, to develop measures for the specific computer self-efficacy construct, the recommendations provided by past work were closely followed[1] [11, 13]. Participants could answer these 5 questions, by choosing an option on a 7-point rating scale, ranging from 1 (strongly disagree) to 7 (strongly agree). We constructed a reliable measure (Cronbach's α = 0.80) of specific computer self-efficacy by averaging participants' answers to this set of questions.

General computer self-efficacy was assessed by asking participants to answer 8 questions regarding their perceived ability to use unfamiliar computer technologies in general. This 8-item scale was originally created by [11]. Participants could answer these questions by choosing an option on a 7-point rating scale, ranging from 1 (strongly disagree) to 7 (strongly agree). We constructed a reliable measure of general computer self-efficacy (Cronbach's α = 0.75) by averaging participants' answers to this set of questions.

The main dependent variable for the second hypothesis was system-specific perceived ease of use. Perceived ease of use was assessed by asking participants to answer 4 questions regarding their personal evaluation of the mental effort that is needed to use GTW. This 4-item scale was originally created by [21, 22]. Participants could answer these questions by choosing an option on a 7-point rating scale, ranging from 1 (strongly disagree) to 7 (strongly agree). We constructed a reliable measure of perceived ease of use (Cronbach's α = .81) by averaging participants' answers to this set of questions.

For exploratory reasons we also assessed whether there was any effect of the two agent-delivered instructions methods on participants' judgments about qualities of the artificial agent. The "Godspeed" questionnaire [23] was used to measure three key concepts of Human-Computer interaction, namely, anthropomorphism, animacy, and likability. This questionnaire was administered in a 7-point semantic differential, scale. We constructed reliable measures of anthropomorphism (Cronbach's α = .81), animacy (Cronbach's α = .91) and likeability (Cronbach's α = .82) by averaging participants' answers to each set of questions.

Lastly, demographic questions of age, gender, education, and level of computer use were asked.

2.5   Procedure

Participants were welcomed in the central hall of the lab building. Each participant was asked to read and sign an informed consent form, stating the general purpose of the research and their willingness to participate in this study. Then, participants were randomly assigned to one of the 3 outlined experimental conditions and they were asked to watch an instructional video (split into two screens) on how to perform a web search using GTW. It was while the participants watched the video that the manipulation of the agent-delivered modeling took place.

In more detail, the video in the agent-delivered modeling condition was split into the following two screens: on the right-hand side, an artificial agent appeared to use the GTW system to demonstrate a computer task (e.g. web search) by moving the head and eyes, while verbally explaining the system features involved in such a task; the

---

[1] The measure for specific computer self-efficacy can be requested from the first author.

left-hand side of the screen contained a display of the system, exposing participants to the progressive effects of the agent's web search actions in real time (see a, Fig. 1).

The video in the agent-delivered instructional narration condition was split into the following two screens: on the right-hand side, the (same) artificial agent appeared to be motionless, with his main function being the provision of (the same) verbal instructions on how to conduct a web search using GTW (i.e., explaining the task-related features of the system); the left-hand side of the screen contained a display of the system, exposing participants to progressive screenshots of the system with labels highlighting the commands the verbal explanation was referring at every time (see b, Fig. 1).

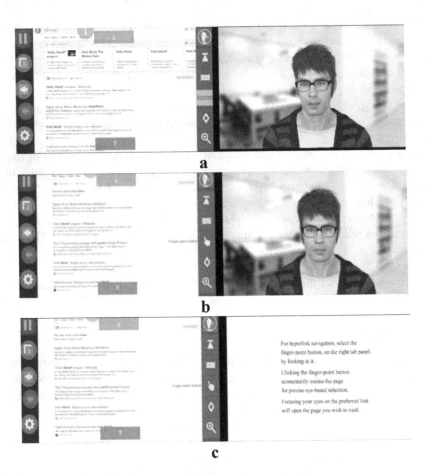

Fig. 1. Different types of instructional methods: (a) Agent-delivered behavior modeling; the agent tilts the head to focus its gaze to the system feature, which, as a result of this action, becomes activated (blue button on the left-hand side) (b) Agent-delivered instructional narration; the agent is motionless while explaining the system feature, which is highlighted in the left-hand side screenshot (c) No-agent, text-only instruction; the agent has been substituted by a text-box, which provides instructions of the function of the system feature, highlighted in the left-hand side screenshot. (Color figure online)

Finally, the no-agent text-only instruction was identical to the agent-delivered instructional narration, with the only difference being that the left-hand side of the screen contained a text-box, with written instructions. Thus, participants in this condition were provided with the same system instructions, but they could not see or listen to the agent. The left side of the screen was identical to the agent-delivered instructional narration condition (i.e. labels highlighting the system's commands) (see c, Fig. 1).

After the end of the instructional videos, participants were requested to answer an online questionnaire. Lastly, they were debriefed, paid and thanked for their contribution.

3 Results

Specific computer self-efficacy: A one-way analysis of covariance (ANCOVA) was conducted to determine the effect of the type of instructional method on participants' specific computer self-efficacy, after controlling for their general computer self-efficacy[2]. Results showed that the covariate general computer self-efficacy was significantly related to the specific computer self-efficacy, $F(1, 193) = 38.68, p < .001$, $\eta_p^2 = .16$. After controlling for general computer self-efficacy, the significant main effect of the type of instruction on specific computer self-efficacy remained, $F(2, 193) = 6.83, p < .01, \eta_p^2 = .06$. Planned contrasts revealed that specific computer self-efficacy was significantly higher for the participants in the agent-delivered modeling condition ($N = 66, M = 6.1, SD = .8$), as compared to the participants in the agent-delivered instructional narration condition ($N = 66, M = 5.6, SD = .9$), $t(193) = -3.48, p < .01$, and as compared to participants in the text-only instruction condition ($N = 65, M = 5.7, SD = .9$), $t(193) = -2.82, p < .01$. No significant difference was found between participants in the two non-modeling conditions after controlling for general self-efficacy.

Perceived ease of use: A one-way ANCOVA was conducted to determine the effect of the type of instructional method on participants' perceived ease of use, after controlling for their general computer self-efficacy[3]. Results demonstrated that the covariate general computer self-efficacy was significantly related to perceived ease of use $F(1, 193) = 27.20, p < .01, \eta_p^2 = .12$. The findings revealed a marginally significant main effect of the type of instruction on perceived ease of use after controlling for the general computer self-efficacy, $F(2, 193) = 2.88, p = .058, \eta_p^2 = .029$. Planned contrasts revealed that perceived ease of use was significantly higher for participants in the agent-delivered modeling condition ($N = 66, M = 4.7, SE = .12$), as compared to participants in the agent-delivered instructional narration condition ($N = 66, M = 4.3, SE = .12$), $t(193) = -2.3, p < .05$. Nonetheless, results showed no evidence for a

---

[2] When we did not include the general self-efficacy covariate in the analysis (i.e., ANOVA), the results were comparable and in line with our first hypothesis, $F(2, 194) = 5.10, p = .007, \eta^2 = .05$.

[3] When we did not include the general self-efficacy covariate in the analysis (i.e., ANOVA), the results were comparable and partially supported our second hypothesis, $F(2,194) = 2.23, p = .11$.

significant difference in perceived ease of use, between participants in the agent-delivered modeling condition and participants in the text-only instruction condition ($N = 65$, $M = 4.5$, $SE = .12$), $t(193) = -1.34$, $p > .05$. Similarly, no significant difference was found between participants in the two non-modeling conditions after controlling for general self-efficacy.

Judgments of the agent's qualities: For exploratory purposes, a one-way multivariate analysis of variance (MANOVA) was conducted to examine whether the agent functioning as a behavior model while providing more social cues, would affect individuals' judgments about the agent's qualities of likeability, animacy, and anthropomorphism, as compared to the agent functioning as a verbal instructor only. The results revealed a statistically significant MANOVA effect of the type of agents' instructional method on the three dependent variables combined, Wilk's $\Lambda = .926$, F (3, 128) = 3.401, $p = 0.02$, $\eta_p^2 = .074$. A series of one-way ANOVA's on each of the three dependent variables was conducted as follow-up tests to the MANOVA. We found a significant difference between participants in the two conditions on their agent's likability judgments, $F(1,130) = 5.50$, $p = .02$, $\eta_p^2 = .041$, with participants' liking of the agent to be higher in the agent-delivered behavior modeling condition ($N = 66$, $M = 3.8$, $SD = 1.1$), as compared to the agent-delivered instructional narration condition ($N = 66$, $M = 3.3$, $SD = 1.0$). Findings showed no evidence for a significant difference between participants in the two conditions on agent's animacy judgments, $F(1,130) = .08$, $p = .77$, $\eta_p^2 = .001$, as also, on agent's anthropomorphism judgments, $F(1,130) = 2.32$, $p = .13$, $\eta_p^2 = .018$.

Mediation effects on perceived ease of use: Our aim was to test whether specific computer self-efficacy could explain part of the anticipated effect of the type of instructional method on perceived ease of use. Since we found differences in perceived ease of use only between the two agent conditions, the mediation analysis compared these conditions. In addition, we also included the agent likeability judgment as a potential mediator. That is, we could not ignore that the difference found in participants' affective state towards the agent (likeability judgments) might have influenced their perceptions of the system's ease of use.

A regression analysis was conducted, using dummy coding-behavior modeling and instructional narration. The analysis was performed using the PROCESS custom dialog for SPSS, as developed by [24]. The results are reported in Fig. 2. Below we provide a summary of the main findings.

The analysis showed the type of the agent instructional method was a significant predictor of perceived ease of use, $R^2 = 3.6\%$ (i.e., the c path in Fig. 2), as well as of, both, specific computer self-efficacy, $R^2 = 6.9\%$, and agent's likeability judgments, $R^2 = 4.1\%$ (i.e., a paths in Fig. 2). In turn, participants' stronger specific computer self-efficacy beliefs and agent likeability judgments were found to associate with stronger perceptions of ease of use of the system (i.e., b paths in Fig. 2). After the inclusion of the mediators, the effect of the type of agent instructional method on perceived ease of use became non-significant (i.e., c' path in Fig. 2), indicating full mediation. Together the b paths and the c' path explained $R^2 = 31.5\%$ of the variance in perceived ease of use.

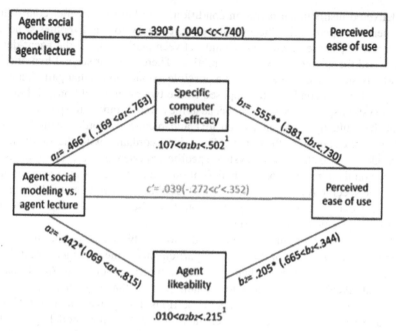

Fig. 2. Mediation analyses of the difference in people's perceived ease of use towards the agent's type of instructional method (behavior modeling and instructional narration). All estimates are in unstandardized units (7-point scale, ranging from 1 to 7). [1]Based on 1000 bootstrap samples (bias corrected). Grey lines indicate statistically non-significant paths, *p < .05. **p < .01.

4   Discussion

The current study investigated the influence of an artificial agent as a behavior model, as compared to two non-modeling instructional methods (with and without an on-screen agent), on users' computer self-efficacy and perceived ease of use of a system, in the context of a novel AT training.

The results of the current study supported our first hypothesis, showing that participants in the agent-delivered modeling condition reported higher computer self-efficacy, as compared to participants in the two non-modeling conditions. This effect remained even when controlling for participants' general computer self-efficacy. We found no difference between participants' scores of self-efficacy in the two non-modeling conditions. This finding is in line with earlier research that showed the effect of behavior modeling (conducted by a human agent) on users' computer self-efficacy, as compared to other non-modeling methods (i.e., lecture training and self-manual) [14, 16]. These findings indicate that an agent that models an observed behavior (rather than when merely explains such a behavior) can increase participants' beliefs about their own capabilities to use an AT.

Furthermore, we found that participants in the agent-delivered modeling condition had higher scores of perceived ease of use compared to participants in the agent-delivered instructional narration condition, both before and after controlling for their general computer self-efficacy. However, contrary to our hypothesis, no differences in perceived ease of use were found between participants in the agent-delivered modeling and the no-agent, text-only condition. Therefore, our second hypothesis was only partially supported. We argue that a possible explanation is that participants in the text-only instruction condition (as opposed to the two agent conditions) did not gather sufficient system-specific experience, because they were required to split their attention between the mutually referring written text and pictures, in order mentally integrate them (e.g., split attention effect) [25]. Thus, in accordance with the rationale of the TAM model, due to the lack of system-specific experience, these participants could have relied on their general positive beliefs about technologies when assessing the ease of use of the specific AT [26]. Future research could examine the general factors, other than general computer self-efficacy that could be used as anchoring beliefs in the absence of a system-specific experience.

In line with past literature [12], our mediation analysis showed that the difference we found in perceived ease of use between participants in the two agent conditions was explained by the differences in their specific computer self-efficacy. Additionally, we found agent likeability judgments to explain part of the difference in ease of use between participants in the two the agent conditions. Lastly, we found no difference in perceived ease of use between participants in the two non-modeling conditions. Overall, the results suggest that an agent that models an observed behavior (rather than when merely explains such a behavior) can enhance participants' beliefs about the easiness of an AT.

Although the effectiveness of the agent-delivered behavior modeling was not tested with physically disabled individuals for reasons related to practicality (i.e., transportation-related issues) and convenience (i.e., statistical power), we are convinced that the findings can also be generalized to this population. The study's results provide evidence that agent-delivered modeling can enhance individuals' computer self-efficacy and perceived ease of use of the system, as compared to other non-modeling methods, even after controlling for their general computer self-efficacy. Modeling has been shown to be a more effective instructional method for people with minimal prior system experience [16]. The fact that the study's participants had high general computer self-efficacy and extensive computer experience is an indicator that modeling could likewise be effective (if not more effective) for those with low general computer self-efficacy and/or minimal general computer experience.

Lastly, although the study's findings provide evidence that an artificial agent can be an effective behavioral model, the study's design does not allow to make inferences about the mere influence of the agent on individuals' beliefs. However, the fact that participants in the agent-delivered modeling condition perceived the agent as more likable than those in the agent-delivered instructional narration, provides some evidence that they agent modeling manipulation was both successful and effective. Future research should examine the mere effect of an artificial model on people's beliefs and other learning gains (i.e., performance), as also conditions of their use as models.

Overall, the current research revealed that an artificial agent, embedded in an AT, can serve as an effective behavior model, increasing individuals' computer self-efficacy, which also leads to higher perceptions of ease of use of this AT. Thus, this study adds to earlier work by providing evidence for the use of an artificial behavior modeling as a strategy to maximize AT adoption. Such findings are important for AT acceptance, as well as technology acceptance in general.

Acknowledgments. This work was supported by project MAMEM that has received funding from the European Union's Horizon 2020 research and innovation program under grant agreement number: 644780.

References

1. Hurst, A., Tobias, J.: Empowering individuals with do-it-yourself assistive technology. In: Thirteenth Annual ACM SIGACCESS Conference on Assistive Technologies 2011, pp. 11–18. ACM Press, Dundee (2011)
2. Eurostat. http://ec.europa.eu/eurostat/statistics-explained/index.php/Disability_statistics_-_need_for_assistance. Accessed 09 Nov 2017
3. Kintsch, A., DePaula, R.: A framework for the adoption of assistive technology. In: Supporting Learning Through Assistive Technology, SWAAAC 2002, pp. 1–10 (2002)
4. Wessel, R., Dijcks, B., Soede, M., Gelderblom, G.J., De Witte, L.: Non-use of provided assistive technology devices, a literature overview. Technol. Disability **15**(4), 231–238 (2003)
5. Hamari, J., Koivisto, J., Pakkanen, T.: Do persuasive technologies persuade? - a review of empirical studies. In: Spagnolli, A., Chittaro, L., Gamberini, L. (eds.) PERSUASIVE 2014. LNCS, vol. 8462, pp. 118–136. Springer, Cham (2014). https://doi.org/10.1007/978-3-319-07127-5_11
6. Ham, J., Midden, C.J.: A persuasive robot to stimulate energy conservation: the influence of positive and negative social feedback and task similarity on energy-consumption behavior. Int. J. Soc. Robot. **6**(2), 163–171 (2014)
7. Reeves, B., Nass, C.: The Media Equation. Cambridge University Press, New York (1996)
8. Fuhrer, M.J., Jutai, J.W., Scherer, M.J., DeRuyter, F.: A framework for the conceptual modelling of assistive technology device outcomes. Disability Rehabil. **25**(22), 1243–1251 (2003)
9. Bandura, A.: Social Foundations of Thought and Action: A Social Cognitive Theory. Prentice-Hall, New York (1986)
10. Bandura, A., Freeman, W.H., Lightsey, R.: Self-efficacy: the exercise of control. J. Cogn. Psychother. **13**(2), 158–166 (1999)
11. Marakas, G.M., Yi, M.Y., Johnson, R.D.: The multilevel and multifaceted character of computer self-efficacy: toward clarification of the construct and an integrative framework for research. Inf. Syst. Res. **9**(2), 126–163 (1998)
12. Venkatesh, V., Bala, H.: Technology acceptance model 3 and a research agenda on interventions. Decis. Sci. **39**(2), 273–315 (2008)
13. Agarwal, R., Sambamurthy, V., Stair, R.M.: The evolving relationship between general and specific computer self-efficacy—an empirical assessment. Inf. Syst. Res. **11**(4), 418–430 (2000)
14. Compeau, D.R., Higgins, C.A.: Computer self-efficacy: development of a measure and initial test. MIS Q. **19**(2), 189–211 (1995)
15. Venkatesh, V., Davis, F.D.: A model of the antecedents of perceived ease of use: development and test. Decis. Sci. **27**(3), 451–481 (1996)

16. Gist, M.E.: The influence of training method on self-efficacy and idea generation among managers. Pers. Psychol. **42**(4), 787–805 (1989)
17. Kim, Y., Baylor, A.L.: A socio-cognitive framework for pedagogical agents as learning companions. Educ. Technol. Res. Dev. **54**(6), 569–596 (2006)
18. Baylor, A.L., Plant, E.A.: Pedagogical agents as social models for engineering: the influence of agent appearance on female choice. In: Looi, C.K., McCalla, G., Bredeweg, B., Breuker, J. (eds.) Artificial Intelligence in Education: Supporting Learning Through Intelligent and Socially Informed Technology 2005, vol. 125, pp. 65–72. IOS Press, Amsterdam (2005)
19. Plant, E.A., Baylor, A.L., Doerr, C.E., Rosenberg-Kima, R.B.: Changing middle-school students' attitudes and performance regarding engineering with computer-based social models. Comput. Educ. **53**(2), 209–215 (2009)
20. Kumar, C., Menges, R., Staab, S.: Eye-controlled interfaces for multimedia interaction. IEEE Multimedia **23**(4), 6–13 (2016)
21. Davis, F.D.: Perceived usefulness, perceived ease of use, and user acceptance of information technology. MIS Q. **13**(3), 319–340 (1989)
22. Davis, F.D.: User acceptance of information technology: system characteristics, user perceptions and behavioral impacts. Int. J. Man-Mach. Stud. **38**(3), 475–487 (1993)
23. Bartneck, C., Croft, E., Kulic, D.: Measuring the anthropomorphism, animacy, likeability, perceived intelligence and perceived safety of robots. In: Metrics for HRI Workshop 2008, Technical report, vol. 471, Amsterdam, pp. 37–44 (2008)
24. Hayes, A.F.: Introduction to Mediation, Moderation, and Conditional Process Analysis. Guilford Press, New York (2013)
25. Ayres, P., Sweller, J.: The split-attention principle. In: Mayer, R.E. (ed.) Cambridge Handbook of Multimedia Learning, pp. 135–146. Cambridge University Press, New York (2005)
26. Venkatesh, V.: Determinants of perceived ease of use: integrating control, intrinsic motivation, and emotion into the technology acceptance model. Inf. Syst. Res. **11**(4), 342–365 (2000)

Understanding Home Energy Saving Recommendations

Matthew Law[1], Mayank Thirani[2], Sami Rollins[2], Alark Joshi[2],
and Nilanjan Banerjee[3(✉)]

[1] Cornell University, Ithaca, NY, USA
[2] University of San Francisco, Fulton Street, San Francisco, CA 2130, USA
[3] University of Maryland, 1000 Hilltop Cir, Baltimore, MD, USA
nilanb@umbc.edu

Abstract. Energy recommender systems attempt to help users attain energy saving goals at home, however previous systems fall short of tailoring these recommendations to users' devices and behaviors. In this paper we explore the foundations of a user-centered home energy recommendation system. We first conduct a study on a set of recommendations published by utility companies and government agencies to determine the types of recommendations may be popular among typical users. We then design micro-models to estimate energy savings for popular recommendations and conduct a followup study to see if users are likely to carry out these recommendations to achieve estimated savings. We found that users prefer low-cost but potentially tedious recommendations to those that are expensive, however users are unwilling to adopt recommendations that will require long-term lifestyle changes. We also determine that a subset of popular recommendations can lead to substantial energy savings.

1 Introduction

Recommendation-based approaches for saving energy in the home have historically been, and continue to be, widely used. Though automated solutions, for example the Nest thermostat, are becoming more common, utility companies and governmental agencies such as the U.S. Department of Energy still aggressively encourage individual energy saving through a wide variety of behavioral recommendations. Additionally, the research community has advocated technology-enhanced systems to persuade users to adopt energy-saving recommendations, for example by making it easy to set goals, providing timely nudges, or offering feedback on progress. Some popular recommendations, for example `Consider installing a solar water heater` are expensive home upgrades while others, such as `Clean the lint screen in the dryer after every load` are small behavioral changes that may or may not be adopted by users.

For energy-saving recommendations and recommendation-based systems to effectively influence user behavior it is necessary to understand which recommendations users prefer and are likely to adopt; how best to communicate recommendations and feedback to the user; and whether the recommendations a

© Springer International Publishing AG, part of Springer Nature 2018
J. Ham et al. (Eds.): PERSUASIVE 2018, LNCS 10809, pp. 297–309, 2018.
https://doi.org/10.1007/978-3-319-78978-1_25

user is willing to implement are likely to have an impact on energy usage. Unfortunately, these areas are not well understood. Utility companies offer banks of static recommendations, some of which may be generally unpopular and some of which may only apply to some users, for instance home owners rather than renters. Moreover, some recommendations may be popular, but have little potential for energy savings in all or some homes.

In this work, we conduct a three-pronged study that (1) identifies user perceptions and barriers to adoption of common energy-saving recommendations; (2) proposes personalized models to quantify savings of popular recommendations; and (3) applies the models to understand potential energy savings in typical homes. Our initial study, a survey completed by approximately 650 participants on Amazon Mechanical Turk, asked users to provide feedback about 181 common energy-saving recommendations. The survey found that users prefer low-cost but potentially tedious recommendations to those that are more expensive, however users are unwilling to adopt recommendations that will require long-term lifestyle changes. From the study, we identified 13 of the most popular recommendations pertaining to the refrigerator, computer, lighting, and heating and cooling, and designed a set of micro-models that accept user-specific input and calculate personalized potential savings of each recommendation. Finally, we conducted a follow-up survey that used our models to determine potential savings for each participant. The study asked participants to provide energy usage profile and rate his/her willingness to adopt popular recommendations. We found that a small subset of popular recommendations can lead to substantial energy savings.

2   Understanding User Preference for Energy-Saving Recommendations

Energy-saving recommendations, for example those offered by utilities companies, span a wide spectrum. Expensive recommendations, such as `replace windows`, may have a significant potential for savings but are relevant only to home owners and not renters. Similarly, minor behavioral changes such as `wash full loads of clothes when possible`, may be broadly applicable but unpopular or unlikely to be adopted.

The goal of our initial study is twofold. First, we explore the kinds of recommendations users prefer and would be likely to adopt. Second, we explore how users would prefer to receive recommendations and feedback in order to encourage energy savings. This section describes the setup and results of a survey completed by 650 Amazon Mechanical Turk (AMT) participants.

Setup: The recommendation survey consists of four components. The **background and goals** portion of the survey asks users general questions about their awareness of energy usage in their homes; their goals for saving energy; and how they would prefer to receive recommendations and feedback regarding their goals. Next, we ask users to choose which **general category of recommendation** would be most useful from the options *Specific Appliances, Activities, Rooms in the Home,* and *Seasons.* Based on the category selected, we then

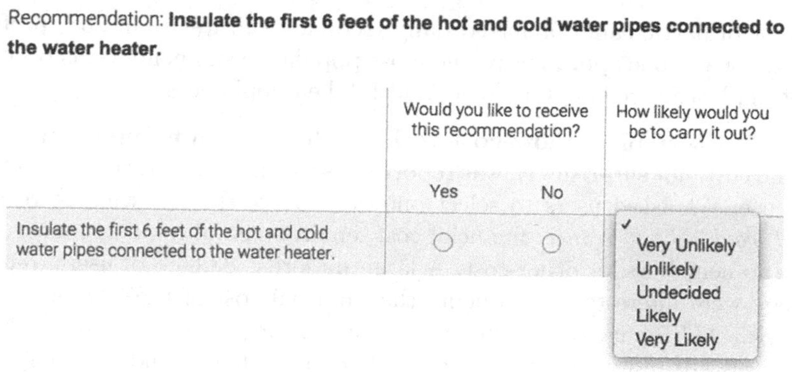

Recommendation: **Insulate the first 6 feet of the hot and cold water pipes connected to the water heater.**

	Would you like to receive this recommendation?		How likely would you be to carry it out?
	Yes	No	
Insulate the first 6 feet of the hot and cold water pipes connected to the water heater.	○	○	✓ Very Unlikely Unlikely Undecided Likely Very Likely

Fig. 1. Participants were asked whether they would like to receive a particular recommendation as well as how likely they would be to carry out the recommendation.

present the user with a set of five **specific recommendations** taken from existing sources including the U.S Department of Energy website and several utility company sites. Our bank of recommendations, which is an aggregate of all of the resources we were able to identify, includes a total of 181 recommendations. As shown in Fig. 1, for each recommendation, we ask the user (1) whether he/she would like to receive such a recommendation and (2) to rate the likelihood of carrying out the recommendation on a scale of 1 (Very Unlikely) to 5 (Very Likely). Finally, we collect **demographics** including age, education, and household income.

The survey was available on AMT from August 3 through September 6, 2015. Though a total of 748 people started the study, some questions were not answered by all participants—a total of 650 participants completed the survey. Most general questions received between 700 and 705 responses, and since each user only saw five of 181 recommendations, each specific recommendation received an average of 18.5 responses.

To better understand the general types of recommendation that were popular or unpopular, we manually tagged each of the 181 recommendations in three categories. Category 1 identified recommendations as behavioral, infrastructural, or both; Category 2 identified easy, medium, or hard recommendations; and Category 3 identified low, medium, high, or no cost recommendations.

2.1   Findings

The results of our survey provide insight into the types of recommendations participants find most useful as well as how they would prefer to set goals and receive feedback. Users were optimistic about goal-setting with the majority preferring a goal of reducing energy usage by 20% or more. We hypothesized that frequent feedback via smart phone application would be popular, however our results indicated otherwise. When asked how often they would like feedback on their progress, most users preferred monthly or weekly feedback. When asked about the medium for feedback, users strongly preferred email or a website.

Only 12% of participants preferred daily feedback and less than 25% preferred feedback via a phone app. Finally, the most popular recommendations pertained to lighting, heating, computer usage, and kitchen appliances.

Insight 1: Users prefer low-cost to low-effort recommendations

Financial cost, not surprisingly, was reported as the main motivation for reducing energy use. We asked users to select one or more of the following in response to the *I would like to reduce*: financial cost, environmental impact, energy usage relative to neighbors, or other cost. A large majority, 83.86% of users, reported that they were interested in reducing the financial cost of their home's energy usage with 47.57% caring about environmental impact. Moreover, with $p <$ 0.001, users are more aware of how much money they spend on energy bills each month than either how much energy their home uses each month or the environmental impact of their home's energy usage.

When asked whether they would like to receive specific recommendations, users preferred inexpensive or free recommendations over expensive recommendations even though many low-cost recommendations require significant effort. Many highly rated recommendations included tedious tasks, such as weatherstripping or caulking gaps around doors. Similarly, recommendations such as `install ENERGY STAR-rated routers and modems`, which are cheap investments, were more popular than more expensive upgrades, such as replacing windows.

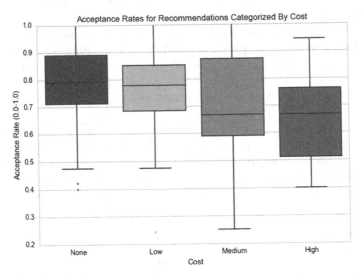

Fig. 2. Percentage of *Yes* responses in reply to the question *Would you like to receive this recommendation?* broken down by cost category.

Figure 2 shows the distribution of acceptance rate for recommendations in each of the categories: no cost, low cost, medium cost, and high cost. The acceptance rate is defined as the percentage of responses indicating *Yes* in reply to the

Table 1. Popular recommendations and mean expected savings for the follow-up study participants.

Appliance	Popular recommendations	Expected savings kWh	Expected savings $
Lighting	Use natural light during the day	40.14	4.81
	Decrease the light to a desired level by installing and using dimmer switches	93.98	11.28
Computer	Use the power management features of your operating system to put your computer to sleep	1.08	0.13
	Turn off the computer/laptop/monitor when idle	0.52	0.06
	Turn off your screen saver	0.10	0.01
	Close applications not in use while using your computer	1.24	0.15
Refrigerator	Increase the temperature of your fridge to 40°	9.27	1.11
	Cover your food before putting it in the fridge	0.12	0.01
	Reduce the number of times you open the door	3.61	0.43
	Reduce the length of time you prop your door open	0.07	0.01
HVAC	Adjust the thermostat down in the winter and up in the summer when you go to sleep	9.42	1.13
	Caulk or weatherstrip gaps and seams around windows, doors, vents, etc. to reduce air leakage	166.01	19.92
	Turn off your fans when you physically leave the room	37.68	4.52

question *Would you like to receive this recommendation?*. The median acceptance rate for recommendations in the no-cost category was nearly 80%, in contrast to a median acceptance rate of 67% for recommendations in the high-cost category. Only 6.1% and 2.7% of recommendations classified as no and low cost, respectively, had low acceptance rates at or below 50%, while a more significant 26.7% of those recommendations classified as high cost were rejected by participants.

Insight 2: Users are unwilling to make lifestyle changes to save energy Table 1 shows the most popular recommendations of the survey. Many popular recommendations were in the infrastructural category and have little or no impact on a user's lifestyle. In contrast, unpopular recommendations, for example, `Go to sleep earlier to require less lighting at night`, often require users to change the way they schedule or perform daily activities. As another example, covering drafty windows with plastic was popular, while repainting house walls to better reflect light was not; the latter affects the user's daily life much more than the former. We found that many of the least popular recommendations were those that had an impact on entertainment activities. `Use a Wii instead of XBox One or PS4`; `Use a smaller TV`; and

Watch less TV all had an acceptance rate of of lower than 50%. The least popular recommendation was Consider spending more time with family and friends in the same room when planning activities.

Discussion: This initial study demonstrates that while many common energy-saving recommendations are popular, other recommendations commonly provided by utility companies and other energy-focused websites are unlikely to be adopted. Some popular recommendations have a large potential for energy savings, though the potential savings for several other popular recommendations, for example Cover liquids and foods you put in the fridge is less clear. In the next sections, we design a set of models and carry out a follow-up user study to quantify the likely energy savings of a user who applies the popular recommendations identified in Table 1.

3   Modeling Consumption

Based on the responses to the initial study, popular recommendations most frequently pertained to refrigerators, home lighting, computer usage, and heating and cooling. To understand the impact of these recommendations on typical users' energy consumption, we built micro-models of energy consumption for each of these appliances using a combination of prior work and experimentation. Each micro-model was dependent on a set of appliance-level and behavioral parameters. Appliance-level parameters were used to characterize the device while behavioral parameters described its usage. These parameters were used in combination to estimate the current consumption of the device as well as the potential savings achievable using each of the popular recommendations. To make the models more applicable to typical users, parameters were chosen in such a way that ordinary homeowners would be able to estimate them with minimal effort.

Refrigerator: The device parameters for the refrigerator model included refrigerator age, size, and configuration, which were used as inputs to an Energy-Star model to estimate an average baseline energy consumption. Further, experimentation was done on a single refrigerator to determine a linear relationship between temperature settings and energy consumption, a curve which was shifted based on the output from the Energy-Star model. Based on recommendations regarding internal temperature, door-opening, and covering liquids and foods, the behavioral parameters included temperature setting; door opening frequency and the duration of door-propping; and whether the user tended to cover food before storing it. Potential savings were calculated by determining the baseline consumption and then subtracting the estimated consumption using the recommendations.

Home Lighting: Assuming it would be difficult to recall the number and wattages of every light bulb in a user's house, the lighting model takes as device parameters the number of rooms that are typically lit and an average size for each room. It then uses a well-known rule of thumb to calculate the `lux` level that would typically be used to light that amount of space in a residential setting by multiplying the number of square feet by 1.5 [1]. Savings are calculated for two recommendations, one regarding natural light, and one involving dimmer switches. The natural light savings are calculated by simply restricting the baseline calculation to the number of rooms that are both occupied during the day and receive natural light. The dimmer savings are calculated by determining the number of `Watts` necessary to light the occupied square footage to several different light levels recommended for different tasks.

Computer Usage: To calculate the usage of a computer we parameterize the model using the following inputs: (1) whether the system was used as a desktop or a laptop; (2) whether the computer was an Energy-Star system; (3) whether the monitor used is LCD or not; (4) whether the user uses multiple applications simultaneously; and (5) whether the computer is kept in sleep mode when not used. Based on these inputs, a baseline power consumption of the computer (200 W for a desktop and 40 W for a laptop) is multiplied by a preset factor. These factors are based on measurements performed on a computer as part of prior work [2]. For example, if a computer is Energy-Star the power consumption is assumed to be 50% of the baseline [3].

Heating and Cooling: We have developed simple models to calculate the energy savings for recommendations involving the heating and cooling system. For instance, to quantify the energy savings when adjusting the indoor home temperature at night, we first calculate a coarse estimate of the external wall area of the house by dividing the total square footage by the number of floors and taking the square root. Our model then calculates the ideal temperature differentials for the winter and summer using indoor, outdoor, and the minimum and maximum temperature in a user's comfort zone. We then use the model described in [4] to calculate the difference in heat loss rate in BTU/hr between boundary and current temperature. Consequently, we multiply the heat loss rate by the number of hours the user is asleep in a month and convert that value to Kilo-Watt-Hours. In our model, we perform the calculations for summer and winter seasons and provide an average of the two.

For the second recommendation (sealing air leakages) the energy savings are calculated using the following equation: `Savings` $= \Delta_T \cdot$ `ACHact` $\cdot$ `Volume` $\cdot 0.018$ where `ACHact` is air changes per hour and is dominated by `ACHnat`, the natural air changes per hour, when `ACH50`, a measurement of air changes induced during a standard blower test at 50 Pascals, is greater than 1 [5,6]. Further, `ACHnat` can be calculated using a conversion factor, `lblfactor`, as $\frac{ACH50}{lblfactor}$, so savings can be described by: $\Delta_T \cdot \frac{ACH50}{lblfactor} \cdot Volume \cdot 0.018$ where 0.018 is the heat capacity of air at sea level on average and Δ_T is the temperature differential between indoors and outdoors. We estimate the volume of the house, and `ACH50` for leaky, moderate and tight houses using the estimates provided in [7] and a combination of the age and the amount of effort the user has put into sealing leaks in the house. As a rule of thumb, we use 20 for `lblfactor`. For the third recommendation (Turning of fans when not in the room) the savings are calculated as `numfans` · `numhours_fans_run_unattended` · `fan_powerusage` · `dayspermonth` where `fan_powerusage` is set to 75 W [8].

4   Quantifying Potential Savings

We conducted a follow-up study that uses our models to quantify the potential savings of the popular recommendations identified by our initial study.

Setup: The follow-up study focused on four areas: **refrigerator**, **lighting**, **computer usage**, and **HVAC**. For each appliance, the study asked users to provide a usage profile then to rate how likely they would be to modify their usage according to the recommendations. In the case of the refrigerator, for instance, we asked the participants several questions about their fridge itself (e.g., its age), then several questions about its use (e.g., how cold is it?). We then applied our micro-model to generate and display potential energy savings per recommendation. Finally, we asked users to indicate if they would be willing to apply any of the recommendations that would lead to savings and to provide an explanation if not.

The survey was available on AMT from March 19, 2016 to March 24, 2016. We collected a total of 110 complete responses. Some users started the survey but did not complete it and their results were not included in our analysis.

4.1   Findings

Insight 1: Applying a few popular recommendations can lead to substantial energy savings.

Our results indicate that an average user could expect to save up to 27.9% on a monthly bill, based on the 2014 US average monthly energy cost of $114.09 [9]. Since some of the recommendations for each appliance could lead to overlapping savings, this is a conservative estimate that first averages the savings for each recommendation, then takes the maximum average for each appliance group, and sums the four results.

Figure 3 shows, from left to right, the total number of users, the number of users who saw at least one recommendation in each appliance category, the number of users who saw each specific recommendation, and percentage of users who indicated they were willing to adopt the recommendation. For instance, 110 users received at least one recommendation related to the refrigerator, however only eight saw the recommendation to cover food and, of those eight, 87.5% said they would be willing to adopt this recommendation.

The acceptance rate of all recommendations was very high, with most users indicating they would adopt a recommendation if they were given that recommendation. The recommendation to put a computer to sleep when not in use had the lowest acceptance rate—one user indicated he runs a twitterbot on his

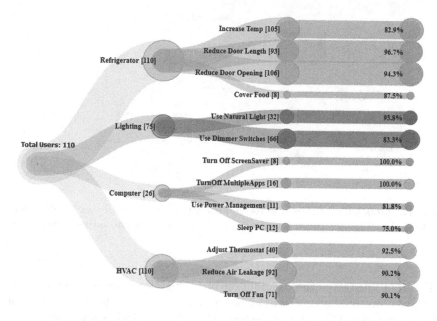

Fig. 3. This figure illustrates how many users saw each recommendation for each appliance and the percentage of users willing to adopt the recommendation.

computer and therefore cannot put it into a sleep state. Note that users were only asked to evaluate a recommendation if it offered potential savings based on their profile. Several recommendations were seen by a small number of users because the users already performed the recommended behavior. For example, 102 users indicated that they already cover their food before putting it in the refrigerator, 74 users said they already use natural light during the day, and 58 users said they already adjust their thermostat when they go to sleep. Less than 25% of users' profiles offered potential savings through at least one of the computer-related recommendations.

As illustrated in Table 1, the expected savings calculated by our models falls into four clusters. Expected savings per user were calculated as the mean savings across all 110 users for each recommendation, including those users who rejected the recommendation or whose profiles offered no potential savings. Infrastructural changes including sealing air leaks and using dimmer switches yield the greatest savings of more than **90 kWh**. Using natural lighting and turning off fans fall into the next cluster at savings in the **high-30 kWh** range. Increasing the refrigerator temperature and adjusting thermostats had a low, **9–10 kWh** average savings, and savings of **less than 4 kWh** was estimated for keeping the fridge door closed, covering food, turning of screensavers, minimizing applications running on a computer, and using computer power management and sleep features.

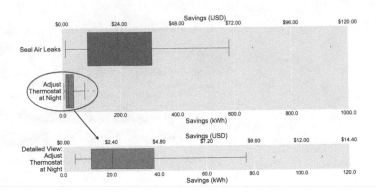

Fig. 4. For users who accepted the recommendation, the figure shows the distribution of potential savings for the recommendations seal air leaks and adjust thermostat at night.

Figure 4 illustrates the distribution of savings for a recommendation with the highest overall savings (seal air leaks) and one in the third tier of savings (adjust thermostat). The figure *excludes* the zero-savings cases where a user did not accept the recommendation or did not see the recommendation based on profile responses. This figure illustrates the wide variance of savings, with many users seeing savings significantly higher than the average. Even in cases where average savings is small, some users may see significant benefit. Other appliances showed similar distributions.

Insight 2: Reasons for rejecting recommendations were consistent with the initial study findings and insufficient savings discouraged some recommendation acceptance.

Users who rejected recommendations were asked to explain their reasoning and most comments were consistent with the findings identified in our initial study. Several users demurred from installing dimmer switches or sealing air leaks in their homes for the sake of cost, supporting our finding that users prefer low-cost to low-effort recommendations. Some users also expressed concern about effort required, for example *I have no idea how to install that in my house and I don't have the time or upfront money.* Investment was also, understandably, a concern for users in rental properties—67% of users who rejected the recommendation to seal air leaks cited the fact that they are renters or do not own the house that they live in. Many comments also reinforced the finding that users are unwilling to make lifestyle changes to save energy. Multiple users rejected the idea of installing dimmer switches because they liked brightly lit rooms. Similarly, when declining a recommendation to reduce fridge door openings one user wrote, *That will be a hard habit to break and I often need to open in quite often.*

In some cases, users found the predicted savings to be too low to justify the cost or effort involved in carrying them out. One user worried that increasing refrigerator temperature would cause food spoilage losses that would not offset the savings. Similarly, a user who had very low savings for reducing the amount the refrigerator is propped open responded, *a penny a month is not enough for me to change*. Another user made a similar comment about the fridge door recommendation, *Because we open it when we want something. It's hardly worth 55 cents a month to try to coordinate family members' thirst or hunger*. Overall, the implication in these cases was that higher savings would have made the recommendation more appealing.

Discussion: Our findings demonstrate that there is ample opportunity to design persuasive systems to encourage users to apply unsurprisingly. Users are, unsurprisingly, interested in saving money, and our findings suggest they are willing to put in effort to do so. Though our study identified many recommendations that are unlikely to be adopted, many of the the most popular recommendations, for example dimming lights and turning off fans when leaving a room, require behavioral change. We acknowledge that this work does not consider whether users follow through on the recommendations they report to be appealing, but suggest that our results offer insight into the design of systems to encourage user adoption.

5   Related Work

In this section, we compare our work with relevant literature in home energy recommendation systems and modeling energy consumption of home appliances.

Persuasion and Home Energy Recommendation Systems: Home energy and resource consumption has received focus as a natural behavioral target for persuasive technologies. Midden et al. suggested that technology could take on the important role of *promoter* to affect change in home energy consumption behavior through feedback [10]. Some have argued that behavioral change is necessary to achieve consumption reductions beyond what technological advances alone can provide [11]. Others have explored the potential of persuasive feedback through embodied agents to affect home energy usage [12].

Prior art suggests that technological interventions like in situ energy saving recommendations may be worth exploring as persuasive. Shih and Jheng identify both the breaking down of desired behaviors into simple tasks and offering fitting suggestions as effective persuasive strategies for affecting energy consumption behaviors [13]. But timing and matching relevant context may also be critical. Immediacy, for example, has been cited as a critical affordance of product-integrated interactive feedback [11]. The Fogg Behavioral Model (FBM) posits three drivers of human behavior: motivation, ability, and triggers [14]. Even with sufficient motivation and ability, a timely trigger is needed for a desired behavior to occur.

Several papers study what recommendation attributes are effective for long term adoption. For instance, in [15], the authors study several types of interventions: goal-setting, information tailoring, modeling, and feedback. In [16], the authors study personalized recommendations based on historical usage patterns and demographics. Pisharoty et al. investigate the effect of personalized recommendations on more efficient thermostat scheduling [17]. In [18] the authors prototype a context-based recommendation system on a smartphone while [19] and [20] discuss the effectiveness of nudging and social cognition and persuasion in increasing the effectiveness of recommendation systems. Our work takes a more fundamental look at which recommendations users are likely to follow and how much savings they may yield.

Modeling Appliance Energy Consumption: These are several tools available for predicting appliance energy consumption and usage [5,21–27]. These tools take usage patterns as input and estimate the energy consumption of the appliance. In this work we utilize these tools to estimate the energy savings of popular recommendations.

6   Conclusion

In this paper, we perform a three step study to understand the feasibility of home energy saving recommendations. First, we use survey results from approximately 650 AMT users to determine the most popular recommendations from a set of 181 popular recommendations published by utility companies and government agencies. Secondly, we design micro-models to estimate the energy savings of these recommendations. Finally, we perform a followup study to determine the actual energy savings for these popular recommendations based on typical usage patterns. We show through our study that a few of the popular recommendations can lead to significant energy savings. Our insights into which recommendations are popular and useful in terms of energy savings can form the basis of home energy recommendation systems.

References

1. Professional lighting services: Frequently asked questions. http://www.professionallightingservices.com/faqs_ad7449e4b1c05f8276d23fac050.html (2016)
2. Power PC technology explained. http://www.makeuseof.com/tag/power-pc-technology-explained/ (2016)
3. How do you save energy when using your computer. http://www.osnews.com/story/25017/How_to_Save_Energy_When_Using_Your_Computer (2016)
4. Heat loss model. http://hyperphysics.phy-astr.gsu.edu/hbase/thermo/heatloss.html (2014)
5. Energy star home sealing specification. https://www.energystar.gov/ia/home_improvement/home_sealing/ES_HS_Spec_v1_0b.pdf (2014)
6. Green building advisor. http://www.greenbuildingadvisor.com/community/forum/mechanicals/23757/what-correct-way-manually-calculate-air-infiltration-heat-loss (2015)
7. Blower door testing. http://www.waptac.org/data/files/Website_docs/Technical_Tools/PAWTCBlowerDoorTesting.pdf (2015)
8. Electricity consumption of ceiling fans. http://energyusecalculator.com/electricity_ceilingfan.htm (2015)
9. Eia: 2014 average monthly bill-residential. https://www.eia.gov/electricity/sales_revenue_price/pdf/table5_a.pdf (2014)

10. Midden, C.J., Kaiser, F.G., Teddy McCalley, L.: Technology's four roles in understanding individuals' conservation of natural resources. J. Soc. Issues **63**(1), 155–174 (2007)
11. McCalley, T., Kaiser, F., Midden, C., Keser, M., Teunissen, M.: Persuasive appliances: goal priming and behavioral response to product-integrated energy feedback. In: IJsselsteijn, W.A., de Kort, Y.A.W., Midden, C., Eggen, B., van den Hoven, E. (eds.) PERSUASIVE 2006. LNCS, vol. 3962, pp. 45–49. Springer, Heidelberg (2006). https://doi.org/10.1007/11755494_7
12. Ham, J., Midden, C.J.: A persuasive robot to stimulate energy conservation: the influence of positive and negative social feedback and task similarity on energy-consumption behavior. Int. J. Soc. Robot. **6**(2), 163–171 (2014)
13. Shih, L.H., Jheng, Y.C.: Selecting persuasive strategies and game design elements for encouraging energy saving behavior. Sustainability **9**(7), 1281 (2017)
14. Fogg, B.J.: A behavior model for persuasive design. In: Proceedings of the 4th international Conference on Persuasive Technology, Article No. 40. ACM (2009)
15. Abrahamse, W., Steg, L., Vlek, C., Rothengatter, T.: A review of intervention studies aimed at household energy conservation. J. Environ. Psychol. **25**(3), 273–291 (2005)
16. Allcott, H.: Social norms and energy conservation. J. Public Econ. **95**(9), 1082–1095 (2011)
17. Pisharoty, D., Yang, R., Newman, M.W., Whitehouse, K.: Thermocoach: Reducing home energy consumption with personalized thermostat recommendations. In: Proceedings of the 2nd ACM International Conference on Embedded Systems for Energy-Efficient Built Environments, pp. 201–210. ACM (2015)
18. Castelli, N., Stevens, G., Jakobi, T., Schönau, N.: Switch off the light in the living room, please!-making eco-feedback meaningful through room context information. In: EnviroInfo, pp. 589–596 (2014)
19. Costa, D.L., Kahn, M.E.: Energy conservation "Nudges" and environmentalist ideology: evidence from a randomized residential electricity field experiment. J. Eur. Econ. Assoc. **11**(3), 680–702 (2013)
20. Gonzales, M.H., Aronson, E., Costanzo, M.A.: Using social cognition and persuasion to promote energy conservation: A quasi-experiment. J. Appl. Soc. Psychol. **18**(12), 1049–1066 (1988)
21. Energy calculator. http://energyusecalculator.com/electricity_computer.htm (2015)
22. How to save energy when using your computer. http://www.osnews.com/story/25017/How_to_Save_Energy_When_Using_Your_Computer (2015)
23. Power PC explained. http://www.makeuseof.com/tag/power-pc-technology-explained/ (2015)
24. Default energy consumption of appliances. http://hes-documentation.lbl.gov/calculation-methodology/calculation-of-energy-consumption/major-appliances/miscellaneous-equipment-energy-consumption/default-energy-consumption-of-mels (2015)
25. Saidur, R., Masjuki, H., Mahlia, T., Nasrudin, A.: Factors affecting refrigerator-freezers energy consumption. Asean J. Sci. Technol. Dev. **19**(2), 57–68 (2002)
26. Khan, M.I.H., Afroz, H.M., Rohoman, M.A., Faruk, M., Salim, M.: Effect of different operating variables on energy consumption of household refrigerator. int. J. Energy Eng. **3**(4), 144 (2013)
27. Hasanuzzaman, M., Saidur, R., Masjuki, H.: Effects of operating variables on heat transfer and energy consumption of a household refrigerator-freezer during closed door operation. Energy **34**(2), 196–198 (2009)

Erratum to: Sustaining Health Behaviors Through Empowerment: A Deductive Theoretical Model of Behavior Change Based on Information and Communication Technology (ICT)

Ala Alluhaidan, Samir Chatterjee, David Drew, and Agnis Stibe

Erratum to:
Chapter "Sustaining Health Behaviors Through Empowerment: A Deductive Theoretical Model of Behavior Change Based on Information and Communication Technology (ICT)" in: J. Ham et al. (Eds.): *Persuasive Technology*, LNCS 10809,
https://doi.org/10.1007/978-3-319-78978-1_3

Figure 1 of the original version of the paper showed all arrows going into **General Self Efficacy** which is not what is referred to in the article. The corrected version of the figure shows an arrow from **Technological Tools** to **General Self Efficacy** and arrows from **Message Alignment with a Goal, Experientially Rewarding Content, Social Connection, and Community Support** to **Feeling Empowered**.

The updated online version of this chapter can be found at
https://doi.org/10.1007/978-3-319-78978-1_3

© Springer International Publishing AG, part of Springer Nature 2018
J. Ham et al. (Eds.): PERSUASIVE 2018, LNCS 10809, p. E1, 2018.
https://doi.org/10.1007/978-3-319-78978-1_26

Author Index

Printed in the United States
By Bookmasters

Printed in the United States
By Bookmasters